TABLE OF CONTENTS

At Goldfield in 1904, Red Ricker tilts the pan for the photographer so that we can see "the color" rimming the pan. The amount of color showing in this very small pan would indicate ore of a value of as much as $1,000 a ton.

Prospectors became very deft in swirling test loads of ore and water so that the heavy gold particles remained, but the lighter gravel and water were ejected in the panning process.

PREFACE

The object of this book is to record the histories of over 575 towns and settlements now entirely abandoned or ones that have dwindled in importance from their former status. Almost all the places included had over fifty inhabitants, a business or two, perhaps a post office, or they were on established mail routes. In addition to mining camps, important stage stations are included as well as railroad towns, agricultural communities, military forts, a few ranches, a mission, a socialist colony — any place where people settled for a time and made homes.

The exhaustive research this has entailed has been augmented by remarkable and never-before published photographic illustrations which bring validity to the record.

These places are grouped in seventeen chapters, one for each county in Nevada. Listings have been arranged in a series of tours so that towns geographically related will be found near each other in the text. Tours are routed from established cities (usually the county seat) via numbered highways and named roads; compass directions and approximate airline distance from an easily identifiable point are sometimes added for quick reference to more obscure points. Tours do not end at a county line; towns over a boundary are included next and after their names a parenthetical insertion identifies the name of the county. Over a dozen border communities in California, Arizona and Oregon are included and treated in the same way.

Confusion about names and locations is inevitable; duplication of names or parts of names exists all over the state. Modern maps show names of listed places applied to newer communities in quite different but not too distant locations. The exact sites of some towns cannot be determined. Variant spellings abound. In several instances notations in the text warn the reader of such confusion.

Most of the towns prospered during the two great Nevada mining eras before World War I. The first one was the Comstock bonanza from 1859 to 1878. Then the state suffered depression until the discovery of silver at Tonopah in 1900. This sparked a resurgence of mining activity which reached its peak in 1918. New mining methods and the discovery of vast deposits of base metals attracted astute promoters with money for large refining plants and interested the world's finest mining engineers. Mineral production, which had dropped from a peak of $46.7 million in 1877 to a mere $2.5 million in 1900, thereafter multiplied more than 19 times, reaching a recorded $48.6 million in 1918.

In 1850, California-bound emigrants discovered gold near Dayton, which led to the state's first settlement at Mormon Station (Genoa) in 1851. It was not until 1859 that mass migration to the Comstock (then known as Washoe) took place, following the discovery of the Comstock Lode in Virginia City. In less than two years over 20,000 Californians rushed there; over half of them stayed but others moved on to Esmeralda (Aurora), Humboldt (Unionville), Reese River (Austin) and elsewhere. This influx and settlement made it possible for Congress to admit Nevada as the 36th state in October, 1864.

After the Comstock's rich surface ores diminished that same year, the mining crowd flowed to eastern Nevada, washing up against the high mountain ridges of central Nevada and finally up onto Treasure Hill (Hamilton) by 1868. The new camps of Belmont, Hamilton, Pioche and Eureka all developed into large influential towns and county seats, the pinnacle of success for mining camps.

When deep ore bodies were found on the Comstock in 1871, interest in Virginia City was renewed. Developments there, together with Eureka and Pioche, enabled Nevada to take the lead in national mineral production for the first time, even surpassing California. With the discovery and development of the "Big Bonanza" in 1873, the Comstock boom intensified, enabling that district to assume an even more dominant position in Nevada mining. Production peaked in the mid-1870s, but the failure to open up new Comstock ore bodies despite costly exploration brought Nevada's first mining era to an end. With a few important exceptions, production throughout the state also fell; no new developments were in sight and in only about a half-dozen districts did mining continue on a profitable scale.

The census of 1890 and that of 1900 recorded successive population losses, reflecting Nevada's economic decline. After the discovery of silver at Tonopah in May 1900, another series of mining booms followed. From there the mining craze tipped over the hills into Goldfield in 1903 and slipped down into Bullfrog (Rhyolite) the following year, and the remarkable growth of these three districts stimulated prospecting for overlooked mineral deposits throughout the state.

In addition to the usual bearded prospectors with their burros, this new mining era saw clean-shaven geologists and mining engineers crashing through the sagebrush in early automobiles. A few would be bad men showed up, but they commanded little attention or fear. Few six-shooters were visible. In the largest camps law enforcement prevailed almost from the start and only in remote

areas were vigilantes such as those of the Comstock era occasionally needed.

The modern rushes made the old-timers dizzy. In addition to horse-drawn stages, autos and trucks were used everywhere, and the building of new railroads linked northern Nevada with the booming south. Many shortlines and branch lines were built to facilitate mining. Telephone and telegraph lines webbed the state, and newspapers and magazines throughout the nation spread the get-rich-quick fever, drawing thousands from every trade to seek bonanzas in the Nevada wilds.

The second era of growth and mineral development ended in 1918 after Goldfield's big mines closed down. A few rich strikes between the world wars created a half-dozen notable boom towns. Though annual production since World War II has often been far greater than during the best years of the early boom periods, no new mining camps are being created. With the aid of modern machinery a few men now do the work formerly done by many, and these few live in existing towns and drive to the mines. The era of mining that produced the colorful boom camp is a thing of the past.

The Life Cycle of a Mining Camp

With few exceptions, the old-time mining rushes were like the tides of the sea — they ebbed and flowed, leaving ruins to tell of the energy expended in building a town and developing the mines. It all began when prospectors working on a grubstake discovered outcroppings of ore. Claims were staked and samples were gathered; if they assayed well the mining town press spread the news and others flocked to the strike. Sanity took flight and men joined the rush by any means of conveyance. Some even walked, pushing wheelbarrows and carts; some had provisions, others had none. All were hellbent to get to the promised land.

After them came the saloon man, the room-keeper, the small merchant, and all sorts of adventurers and gamblers. At the discovery site the newcomers scurried over the hills; the cold clank of picks and the reverberating thud of hammers echoed through the silence of the desert. Amid the diggings the countryside erupted in a rash of tents, and streets appeared, twisting about at irregular angles. One good prospect started a camp.

Others early on the scene were promoters of active mind and ready tongue, who bought up mining sites for further development or resale through newly formed stock companies. A real estate broker platted an "official" townsite and began selling sagebrush lots. Most men in the camp were prospectors who claimed "millions" untapped in the wilds, yet seldom had two dimes in their pockets. On a rumor's notice these wanderers struck out from civilization to look for rich leads, trailing in restless discontent up and down mountain ranges and along low-lying bluffs or winding canyons, continually searching, tapping, examining, with the hope of finding a deposit before their grubstakes ran out.

Many camps never developed further than the rag-town stage, with names dimly remembered. But if the mines showed promise of depth, sturdy wood-frame buildings sprang up amid graded streets and mining companies erected costly mills, often before determining whether sufficient ore was available to keep them running. A red-light district formed at one end of town. The businesses which fronted the main street were mixed and shuffled together like cards in a gambler's hands; the town's status was measured by the length of this thoroughfare.

A confusion of sounds accompanied the bustle and excitement of camp building. The hee-haw of burros mingled with the rasping of saws and the creaking of mule-driven freight wagons. Bullwhackers cracked whips a dozen feet in length and prospectors milled about studying ore samples while engaging in jawbone. The daily stage arrived with human cargo and mail, then left carrying bullion guarded by stern silent men armed with sawed-off shotguns, who did not always succeed in protecting the treasure.

Amid the chaotic crowds the entire spectrum of mining town society could be found. Everyone from banker to waiter was on the alert; every nerve was tense, every ear was perked to hear the first news of a strike. A discerning stranger might notice a group of swindlers, confidence men, and card cheats patiently awaiting victims. Boisterous wheeler-dealers wearing coats with pockets stuffed with ore specimens, small silver bars, and rolls of duplicate location notices and assay certificates, strolled the streets, buying, selling and talking mine prospects. These men patiently listened for the rumble of the incoming stage, ready to sell a salted mine to a newly arrived greenhorn.

Above the bibulous throng of men, the high-pitched chant of auctioneers was heard, or perhaps the voice of a California vendor peddling fresh fruit from his wagon. Selling space was at times difficult to find, for teams and wagons usurped most of the street. Mexicans with their bands of lean mustangs careened through the streets or bucked their broncos to the delight of the crowd.

Mining and milling were in full blast. Surface explosions of dynamite ripping through the air met the bang and clatter and shrill whistles of quartz mills. Dull detonations of blasts from deep in the earth periodically shook the town. Hoisting engines ceaselessly clanked and rattled. Armies of miners marched to and from the shaft houses, from where the gold and silver ores emerged.

Saloons were flooded with miners, operators, bullwhackers, skinners, swampers, onlookers, whores, drifters, and nondescripts of the seediest class, who swore, talked, fought, swapped dirty jokes, told tall stories about the mines they owned or worked in, and drank at the expense of every stranger who approached the bar. It was the only relaxation for men who had labored long hours, sometimes to no avail.

The rest of the floor was occupied by gaming tables presided over by silent watchful dealers, with hundreds or even thousands of dollars in checks and gold and silver coin piled high in front of each player, and a hidden gun always within reach. In the rear were private cardrooms stale with tobacco smoke, crowded with tables surrounded by miners who drank straight shots of whiskey three or four times an hour.

Quarrels frequently broke out, most of them having their origin in too much whiskey. Tension mounted in a close card game; when ugly words passed, a shove followed, a fist would swing, and then came a display of the revolvers. Occasionally an innocent spectator stepped into the path of a bullet, but the victim was considered partly at fault for being in the way.

The accused was usually freed without a fine on a plea of self-defense, but pre-dawn vigilance committees at times administered due process with bullets and ropes. In a real sense the frequency of violence was an index of a camp's prosperity; each incident demonstrated that the camp was lively. Fights, shootings and claim jumping were news of importance to the mining town press, and in such a setting the journalist created the richest mines in the West.

Though drawing from most segments of society, the mining camp observed only slight social distinctions. Mineral fields held a special fascination for romantic people of culture. Teachers, retired army officers, lawyers, judges and other educated men came in good numbers and might be found digging together in a rocky hole. While females were not conspicuous, more women and children lived in mining camps than one might expect. They lived quiet good lives, and even the worst rowdies had a deep respect for them, seldom insulting or accosting the respectable women or young girls.

With the rise of two- and three-story brick and stone business blocks above the sea of wooden buildings and tents, the camp matured. Newspapers competed for public favor, and rails were extended to the district. Churches and fraternal groups organized and built costly buildings. Itinerant lecturers, minstrels, singers and actors performed in the town theater. Libraries and literary societies were organized as well as debating clubs. The largest mining towns enjoyed such amenities as a water company, fire and school districts, lighted streets, ice plants, and hotels with lavish furnishings. Town government was begun, with mayor, sheriff and judges installed. Property taxes were assessed. Political power was sought by trying to obtain the county seat.

When the boom subsided milling slowed to a trickle and one by one obituaries of the mines appeared in the newspaper before the press itself succumbed. Crowded outbound autos, wagons, and coaches laden with parcels and passengers struck out for virgin bonanzas, distant rainbows; the wild roar of the saloons subsided and finally quieted to the weak whispers of hangers-on; mute

mills were dismantled and moved elsewhere; rails were ripped out of their beds and silence settled like a blanket over the area.

Most towns were abandoned when ore bodies could no longer be profitably worked with existing equipment and transportation facilities. In other instances mines could still produce, but the siren call of favorable finds in distant ranges lured everyone away. Restlessness, exaggerated hopes, false guesses, flood, fire — all these hastened the death of a mining camp. Usually a few die-hards or older people stayed on who worked a low-grade ledge for a meagre living. Often the exodus was so fast that bulkier possessions were abandoned, and merchants closed their doors leaving stock on the shelves. Furniture was left in hotels and cabins, billiard balls and cues lay where they had been dropped on saloon pool tables, and tools and machinery were abandoned beside mills and furnaces.

With the passing of time the graded streets were lost to the encroaching desert growth; sagebrush pushed its way up through rotting floor planks and extended along crumbling walls; and tall imposing smokestacks stood alone near shambles of mills. These caved-in dwellings, brick facades and bare stone walls would continue to break down and crumble until the desert had completely reclaimed the land.

———

In recent years chasing down ghost towns and dead mining camps has become a week-end diversion for city dwellers. Even with a minimum of preparation, dozens of former settlements situated on or very near paved or well-graded roads are easily reached in comfort and safety. Stone, wooden or brick ruins are extant, sometimes protected by a few remaining residents.

Visiting the more accessible places usually leads to an interest in traveling far from main highways to explore the ghostly remains of mines and towns totally abandoned. Finding them often is a challenge, though with persistent searching even the most elusive site can be uncovered. Be sure to read the Appendix material about travel in the desert before you head out for extensive searching.

Late in the afternoon toward sunset is the most beautiful time on the desert, for the coloring is heightened by the setting sun and lengthening shadows add their magic. Moonlight, too, lends an aura to the old ruins, but there are those who believe that in early morning, when the sun rises above the horizon of clearly defined mountains Nevada is at its most beautiful.

Satisfaction gained from exploring one town will make you pack your gear and head for the next one. After a few days of exploring you too will catch ghost town fever — and it is not easy to cure.

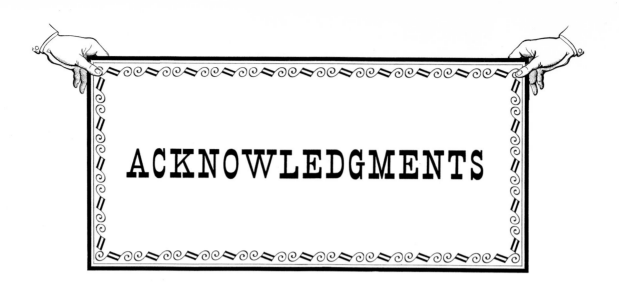

ACKNOWLEDGMENTS

In five years of researching, compiling and bringing to a conclusion this study of Nevada towns, scores of individuals were most helpful. Extraordinary assistance came from Mrs. Myrtle Tate Myles, now of Reno. Born and reared in Nye County, this "Lady of the Toiyabes" lived in Smoky Valley, Belmont and Manhattan, and visited Tonopah and Goldfield during the boom years. Her firsthand knowledge greatly aided my understanding of early Nevada. She helped caption dozens of pictures, loaned me several choice photographs, directed me to many sources of pictures and information and read parts of the text.

Others generous with reference materials who were consulted countless times include: Theron and Frances Fox of San Jose, David F. Myrick of San Francisco, E. W. "Shorty" Darrah of Austin, Nevada, Jack McCloskey of Hawthorne, Tony and Jan Lesperance of Reno, Colonel Thomas W. Miller of Reno, Dorothy Dalton of Las Vegas and Elbert Edwards of Boulder City.

Special help in specific areas came from the following: Mrs. Lillian Ninnis in identifying pictures and in the history of Tonopah and Goldfield; Bert Acree with recollections of Lander County and assistance in field trips; the late George Nelson for histories of towns in Elko County; Clyde Keegel for explanation of mining and milling techniques and picture identification; and Stanley Fine for descriptions of early Eureka and freighting.

Fenton Gass, son of Octavius Gass who founded the Las Vegas Ranch, Henry H. Lee of Panaca, Lloyd Denton of Caliente, and Captain Ray Gibson who freighted to Beatty in 1904 all related tales of southern Nevada before the Salt Lake Railroad was built. Walt Mulcahy's explanations of desert relics were useful, as were Kenneth Carpenter's reflections. Charles Gallagher's pictures and reminiscences of early Ely and the surrounding valleys were entertaining; valuable help with that same area also came from Dr. Russell Elliott.

Northern Nevadans with valuable recollections and knowledge were: Bill Freeman with Lyon County; Zenas Walmsley with Dayton; Miss Hermine "Aunt Min" Bucking with Mason; Walter Van Tilburg Clark with Virginia City and Como; W. G. Emminger with tungsten mining; Mr. and Mrs. Clarence Basso and David Basso with Pershing County; Roy Linsea with the Fallon-Fairview freight run; Ed A. Smith with Humboldt County; Mrs. Roy Primeaux, early Tuscarora; Mrs. Helen Sharp, Tobar; Gene Stoddart, White Pine County towns.

Helping about southern Nevada were: Walter Averett and Richard E. Lingenfelter with Clark County; Mrs. Henrietta Revert with Nye County; James G. Hulse with Lincoln County; Miss Lilly Pepper and T. L. Williamson with Mineral County; and James Corlett with Gabbs area mining. Leo Grutt, one of the "fathers" of Rawhide, recalled the early days of the camp. William Mac Boyle's recollections helped with the Esmeralda County chapter. Leonard Traynor's observations and reference materials aided in writing the Weepah story.

12

The most enjoyable aspect of research was meeting scores of individuals who allowed me to borrow pictures from time to time. In all, over 1600 rare views of Nevada towns were uncovered, most of which have never been published. The following extensive collections deserve special mention: Mrs. R. R. Purdy, John Zalac, William A. Kornmayer, Chester Barton, Mrs. Estelle Funke, Gerald "Casey" Fisher, Douglas Robinson, Jr., Mrs. W. B. Mercer, Willie Capucci, William H. Scott, Orlo Parker, Mrs. Lorena B. Meadows, John Yount, Fritz Buckingham, and the Tonopah *Times-Bonanza*. The files of the Las Vegas *Review-Journal* were made available thanks to Bill Vincent.

Valuable pictorial assistance also came from: Mrs. Ida Le Nord, Mrs. Harry Mighels, Mrs. Nevada Browne, Dr. James R. Herz, Ralph Barrett, Mrs. Jack Burns, Philip R. Bradley, Mrs. Willard Hanson, Emil Billeb, George Barnett, Mrs. Dorothy Jennings, Tony Primeaux, Mrs. Della Phillips, Fred Minoletti, the Kennecott Copper Corporation, the White Pine Museum, Don Cirac, Bob Stewart, *Nevada Highways & Parks* Magazine, Leonard Fayle, William Ellis, Mrs. H. H. Heisler, Charles Hendel, Fred Steen, Bill Metscher, Helen McInnis, Mrs. Della Dodson, Richard C. Datin, George Barnett, Ray McMurry and the late Abraham Kendall and Albert Silver.

Photographic files in nearly a score of libraries and historical societies in six states were also tapped. Dr. Gene M. Gressley, director of the Western History Research Center at the University of Wyoming, made available dozens of unpublished views, especially those of the Henry Curtis Morris collection. Dr. Edwin Carpenter at the Huntington Library assisted in procuring unpublished pictures; Pamela Crowell was particularly helpful at the Nevada State Museum; and at the Northeastern Nevada Museum, Howard Hickson gave generous assistance.

Robert D. Armstrong, Special Collections librarian at the University of Nevada, Reno, and at the same school La Verne Rollin of the Mackay School of Mines extended pictorial help. Other important sources of photographs were the Dickenson Library at the University of Nevada at Las Vegas where Mrs. Celesta Lowe rendered aid; the Death Valley Museum and Pete Sanchez; the History Room at Wells Fargo Bank in San Francisco and Mrs. Irene Simpson Neasham; the Bancroft Library; the Nevada Historical Society; the California Historical Society; the United States Geological Survey; the Smithsonian Institution and the National Archives.

The quality of photographic reproduction was enhanced by the skill of Las Vegas photographer Frank Mitrani; his contemporary views also grace these pages. Gary Allen also furnished modern ghost town scenes. Other pictures not credited were taken by the author. Jimmy Smith, Adrian Atwater and Al Jennings processed several western Nevada pictures.

The best sources of mining town history and description are the files of boom town newspapers. Numerous volumes were read at the Nevada Historical Society, University of Nevada in Reno, and at the Bancroft Library. At those places and at the Huntington Library rare manuscript materials were examined; the assistance of the staff at each place made research a pleasant task.

Numerous field trips into Nevada's back country gave the visual setting for writing the town histories. Many friends, including my brothers Roger and Ken Paher, joined me in search of ghost towns. Thanks, too, are due my parents, Mr. and Mrs. Stanley M. Paher for extended assistance while the manuscript was revised and prepared for publication. To them this book is dedicated.

There are others — many, many more — who helped or gave encouragement along the way. To all a thanks as deep as sunset shadows in the desert!

STANLEY W. PAHER

Las Vegas, Nevada
January, 1970

At the 2600 foot level station, miners wait for the cage to take them to the surface. *(Mackay School of Mines, University of Nevada)*

This panorama of Virginia City in 1861 shows restaurants, saloons, and stores extending the full distance of B and C Streets. By then pioneer businesses had replaced their hastily constructed offices, built during the camp's early expansion, with frame buildings having imposing facades. *(National Archives)*

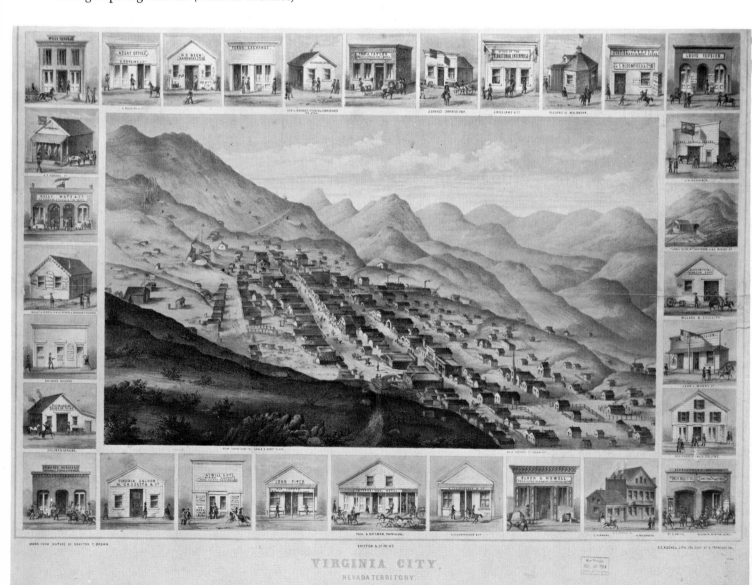

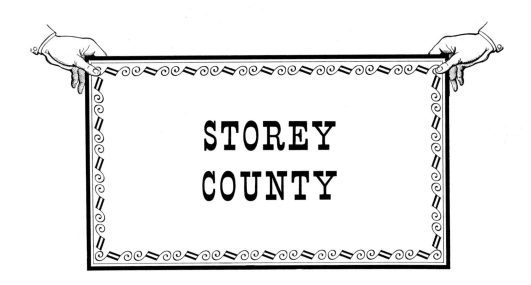

STOREY COUNTY

Nevada's most famous lode, the Comstock, and the important mining camps of Virginia City and Gold Hill both prospered from the beginning of the boom in 1859 until the last year of bonanza production, 1878. Irregular but valuable outputs have since been recorded. The 20th century state-wide boom did not revitalize the Comstock, although companies such as those in American Flat in the 1920s worked the old mines with varying success. The last important periods of sustained mining came just before and after World War II.

VIRGINIA CITY, on SR 17, 8 miles north of US 50 at a point 8 miles east of Carson City.

Virginia City is the home of the fabulous Comstock Lode, the greatest 19th century silver mining center in North America. That lode was directly responsible for the creation of Nevada Territory in 1861 and its ascendancy to statehood three years later. The outpouring of the Comstock helped finance the Civil War and provided a fresh source of capital for new projects after the rebellion had ceased, stimulating in part the early nationwide cycles of inflation after 1865.

The Comstock occupies a most resplendent place in history. No single ledge anywhere in the world has been so prolific of romance as the Comstock, the true fissure of Nevada. It built transcontinental railroads, great steamship lines, and telegraph cables across the Atlantic; it endowed universities and colleges and art museums; it built palaces in Italy and France overlooking the blue Mediterranean; it helped build towns and cities,

the outstanding example being San Francisco; it made men nationally famous in finance and politics including United States Senators, railroad and bank presidents; it fixed into history the names of Mackay, Fair, Flood, O'Brien, Sharon, Jones, Ralston, Stewart, Hayward and Sutro!

Comstock mining dominated the development of 19th century Nevada. The high early production after discoveries in 1859 encouraged intense prospecting for several hundred miles around and resulted in the discovery of such bonanzas as Esmeralda (Aurora), Humboldt (Unionville), and Reese River (Austin). Satellite towns such as Dayton, Washoe City, Empire City, and Reno all prospered in serving the Comstock. Indeed, that single lode was the principal reason why Nevada's population rose from less than a dozen in 1850 to 6,857 in 1860 to 42,491 a decade later to an estimated 75,000 in 1875.

Discovery of the Comstock Lode cannot be attributed to any individuals nor assigned an exact date, for it was the culmination of activity of many individuals over a period of at least nine years. Events directly leading to discovery of silver began in 1852 when Hosea and Allen Grosh came to Gold Canyon to join others in placer mining. Ultimately the brothers found silver in the placer gold and continued work until 1857, but both died separately that year before exploiting their deposits. Probably few besides the Grosh brothers knew the existence of silver in the area; most of the miners were strictly looking for placer gold.

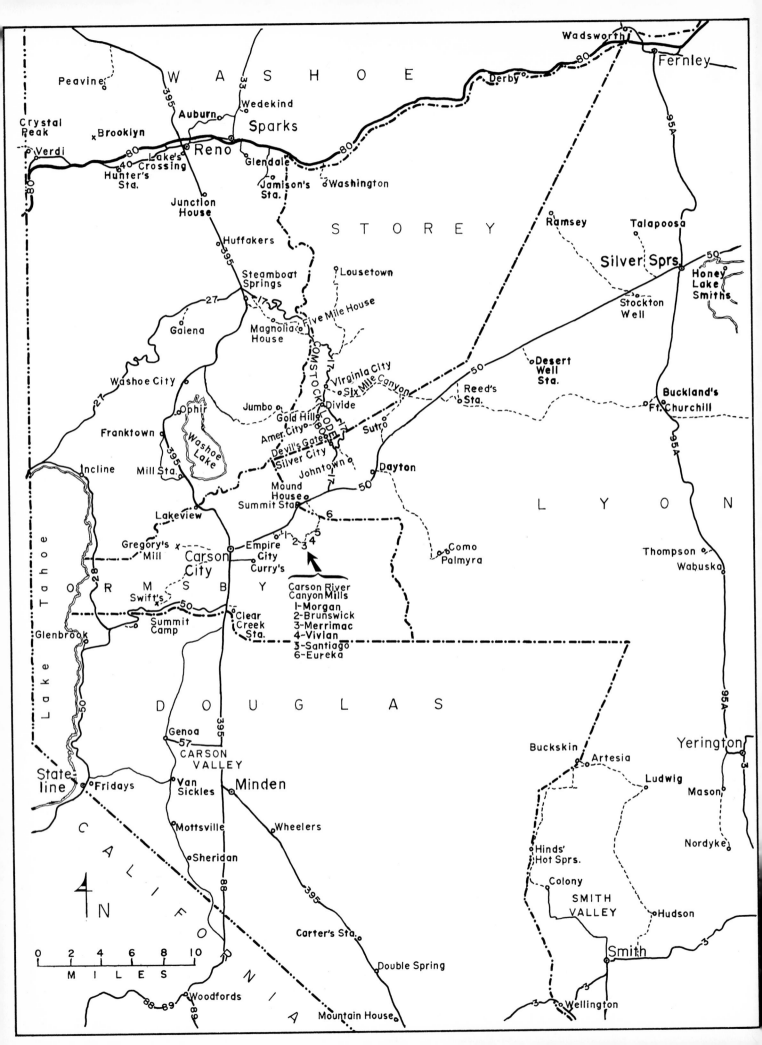

A heavy metallic substance persisted in covering the quicksilver in the bottom of their rockers, interfering with the recovery of gold. This "blasted blue stuff"—soon to be identified as rich sulphurites of silver—was cursed from the rising of the sun until dark, trodden underfoot, washed away, sluiced out, and discarded as totally worthless. By the mid-1850s a helter-skelter settlement known as Johntown (which see) had appeared among the diggings and especially after 1856-57 many new arrivals were on the scene with more of them remaining during the winter. All nearby ravines were worked for placer gold, especially Six Mile Canyon, and in the spring of 1858 that canyon received most of the attention of the Johntowners.

Until 1859 all work met with indifferent success with the miners averaging about five dollars a day for their efforts. In January 1859 James Fenemore and Henry T. P. Comstock prospected the upper end of Gold Canyon and located many placer claims, not realizing that rich gold- and silver-bearing quartz veins were below the surface croppings they had found. This discovery was the first location on what was soon to be known as the Comstock Lode. When pay dirt became richer there, the Johntowners came to stake additional claims, and shortly a crude camp which took the name Gold Hill formed around the new activity.

In the spring of 1859 Peter O'Riley and Patrick McLaughlin set up their rockers at the head of Six Mile Canyon in the shadow of sage-covered Sun Mountain (Mount Davidson). For most of the decade miners had been gradually approaching that mountain and the rich lode which lay beneath its base and on its east slope. These two Irishmen while digging a reservoir for placering, uncovered the top of what became the Ophir bonanza and began washing gravel for gold. Within days their rockers were recovering $500 to $1000 in gold per day from the deposit, and news of this strike brought a rush from Gold Hill, Chinatown (Dayton), and from farms in surrounding valleys to the west.

A Truckee Meadows rancher who visited the diggings early in July before going to California carried away a specimen of the ore as a curiosity. An assay in Grass Valley disclosed that the blue-gray ore which the miners considered worthless actually contained sulphurites of silver of up to $3000 a ton, in addition to $876 per ton in gold! In a night Grass Valley was charged with the news, and in the midst of a mining excitement unparalleled since the days of '49 a stampede was on to "Washoe," as the region was then called.

This rush emptied California's worked-out gold towns of thousands of merchants, farmers, miners and prospectors who flocked over the Sierra Nevada late that summer, despite the approach of cold weather. Numerous locations were made for miles on the supposed course of the lode. The camp which formed near the strike was initially called Pleasant Hill or Mount Pleasant Point, then Ophir, and finally Virginia, after "Old Virginny," a sobriquet borne by James Fenemore, one of the discoverers of the lode.

As early as August a four-stamp mill was dragged by oxen over the mountains from Sacramento, and that October it began running on the Carson River. But it was soon evident that the softness of the silver ore presented difficulties in milling. Almirin B. Paul experimented with the rock and in 1860 built a mill near Silver City to treat ore by a modification of the old Mexican process, which came to be known as the Washoe process, amalgamation without roasting. Another Comstock innovation was the introduction of square-set mine timbering, as designed by Philip Deidesheimer.

After 1860 good roads were built over the Sierra, and Virginia City grew rapidly as supply center for most of Nevada territory. A period of financial promotion followed and another of mill building; over eighty mills were built by 1862. The population of this flourishing town increased to 15,000 or 18,000 by 1863 and rose to stature of the second city west of the Rockies. Large as the city was, mining excavations underneath were much larger; any one of a half-dozen mines contained more timber than all of the structures on the surface.

Even at that early age Virginia City had costly public buildings, fraternal orders and organizations, stores and shops of every description, and competing daily newspapers. Its turbulent society drew from every conceivable occupation, including gamblers, thieves, swindlers, prostitutes, and hired guns. Every major nationality was represented in the money-mad crowd that swarmed the

Although Mark Twain jocosely reported in 1862 that amid the gambling dens and whiskey mills there was only "some talk of building a church," by the middle of the decade Virginia City had at least three fine houses of worship. From left to right are St. Paul's Episcopal church, the wood-frame St. Mary's Catholic church and the Methodist church. *(Abraham Kendall Collection)*

The 1875 view (below) demonstrates how steep the streets were. The churches appear in a different arrangement, and the city had extended far up the barren slopes of Sun Mountain (Mt. Davidson). *(National Archives)*

city's steep avenues. Aside from mining and milling, heavy drinking, fighting and gambling were the order of the day; indulgence blossomed into crime and the vigilante's tree soon bore fruit. Times were flush—excitement ran high.

After the winter of 1864 the Comstock boom began to slacken. New discoveries ceased, ore began to give out in a few mines, and California investors grew tired of investing in sagebrush. As production declined, miners scattered eastward across central Nevada where new discoveries offered opportunities and employment. Production continued to fall until 1869; output that year was only about 45% of the high recorded five years earlier. The thinning of surface bonanzas, expensive mining litigation, and the morale-destroying Yellow Jacket fire which took 37 lives—these all brought on a recession.

Two years earlier, in 1867, the Bank of California represented by William Sharon, organized the Union Milling & Mining Co., and the Bank of California Ring exerted a powerful influence on Comstock affairs for the next decade. That company built the Virginia & Truckee Railroad from Carson City to the Comstock in 1869, the same year that Adolph Sutro began work on the Sutro Tunnel, designed to drain and ventilate the mines at a depth of over 1000 feet.

Toward the end of 1870 a welcome discovery in the Chollar-Potosi gave a little vitality to the moribund town. A few other finds were made early in 1871, and in November of that year rich veins were discovered at a depth of over 900 feet in the Crown Point mine. Its superintendent John Jones and Alvinza Hayward, a member of the Bank of California Ring, reportedly obtained advance information and reaped immense fortunes when in less than seven months Crown Point rose from $2 to $1825 a share.

After that strike new discoveries came like firecrackers, one by one, culminating in one big detonation, as though the remainder of the pack went off together. The Crown Point bonanza, ultimately yielding about $35 million, was followed the next year by the discovery of rich silver in the Belcher, which yielded a similar amount. The crowning achievement in the history of the lode was the discovery early in 1873 of the deep-lying Consolidated Virginia ore body—the Big Bonanza. From

that mine alone $105 million was taken, out of which about $75 million was paid in dividends. Never had so few mines produced so much wealth for so many stockholders!

By the mid-1870s Virginia City's 25,000 population supported 110 saloons, over fifty dry goods stores, four banks, twenty laundries, six churches, public and private schools, a railroad with 32 arrivals and departures daily, and five newspapers including the daily *Territorial Enterprise* unsurpassed by any inland paper in the West. Then the great fire of October 1875 swept away three-fourths of the city and damaged mills and mine timbers. Rebuilding began at once amid the smoking embers and within a year most of the city had been rebuilt, but it never did regain its former influence and glory. The mines still produced well but the ore was not as rich.

Besides the mines mentioned above, the Potosi, Yellow Jacket, Ophir, Gould & Curry, and the Savage had joined the $10 million production club before the decline of 1878. During the previous 19 years production of nearly $300 million had been recorded—an unparalleled record. Large unrecorded production in the early years cannot be estimated.

The costly problem of draining the mines was partially solved with completion of the Sutro Tunnel in 1879, although pumping was still required in shafts that had been sunk to deeper levels. The tunnel did not reverse the decline in production, which fell sharply from $38 million in the peak year of 1876 to only $1.4 million in 1881.

For the rest of the century low-grade veins were worked systematically, and annual productions ranged from a maximum of over $7 million in 1888 to a mere $172,000 in 1899. Total yield during this period was almost $50 million — less spectacular than the bonanza era but more than the total production of most districts in the state. An immense flow of hot water inadvertently struck in 1882 drowned out the Gold Hill mines below the Sutro Tunnel level and deep work was suspended four years later in the Virginia City mines. Pumping resumed in 1899 and almost $18 million in irregular production was taken out before pumping was again discontinued in 1922. The better than a million a year record occurred during 1923-

A recital at St. Mary's School featured twin pianos and a duet. Music was stressed as an accomplishment for young ladies enrolled there. Note the library and the potted plants. (Willie Capucci Collection)

The panorama (below) shows the city as rebuilt after the fire of 1875 had swept through the central portion. Palatial saloons, costly hotels, including the six-story 100 room International (at the extreme left edge), restaurants with excellent cuisine and comfortable homes had been built. The shaft house of the C&C is seen at the extreme left edge. St. Mary's church is situated to the right of the International Hotel. Behind the town is Six Mile Canyon, a satellite mining and milling area. (John Zalac Collection)

Still very much in evidence after the turn of the century is the Virginia & Truckee Railroad, bringing passengers and freight to the Comstock. The Hale & Norcross trestle is in full view, and the Fourth Ward School, built during the boom days, dominates the slope. *(William H. Scott photo)*

Important surface buildings such as the Savage and the Hale & Norcross works are shown in the picture below. In the center distance are the works of the Combination shaft, a project intended to intersect the Lode at a depth of about 3000 feet. Excessive flows of hot water and mud defeated it. *(John Zalac Collection)*

By the 1880s a few paid firemen easily contained minor blazes such as this one on C Street because water mains and hydrants had been installed throughout the city. Horse-drawn hose carts (below) were also part of the fire-fighting equipment, although early carts were pulled by men. *(Top: Mrs. Jack Burns Collection; bottom: William H. Scott photo)*

22

In this view looking north on C Street (above) early one afternoon in 1866, wagons make mid-day deliveries. *(Abraham Kendall Collection)*

Though in decline in the late 1880s, dignified and orderly Virginia City looked impressive from Cedar Hill north of town. *(Mrs. Jack Burns Collection)*

Composite view of a Comstock Mine, illustrating miners' tools, shafts and a remarkably clear concept of the square set stoping method. This method of mining was developed in Virginia City in 1860 by Phillip Deidesheimer for the Ophir mine. The system was so successful it was used all over the world and still is where very soft ground has to be mined. (*Nevada State Museum*)

James Fair discovered the Big Bonanza when he ran a drift from the 1200 level of this shaft into his Consolidated Virginia ground. This was the Bonner shaft of the Gould & Curry. *(Mrs. Jack Burns Collection)*

The Comstock mines employed Cornish pumps for handling the great volumes of water encountered in deep mining. This is the pump engine at the Hale & Norcross. *(Mrs. Jack Burns Collection)*

In the late 1880s, during the days of low-grade operations at the bonanza mines, local photographer J. H. Crockwell visited the dynamo room (above) at the 1600 foot level of the Chollar mine and photographed it by electric light. The electricity produced ran the Chollar mill, shown below. *(Both photos: Mrs. Jack Burns Collection)*

The Sierra Nevada mine was one of the least successful of the Comstock mines. Its hoist was both crude and primitive compared with the rest of the mines. The flat cables can be seen running from the reels up into the headframe. (*Mrs. Jack Burns Collection*)

The view of Virginia City (below) from the cemetery shows the Ophir Mill in the foreground, the Gould & Curry's Bonner shaft house at the left, and C Street and Mt. Davidson in the background. (*Mrs. Jack Burns Collection*)

In 1862 Gold Hill had a long narrow business street which followed the contour of the Gold Canyon Ravine. Early hoisting works are in evidence, as is the flume to Virginia City, high on the mountain slope. Below the flume a jungle of over a dozen ore chutes extends from shaft houses to bins from which wagons hauled ore to mills on the west shores of Washoe Lake and on the Carson River. Original locators such as Sandy Bowers and Eilley Orrum owned small claims of ten to twenty feet, but these sections were later consolidated to form the Imperial mine. *(Getchell Library, University of Nevada)*

In the early 1870s (below), in a view taken from an opposite direction from the above, the Crown Point mine had a handsome shaft house, and the Virginia & Truckee had built a trestle across the ravine. The town had grown far down Gold Canyon, where many other important mines were active. The Crown Point Trestle, regarded as the pattern for the great seal of the State of Nevada, was torn down in the 1930s to permit mining the ground beneath it. *(Nevada State Museum)*

26 and again during 1936-40. The big mines are now idle.

Many important historic buildings remain in Virginia City, the West's most famous mining town. Leftovers from the Comstock era include Piper's Opera House and the Courthouse on B Street, St. Mary's church and the Episcopal church, Savage mine office, Fourth Ward School, brewery and graveyards below C Street, and several commercial buildings on C Street itself, including the *Territorial Enterprise* building, where the visitor for a small admission can sit at the desk used by cub reporter Mark Twain.

THE DIVIDE, ½ mile south of Virginia City, at junction of SR 17 and SR 80.

This area was appropriately named. Initially, the Divide separated Virginia City and Gold Hill, but as mining activity increased in the 1870s the Divide, also known as Middletown, developed into a densely populated suburb of over 1000. Old houses and ruins of others remain in this area today.

JUMBO (Washoe County), via Ophir Grade, 4 miles west of SR 80 at The Divide.

After mines opened in the Jumbo district in 1907, a camp formed and soon had a mill, a couple of saloons, hotels, an assay office and a grocery store. A post office opened in April 1908. A small mill, built in 1910, and a ten-stamp mill built in 1915 produced until 1921. A wooden building of later origin marks the site.

GOLD HILL, on SR 80, ¾ mile south of Virginia City.

Among the prospectors whose activity in Gold Canyon led to the discovery of the Comstock Lode were those who in 1859 initially occupied this community at the head of the canyon and named it Gold Hill. The first inhabitants camped out under trees and erected crude huts and log houses. The actual discovery of silver in the Lode came five months later and as the news reached mining communities in California, large influxes of Californians settled here, so that by the end of 1859 Gold Hill briefly rivaled Virginia City.

The camp then consisted of frame shelters pitched together as if by accident, canvas tents, and other dwellings made of blankets, potato sacks, and old shirts, with empty whiskey barrels serving as chimneys. Other structures were mere hovels of mud and stone. During 1860-64 Gold Hill expanded because it was at the lower end of the Comstock Lode. The Gold Hill *News,* published in this distinct suburb of Virginia City, often engaged in vitriolic "educational" duels with the larger town's newspapers. The rivalry grew to the extent that Virginia City in 1864 tried to enlarge its boundaries and annex Gold Hill and nearby American Flat. To stop the move, Gold Hill incorporated all of the south end of the county, and then attempted to create its own county, but the Virginia City press fought the move and eventually the plan died.

Gold Hill quieted after 1864, with subsidence of the Comstock boom, but construction of the Virginia & Truckee Railroad from the Comstock to Carson City in 1869 was the harbinger of a decade of increased mining activity which saw more ore being shipped out than ever before. By 1873 Gold Hill was as up-to-date as any western city, and its 8000 citizens supported public and private schools, a high school, three fire companies, town hall, banks, halls for societies and lodges, Miners Union

Below is the office of the Gold Hill *Daily News* in 1880, one of the state's most influential newspapers during the Comstock's heyday. (*Mackay School of Mines, University of Nevada*)

The 3000-ton mill of the United Comstock Merger Co. was the nation's largest cyanide plant at that time. From back of the mill a tunnel was driven into the Comstock Lode, where a drift was extended north into the old mines under Virginia City. Because the mill was built of concrete, metallurgical changes were nearly impossible. When the price of silver dropped in the mid-1920s, the venture failed. *(Roy A. Hardy Collection)*

The camp (below) was situated immediately to the north of the mill. From left to right are company houses, post office and store, large dining hall, hospital and recreation hall. *(Mrs. Emma Robertson Collection)*

hall and churches. Gold Hill also boasted such amenities as street lamps, fire hydrants and a water company.

During the 1870s millions in silver were taken from the lower portion of the Comstock Lode, from the Crown Point, Belcher, Yellow Jacket, Imperial, Kentuck and Confidence mines. But as production slowed after 1878, Gold Hill inevitably declined. Alf Doten ended a 14-year connection with the Gold Hill *News* late in 1881 and early the next year that paper, the last one published here, found a more profitable field in Idaho. The old town slowly died over the decades and finally by 1943 its remaining symbol of urbanity, the post office, closed. Ruins of many buildings flank the road up the canyon amid a few modern homes, and old mine buildings cling to the side of the ravine.

AMERICAN CITY, later Comstock, 1 mile west of SR 80 at Gold Hill.

Gold and silver mining began in American Flat after 1860 when the Comstock discoveries extended beyond the Gold Canyon ravine. By 1864 American City had become a town and its citizens tried to secure the territorial capital from Carson City, because at that time Ormsby County was in disfavor for charging $4500 each legislative session for room space instead of providing rent-free quarters. Promoters at American City offered $50,000 to the Nevada territorial government if it would relocate here. The Storey County papers backed the removal attempt, but the legislators rejected the offer.

During 1864-66 this thriving town had two large hotels amid other businesses and had its own township officers. In March 1866 a post office was established. But the community never took root and late 1867 American City gave way to sagebrush and the coyote.

The area remained relatively quiet until 1920, when the United Comstock Mining Co. constructed a $1.5 million four-story cyanide mill of reinforced concrete to process low-grade ores at the south end of the Comstock Lode. A two-mile-long spur was built from the mill to the Virginia & Truckee's main line. Three years later the Comstock Merger Mines, Inc. was formed to operate a group of Comstock mines in the middle of the lode and in 1923 acquired the U.C.M.C.'s mill when that company went out of business. The small company camp of Comstock just below the mill included a store, houses, a post office and other buildings until December 1926, when the Merger Mines company terminated operations because of the low price of silver. A San Francisco firm bought all equipment and salvaged removable parts, but large concrete mill remnants are left.

DEVIL'S GATE, 3¼ miles south of Virginia City on SR 80.

With beginnings as early as November 1859, when this section of Gold Canyon became the second mining district organized in Utah territory, Devil's Gate soon developed into a small community. On a journey in 1860, J. Ross Browne complained that the place was unsafe for travel because of "inexorable imps." He probably meant that the gate was a favorite hangout for robbers. On a return trip to the Comstock three years later, Browne noted that Devil's Gate contained a continuous line of mills, tunnels, sluices, water wheels, buildings, grog-shops, stables, hotel, barber shop, brewery, express office and a tollkeeper's station. With the decline of the Comstock, this straggling village died.

SIX MILE CANYON, 2 miles east of Virginia City.

Gold had been panned in this canyon before the organization of the Flowery district in the fall of 1859, and a settlement known as Flowery functioned briefly but did not grow, because of the rapid rise of Virginia City. In the 1860s and 1870s several mills flanked the road through the canyon, the largest being the Gould & Curry. Attractive houses with gardens were built for mining officials and miners with families as well as rock cabins for transients. Six Mile Canyon took the spillover from Virginia City, and not until well into this century was the area devoid of mills and residences. In 1902 the Butters mill, the nation's largest cyanide plant at that time, began refining tailing piles; but with its closing 25 years later, Six Mile Canyon's industrial days ended. The refreshing back road through the canyon today leads past groves of cottonwoods, old bridges, stone ruins, and mine dumps.

The Devil's Gate toll house stood at the southern terminus of a road to Gold Hill. This narrow pass is an extremely important Comstock landmark. Beginning in the summer of 1859 this gate was the entrance for thousands of silver-mad Californians to the famed Lode three miles above. J. Ross Browne described the traffic as an "almost continuous string . . . which stretched like a great snake dragging its slow length along as far as the eye could reach." In the moving pageant the aged competed with the young and even sick men joined in this race of avarice. In the rear is part of Silver City. (*Mackay School of Mines, University of Nevada*)

LOUSETOWN, 7 miles north of SR 17 at a point 2 miles north of Virginia City.

Early in the 1860s Lousetown, corruption of Louisa Town, began as a toll station on the turnpike from Virginia City to Stone & Gates crossing in the Truckee Meadows. Another road was later built almost directly north to connect with the Truckee River. Lousetown eventually consisted of about a dozen buildings which contained lodging facilities, wagon shop and blacksmith shop, and here teamsters, cattlemen, sheepherders and miners met each other in coming and going.

Tradition in Virginia City has associated Lousetown, with race tracks. The first one at nearby Ice Lake was replaced toward the end of the 1860s by a larger and better-known track in a flat in Long Valley two miles north of Virginia City. The latter track developed into a tough little sporting center for the Comstock crowd, and saloonkeepers and crooked gamblers mingled with other sports who hung out there. Prize fights which were illegal in Virginia City were held here.

Stage and freight traffic declined as early as the mid-1860s when the Geiger Grade assumed most of the traffic northwest to and from Virginia City and racing probably ceased in the 1870s. Foundations mark the site of Lousetown and traces of the race track oval also remain.

FIVE MILE HOUSE (Washoe County), 5 miles north of Virginia City, on the old Geiger Grade.

This station and teamsters' hangout at the summit of the original Geiger Grade was an important stop on that road during the 1860s. It was also known as Summit House.

Early in this century Six Mile Canyon had quieted considerably since the Comstock boom days. Tramway towers extend from the center of town east to the Butters cyanide plant (below), situated at the foot of Sugar Loaf. Tonopah ores were also treated there in the early years of that camp before local facilities could be constructed. *(Both photos: William H. Scott)*

BUTTERS PLANT
VIRGINIA, NEV.

The Wedekind mine and mill were operating before the City of Sparks came into existence. *(Nevada Historical Society)*

This small country school is the only evidence remaining of the former community of Glendale. It was built just before Nevada became a state and remained in use for nearly a century. *(Frank Mitrani photo)*

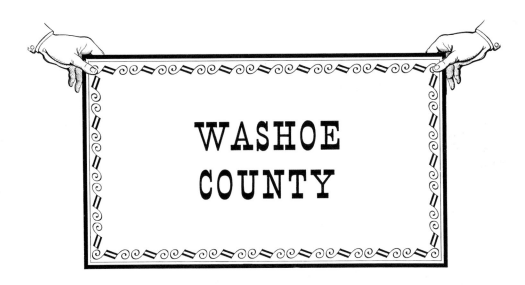

WASHOE COUNTY

Since its creation in 1861, Washoe has been one of the state's most influential counties because of its strategic location and large population. Settlement dates to the 1850s when Mormons established farms in Washoe Valley. When the Comstock boom spread after 1860, such towns as Franktown, Ophir and Washoe City grew up around farming and lumber and quartz mills. That activity peaked in the mid-1860s, when the county had more voters than at any time until Reno's growth after 1904.

The building of railroads in Nevada during 1868 and 1869 restructured the county's economy. Reno on the Central Pacific became the supply depot for the Comstock, while the county's quartz milling industry was virtually killed by the competition of the great new milling center on the Carson River in Ormsby County, which became easily accessible on completion of the Virginia & Truckee Railroad. The mining camps of Peavine and Pyramid were active in the 1870s. Olinghouse emerged after 1897, and in this century Wedekind and smaller mines produced briefly.

AUBURN, on Wedekind Road, 2½ miles northeast of downtown Reno.

After an English mining and milling company built a 20-stamp mill at the north end of Truckee Meadows in 1865, the mill camp of Auburn sprang up. It died when Reno was founded in the spring of 1868, though the mill continued to operate during the 1870s and occasionally in the 1880s. Reno's later growth had overtaken the site by 1951 but mill ditches still remain.

WEDEKIND, east of SR 33 at a point 2 miles north of downtown Sparks.

George Wedekind, a piano tuner who spent his idle hours prospecting in the hills northeast of Reno, discovered gold in 1896 by tracing float from the Reno-Spanish Springs Valley road to a nearby source. Hopeful Renoites spent their weekends searching for leads, and by 1901 various individuals had sunk about fifty shafts. Wedekind himself took out about $100,000 before selling out to Governor John Sparks for $175,000. In the summer of 1901 the small camp of Wedekind City, briefly called Bryan City, had a store, machine shop, assay office, boarding house, and a year later a post office as well. Sparks built a thirty-ton mill but made only a few bullion shipments before stopping operations about a year later because of excessive losses in milling.

PYRAMID CITY or Lower Pyramid, 1 mile south of SR 33 at a point 25 miles north of Sparks.

Though silver ledges had been found as early as 1860, the Pyramid district did not attract outside attention until the spring of 1876 when a mineral-conscious Reno physician spotted an interesting ore specimen on the table of a sick miner. Since the assay promised high returns, the alert doctor made locations. A rush developed after news of this discovery had circulated and Pyramid City sprang up from the sagebrush. A two-stamp mill was erected nearby to crush ore.

Of the five townsites eventually platted in the district, Pyramid City in the delta of Perry Canyon became the most important and in March 1877

In Wadsworth before 1884, an 18-horse team with three wagons laden with whiskey, other supplies and equipment is about to depart for central Nevada mining camps. The smallest wagon contained camp supplies and animal feed. Note the "wheeler" in front of the largest wagon; he controlled the team by a single jerkline that ran from the lead team at left.

The relocated main street early in this century (below) shows depot fountain across from tobacco shop, ice cream parlor, grocery and provision store (which had a fraternal hall on the second story), barber shop, and lodging house. *(Top: Northeastern Nevada Museum; bottom: Nevada Historical Society)*

WADSWORTH, NEV.

possessed two saloons, a Chinese washhouse, store, boarding house and a stage line with daily service to Reno. Several hailed the boom as a "new Comstock," a certain extension of that rich mineral area. In the winter of 1877 sixty miners prospected the district but only one woman graced the camp. She dressed in masculine apparel for awhile until acquiring a pullback of the latest pattern. The local miners had hopes that with the coming of spring, more pullbacks would find their way into camp.

Two miles above Pyramid City, a smaller camp called Jonesville or Upper Pyramid grew around the district's most important mine, the Jones & Kincaid. That mine produced ore for eight years after 1877 and the camp contained a hotel, store and several rock dwellings. Both Pyramid City and Jonesville died toward the end of the 1880s and the Pyramid City post office closed in 1889. No structures mark the site of Pyramid City; at Jonesville several rock walls remain in a picturesque canyon, accessible only by high axle cars.

GLENDALE, on Boynton Lane 1 mile southeast of Sparks.

Glendale started in 1857 as a station and trading post for westbound emigrants, operated by Stone and Gates. During Nevada's pre-territorial days many travelers crossed the Truckee River at this point, and in 1860 these men operated a toll bridge and ferry. Glendale was also the terminus of a turnpike which extended almost to Virginia City. A school opened in 1864 to serve the families in Truckee Meadows.

By 1866 Glendale had two stores, a hotel, market, blacksmith shop and saloons, and the village was considered the literary and social center of Truckee Meadows. A post office was officially established in 1867. After Reno was founded in May 1868, most of Glendale's commercial activity moved there within the year. At least one druggist remained and prepared the meadows' favorite remedy—syrup of figs—which was so popular that it had replaced the community's other popular remedies such as Ayer's Pills, Perry Davis' Pain Killer, Mrs. Winslow's Soothing Syrup for children, and Hostetter's Stomach Bitters. Nevada's oldest school house stands on the original Glendale site.

JAMISON'S STATION, near Steamboat Creek 3 miles southeast of Sparks.

In 1852 a Mormon trader named Jamison established a station on the east edge of Truckee Meadows between marshes bordering the Truckee River and the foothills of the Virginia Range at a point where every westbound emigrant train had to pass by. Thousands of emigrants traveled through the meadows, and with all traffic immediately at his doorstep, Jamison exchanged provisions and healthy cattle for exhausted stock, overworked and undernourished after the long journey through the deserts to the east. Emigrants rested here, preparing for the final struggle over the Sierra. Fenced-in rock foundations are left.

WASHINGTON (Storey County), 3½ miles south of I-80 at Lockwood exit, 10 miles east of Reno.

This settlement and station of the 1860s was supposed to develop into a thriving town when the nearby silver mines opened up. Mining never got started and Washington was probably abandoned in the 1870s. Remnants of two stone buildings remain.

DERBY, south of I-80 at Painted Rock exit, 5 miles west of Wadsworth.

Gold strikes in the fall of 1904 led to the founding of a camp which by mid-1906 had a post office and Southern Pacific station. In 1907 the San Francisco *Recorder* described Derby as a promising camp where a mill might soon be built. Stages ran to Olinghouse and the round trip fare was $1.50. Nothing came of the mines and the post office closed in 1922. Seven years later Roderick post office opened here. It closed in 1936 and nothing remains to be seen.

WADSWORTH, one mile northeast of Wadsworth exit on I-80 at a point 31 miles east of Reno.

Situated on the big bend of the Truckee River at a point where it turns north toward Pyramid Lake, this locality was the first source of pure water for emigrants who had come across the harsh deserts to the northeast. After 1854 crude trading posts were maintained during months of heavy emigrant travel, and the few settlers who homesteaded in the 1860s saw the Central Pacific built to here in the summer of 1868. When the railroad established a supply camp for construction northeastward across the deserts, a community developed on the east bank of the Truckee River and had a post office by August. The C.P. made Wadsworth headquarters for its Truckee division with a twenty-stall roundhouse and machine shops for rebuilding engines. In front of the big freight depot an enclosed park soon had trees, fountain and a carefully kept lawn, later described by west-bound travelers as a delightful sight after miles of barren, monotonous desert.

Because of Wadsworth's geographical position, an important freighting trade developed with Columbus, Ellsworth, Belmont and many other mining camps to the south and east. The huge animal-driven outfits, trailing from two to four wagons loaded with supplies and equipment, attracted the curiosity of eastern tourists. Soda and borax from Churchill and Esmeralda counties were teamed into Wadsworth for shipment to distant markets. With extensive facilities for both freighting and railroad maintenance, Wadsworth became the state's most important railroad town east of Reno.

During the 1870s Wadsworth contained several large stores, hotels, saloons and "china houses *ad libitum*," as an 1882 tourist guide archly referred to certain establishments. The town's sizeable tax roll became a bone of contention in 1869-70 between Storey, Lyon and Washoe counties. The latter had always exercised jurisdiction and Wadsworth was officially placed in it by the Humboldt County district court in May 1871. That year the town made an unsuccessful attempt to become a part of sparsely-populated Churchill County, in hope of attaining the status of county seat. Wadsworth's population of about 700 in 1871 was greater than that of all Churchill.

For the next thirty years Wadsworth continued as a prosperous freighting center, and even after the Carson & Colorado Railroad was built into southwestern Nevada in 1881, teamsters still maintained a fair trade with that area. A fire which originated in the railroad depot in April 1884 quickly spread through town destroying four-fifths of the buildings. Ground was then broken for new yards on the west side of the Truckee River and Wadsworth was rebuilt in its present location, prospering for the rest of the century.

The town's days were numbered after 1902 when the Southern Pacific chose to relocate its shops east of Reno in what is now Sparks, rather than to remodel Wadsworth's outmoded facilities. Transfer of shop equipment which began in 1904 was followed by removal of stores and dwellings. Trees near the depot and roundhouse were uprooted and hauled to the new location, and the Wadsworth *Dispatch* became the Sparks *Dispatch*. Thereafter Wadsworth declined to a scattered village wholly dependent on tourists, and since Interstate 80 bypassed the town in the 1960s, it has become very sleepy indeed.

OLINGHOUSE, 5½ miles west of SR 34 at a point 2 miles northwest of Wadsworth.

Though prospected as early as 1860, with some activity also in 1864, 1876 and 1893, Olinghouse's first sustained mining development began in 1897 when placer miners worked deposits in ravines tributary to Olinghouse Canyon. The White Horse district was organized in January 1899, and with enthusiasm running high several prospectors drifted into the camp to locate claims. A post office, first called Ora, opened in January 1898; a small mill was installed near the canyon creek; and in time saloons, assay office, restaurants and lodging houses were in business. Production peaked in 1902, but a decline set in during the next year.

Many individuals gave the district a second look in 1906 and a new corporation built a huge fifty-stamp mill a mile west of Wadsworth. The Nevada Railroad connected mines and mill after February 1907, and on May 29 Olinghouse celebrated Railroad Day with speeches, sports, barbecue and an evening dance. By fall, however, it was evident that the mines could not deliver enough gold to keep the mill running, and at year's end the railroad was dismantled with the mill soon following suit. Some production is reported for several years between 1910 and 1940. Wooden buildings remain at Olinghouse while mill foundations are to be seen west of Wadsworth.

PEAVINE, earlier Poe City, via graded road 3 miles south of US 395 at a point 9 miles northwest of Reno.

Poe City was laid out after extensive copper and gold veins were discovered on the east side of Peavine Peak early in 1863, and within a year it had 200 inhabitants. Specimens of rich copper ore were exhibited in 1864 at the state fair in Carson City. Ore was not shipped in quantity until late 1866, when wagons took it to Cisco, California, from which the new Central Pacific trains carried it to a smelter at Sacramento. During 1867 the C.P. was completed over Donner Summit, and the closeness of the railroad gave considerable impetus to increased prospecting. Early in 1868 some 13 veins were being exploited.

Activity peaked about 1873-74 when Peavine had a few hundred inhabitants, a ten-stamp mill, brick and log houses and a post office known as Poeville. By 1880 the population had declined to a mere dozen, and only limited work was done thereafter. Mine dumps remain to mark the site of "Podunk" as some people used to refer to the place.

BROOKLYN, approximately 6 miles west-north-west of Reno.

Initial mining efforts began in 1875 when the New York Co. opened a tunnel on the south side of Peavine Mountain and laid out a townsite. Before its abandonment a year or two later, the camp contained a boarding house, company shops, shanties and stables. Though the company spent much money and time in development, little ore was actually found.

HUNTER'S STATION, south of old US 40 at a point 5 miles west of Reno.

This Truckee River crossing of the 1860s consisted of hotel and store and, from 1867 to 1870, a post office. Later this settlement was known as Mayberrys.

CRYSTAL PEAK, half-mile northwest of Verdi via graded road.

Beginning in 1864 this rowdy lumber camp flourished for about five years after the Crystal Peak Co., the principal lumber and mining firm in the area, laid out a townsite in a pleasantly-situated meadow north of the Truckee River. The site was selected because it was a natural outlet for shipment of timber to California markets. The company's main timber stands were located 10 to 15 miles west in California where gold and silver veins were uncovered. Low-grade coal was also found nearby, and several companies were formed to work those deposits. A post office was established in the summer of 1864 and a modest business district developed.

Crystal Peak's best year was 1868 when the area's 1500 people supplied immense quantities of lumber required for building the Central Pacific across northwestern Nevada. After the railroad laid out Verdi and placed its depot facilities there in 1869, Crystal Peak swiftly declined. Its post office was officially moved to the new town that November, and by 1870 nearby sawmills were considered as belonging to Verdi. Logging continued for another half-century, and increased to the extent that in 1902 the Verdi Lumber Co. extended a shortline railroad into the California timberlands. By the 1920s area lumbering activity practically ceased. Verdi lives on as a small town, but only a few graves and foundations indicate the site of Crystal Peak.

LAKE'S CROSSING, on the site of the Riverside Hotel in downtown Reno.

During the 1860s four important bridges carried traffic across the Truckee River at strategic points in the Truckee Meadows, and the most important of these was Lake's Crossing. This crossing was first settled in 1859 when a Mr. Fuller built a shelter on the south side of the Truckee and operated a ferry service. He added a toll bridge in 1860, but it was wiped out by a flood in the winter of 1862. Fuller then traded his property and bridge location for a ranch in the Honey Lake area of California owned by M. C. Lake, who rebuilt the old bridge in 1863 and eventually constructed a hotel with tavern and store. The bridge then took the name Lake's Crossing, and Reno townsite was platted nearby in April 1868. Two years later Lake built the Lake House in Reno, a fine two-story wood-frame hotel.

JUNCTION HOUSE, on US 395, 3 miles south of downtown Reno.

Initially a ranch was started here sometime in the early 1850s, probably the first one in the Truckee Meadows. Gradually roads were built through here and a station house was started. By mid-1861 Junction House was a busy crossroads

Charcoal drawing of Crystal Peak shows a street of this scattered camp. A shingle mill appears in the right corner while Verdi Peak and Crystal Peak Ridge are in the distance. *(Nevada Historical Society)*

Important crossing during the rush to "Washoe" after 1859 was Lake's (Fuller's) Crossing, here depicted in the mid-1860s after a roadhouse had been built. Charges for cross-ing the bridge were ten cents a head for pack animals and loose stock, fifty cents for each horseman, a dollar for each carriage or small wagon, and $1.25 or more for larger rigs. On All Fools' Day, 1868, Reno townsite was laid out on the other side of the bridge, and after an auction on May 9 Reno was officially born. Lake replaced his tavern-inn shown here with a commodious hotel which opened on New Year's Day, 1870. *(Nevada Historical Society)*

settlement; toll roads from Virginia City and Washoe Valley as well as the Henness Pass road from California, the old emigrant road from the east and a road from Oregon all converged here. A post office known as Truckee Meadows was established in September 1862 which served nearby ranches until it was officially discontinued almost exactly a decade later. When the Virginia & Truckee Railroad was built through here in 1871 the station took the name Andersons. A historical marker indicates the site.

HUFFAKERS, on US 395, 7 miles south of downtown Reno.

At the terminus of the Pacific Wood, Lumber & Flume Co.'s six-mile-long flume, the community of Huffakers consisted of an unofficial post office, store, school and produce station on the Virginia & Truckee Railroad in 1871. Later in the decade it was also the home of the Athenian Literary Society where recitations, songs and eulogies were presented in addition to debates on such topics as Mormonism and polygamy.

STEAMBOAT SPRINGS, east side US 395 at a point 12 miles south of Reno.

Nevada's best known mineralized hot springs were permanently settled in 1860, though for years they had been a welcome oasis and campground for westward bound wagons. A bathhouse, cottages and hospital were built early in the 1860s, but most buildings were destroyed by a fire in 1867. Early in 1871 a fine hotel was erected to accommodate fifty guests, and a drugstore, cottages and 15 sets of medicinal baths made this a fashionable spa for Comstockers, tourists and invalids.

The Virginia & Truckee Railroad reached here from Reno in November 1871, and for nearly a year thereafter Steamboat Springs was a busy transshipping point for freight bound for the Comstock and points south, with extensive wagon yards and storage buildings. The V.&T.'s completion to Carson City in August 1872 quickly extinguished the commercial light of Steamboat Springs, but resort facilities have remained in operation to the present time. The springs cover an area a mile long and about a third of a mile wide. Many springs still shoot clouds of steam at intervals, but others are now dry, yawning vents.

MAGNOLIA HOUSE, 2¼ miles east of Steamboat Springs.

Here at the foot of the old Geiger Grade was the largest toll station on the turnpike from Virginia City to Steamboat Springs. In the 1860s and 1870s this station consisted of a blacksmith shop, wagon yard, corrals, tollhouse and possibly a farm. Little of interest remains.

GALENA, 1½ miles south of SR 27 at a point 4 miles west of its junction with US 395.

Founded in 1860 as a mining camp when silver was discovered in the eastern foothills of the Sierra Nevada, Galena grew in importance after 1862 when nearby groves were cut for use on the Comstock. Activity peaked in 1863-64 when a dozen sawmills encircled the town. Lumbering took place 24 hours a day, and Galena's crowded streets and grog shops overflowed with charcoal burners, wood choppers, timbermen, millers, miners, bullwhackers and teamsters. The camp had the reputation of being the gayest in Nevada territory; all incoming liquors were strengthened with "powerful ingredients" until they satisfied the taste of the most exacting bullwhacker.

Galena's 300 residents watched Civil War developments closely. Union victories were celebrated with songs, cheers and patriotic addresses around huge bonfires. This solidly Republican town gave President Lincoln 381 out of 384 votes in the 1864 election, in sharp contrast to its Democratic rival, Washoe City, four miles down the slope.

The locals faced bad weather without flinching, not daring to carry umbrella or parasol because neither was a match for the Washoe zephyr, a gale-like wind that regularly visited the camp. Flames spread by these zephyrs in 1865 and 1867 destroyed most of the camp's wooden buildings at about the time that nearby timberlands were depleted by excessive cutting. Only a few weathered graves and foundations now remain at the site.

INCLINE, on SR 28, 2 miles east of its junction with SR 27 (22 miles south of Reno).

This settlement began about 1879 when the Sierra Nevada Wood & Lumber Co. installed a sawmill on the northeast shore of Lake Tahoe to

41

This map of the "Washoe" region in 1862 shows route of the projected Railroad from the Comstock to the Ophir mill. The camp adjacent was Ophir, incorrectly called "Washoe" on the map. The original map also indicates a "Lake City" at the north end of Washoe Lake; a correction inserted here shows Washoe City in its true location.

(*National Archives*)

take advantage of a plentiful supply of timber. By the summer of 1881 a company narrow gauge railroad began hauling timbers to the mill, and the cut lumber and cordwood was then carried in wooden cars up a 4000-foot-long inclined hydraulic tramway to the summit of the Carson Range. From there the wood was flumed to Lakeview where it was dumped and loaded on Virginia & Truckee cars for shipment to the Comstock.

The settlement of Incline was a minor supply center for the workers in the area, who numbered up to 200 men at peak periods, and a post office was open from 1884 until the lumbering activity ceased in 1895. Machinery was then dismantled but wooden ruins of the incline railway still remain.

WASHOE CITY, on US 395 at a point 18 miles south of Reno.

Washoe City was born of necessity. Virginia City needed timber for its mines, and foothills west of Washoe Lake were covered with trees. Unlimited water power was available to run mills for reducing ore. Washoe City emerged early in 1861 north of Washoe Lake and quickly became a commercial center for nearby farms, sawmills, and quartz mills including the twenty-stamp Atchison mill. Dozens of mule-driven ore wagons plied daily to Virginia City hauling farm produce and freshly cut timbers, while downward runs brought Comstock ore for milling.

Washoe City gained additional prestige when it became county seat in November 1861 and judges, lawyers, doctors and a dentist soon settled here. Restaurants, stores, saloons, livery stables, feed yards, drugstores, post office, bath house and shaving emporium all opened up, and in October 1862 the Washoe *Times* made its first appearance. Eventually Masonic and Odd Fellows lodges erected substantial meeting halls; churches, a school and a hospital were built and in 1863 the county constructed an imposing brick courthouse and jail.

By the mid-1860s Washoe City had a large floating population which may have reached 6000 at times, with less than half that many permanent residents. In the local bistros bullwhackers and lumberjacks from Galena often had it out with Comstock teamsters and miners in fisticuffs and shootings, but less pugnacious individuals also came for the amusements, dances, theater and horse racing. John C. Lewis' *Eastern Slope* began publication in 1865, lasting until June 1868 when he moved it to Reno.

Milling and lumbering activity faltered as early as 1865, and the completion of the Virginia & Truckee Railroad to the Carson River in 1869 destroyed what was left of the town's twin mainstays. After two lengthy court fights with Reno during 1870-71, Washoe City lost the county seat, and the brick courthouse was taken apart and sold. The economy of Washoe City soon collapsed. By 1880 the town had become a dilapidated hamlet with a population of only 200. In 1894 the post office closed. Only one of the old commercial structures is left, but old residences and a well-preserved cemetery remain.

OPHIR, quarter-mile east of US 395 at a point 20 miles south of Reno.

Ophir derived its name from the mythical land from whence came all gold. After the Ophir Mining Co. of Virginia City erected a large $500,000 72-stamp quartz mill complex in 1861, the camp of Ophir grew around the operation and acquired a few hundred residents. The mill building covered over an acre of ground and employed 165 men. Its superintendent earned a salary of $30,000 and a furnished house. The camp grew to almost 300 residents in 1862-63, and construction of a railroad from Virginia City west to Ophir was planned but not started. Instead, ore-laden wagons came bumping down from the Comstock over a toll road, reaching Ophir by way of a $75,000 mile-long wooden causeway across marshes at the north end of Washoe Lake. Besides milling, the camp thrived due to the extensive shipping of cordwood.

Accidents in the mills, people falling under wagons, and teamsters taking swings at each other kept many doctors busy. Businesses included saloons, lawyers, the post office, first called Washoe, which opened in November 1861, and several blacksmith and wagon shops to repair wagons damaged on the grueling journey from the Comstock. The quick decline of lumbering and mill activity in the mid-1860s led to the end of Ophir, and only 41 voters remained in 1871 when the post office was removed. During the next year the big mill was dismantled. Its walls remain in a private field; ask owner's permission to visit.

Just right of Judge J. W. North's quartz mill at Washoe City was Washoe County's $25,000 brick courthouse, built early in 1863. This rare view looks east, about 1864, when Washoe City was among Nevada's leading towns. *(Henry E. Huntington Library)*

The shipping and milling town of Washoe City appeared impressive from the Sierra foothills in the mid-1860s.

Though it was laid out in a grid, zoning and city ordinances were probably unheard of. Mills, commercial building, churches, residences and the courthouse were built where convenient, and animals and livestock roamed at will. Shooting chickens on the street was a local sport. A contemporary editor said that the town resembled a huge unattractive woodyard. *(E. M. Mack Collection, Nevada Historical Society)*

FRANKTOWN, on US 395 at a point 21 miles south of Reno.

Mormons started Franktown in 1852, only a year after Nevada's first settlement at Genoa. Four-acre lots were laid out in 1855 and the community built up rapidly, but in 1857 over 350 Mormon families sold their property here and left for Salt Lake City in response to the call of Brigham Young. When Orson Hyde, wishing to obey the edict, received very little for his sawmill and farm, he cursed the area before departing: "Ye shall be visited with thunder and . . . with floods, with pestilence and with famine, until your names are not known amongst men."

Nevertheless, by 1860 Franktown was more prosperous than ever. The $250,000, sixty-stamp Dall mill was erected that year to refine Comstock ores; two smaller mills operated south of Washoe Lake and sawmills west of town supplied Virginia City with lumber.

Nevada's first millionaires, Sandy and Eilley Bowers, completed a lavish two-story mansion north of Franktown a few years later. European furniture and marble mantles were shipped around the Horn to add opulence to the Bowers' bid to impress the social elite of the Comstock.

Franktown had a number of neat dwellings and prosperous farms by the mid-1860s, but the town thereafter declined with a falling off of milling and lumbering activity. In 1871 an arsonist started a fire that burned the Dall mill to the ground. The next year the Virginia & Truckee Railroad made Franktown a produce station, but by 1880 only five businesses remained. Foundations and the V.&T. water tank mark the site. The Bowers mansion, a mile north, is a museum and county park open to the public.

MILL STATION, west of US 395 at a point 24 miles south of Reno.

This was a settlement near sawmills and two quartz mills, and after 1871 Mill Station became a lumber stop on the Virginia & Truckee. The place never grew large and nothing of interest remains.

Buildings housing machinery covered over an acre in this artist's conception of the huge $500,000 Ophir Quartz mill, built in 1861. Its stamps fell silent in 1867 because of competition from mills in Carson River Canyon. During 1873 the mill was dismantled, and now only walls remain in a private field. (*Abraham Kendall Collection*)

45

The hotel at Curry's Warm Springs, a popular resort for settlers along the Carson River, was still in use early in this century. *(Mrs. Jock Taylor Collection)*

In 1880 Empire City was an important village between Carson City and Dayton. A spur of the Virginia & Truckee Railroad extends from the main line on the right alongside the long woodpile in the center of the picture and past the Mexican Mill (in background at the left) to woodyards across the Carson River. Another V&T spur served the Mexican mill. Behind the trees in back of the mill was the home of the mill superintendent, in use in the early 1970s. *(Ralph H. Barrett Collection)*

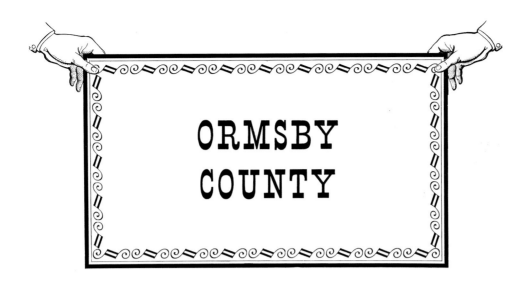

ORMSBY COUNTY

No mining developments of any importance have been undertaken in Ormsby County, but Nevada's most important milling complex was built on the Carson River during the early part of the Comstock boom in the 1860s. The county seat, Carson City, has been since 1861 the territorial and state capital of Nevada. The only other town of importance was Empire City, a milling and lumbering satellite of the Comstock which prospered until the decline of mining in 1878. Milling all along the Carson River thereafter also slowed, ceasing entirely by 1920.

LAKEVIEW, west side US 395, 5 miles north of Carson City.

Initially established by the Virginia & Gold Hill Water Co. about 1870, Lakeview was also made a post office and flag station by the Virginia & Truckee Railroad. A post office operated during 1881-83 and 1890-94.

CURRY'S WARM SPRINGS, 1¾ miles east of Carson City.

In the early 1860s a prominent early Nevadan named Abraham Curry operated a hotel with swimming pools at the warm springs which were used by the local miners, loggers and others. The territorial legislature also met here through Curry's generosity. A nearby quarry supplied sandstone for buildings in Carson City, Virginia City, Reno and the Brunswick Mill. Later Nevada built its state penitentiary at the warm springs.

EMPIRE CITY, one-half mile south of US 50 at a point 3¾ miles east of Carson City.

As early as 1855 a ranch with station and tavern known as Dutch Nick's was opened on the north bank of the Carson River for overland travelers. Its proprietor, Nicholas Ambrose, moved to Johntown about 1857 and then to Six Mile Canyon the next spring where he set up a saloon-boarding house in a large tent, charging the miners $14 a week for food and blankets. The small frame establishment he erected in 1859 at Gold Hill was that camp's first building. Nick then returned to the sage desert he knew five years earlier to operate a commodious hotel on Main Street of the new town of Empire City.

Streets and lots were surveyed in March 1860, and the rapidly-growing town thrived on silver mining and logging. The town soon was given the nickname of "seaport" because of the water-borne traffic in timber which was driven down the Carson River, having first been hauled over the mountains from groves in Alpine County and the Lake Tahoe area. Great booms caught the wood on the river, sawmills cut it for timbering the mines, construction and fuel, and local woodyards stored it for wagon delivery to the Comstock.

Quartz milling began in 1860 after completion of a small mill. During the next three years three important mills were constructed: the 44-stamp Mexican, Mead's with 16 stamps, and Baldwin, 16 stamps. In 1863 J. Ross Browne noted that quartz mills and sawmills completely usurped the banks of the Carson River, and that the "hammering of

47

To satisfy the Comstock's demand for steam, gigantic wood drives extending up to four miles or more took place on the Carson River each spring after the first rush of high water. At Empire City the drive ended and railroad cars of the Virginia & Truckee completed the delivery. After wood was cut and stored in booms (above), ropes and chains were released on a certain date and the drive began. (In other drives large logs were sent down the river for the sawmills at Empire City.) Because the mighty Carson could not be controlled, log jams (below) were inevitable. They afforded excitement to the local inhabitants.

Even more often, stray timbers were caught in a sand bar, as shown in an eddy near the Cradlebaugh Bridge (middle right) south of Carson City. Each logger holds a long hooked pole known as a picaroon with which logs were nudged to keep them moving along and to prevent jams. Behind the men the pirogue follows the drive. At the stern a man with a large pole steered and propelled the canoe.

Normally the pirogue sailed ahead of the loggers to a designated spot to set up camp. In the close-up view (above, right), some of the cooking supplies, food, tents, bedrolls and spare tools are shown.

Wood was teamed ashore near Empire City (lower right). While wood was laid crosswise on the bed of one wagon, another is ready to move forward. *(Lower right: Mackay School of Mines, University of Nevada; all others: Nevada State Museum)*

The $200,000 Morgan mill (above) built in 1865, handled 75 tons of ore daily. Behind the large trestle carrying tailings to a pond off to the right, the Virginia & Truckee tracks lead to Empire City in the distance. A small cyanide plant was active here around World War I, but the area now is a vast clump of cottonwoods. *(Bancroft Library)*

The Vivian mill, 16 stamps and 40-ton capacity, was in the very heart of the Carson River Canyon mills. During the 1860s and 1870s the thundering noise of stamps echoed almost 24 hours a day along these walls. The Vivian received its ore from V&T cars (which ran above the steep grade at the left) down a chute and across a bridge.
(Fannie Spurgeon Collection)

stamps, the hissing of steam, the whirling of clouds of smoke belching from tall chimneys, and the confused clamor of voices from a busy multitude" all reminded him of a manufacturing city. By the mid-1860s the lumbering activity overtook the important Galena-Washoe City area in furnishing cut wood for Virginia City while the Carson River mills assumed most of the Comstock milling.

Empire City had grown to extend three-fourths of a mile by a half-mile, and it contained stores, hotels, real estate offices, carpenter shops, grocery stores, post office and several saloons. Large stables and blacksmith shops occupied the south side of town near the river for easy access for watering stock. A fine public school served this town which had over 700 inhabitants during peak times, between 1865 and 1875.

The Virginia & Truckee Railroad was completed through here in 1869 and in the next year lumbering activity decreased somewhat because a large woodyard opened south of Carson City. (See Glenbrook.) But the railroad brought increased business to the local quartz mills and they were enlarged to handle the carloads of ore that came on the downhill runs. Quartz milling reached its peak in the early 1870s. With the decline of the Comstock in 1878, Empire City also diminished and the town had only 150 in the 1880 census. The post office closed in 1910 and only one family remained in the 1960s.

MILLS IN CARSON RIVER CANYON, from ½ to 3 miles east of Empire City.

A century ago the seven-mile portion of the Carson River canyon, from east of Empire City and into Lyon County toward Dayton, was virtually a continuous strip of mills and settlements housing hundreds of people. During the years of heavy Comstock mining activity, 1860 to 1878, several mills and arrastras opened in the canyon to take advantage of the water power of the Carson River. A few of the mills ran on steam and required wood shipped by wagons from Empire City. Houses and shanties clustered at each mill, as well as immense wagon yards and stables for animals and equipment.

Nevada's greatest and most important milling complex began to form in 1860 when two big mills were built, and the erection of other large stamp mills took place annually until 1865. Through that decade an almost continuous stream of mule-driven ore wagons from the mines at Virginia City deposited their precious cargoes at the mills until the Virginia & Truckee Railroad was built in 1869, displacing most wagons. Mills were altered and enlarged to handle bonanza Comstock outputs during 1871-75. When production slowed after 1878, the mills closed down, one by one. No one lives in the canyon today.

Five of the largest mills were served by the Virginia & Truckee. Following the river road downstream on the old V.&T. railroad grade from Empire City, the Yellow Jacket or Morgan mill was a half-mile east on the north bank of the Carson River; a mile further was the Brunswick. Three-quarters of a mile to the east was the Merrimac, and the same distance beyond on the south side of the river was the Vivian mill. East of this a quarter mile was the Santiago mill, and another half-mile east, 4¼ miles from Empire City, where the river road begins to swing north, was the terminus of the narrow gauge line that came from the Eureka mill in Lyon County.

From the river road segments of the Eureka Mill railroad grade are visible far down the canyon to the east. Its gradient is still traceable but only on foot, and big stone abutments stand where trestles spanned gullies.

With barren cliffs and colorful rock formations as well as mill foundations, this canyon byway is the most interesting short river road in Nevada. Certainly none other has such memories.

GREGORY'S MILL, approximately 3 miles west of of Carson City.

Three sawmills were constructed on Mill Creek before 1861 at an aggregate cost of $60,000. The largest was Gregory's, erected in 1859 as the first steam-powered mill in western Utah territory. The other mills took power from the creek's rapid fall. Gregory's cut 15,000 feet of lumber per day while the others had smaller capacity. Even before the Comstock discovery, several families had located at Gregory's and early in the 1860s these mills employed 100 men, but all declined later in the decade.

51

In the foreground, water is being diverted from the Carson River into the ditch to be used by the next mill downstream, the Merrimac. A Virginia & Truckee train heads westward toward the Brunswick mill in the background. That mill with 56 stamps and 155-ton daily capacity, the Carson River Canyon's largest, was shut down in 1904.
(Mrs. Jack Burns Collection)

Originally built in 1861, the Eureka mill (below) ultimately had 60 stamps capable of processing 120 tons of ore daily. Without direct benefit of the Virginia & Truckee Railroad, the mill constructed its own 1.1-mile narrow gauge from a point below the V&T's Eureka siding in 1872 so that Comstock ores could be expeditiously sent. Transfer of ore at Eureka siding was accomplished by a chute which sent ore into horse-drawn cars (later replaced by a steam locomotive). This view of the mill around 1910 shows tracks of the Eureka Mill Railroad entering from the left. Behind the mill and to the right was the superintendent's home. *(William H. Scott photo)*

CLEAR CREEK STATION, east side US 395 at a point 4½ miles south of Carson City.

This station was founded in the late 1850s at a point on Clear Creek where emigrants, stage teams and freight wagons stopped for water. Eventually a large wagon yard, blacksmith shop and telegraph office were added to the station.

To the west, three important sawmills were active in Clear Creek Canyon before 1861; Haskell & Co.'s mill was the largest. These mills originally cost $33,000, employed about 100 men and produced 50,000 feet of lumber per day. Each mill had its own settlement and enough people lived in the canyon and at Clear Creek Station to warrant the establishment of a polling place at Haskell's during territorial elections. By 1864 other sawmills had displaced local lumbering, and when the toll road to Lake Tahoe saw less frequent traffic the station was abandoned.

SWIFT'S STATION, via Kings Canyon Road, approximately 10 miles southwest of Carson City.

On the road to Lake Bigler, as Tahoe was then known, S. T. Swift established this station in Kings Canyon before his days as sheriff of Ormsby County began in 1872. With the decline of that road, Swift's Station fell into disuse.

Swift's Station in King's Canyon was a busy eating and overnight stop on the toll road from Carson Valley to Lake Bigler (Tahoe). Around 1861-62 a Lake Bigler Lumber Co. wagon approaches an area where larger rigs are gathered. *(California Historical Society)*

Two of Glenbrook's hotels, shown here before the turn of the century, are crowded with summer guests. The Lakeshore House later became part of the Glenbrook Inn, a popular 20th century resort. *(Top: Ralph Barrett Collection; bottom: Nevada State Museum)*

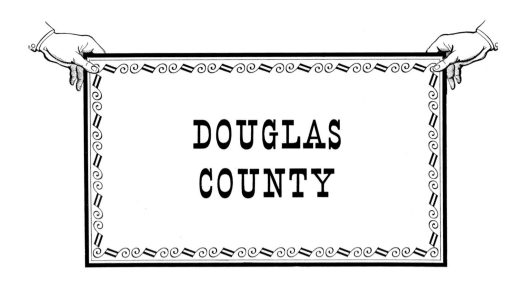

DOUGLAS COUNTY

In agricultural Douglas County is Nevada's oldest community, Genoa, which was settled in 1851. Lumbering started at Glenbrook in the 1860s and became a prosperous industry in the 1870s; by 1900 it had completely declined. Only in this century did a few small mining efforts make a showing, and these ceased after the end of World War I.

SUMMIT CAMP, south of US 50 at a point 1½ miles east of its junction with SR 28 (8 miles southwest of Carson City).

During the 1870s Summit Camp thrived as a stage stop and wood camp where the Carson & Tahoe Lumber & Fluming Co. railroad from Glenbrook met a flume which sent the cut wood to the company woodyard south of Carson City. Another stage station nearby was Spooner's, three-quarters of a mile to the west.

GLENBROOK, ½ mile northwest of US 50 at a point 11 miles north of Stateline.

The first permanent settlement on Lake Tahoe was here on the east shore, where Captain A. W. Pray built a sawmill in 1861. It had a post office as early as August 1871. Glenbrook became important as an industrial area of logging camps, sawmills, railroads, barges and flumes, all busily engaged in producing and delivering lumber for the Comstock. From timbered areas around the lake, logs were floated or barged to Glenbrook mills which during the mid-1870s were turning out about 25 million feet of sawed lumber annually.

In 1875 Glenbrook had four sawmills, a store, a billiard hall and bowling alley regarded as the finest in Nevada, two hotels and a summer population of 400. The first-class Lakeshore Hotel had a large dance hall and hired out boats for fishing and excursions as well as teams for pleasure riding. Comfortable accommodations cost twenty dollars a week. During warmer months curious sightseers ascended Spooner's Summit on the lumbering company railroad to watch the unloading and fluming of lumber. By 1880 logging activity had slumped to less than 50% of the high recorded five years earlier, and all lumbering ceased late in the century. Today Glenbrook is a modern resort and residential community.

FRIDAYS, or Small's Station, 1 mi. east of Stateline.

Originally a Pony Express stop in 1860-61, Fridays gained considerable importance as a station on the Lake Bigler toll road after its completion in 1863. In later years, about 1895, this place became known as Edgewood. A blacksmith shop remains on the site.

GENOA (pronounced Ge-no'-a) at western terminus of SR 57, 4 miles west of its junction with US 395 at a point 4 miles north of Minden.

The west side of the Carson Valley along the base of the Sierra is the cradle of civilization in Nevada, and in its midst is the town of Genoa, initially settled permanently in 1851 as Mormon Station. As early as 1848 and 1849 this locality was a camping spot on an emigrant trail to California, and in June 1850 H. S. Beatie and other Mormons built a crude roofless log enclosure and corral near a stream as a trading station. Here emigrants obtained clothing, tobacco, meat, sardines, fruit, tea, coffee, sugar, beans, flour and bacon. The latter two items sold for two dollars a pound while a pound of beef sold for a dollar. After travel slowed in September the station was abandoned. The oft-written date of 1849 for the year of Beatie's arrival has not been substantiated by scholarship.

In the spring of 1851 John Reese came with about a dozen wagons loaded with supplies and a herd of stock and horses to start a permanent trading post. Reese completed the unfinished building and also put into cultivation wheat, barley, corn, watermelons, turnips, and other vegetables. His nearest neighbors were a few placer miners in Gold Canyon 25 miles northeast, but that summer other Mormons had taken up small farms and ranches nearby. In November a crude squatters' government was set up to handle titles to farm land and adopt laws and regulations for governing Carson Valley. These people were either unaware that they were within Utah territory or considered the distant territorial government inadequate to their needs.

During 1852 emigrant travel was heavy and the new settlement grew. A blacksmith shop was built and in December Carson Valley post office opened here. With such natural advantages as rich soil, ample water for irrigation and an abundance of timber nearby, Genoa prospered. Saw and grist mills were erected in 1854, the same year that Utah territory displaced the citizens' government by creating Carson County with Mormon Station as its seat. The new county embraced the settled portion of western Utah — Carson, Eagle and Washoe valleys and Gold Canyon.

In the spring of 1856 Orson Hyde laid out a townsite and named it Genoa. In December 1858 the *Territorial Enterprise* was founded and was published here before moving on to Carson City and finally to Virginia City. During 1859 Genoa had about 200 inhabitants; the next year one of them, John Reese, left to join Captain Simpson in surveying a road through what is now central Nevada and over the Sierra. That pioneer had come here following an Indian trail but left over well-used roads.

During 1860-61 the Pony Express ran through here. The town grew with the development of the Comstock after 1859, although the seat of Carson County was moved to Carson City early in 1861. When Nevada territory carved out counties later that year, Genoa was made the shire town of Douglas County. A fine two-story brick courthouse was built in 1865, and in the 1870s the town also had schools, churches, town hall, and several stores and shops. Attractive homes with fine gardens had been built, and prosperous ranches surrounded the town. David Walley's forty-room hotel with adjoining bathhouses, at the hot springs nearly two miles south of town, was a fashionable resort.

In all Genoa had about 1000 inhabitants. An important early newspaper was the Carson Valley *News* established in 1875, replaced by the weekly *Courier* which ran until the end of the century. The town's conservative prosperity continued well into this century, although by 1915 the county seat was moved to nearby Minden. This picturesque town still has several interesting buildings including many occupied residences, courthouse-school, and restored Mormon stockade. The cemetery contains the grave of "Snowshoe" Thompson who took the mail over the Sierra before completion of the telegraph line in 1858.

VAN SICKLES, 2½ miles south of Genoa.

This station at the foot of the Kingsbury Grade occupied a stategic point on the road between the Carson Valley and Lake Tahoe via Daggett Pass. The owner of the hotel, Henry Van Sickle, killed the notorious desperado Sam Brown in 1860 and this station became a noted place because of that association.

MOTTSVILLE, 5 miles south of Genoa.

Nevada's first school was here in 1854-55 and a post office from 1858 to 1860 served nearby farms. The community was named after Hiram Mott who came in 1852 with his wife, the first permanent woman settler in Carson Valley.

SHERIDAN, 8 miles south of Genoa.

The first settler in this locality at the base of the Sierra Nevada was Moses Job who opened a small store there in 1854. It had a post office briefly in 1858 and a small settlement grew up about it which had come to be known as Sheridan by the time the post office was re-established in 1865. Within a decade the community had a saloon,

Friday's Station, located less than a mile from the south shore of Lake Tahoe, was captured by a photographer around 1864 and put on a stereo slide. Five sets of freight teams are shown, including the familiar prairie schooner arriving at the left. The station house still stood in the early 1970s. *(California Historical Society)*

When Captain James H. Simpson surveyed central Nevada in 1859 for wagon routes, he came to Genoa. Because of its fine agricultural and grazing advantages, the town thrived where other small settlements and stations were often left abandoned. Here miners from as far south as Mono County, California obtained supplies. Simpson reported that the village embraced a couple of stores and hotels, 28 houses, telegraph office, office of the *Territorial Enterprise,* four sawmills and two grist mills. *(National Archives)*

Genoa, nestled at the foot of the Sierra Nevada, was nearly a third of a century old when this picture was taken. Looking south on Main Street, this picture shows the livery, hotel and Odd Fellows hall on the left, while the courthouse is the stately brick building on the right. In the view below, the buildings farther down the street are shown more clearly. *(Top: Dr. James Herz; bottom: Ralph H. Barrett)*

Nevada's first permanent building (above), a trading post and protective stockade built in 1850-51, was initially known as Mormon Station. This building succumbed to flames in 1911, but a restoration that was made in 1947 still stands. From a camping spot on the California emigrant trail, Genoa grew to be quite a settlement late in the last century. Hansen's Saloon (below) was a typical establishment of that era, with its potbellied stove, card table, fancy wallpaper and pictures behind the bar.

(Top: Ralph H. Barrett; bottom: Nevada Historical Society)

Situated at the foot of Kingsbury Grade, Walley's Hot Springs (above) was a popular resort for many decades. The hotel had fine accommodations, and stages ran regularly from Carson City to bring the ailing to benefit from mud baths which were thought to be helpful in cases of chronic rheumatism.

When not delivering groceries and supplies, the sleigh at Sheridan was used for pleasure riding. (*Getchell Library, University of Nevada*)

blacksmith shop, wagon shop, store of general merchandise and two hotels to serve 100 people.

Modern structures have obliterated the site, although a former hotel is now a residence.

WOODFORDS (California), 13 miles south of Minden via SR 88.

The wayward Mormon bishop Sam Brannan established the first settlement in what is now Alpine County in 1847 when he built a cabin and storage dugouts. Two years later Daniel Woodford erected a station, and in 1853 John Carey built a sawmill. By 1860 Woodfords had become an important trading post and station where freight from Woodfords Canyon was reloaded from sleigh to wagon for delivery to Genoa and the Comstock. For six weeks in the spring of 1860 Woodfords was a temporary station on the Pony Express, and a telegraph line ran to this village which contained a toll station, mill, saloon, blacksmith shop and wagon yard, a large hotel, unofficial post office, and several residences. Numerous westbound travelers stopped at the Woodford station house, an inn noted for the sign with an elephant on the front of the building. Billboards at Ragtown and in other places east urged the traveler to "stop at the sign of the elephant" for accommodations for man and beast. These billboards may have been the first in the West.

During the 1860s surrounding ranches and farms grew hay, wheat, and cereals for the Comstock and other nearby mining districts. By 1867 this place also became quite a resort and possessed a fine dance hall which had a spring floor. This versatile settlement declined around 1873, when nearby mining activity slowed. A fire destroyed most structures in 1881, but one house built in 1854 from timber from Carey's mill still stands. This town of 150 people has two cemeteries and interesting old residences.

WHEELERS, on US 395, 4½ miles southeast of Minden.

During the 1860s this was a station twelve miles from Genoa on the road to Aurora. Later it was known as Tisdell and finally in the 1870s as Twelvemile House.

CARTER'S STATION, on US 395, 12 miles southeast of Minden.

Stages stopped here halfway between Twelvemile House and Double Spring during the 1870s. This station may have replaced Mammoth Lodge, a mile to the southeast, which also had a post office most of the time between 1863 and 1869. Silver was discovered near that point in 1860.

DOUBLE SPRING, on US 395, 15 miles southeast of Minden.

This was an important stage station on the Carson City-Aurora road beginning in 1861. Around 1880 it was also known as Spragues.

MOUNTAIN HOUSE, west of US 395, 19 miles southeast of Minden.

Initially known as Burnt Cabin, Mountain House was a station on the Carson City-Aurora stage run in the 1860s, but the post office took the name Holbrook in 1883. To serve prospectors in nearby hills early in this century, Mountain House had hotels, a saloon and from 1904 to 1915 a post office.

Dayton, around 1900, was a firmly established community on the north bank of the Carson River. Since the Comstock days Dayton thrived on teaming, farming and milling — with most of its services sold in Virginia City. Its business district served outlying farms and ranches. The two-story Lyon County courthouse is hidden amid the grove of poplars opposite the church; the school (below) built in 1865 north of the courthouse still stood a century later. Though always overshadowed by the Comstock, Dayton nevertheless is one of the state's most important historic towns.

(Two photos: William A. Kornmayer Collection)

LYON COUNTY

Nevada's first mineral discovery was in Gold Canyon north of Dayton in the spring of 1850. Johntown emerged there by 1854, the state's first mining camp. During the Comstock boom after 1859 Dayton prospered with extensive milling and freighting, and Como, Pine Grove, Sutro, Silver City and Fort Churchill were also important early mining camps and settlements.

After 1900 mining revived at Como and Pine Grove, and Ramsey rose as a gold camp. Ludwig, Mason and Yerington became copper centers and were aided by the Nevada Copper Belt Railroad which terminated at Wabuska and Ludwig. The copper districts boomed during World War II as well as in later years, and there was renewed activity in Gold Canyon between the world wars. Since 1950 Yerington has been the county's most important mining center.

DAYTON, 12 miles northeast of Carson City via US 50.

After westbound emigrants discovered gold in nearby Gold Canyon in 1849 a tent trading post catering to emigrants was set up each year on the north bank of the Carson River. Sometime in the early 1850s a permanent building was erected and by 1857 or 1858 a straggling hamlet emerged, known by the impromptu name of Chinatown because of the many Orientals mining placer gold in nearby streams. In the fall of 1859 most of the settlers moved their buildings to the center of Comstock activity seven miles north, leaving only a few families by early 1860. Sir Richard Burton de-

scribed this village later that year as a line of ranches and frame houses, a kind of length-without-breadth place, looking dreary and grim in the evening gloom.

By November 1861 Chinatown again contained a few hundred residents and was renamed Dayton. This same month Nevada Territory organized counties and made the town seat of Lyon County. Because of its strategic location, Dayton became a busy commercial center for the Comstock, trans-shipping freight from east and west. The rival camp of Mineral Rapids, immediately to the east, had been absorbed in the course of Dayton's early growth. The Pony Express had a station on the eastern edge of town. In January 1862 Dayton gained its post office.

After the first major quartz mill was built in 1861, other stamp mills as well as arrastras were erected nearby on the Carson River, notably the Rock Point, Woodworth and Douglass mills. Peak population was attained in 1865 when Dayton had 2500 people. A visitor that year described the place as a neatly-built, friendly mining town on the Carson River where a bridge 200 feet long led the traveler to the main street, flanked by storehouses, businesses, restaurants and a German brewery.

After the mid-1860s population dwindled until increased Comstock mining and heavy construction of the Sutro Tunnel between 1872 and 1878 brought renewed prosperity. During the height of milling early in the 1870s Dayton and vicinity boasted a dozen mills with 180 stamps. The stone schoolhouse was among the finest in the state.

The Rock Point, or Nevada Reduction Works, was one of Dayton's three important mills. C. C. Stevenson, state governor in the 1880s, originally built the mill in 1861 with forty stamps at a cost of $75,000; later additions brought the number of stamps to 56 and the cost of equipment to $170,000. (*William H. Scott photo*)

Early in May 1909 the mill (below) burned down. Rebuilding began immediately, using galvanized iron.
(*William A. Kornmayer Collection*)

Thirteen days after the Rock Point mill burned, fire gutted the courthouse (upper right), a classic structure built in 1864. Like many other courthouses in Nevada, ill-advised financing and extravagant building costs made it a burden on county taxpayers for decades. Beginning that very summer more prosperous Yerington began to agitate for the county seat, securing it by legislative act two years later.
(*Chester Barton Collection*)

The Union Hotel (lower right), built in the early 1870s, was still standing a century later. Steady boarders were charged a dollar a day, while occasional meals were available for fifty cents — all you could eat. In the wooden building next door, haircuts cost 25 cents.
(*Chester Barton Collection*)

64

This large blacksmith shop (top left) at Dayton in the early 1880s attests to the importance of freighting in the vicinity. Another early business was a butcher shop (upper right), pictured here around 1905.

This dredge with a clam shell bucket functioned just southwest of Dayton around 1897.

Holly the Chinese peddler walked daily (except Sunday) from Dayton to Virginia City with filled baskets of vegetables to sell en route. In Virginia City he stocked the baskets with fish and other commodities brought in by railroad and peddled them on the return trip. *(Top left: Mrs. W. B. Mercer Collection; bottom left and top right: Chester Barton Collection; bottom right: William H. Scott photo)*

67

Silver City, looking down Gold Canyon from a point above Devil's Gate, presented an imposing appearance late in the last century. Many of the residences shown here were still inhabited over a century later, including the Bonanza House (below), a popular establishment around 1905. A few bars still relieve thirst, but the mills have all closed.
(Top: Nevada State Museum; bottom: Chester Barton Collection)

Blackboards and appropriate mottoes and pictures covered all walls, the floor was matted, and flowers and vines grew in all of the windows.

With the decline of the Comstock after 1878 Dayton faded. Even the arrival of the Carson & Colorado Railroad in 1881 did not stimulate the town until early in this century when railroad traffic increased because of mining activity in southern Nevada. During peak periods of activity, Dayton had several businesses and a population of 700, but in 1909 fire destroyed the courthouse. Two years later the county seat was removed to Yerington.

Placer mining resumed in earnest between 1920 and 1923, when the Gold Canyon Dredging Co. recovered over $300,000 from three million yards of gravel with its floating dredge. The operation shut down because boulders and continued loss of water from the dredge pond hindered work. As late as 1939-1940 and 1941-1943 two companies worked the placers, leaving an immense rock pile in the north part of Dayton, almost exactly where gold was first discovered in 1850.

Dayton is now a small community of about 400 and its many old buildings and mill ruins remain unspoiled as a historic site.

SILVER CITY, on SR 80 at a point 3½ miles north of its junction with US 50 (3 miles northwest of Dayton).

Though placer miners had worked their way up Gold Canyon during the late 1850s past this locality, not until after the Comstock discovery in 1859 were locations made in the Silver City district. A camp arose late that year which within a year had become an important place with four hotels, boarding houses, saloons, and vast facilities for wagons and horses. By 1861 the population reached 1200 and Silver City served as the main boarding place for animals used in hauling ore-laden wagons between the Comstock and mills on the Carson River. A directory published that year listed 260 Silver Citians engaged in businesses of all kinds, including many teamsters and carpenters. A crude foundry, the first iron works in Nevada, was moved from Johntown and re-established here in 1862. Silver City also had the Comstock's first silver mill — Paul's Pioneer. During the 1860s other mills were erected and by 1871 Silver City boasted eight mills with 95 stamps.

Virginia City and Gold Hill on the Comstock always overshadowed this town. Silver City challenged them in 1860-61 but quickly fell behind because the district's low-grade veins did not interest large stock companies. Nearly every family had its own mine and developed it only when money was actually needed. In 1869 the place declined after the Virginia & Truckee robbed it of its extensive freighting business. Nevertheless this district has been one of Nevada's most consistent ore producers; some sort of mining or milling has been reported almost every year since 1860, and the camp had at least a few hundred people until well into this century. Many old houses and a small population remain.

JOHNTOWN, ¾ mile southeast of SR 17 at a point ½ mile south of Silver City.

This small placer camp first appeared along the road through Gold Canyon in the early 1850s. As early as 1851, two years after passing emigrants first discovered gold at the mouth of Gold Canyon, a bibulous teamster named James Fenemore built his tent into the side of a hill and began to wash gravel in a small reservoir. For the rest of the decade a band of miners sluiced the placer deposits with primitive rockers and long toms, recovering limited amounts of gold. The canyon was worked only a few months each year when enough water was available; the locals spent the rest of their time prospecting, and foraging on Mormon ranches in Carson and Washoe valleys for supplies. Many Chinese who had come over the Sierra also worked in the diggings, placering gravel abandoned by whites, and this camp got its name from the presence of "John Chinaman."

A small handwritten newspaper, the Gold Canyon *Switch*, appeared on foolscap for awhile in the mid-1850s, the first journalistic effort within modern Nevada. From 1857 until February 1859 Johntown was the "big mining camp" in western Utah territory's only significant mining area, with up to 180 inhabitants during the summers. The Comstock had its beginnings in this primitive outpost in the winter of 1859 when local miners ventured up Gold Canyon to become the first to placer gold at the present site of Gold Hill, where the Comstock silver discoveries were made in June (see Virginia City). Stone ruins and a historical marker on state route 17 indicate the site.

Placer mining took place in Gold Canyon below Silver City in the 1880s in an area which was mined for gold as early as the 1850s. Several sluice boxes are shown in the foreground. Large-scale mining took place here right up to World War II, when a dredge operated out of nearby Dayton. *(Nevada Historical Society)*

Mound House was a busy interchange between the Virginia & Truckee and the Carson & Colorado Railroads. The small settlement around the station never grew to any extent.
(William A. Kornmayer Collection)

MOUND HOUSE, north side of US 50 at a point 5 miles west of Dayton.

This locality was first settled sometime in the late 1860s when tolls were collected at Mound Station on the Carson-Comstock stage road. After the arrival of the Virginia & Truckee Railroad in 1869, Mound House was established as the transfer point to coach and wagon for passengers and freight destined for Dayton, Pine Grove and eventually Sutro. Tents and wooden houses made up the village, and the V. & T. brought fresh water from Carson City. With the decline of the Comstock this community languished, but in April 1881 the narrow gauge Carson & Colorado Railroad began running from here to Hawthorne. As northern terminus of that line, Mound House thrived as a transshipping point and had a post office after 1884.

Activity increased as booms developed at Tonopah and Goldfield between 1902 and 1905, to the extent that transshipment between gauges at Mound House became an intolerable bottleneck. The Southern Pacific, which had acquired the C. & C. in 1900, built a 28-mile connection between its transcontinental main line at Hazen and Churchill siding on the C. & C. which was at the same time converted to standard gauge as far as its Tonopah connection, and was reorganized as the Nevada & California Railway. Mound House as interchange ended September 1905, and two months later the post office was removed.

About this same time nearby ground was located for gypsum mining, but not until the Pacific Portland Cement Co. erected a large plant in 1913 did mining begin. An aerial tramway transported gypsum from quarry to mill immediately north of here, and a camp of about 20 buildings was in evidence. After 1921 company operations were transferred to Gerlach and the Virginia & Truckee finally ended operations in 1939. Modern construction and buildings have obliterated the site of Mound House.

SUMMIT STATION or Halfway House, north side of US 50 at a point 4 miles west of Dayton.

Summit Station was established after 1860 as the midway stop on the stage road between Carson and Virginia City. A polling place for the 1861 election was set up here. The station was active until 1866, when increased business led to its relocation at Mound House Station (see above). Rock foundations remain.

COMO, 11 miles southeast of Dayton.

Gold discoveries in the Pine Nut Mountains in June 1860 led to the establishment of a district and camp which were soon given a name out of Syrian antiquity, Palmyra. A mild rush ensued, and by fall a saloonkeeper and a few other merchants had set up shop to serve over 100 miners working and locating claims. Though 1861 slipped by with only limited development, Palmyra got a post office the next year and a business district had developed large enough to serve 400 people. As 1862 progressed, attention gradually focused on newly found ledges in a narrow cave a half-mile east, and there the town of Como was platted. Soon Palmyra was drained of all business except three saloons and a hotel.

Como boomed for the next two years. Rancher-politician J. D. Winters opened tunnels and built a small steam-driven mill southeast of the camp early in 1864, only to shut down by the year's end when his test operation did not even cover costs. Later he became boss of the Comstock's Yellow Jacket mine.

Others formed corporations at Como, usually the same people, issuing certificates handsomely engraved in San Francisco, and agents peddled the stock on the Comstock. A versatile citizen of Como and the camp's chief organizer was Alf Doten — doctor, carpenter and player of guitar, violin and flute. He presided over six mining corporations, all promotional, and wrote the "Como Letters" which were fed to the Comstock once or twice a week. Convinced as he was that Como would develop into a big mining center, Doten eventually went broke here.

The camp's small business district varied from small saloon dives to the Cross Hotel, first class all the way, with parlor, gentlemen's bar, carpeted sleeping rooms, and a meeting hall on the second floor for lectures, parties, and Sunday services conducted by ministers from Gold Hill.

Of the defunct Palmyra, Doten said little in his famous diaries, only that the local hotel's daughters were good looking and that he occasionally went down to see them. During the district's active years woodcutters obtained timber from the

The old mining camp of Como, lively in the territorial days, revived significantly in 1902 when new buildings and a mill were built.
(Top: William A. Kornmayer Collection; bottom: Nevada Historical Society)

Picturesque ruin of this five-stamp mill still stood on the road to Como in the early 1960s but is gone now. *(Theron Fox photo)*

The whim was a very efficient machine for prospecting and production at small mines. Here is one in operation at Como. *(William A. Kornmayer Collection)*

The town of Sutro (above, looking east) was a substantial settlement during the mid-1870s when the Sutro Tunnel was being built. The usual stores and shops were here to serve several hundred people. With completion of the tunnel in 1878, the town declined, and by 1890 (below) many buildings had been removed. To the right is the tunnel entrance, the town below was laid out in a grid with tree-lined streets and four parks. Extending across the photograph (west and east) is Tunnel Avenue; intersecting in the background is Florence Avenue. The magnificent Sutro mansion is shown, which met its end in a fire in 1941. Only stumps and trees indicate the site of parks and streets. (*Above: Willie Capucci Collection; below: Nevada State Museum*)

piñon-studded plateaus for fuel, building and for use in mines and mills. Cutting these trees sometimes brought the Indians on the warpath, for they depended on the pine nuts for food during the long winters.

Como also contained a pocket of Confederate sentiment in pro-Union Nevada; almost half of its citizens were "copperheads." Before elections took place, secret meetings were held to figure out measures to determine who was eligible to vote. Como briefly had a weekly, the *Sentinel*, during the spring of 1864 before it was moved down to more prosperous Dayton. The district was thoroughly prospected by the end of 1864, but thereafter Como's merriment grew fainter and the town was finished early in the next year. Como experienced important revivals in 1879-1881 and 1902-1905, and the camp had a post office. Production was richer each time than in the early era, but the revivals lacked the color of the territorial boom. In the 1930s a large mill was built. It ran but a few days until it was discovered that there was no ore, a fact that promoters had overlooked. Cellars and foundations are left at Como.

SUTRO, 1 mile north of US 50 at a point 2¼ miles northeast of Dayton.

A few years after Adolph Sutro arrived on the Comstock in 1860, he conceived the idea of building a tunnel to drain the mines, and as early as 1864 he petitioned the state legislature for a franchise. Despite the bitter opposition of the Virginia City "Bank Ring" and organized mine owners, he was able to break ground for the project in October 1869. He had difficulty in raising capital, a proposed federal subsidy failing to pass Congress. In August 1871 he succeeded in obtaining loans totaling $1,450,000 from London bankers. The tempo of construction thereupon increased, and ultimate completion was assured by additional foreign capital. The cost of all this financing over $5 million, was never repaid in royalties received after the tunnel was in service.

A cluster of buildings thrown up at the tunnel entrance in 1870 was the first hint of a town, but in 1872 Sutro laid out a model city. He claimed that Virginia City would become a ghost town, given over to bats, owls and coyotes, after the mills were relocated in his city, and that miners would prefer to reside at Sutro, passing through the tunnel to and from the mines.

Mr. Sutro seemed to carry the mantle of an ancient prophet and many individuals settled in his town, numbering between 600 and 800 by 1876. A school was here, and a church, post office, the weekly *Independent*, Sutro's Victorian mansion and other fine residences. Many accidents occurred during tunnel construction and a hospital was built out of necessity.

The tunnel connected with the Savage mine in July 1878 and was completed during the next year. In 1880 there were still 435 residents in Sutro, but most of these had left by the end of the century. The tunnel was used for over fifty years, especially for draining the mines. But, being completed after Comstock production had started to decline, the tunnel was never used for bringing out ore as Sutro had hoped. Left today are several wooden buildings and the barred tunnel entrance.

REED'S STATION, 1 mile east of US 50 at a point 6 miles northeast of Dayton.

Beginning as a Pony Express station in 1860-61, Reeds remained a small station for a few years because at this point on the Carson River important roads converged—from Virginia City via Flowery Canyon, Fort Churchill, Dayton and a road heading north. Not even a foundation is left.

DESERT WELL STATION, ¾ mile south of US 50 at a point 15 miles northeast of Dayton and 11 miles west of Silver Springs.

Early in the 1860s an Overland mail and stage station was here and a well where east-west travelers obtained water. Mark Twain supposedly stopped nearby one night during a furious snowstorm. In *Roughing It* he tells with tongue in cheek about Ollendorf, one of his two companions, who "claimed an instinct as sensitive as any compass," and who was guiding the party on horseback through the storm, west to Carson City. They spent most of the day wandering aimlessly in the snow, even following their own tracks. Eventually an Overland stage passed them and they followed it as fast as the tired horses would permit. When night overtook them after losing the road again, the three decided to stop and build a fire to keep from freezing. With only four wet matches among

The top picture shows Ramsey when the camp was only months old. New operators gave the district another chance in the late 1930s (above) when considerable development was done. Below is Talapoosa as it appeared during its revival just before World War II. *(Top: U. S. Geological Survey; middle: Mrs. Parker Liddell Collection; bottom: Mrs. Ida Le Nord Collection)*

Twain and his companions had given up their bad habits in anticipation of dying in the blinding snowstorm. The next morning each revived his vice: Twain his smoking, Ballou his card playing and Ollendorff his drinking.

them, none of the matches would strike. Ollendorf's effort to start a fire by firing his revolver into a pile of sagebrush scared the horses away. In the face of anticipated death, Twain and his friends lay down in their blankets and made serious reforms; but they survived the night and awoke early in the morning to find the comfortable inn of Desert Well Station only a few steps away! Well and corral ruins are left.

RAMSEY, 7 miles northwest of US 50 via unimproved road at a point 3½ miles west of Silver Springs.

Initial discoveries were made by Tom and Bladen Ramsey, two Texans who sold out too soon their properties in Goldfield, ground which later became part of the Mohawk, one of the world's most productive mines. The early 1906 gold discovery quickly circulated via the mining grapevine and by midyear three townsites were platted and promoters commenced selling lots. The few original tent-dwellers were rapidly augmented by arrivals from Reno, Goldfield and Carson City, and several eight-horse teams hauled in supplies from Apache siding on the Southern Pacific. Daily auto service from Carson City commenced, and autos met the train west of Wadsworth. Ramsey was one of the most accessible of the new mining camps.

By mid-July the population bunched in the 12-block Ramsey townsite and the other two townsites died a-borning. In August the Ramsey *Recorder* told of rich ledges in the bosom of nearby hills and boasted of the prices paid for lots — $400 to $600. One 25-foot lot sold for $2500! At year's end the young town had eight saloons, three restaurants, two hotels, daily newspaper, post office, brokerage and assay offices, as well as other stores for 500 residents. Regular stage runs connected the camp with Carson City and Virginia City.

The boom subsided in 1907 but two years later a thirty-ton amalgamation and cyanide mill was built and large-scale mining began. This mill operated only a year, shutting down after producing about $80,000. Ramsey officially lost its post office in 1913. Some work was done in the 1920s and 1930s, and a significant revival in 1939 did not outlast 1940. Mill foundations and scattered wooden debris remain.

STOCKTON WELL, 1 mile southeast of US 50 at a point 3½ miles west of Silver Springs.

Established in the territorial days, Stockton Well was the first important station east of Virginia City on the road to Humboldt. Later it was a trading station.

TALAPOOSA, by primitive mountain roads 4½ miles north of US 50 at a point 1¼ miles west of Silver Springs.

Prospectors from Virginia City made initial silver discoveries in 1863, but development work did not follow. Leasers made occasional unrecorded productions thereafter, and during 1938-1942 over $300,000 in silver and gold was taken out and treated at a cyanide plant in Silver City.

HONEY LAKE SMITHS, earlier Williams' Station, now under Lake Lahontan, 2¼ miles east of Silver Springs.

During Nevada's preterritorial days Williams' Station served as an isolated inn and trading post for westbound emigrants. In a raid one evening in April 1860, Paiutes massacred five men and burned the station to the ground. This incident created considerable excitement in Carson and Virginia cities and a volunteer army of 105 men was organized to track down the Indians. The men or-

Above is an artist's conception of Fort Churchill, the heart of a 1384-acre military reservation. Sam Buckland's famous hotel (left) was in use as a farm residence until the mid-20th century; this house may at a future date be moved to Fort Churchill State Park. *(Top: Nevada State Museum; left: Frank Mitrani photo)*

ganized under experienced Indian fighter Major Ormsby at Bucklands and in a few days traced the Indians to Pyramid Lake. In an ambush, four or five dozen volunteers were slain, including Major Ormsby.

Shortly afterward, "Honey Lake" Smith rebuilt the inn on the same spot and added large brick stables. The two-story log inn sat on a small knoll, according to Mark Twain, who stopped for the night on a journey to Unionville in the winter of 1861-62 and remained eight long days because of the flooding Carson River. The station prospered until 1869 when the Central Pacific Railroad began service. The tumbled-down, partly buried walls of the station now lie submerged under Lake Lahontan and these faint ruins last appeared above water in 1960.

FORT CHURCHILL, half mile southwest of US 95A at a point 8 miles south of Silver Springs.

Nevada's first, largest and most important military post was Fort Churchill. Destruction of nearby Williams' Station early in 1860 and raids on other stations along emigrant routes, interruption of mail service and general harassment of travelers by warring Paiutes moved the federal government to order construction of this outpost in Western Nevada. Some troops arrived in July, a post office was established in October, and at the end of 1861 the fort garrisoned about 600 men.

For the rest of the decade the fort protected Western Nevada settlements and main emigrant routes from Indians. During the Civil War, volunteers from California occupied the fort when regulars were transferred to the East. The fort also served as a recruiting station for the Union army. By the mid-1860s various army company units replaced the volunteers, and in 1867-69 only one company maintained the fort.

Most Indian trouble ceased by 1869, and the completion of the Central Pacific displaced most stage travel on the central Overland Trail. In September of that year Fort Churchill was abandoned, and six months later buildings originally costing several hundred thousand dollars were sold at auction to Sam Buckland for a mere $750 (see below). The fort is now a state park which in 1964 was declared a national historic landmark. Camping facilities are available.

BUCKLANDS, east side US 95A, 9 miles south of Silver Springs.

A tent road house opened in 1859 for travelers in ox-team caravans coming from Ragtown and other points east. Sam Buckland built a more substantial ranch house in the spring of 1860 which contained a trading post, tavern and hotel. A blacksmith shop and wagon repair barn were eventually added, and a toll bridge allowed passage across the nearby Carson River.

In November 1861 Nevada Territory designated Bucklands the seat of Churchill County, a sparsely populated and unorganized area to the east which was administered by the Lyon County commissioners at Dayton. This *de jure* status for the settlement was maintained until Churchill County's organization was perfected in 1864, and a later boundary change placed Bucklands in Lyon County. Corrals, a wagon yard, and a farm had been added to the station before 1870, when Sam Buckland built a large hotel with dining room, bar and dance hall. With a decline in stage traffic after the mid-1870s, this station lost its importance. After the turn of the century the community for a while took the name Weeks. The large station still stands.

DESERT STATION, also known as Houten Well and other names, 11 miles east of US 95A at a point 10 miles south of Silver Springs.

This station began as a Pony Express station in the early 1860s and later in the decade a rock and adobe stage station known as Houten Well was built which was abandoned before the mid-1870s. Remnants of the later station remain.

THOMPSON, ¼ mile west of US 95A at a point 20 miles south of Silver Springs.

Encouraged by the active development of copper mines west of Yerington, the Mason Valley Mines Co. pushed ahead in 1910 with construction of a smelter at the north end of Mason Valley. Plans called for installation of two smelters of 500-ton capacity. In 1912 the first of these was blown in and began treating 700 to 1000 tons of copper daily. After installation of the second furnace in 1913-14, the original two-block townsite had expanded to embrace several blocks of residences, stores, saloons, an auto repair shop, and a popula-

Thompson, around 1913 was a busy copper town and the location of the so-called "million dollar smelter." Ore from mines near Ludwig and Yerington was shipped on the Nevada Copper Belt Railroad for processing into copper matte, with about 30% copper content. The Southern Pacific then hauled the matte to Utah for conversion into blister copper, 98% pure. View looks northwest.

(Getchell Library, University of Nevada)

In its early days, Mason occupied a strategic position as a business center for copper mining and agriculture. Its railroad station (center) was a busy place until the end of World War I. The school at Mason was featured in advertisements which helped lure people to the town. School days ended about 1940 and the building was removed.

(Two photos: Hank Barlow Collection)

tion of 350. Some mill workers also lived at Wabuska and at ranches in Mason Valley. The smelters closed down late in 1914, resumed briefly in 1917, then stopped once more in 1919. One smelter was reactivated in 1926 and ran continuously until the end of 1928 when it was closed and dismantled. Foundations remain.

WABUSKA, on US 95A at a point 21 miles south of Silver Springs.

Settlement around Wabuska began in the early 1870s and in 1874 a post office was established to serve the north end of Mason Valley. The Carson & Colorado in 1881 made Wabuska a station where meals could be obtained, and the settlement grew in importance after 1902 when mining activity heightened in southern Nevada. In 1905 the Southern Pacific standard-gauged the line and workers engaged in the conversion lived here. Wabuska also became a small distribution center for Mason Valley and nearby mining activity.

With the construction of the Nevada Copper Belt Railroad past Yerington to Ludwig in 1911, Wabuska became a true railroad center and an important junction point. At the height of the county's copper boom during World War I, the town boasted a commodious railroad station, a two-room school, grocery stores, seven saloons, and a population approaching 100. Copper mining subsided in 1919 and as trucks and autos displaced railroad traffic, Wabuska shrank to a grocery store and a dozen houses by mid-century. Wabuska as a town is dead, but at this point the Anaconda Copper Co.'s precipitated copper and concentrates from its works at Weed Heights are shipped to its smelter in Montana, and thousands of tin cans are received here to precipitate the copper.

MASON, 2 miles south of 95A at a point 1 mile west of Yerington.

After nearby copper mines in the westerly Singatse Range began development, the community of Mason was founded in 1906 on the west bank of the Walker River. Late in 1908 it acquired a post office, and the young town came of age in the spring of 1910 when the Nevada Copper Belt Railroad was built through the area. A celebration with bands, parade, boxing matches, barbecue, and baseball game marked the beginning of service on

Railroad Day in May 1910. The N. C. B. located its general offices, machine shops, freight yards, round house, and passenger depot in Mason, which served as the station for agricultural products and cattle, sheep, and hogs raised in Mason Valley. The town also provided a place of residence and trading center for nearby miners and mine officials.

With several advantages for growth, the quiet town of Mason by 1914 had a bank, two-story hotel, stores, saloons, post office, brick school, two churches, steam laundry, hospital and a population approaching 1000. A chamber of commerce, women's club and a volunteer fire department were organized. Wide streets were laid out in grid fashion and the town boasted electric lights and a water system.

Above town several mines boomed, especially the Bluestone, and beginning in 1912 a three-mile tramway connected the mines with Mason where ore was loaded on N. C. B. cars for shipment to Thompson Smelter. During World War I at the height of mining at the Bluestone, a 2½-mile-long standard gauge railroad was built to meet the N. C. B. at Mason. Until then the town rivaled Yerington, but after 1918 Mason steadily declined, finally losing the railroad facilities when the Nevada Copper Belt was abandoned in 1947. Banks and other structures remain, as well as a population of about twenty.

NORDYKE, 7 miles south of US 95A at a point 1 mile west of Yerington.

A settlement with post office was here in 1892, gaining importance because a flour and a quartz mill were active. In 1910, the same year that Nordyke gained a station on the Nevada Copper Belt Railroad, the post office served about 150 people. The community declined by 1914 and the post office was removed the following year.

PINE GROVE, 5 miles west of Pine Grove Flat road at a point 20 miles south of Yerington.

An Indian led an untiring prospector named William Wilson to gold-bearing rock in June 1866, and prospectors stampeded the northeastern side of thickly wooded Pine Grove Hills through the summer. The camp briefly took the name Wilsonville and within two years the camp, renamed Pine Grove, had a post office, the weekly News, and a

In 1880 Pine Grove was an attractive mountain village divided into three sections. The upper end of town (top) contained the camp's main five-stamp mill, which was hauled into the district by oxen around 1870. It ran for nearly twenty years. Other buildings opposite were the blacksmith shop, assay office and boarding house.

At the entrance to Pine Grove Canyon, a 12-horse team hauls lumber into the camp. *(Both photos: Mrs. Willard Hanson Collection)*

A primitive steam boiler in the Pine Grove district supplies steam for a small engine, which in turn drives a ventilation fan.

A few of the ladies at Cambridge watch a horse-powered whim in action.

(Both photos: Mrs. Willard Hanson Collection)

83

This general view of the Nevada-Douglas Copper Co. shows the mine and buildings. Ludwig was just below (to the right) of this picture.
(Getchell Library, University of Nevada)

In the 1920s the Standard Gypsum Co. erected this mill (lower) at Ludwig and mined gypsum by open cut. These deposits had aroused interest as early as 1907 but in that year talk of copper filled the air. *(Nevada Historical Society)*

population of 200. Two steam-powered stamp mills and three arrastras treated both gold and silver ores. Stages and freight lines handled traffic to the town, bringing in supplies from Sacramento and other trading centers and hauling out bullion.

In the early 1870s the population reached its peak of 600. The tri-sectioned camp straggled for a mile along a canyon and contained five saloons, three hotels, variety store, hardware store, Wells Fargo agent, dance hall, blacksmith shops, stores of general merchandise, barber shops, shoeshine shop, school, oxen yards, livery stables and two doctors' offices. Toll roads extended in every direction. Pine Grove developed into a regional supply center and recreation spot for ranchers from East Walker, and the Mason and Smith valleys until the latter part of the decade, when the district's mines began to decline. Two mill enlargements were made in 1882 and mining sites were still coveted in the 1880s, but after the demonetization of silver in 1893 the Pine Grove mines were worked only intermittently. A few minor revivals early in this century helped bring the total production to a bountiful $8 million. In the late 1960s work has started again. Mill foundations and a few wooden buildings remain.

ROCKLAND, 6 miles southwest of Pine Grove Flat road at a point 20 miles south of Yerington.

Discovery of gold at the Rockland mine in 1868 was inevitable after choice properties had been claimed at Pine Grove three miles northwest. After a ten-stamp mill was built in nearby Bridgeport Canyon, Rockland grew quickly and had saloons, stores, post office, express office, and a population from 100 to 150 in 1870. In the spring of the next year the miners did not get their pay and operations abruptly terminated. While the owner left temporarily to raise additional capital, a disgruntled miner burned the mill. He was eventually convicted of arson and sent to the state prison at Carson City.

The post office was discontinued in 1872, and thereafter the district had recurrent ups and downs, but early in this century three new mills were erected and Rockland was again large enough to support a post office and a tri-weekly stage to Yerington. The district was especially active during World War I, and operations shut down for good in 1934 after about $1 million was produced in over a half century of mining. A new mill began to roll in 1969. Wooden buildings and stone walls remain — silent reminders of the drunken brawls in the town's bistros during the early mining era.

CAMBRIDGE, 2 miles southeast of Pine Grove Flat road at a point 21 miles south of Yerington.

When gold was discovered in 1861 a district was organized and known as Washington. The Pine Grove discovery revived interest here and production began after the district was reorganized in 1867. The camp was large enough to have a post office during the revival of 1879-1881, and a ten-stamp mill on the East Walker River treated local ores. Other revivals occurred in later years, the one in 1936 large enough to bring another mill into operation. Numerous mine dumps remain.

HUDSON, 3 miles by graded road, north of SR 3 at a point 20 miles southwest of Yerington and 2 miles east of Smith.

After the Nevada Copper Belt Railroad was built past this point on the north bank of the Walker River early in 1913, the community of Hudson grew around newly established freight operations. From here regular auto stages began running to Bodie (fare ten dollars), Bridgeport, Aurora, Wellington and Lundy. By April a post office was established and ultimately about fifty people lived here. Hudson's importance as a transportation terminal diminished a few years later with the decline of mining in the trade area, but in the 1920s this place was a bootleggers' hangout and cattle rustlers' retreat.

LUDWIG, 9 miles north of Hudson by graded road.

A German immigrant discovered high-grade copper on the west side of the Singatse Range. The Ludwig mine produced limited quantities of ore from 1865 until about 1868. Attempts to smelt it were unsuccessful until 1907, when the Nevada-Douglas Co. purchased the mines and invested enough capital for adequate development. A camp named Morningstar formed a half mile below the mines. Soon it was renamed Ludwig and had a post office after 1908.

Wagons hauled ore to the Nevada & California until the Nevada Copper Belt Railroad was completed from Wabuska in October 1911. On December 29 Ludwig celebrated its Railroad Day, and a crowd from Mason and Smith valleys took part. Visitors were guided through the copper mines, gypsum quarry and works that afternoon, and after a supper in the old boarding house, a dance capped the evening's festivities. In 1912 several hundred men worked in the mines and the camp had 65 buildings, including boarding houses, school, hotel, a well-stocked store, infirmary, and residences. The modern company club was the camp's social center, and a dance was held there once a week. On the outskirts of the camp were saloons and brothels.

In the summer of 1913 Ludwig had over 750 people, but its importance waned after mining activity peaked in 1914, despite the building of another mill the next year.

Gypsum was mined during the 1920s but by 1930 Ludwig had closed shop. Through the 1940s many houses, a reducing plant, and several large shells of mills stood virtually intact, but by 1959 all had been removed. Cement foundations and slabs remain.

COLONY, later Simpson, 8 miles northwest of Smith, via graded roads.

Before the turn of the century several Californians came here to form what was to be a model cooperative colony. A townsite was laid out but the promotional scheme failed.

During the height of the Smith Valley land boom of 1919-20, superlative advertising lured many settlers to farm 80-acre tracts, and the new community of Simpson acquired a post office. Many farmers stopped raising hay a decade later, and farms have been consolidated in larger holdings by fewer people. The post office was discontinued in 1943.

HINDS' HOT SPRINGS, 12 miles northwest of Smith, via graded roads.

North-south travelers during the 19th century took advantage of the overnight facilities of this spa and station. The medicinal value of its hot springs attracted tourists and invalids. In later years the place was known as Nevada Hot Springs.

ARTESIA, 18 miles north-northwest of Smith, via graded roads.

Small homesteaders arrived as early as 1907, and by 1910 a change in the Homestead Act and nearby copper mining brought a land rush to the area around Artesia Lake. Many land claims were filed and wells were drilled at a furious pace. Many of the settlers had come to work at Ludwig and some continued to work there while developing their lands. The transfer of the Buckskin post office to Artesia in July 1914 showed its rising importance and a school was soon opened. But after a few years it was evident that the wells could not provide enough water to irrigate lands and support the homesteaders. Many of them sold out or abandoned their farms in the early 1920s. The post office was removed in 1926. Abandoned buildings remain.

BUCKSKIN (Douglas County), 20 miles north-northwest of Smith by graded roads.

After discovery of gold in the spring of 1906, a camp known as Gold Pit emerged below the Buckskin mine and the contemporary press said it had the makings of becoming a big camp. The name was soon changed, and Buckskin rose on a platted townsite on the Douglas-Lyon county line. Beginning in June, Buckskin had a post office and eventually saloons, telephone and telegraph service, and a stage service to Wabuska on the Nevada & California Railway. Operations subsided after 1908 and by 1910 Buckskin was a mere post office station. Copper mining resumed during World War I, and the district was active again during 1933-1938. The Buckskin mine marks the site.

WELLINGTON, 4½ miles southwest of Smith, via SR 3.

After a bridge was built across the West Walker River in 1861, Wellington began as a stage station where routes through Smith Valley converged to form a single road southward to Aurora. A post office was established in 1865, and as traffic to Aurora declined early in the 1870s, the settlement was by 1879-1883 relocated a quarter mile southeast at the present location, where stores, blacksmith shop and hotel were built to serve the surrounding farming area. Stage travel had declined, but Wellington served as supply point for mining camps and prospectors. Later an elementary and high school were built, and with the advent of the auto age a garage and gasoline stations opened. Wellington still has a few dozen families and stores to serve the area.

WALKER RIVER STATION or Rissue's Bridge, (Douglas County), 5 miles southwest of Wellington via Hoye Canyon road.

A station and store with unofficial post office were here in the 1860s to serve travelers on the Carson-Aurora road where they crossed the West Walker River. About 1872 this bridge was replaced by one at Hoye's Station, a mile and a half northeast. That bridge was abandoned in 1883 after its owner moved to Wellington.

WILEY'S STATION, 14 miles south-southeast of Wellington via SR 22.

This stage station in Dalzall Canyon on the Carson-Aurora stage run was active in the 1860s and 1870s. Dalzall Station, a mile south, and Sulfur, three miles north, were also used. The latter is a picturesque rock ruin in a grassy field. A stone house and a wooden house remain at Wileys.

SWEETWATER, 24 miles south of Wellington via SR 22.

Initially called Wahappa, Sweetwater was a stage station beginning in the 1860s, and acquired a post office in 1870. Early in the 1900s a village of fifty emerged in this farming valley, and two stores, hotel and saloon were open for travelers and nearby miners. The post office closed in 1925.

CLINTON (California), 4½ miles west of Sweetwater by road and trail.

Claims were staked in the 1860s at the time when nearby stands of pine were cut for use in Aurora and Pine Grove, but not until 1880 was the Patterson district organized and active mining begun. At the mouth of Ferris Canyon a silver camp named Clinton sprang up below the district's largest mine, and afterwards Cameron was established on Frying Pan Creek near gold mines. The district peaked in 1882-1883 but thereafter declined to one operating mine five years later.

ELBOW, 6 miles east-southeast of SR 22 at a point 4 miles southeast of Sweetwater.

Located where the East Walker River makes a sweeping turn, "Elbow Jake's" stage station in the early 1860s consisted of a frame house, stables and corrals. The station keeper raised cattle and ran a small dairy for Aurora. A post office operated briefly in 1881. A marker indicates the site.

The main ranch house at Sweetwater was located in the midst of the East Walker River ranching and farming area. (*William A. Kornmayer Collection*)

Carry Nevada for Socialism

The Nevada Colony Corporation Begins a Movement to Transform the State

THE *Nevada Colony Corporation is organized under the laws of the State of Nevada, for the purpose of promoting Co-operative Colonies. It is empowered to transact all manner of business in connection with its colonies.*

Its prime object is to actually inaugurate cooperation along conservative business lines, and thus promote the welfare of the Colony investors, insuring them employment and the most favorable surroundings.

A secondary purpose lies in a desire to call together a sufficient number of cooperators from all sections of the United States to enable them to control the politics of a State that is but spacely settled and that almost exclusively by working people, thus making possible the bringing of the entire state under cooperative control. It would require only a little over 5,000 such cooperators from other states to do this work. And in Nevada the women vote.

The ultimate purpose is to afford the world an object lesson of successful cooperation, both in community life and in the life of a great commonwealth of the United States, in order that demonstration may disarm criticism and help to lift the world to better living.

At the last general election a change of 2,000 votes from the dominant party to Socialism would have made Nevada Socialistic. Since that time women of the state have been granted the ballot. A. Grant Miller, then candidate for the U. S. Senate as he is today, made a vigorous campaign for woman suffrage, and thus won friends who will doubtless stand by him this year.

Five thousand new Socialist votes, well distributed, will change the state to Socialism! And the Nevada Colony Corporation provides means of furnishing all who may join it employment amid congenial surroundings while doing the work!

Where is there anything in all the world so full of hope and promise as this plan?

Act, Comrades, act at once. Join the Colony and help.

Carry Nevada for Socialism!

Advertisements such as this one full of superlatives lured idealists to the Nevada City socialist colony, just east of Fallon. But like so many other cooperative schemes in California and the East that failed, this one was doomed from its first year of existence.
(Willie Capucci Collection)

CHURCHILL COUNTY

Although Churchill County was traversed by two important overland trails used by California-bound emigrants beginning in 1849, no minerals were discovered until the early 1860s when the Comstock and Reese River strikes encouraged prospecting in the country between. There were short-lived early silver camps at La Plata and Silver Hill, and salt was mined at Sand Springs, Leete and White Plains. After 1870 lode mining was negligible except at Bolivia and at Bernice from 1883 until 1890.

With the statewide mining boom after 1905, Fairview and Wonder emerged, as well as such lesser lights as Coppereid and Jessup. Nearly half of the county's total production came from Fairview and Wonder during the years from 1912 to 1916, but after 1920 only leasing operations have been active, particularly before World War II. Since then the mines have been relatively quiet.

RAGTOWN, later Leeteville, a quarter-mile south of US 50 at a point 8 miles west of Fallon.

As early as 1854 a crude station on a small ranch was established at this noted place on the Humboldt Overland Trail, the first watering place and patch of green for westbound travelers who had crossed the parched alkali plains of the Forty Mile Desert. That area between Carson Sink and Ragtown was the scene of countless pathetic tragedies told in old diaries, and many more deaths occurred on that horrible segment of the trail in a few short years than in the entire history of Death Valley! Emigrants rested stock on the north bank of the sluggish Carson River before striking west toward the Sierra Nevada. Ragtown derived its name from tattered clothing which the emigrant women hung up to dry on trees by the banks of the Carson.

Toward the end of the 1850s houses of willow poles and canvas were thrown up each summer by traders, gamblers and thieves from California, who annually abandoned this place after emigrant traffic slowed in the fall. Ragtown also served travelers on Captain Simpson's trail across central Nevada especially after the Overland Mail & Stage Co. started running in 1861. Dan De Quille of the *Territorial Enterprise* and Mark Twain separately visited Ragtown that year and each noted a solitary log house.

After an 1862 flood destroyed all structures and disrupted 200 graves of deceased emigrants, the camp was temporarily abandoned, but during the Reese River excitement Ragtown served as an important station on an east-west toll road after 1863. By the mid-1860s about four dozen settlers had established farms and Ragtown acquired a post office. After 1868 soda was recovered at nearby Soda Lake, a half mile north, but stage travel slowed when the Central Pacific started running across Nevada. Later, a farm community with hotel and post office known as Leeteville was here for about a decade after 1895. A historical plaque has been placed near the site on US 95; nothing remains at Ragtown.

HAZEN, on US 95A at a point 16 miles west of Fallon.

When the Southern Pacific realigned its route east of Wadsworth in 1902, Hazen station was a

Local desperado William "Red" Wood was hung at Hazen about March 1, 1905, after weeks of robbing nearby canal builders and citizens of Hazen. A contemporary journalist commented, "Keep the good work up! Ornament all telegraph poles with the carcasses of this type of men." *(Mrs. Agnes Sever Collection)*

stop on the right of way. A town developed and by April 1904 a post office opened, and saloons served workers engaged in digging a 31-mile canal from the Truckee River east and south to the Carson River. Hazen's importance grew after September 1905 when it became the northern terminus of the S. P.'s Nevada & California Railway on completion of the Hazen cutoff connecting the S. P. main line at this point with the N. & C. near Fort Churchill. Thereafter the heavy rail traffic to Goldfield and Tonopah passed through here. A weekly, the *Harvest*, appeared that fall but folded after a few months.

During 1906 large freight wagons teamed supplies from Hazen to the county's outlying camps, especially Fairview and Wonder, but that trade was lost when the S. P. completed a line from here to Fallon early the next year. Hazen then became an important four-way railroad junction point and the S. P. installed a handsome depot and round

house, both of which managed to escape the fire of 1908 which wiped out most of the town.

Hazen rebuilt and became a small trading center with school serving nearby ranches. The showcase of this town of 250 residents was the elegantly furnished Palace Hotel, which had a restaurant and grill. But the advent of the auto age and decrease of railroad traffic on the route to Mina brought the community into a decline. One store is still open, containing a fourth-class post office.

ST. CLAIR, approximately 3 miles west of Fallon.

During the 1860s St. Clair was a popular trading post and station for teamsters on the central Overland Trail. A ranch was started here in 1862 and its owner operated a ferry across the nearby Carson River. A post office was open from 1865 to 1869 and again for nearly thirty years after 1877.

CARSON SINK STATION, by road and trail ¾ mile west of US 95 at a point 14 miles south of Fallon.

Pony Express and stage stations were here. In 1860 the latter consisted of stables and a frame house inside an adobe enclosure that doubled as a fort when Paiutes were on the warpath. When Dan De Quille came in 1861 he noted that an eight-foot fortification wall had been built around the one-story house. The polite station keeper invited him to use the kitchen firewood and anything else he might need. In contrast, Sir Richard Burton, passing through the previous summer, had had to fetch his own water from a pond a mile away and gather his own firewood, though the station keeper had a generous pile. Either the station keeper had softened or the rascal had been replaced! Carson Sink Station was abandoned by the mid-1860s. Little is left except crumbling bricks of a former wall, and a heap of stones which suggest a corral.

WILDCAT STATION, 4 miles east of US 95 at a point 14 miles south of Fallon.

Situated at the north foot of the White Throne Mountains on the route of the Pony Express trail, Wildcat Station was founded two years after the ponies stopped running, and was active for six years until 1869 when the completion of the Central Pacific put it out of business.

TERRILL, by unimproved roads 6 miles southeast of US 95 at a point 24 miles south of Fallon.

After initial discoveries in the summer of 1911 the new camp came to notice when George Wingfield examined the properties. In August Terrill had three saloons, corral and feed yard, other businesses and fifty inhabitants, but it soon died.

NEVADA CITY, about ½ mile south of US 50 at a point 4 miles east of Fallon.

This community was promoted by the Nevada Colony, a socialist organization with roots in California where it had run into trouble. It was able to take root in Nevada, beginning in the spring of 1916, with the benefit of government-watered land under the Newlands project, and the encouragement of a friendly locality and an active Socialist party.

From its very beginning the colony suffered from uncertainty, false hopes, lack of management and a transient population which included Utopians, pacifists, Populists and Marxists from many parts of North America and Europe. The political and ethnic differences made it impossible for the colony to prosper.

The community reached its height in January 1918 when it had a population of 200, a newspaper, the *Cooperative Colonist*, and about three dozen buildings. There were highly publicized plans for a large hotel, library, sunken gardens, croquet grounds and a gasoline station on the highway that is now US 50, none of which were ever built. Many individuals had bought stock in the venture on the basis of articles in the town's promotional newspaper which described these facilities as already existing. By May 1919 company debts were too burdensome and the colony went into receivership and liquidation. Litigation followed, but individuals were unable to recover lost funds. A row of cottonwood trees and remnants of foundations indicate the site.

STILLWATER, 17 miles east of Fallon on SR 42.

In the fall of 1862 several families settled by a large, deep slough, for whose stagnant water the settlement was named. A year earlier the Overland Stage Co. had opened a station here. In succeeding years homesteaders brought many fields under cultivation, and early in 1865 Stillwater got its post office. Farmers cooperated in building roads, irrigation ditches, bridges and fences, and the community prospered. In 1868 Stillwater became an important stop on the Wadsworth-Nye County mail run, and that December the county seat of Churchill County was moved here, the third

The Main Street of Stillwater around 1907 contained the few business houses shown here and offered only overnight accommodations and drink. Even these closed several years later. (*William A. Kornmayer Collection*)

The mine and camp of Coppereid is shown here, about 1913, after the boom.
(U. S. Geological Survey)

Gracefully curved Singing Sand Mountain (below) had been praised for its beauty in diaries of California-bound argonauts for almost two decades before a photographer brought his wagon here late in 1867. (Bancroft Library)

Elmer Huckaby's unique salt harvester scrapes the surface of Eight Mile Flat in such a way that very little silt is picked up while gathering about a ton of salt a minute.

Salt collects under blades from which a continuous bucket line elevates the product to a five-ton capacity bunker. Trucks then carry it away to Fallon and other points where without further treatment it is used for stock and on icy highways and streets. (Elmer Huckaby)

change of headquarters within seven years. Area population was 150 that year.

Farming activity declined so severely after 1870 that Stillwater lost its post office for seven years, but by 1880 it had a wooden courthouse with jail in the basement, store, hotel, saloon, restaurant, post office, blacksmith shop, school, ice house and hay yard. The presence of several trees near the slough gave the town a pleasant appearance. A tri-weekly stage brought freight from Wadsworth for $20 a ton. After 1880 an unchartered temperance organization in the community offered the erring an opportunity to take one of three pledges: to abstain from tobacco, from whiskey or from both.

By 1904, when the county seat was moved to Fallon, the community had barely three dozen residents, though it still had a fine two-story brick hotel and saloon. Stillwater swiftly declined as Fallon grew, and later it became a spot renowned for excellent catfishing and duckhunting. The farming district still continues to thrive, but the town is a ghost.

SHADY RUN, 1½ miles east of Stillwater-Lovelock road at a point 46 miles northeast of Fallon.

Gold discoveries in March 1908 led to Shady Run being staked out and by April's end a feed yard and two saloons were running. In May $200-a-ton ore was being shipped, but the camp folded that summer.

COPPEREID, by road and trail 1½ miles east of the Stillwater-Lovelock road at a point 49 miles northeast of Fallon.

Copper discoveries in White Cloud Canyon early in 1869 led to the establishment of a camp near the mines which briefly contained a provisions store, saloon and about forty people. In hope of further growth, White Cloud City was platted a mile and a half below, at the foot of the range, but the mines did not develop and the camp was abandoned. Early in the 1890s a small smelter was set up at the mouth of the canyon. It ran briefly and some copper ore was shipped in 1893.

Further production was insignificant until March 1907, when the Nevada United Mining Co., under John T. Reid, initiated large-scale copper mining. In April a post office opened, as well as a boarding house, commissary and saloon. A forty-mile railroad was projected to Hazen or Parran on the Southern Pacific, but mining subsided within months. Between 1907 and 1912 the only noticeable production was several carloads of hand-sorted ore from surface workings. No buildings remain.

HILL, or Hill and Grimes, on US 50 at a point 11 miles southeast of Fallon.

This station near the foot of Grimes Point on the old central emigrant road across Nevada had a post office from 1882 to the 1900s, and early in this century it was the first water stop for teamsters east of Fallon on the freight run to Fairview.

SALT WELLS, also Petersons, on US 50 at a point 15 miles southeast of Fallon.

Beginning in 1905 this station was a watering stop for the Fallon-Fairview freight and stage lines. With the coming of automobiles, a gasoline station and restaurant replaced the earlier facility.

SAND SPRINGS, north side of US 50 at a point 26 miles east of Fallon.

The barrenness of this area belies its importance and varied history. Westbound emigrants who traveled the central route of the Overland Trail in the 1850s were followed in 1860-61 by the Pony Express which established a change station housing a station keeper, spare rider and supplies. After 1861 Sand Springs station remained as a facility for east-west travelers.

Periodic salt mining and an era of borax operations have given significance to Sand Springs. After the discovery of salt on the hot, dry Four Mile Flat south of the station, the Sand Springs Co., owners of 1600 acres of the salt bed, built a $175,-000 works on the east edge of the flat. The salt's purity permitted a simple mining operation. Tracts of the marsh were divided into strips whose surfaces were regularly scraped with broad wooden hoes onto large planks. These heaps drained and dried in a few days' time, and then the product was loaded onto wheelbarrows or cars placed on wooden tracks which ran to platforms where the salt was sacked for shipment. Because secretions from the saline clays allowed incrustation to form in only a few weeks, a fresh crop from each strip was assured at least once a month.

This ten-stamp mill built in 1864 at the lower end of La Plata, never treated much ore, as evidenced by a small tailings pile. Lack of ore brought about a swift decline and abandonment in 1868.

Around 1910 the station at Frenchman offered facilities for care of man and beast. More modern service stations have operated here since the 1920s.
(Mrs. Lyle de Braga Collection)

(below) This view of Fairview looking west about 1913 shows the upper camp adjacent to the mines, while on the flat below is the original camp. The large building in the center is the hotel. By 1914 the lower town was completely abandoned in favor of the upper site, where wooden buildings remained protected for another half century.
(Nevada Historical Society)

The Comstock mills consumed great quantities of salt, though no general agreement was evident in the manner of its use or its effectiveness. Some operators applied salt with scientific sophistication; others used it naively in the same manner as early millers who, lacking any knowledge of chemistry, even tried tobacco juice, decoction of sagebrush and other equally absurd ingredients, expecting them to be effective in ore reduction. The succeeding century has not settled the controversy over early use of salt.

The mills bought several thousands of tons of salt each year and though the company invested over $100,000 to outfit seventy large teams to transport the product eighty miles for delivery, others had to be hired to assist in freighting, with extra freight bills of $10,000 to $15,000 per week! The uniform price for salt delivered at the mill was $60 per ton, substantially less than its cost from previous sources at San Francisco and Rhodes, Nevada.

Salt could be delivered still more cheaply from a nearer point, and after discovery of the Eagle salt marsh in 1869 (see Leete), salt production at Sand Springs practically ceased, but that same year newly organized companies began exploiting borax deposits on Four Mile Flat. Great quantities of borax were mined by scraping it from the top of the soil, running it through concentrators and tanks and then crystallizing it. Two large mills were built in the area; one operated by the American Borax Co. could process half a ton of borax daily for eastern consumption, while a smaller mill nearby had a monthly capacity of about five tons. Borax mining here ceased permanently in 1872 because of immense importation of boracic acid from England. This recovery of borax was a pioneer project in the Great Basin, a precursor of an important industry at Columbus and Death Valley.

When heavy freighters from Hazen and Fallon began regular runs to the eastern mining camps after 1906, the Sand Springs stage station revived with a post office. Teamsters spread their bedrolls in the corral next to their rigs and watered animals at ten cents a head. The station fell into disuse after wagons gave way to autos.

Salt mining resumed occasionally, and a four-story salt mill erected in 1928 ran until the early part of the depression. Elmer Huckaby began working the salt flats in earnest during 1938, after

building a salt harvester out of old machine parts and mounting it on the frame of a truck. His family operation continued through the 1960s.

Nothing remains of the early salt company's mill, but rock walls of the larger borax mill stand on the western edge of Eight Mile Flat. Foundations of an old station lie west of the Sand Springs historical marker.

LA PLATA, 13 miles north of US 50 at a point just west of its junction with SR 31 (25 miles east of Fallon). High axle required.

Silver discoveries on the east side of the Stillwater Range in 1862 led to organization of the Mountain Wells district, and a camp with many stone buildings rose early in 1863 amid numerous mining locations. Eastern capitalists bought several claims that year and carried on extensive prospecting and development work with discouraging results. The Silver Wave Mining Co. which owned the La Plata townsite and an adjacent 1500-acre wood ranch built an expensive mill in 1864 in anticipation of sustained products. Early that same year La Plata became the seat of Churchill County.

During the mid-1860s the camp was the county's largest and had a post office, three mills, and businesses. There is no evidence to show that a courthouse was built; the county was too small and poor to afford a permanent building. The district failed after the spring of 1867 when news of discoveries at White Pine and several localities in Nye County promised rich ore. The Monte Cristo Mining Co. relocated in White Pine at the camp of Monte Cristo, and by the end of 1867 the post office was discontinued. The county seat was removed to Stillwater during the next year. Discoveries in the spring of 1906 sent a few miners back to the district but the camp did not revive. Scars of old roads, mill walls and rock ruins remain.

FRENCHMAN, south side of US 50, 35 miles east of Fallon.

For about a decade after 1906 "Frenchy's" served as a teamsters' station with saloon and stables on the Fallon-Fairview-Wonder freight run, and here food and lodging were available. A post office known as Bermond was open between 1920 and 1926, and a gasoline pump served motorists on Highway 50 into the 1930s, when that road was given its first hard surface.

FAIRVIEW, 1½ miles south of US 50 at a point 39 miles east of Fallon.

Discoveries of rich silver float in 1905 encouraged the mineral-conscious to seek additional finds, and important locations were made in January 1906. The purchase of several claims by Wingfield and Nixon in March signaled the beginning of development work, and in June a townsite was platted in the flat below the camp near the mines. Promoters got busy and a furious boom ensued; during 1906-07 several thousand people came and went. The road from the railroad station at Hazen was lined with freighters burdened with all kinds of goods, and competing stage lines brought in additional fortune hunters.

In the early months of the camp most of the mines were in the hands of leasers. Early in 1907 Fairview had hotels, banks, 27 saloons, assay offices, the *News,* which invited investors to "first see Fairview," post office, miners' union hall, and a population of 2000. Sagebrush and sand sold for $100 a front foot, and numerous wildcat companies offered stock. Prices for most goods were high. Ice was $4 per 100 pounds, water $2.50 a barrel, and wood ran $20 a cord.

Optimism shifted into second gear in 1907, and the camp sought to remedy the unhappy situation of being sixty miles from a railroad connection by planning a vast network of lines which would connect Fairview with Austin to the east, Tonopah to the south, and Hazen to the west. Though the state legislature approved these ambitious plans, no ties were ever laid. After 1908 the excitement wore off, most people drifted to other camps, the newspaper ceased publication and mineral production fell to only 12% of the 1907 figure.

Only high grade was mined and all ore was shipped to smelters until 1911, when the Nevada-hills Mining Co. began an era of profitable production which lasted until 1917. Some leasers were active thereafter, but today the camp is dead.

Fairview is shown in flags and bunting on its first Fourth in 1906. Wagons were also wrapped in bunting, bought by the yard and spread liberally. The camp was then barely a month old; the swiftness of its growth is demonstrated by the fact that none of these buildings were here at the beginning of May. The marshal of the day (second from the left) positions vehicles for the parade. *(Theron Fox Collection)*

Animals were important to these prospectors at Fairview. Burros carried their gear and supplies and dogs offered companionship while in the lonely hills far from the camp. Two auto stages (center) have arrived from nearby camps. The freight wagon behind the ladies comes from Hazen or Fallon. An early auto into Fairview (lower) captured the curiosity of some of the men. *(Three photos: Theron Fox Collection)*

Mining in the early years of Fairview was done by leasers. They acquired the right to work a certain portion of ground for a specified amount of time, payment for which was usually on a sliding scale of royalties based on ore extracted. Shown here (top left) is the lease of Henry Curtis Morris, a skilled early mining engineer who later worked mines in central Mexico.

Sacked ore (bottom) at this large lease is ready for shipment, while a hoist brings up additional ore from the shaft. It is then carted out to the bins.

The two views at the top of the opposite page show prospectors looking over the possibilities of a lease and some lady visitors who came to see ore being mined. In the underground picture (lower right), other visitors are inspecting a stope underground. The man in the striped shirt is leaning against the vein, shown at an angle of about 30°. *(Five photos: Theron Fox Collection)*

The Nevadahills mine, initially located in January 1906, was the Fairview district's principal producer. After the Nevada Hills corporation acquired control of an important contiguous property in 1910, it brought in power and water and built this mill the next year. It had a daily capacity of 200 tons. That company operated successfully until 1917, closing down after recovering over $2¼ million in silver and gold. Soon thereafter the mill was dismantled, leaving massive foundations.

(Mackay School of Mines, University of Nevada)

Before a mill was built in the Fairview district, ore was sacked for shipment by teams to railroad stations at Hazen and Fallon. A steady stream of wagons was necessary to move the tons of ore that leasers were producing.

(Two photos: Theron Fox Collection)

WONDER, 14 miles north of US 50 at a point 39 miles east of Fallon.

Prospectors from Fairview discovered veins of rich quartz in a dry wash north of Chalk Mountain, 29 miles north of their home camp, in May 1906 and that month hundreds of people rushed here to make locations. On June 1 the camp of Wonder sprang up from the sagebrush, and soon buildings and tents were rising in every direction. On the morning of August 11 newsboys began selling the Wonder *Mining News'* first issue, which inquired, "Did you know that Wonder has no mosquitoes?" A competing paper set up shop within another month and a post office opened. By fall Wonder had the usual mining town businesses:

drug store, assay office, stage line which ran six-horse coaches into Fairview and Fallon, freight depot, several saloons, cafes, sporting house, hotels and boarding houses. Business lots sold for as high as $8000.

During the camp's first years several mining companies started operations but most of the district's yield came from the Nevada Wonder Mining Co., founded in September 1906. Eastern capitalists ultimately took over that company and began systematic development, especially after building a mill below the mine in 1913. Nevada Wonder's profitable career ended in 1919, and only leasers remained. Foundations, collapsed wooden buildings and dead locust trees mark the site.

Wonder was one of several dozen Nevada camps that emerged near newly found ore bodies during 1906. The camp boomed mightily and by August 1907, when this picture was taken, wooden buildings had already appeared in the heart of the camp. The view looks east.

Pioneer businesses at Wonder included this real estate office and outdoor cafe. Dealers set up shop to sell mining and town real estate almost immediately after discoveries. Under a sheltered counter food was served, with prices posted on the wall menu. Beans, eggs, ham, jerky, biscuits, and canned goods were principal parts of the diet. *(Two photos: Charles Hendel Collection)*

The Wonder Boosters circulated several types of cartoon post cards to help promote their favorite camp. *(Theron Fox Collection)*

HE CAME, HE SAW, HE STUCK

Gasoline engines provided power to hoist buckets up shafts which probably did not go down more than a hundred feet. In the crude shed in the foreground, high-grade ore was sorted out and sacked. *(Theron Fox Collection)*

By 1911, when this panorama was taken, Wonder had settled down to be a stable community of a few hundred people and one large producing mine. The camp had electric power, telephones, smooth side streets, and several neatly painted dwellings.

(U. S. Geological Survey)

Essential to every private camp was a water supply, kept in barrels. Wood-frame canvas dwellings were common in the mining camp because of a scarcity of building materials and the transient make-up of a new camp. Tent dwellers could pack up and move on with a minimum of delay. *(Western History Research Center, University of Wyoming)*

Social life in Wonder during World War I featured the community dance in the town's recreation hall. *(Mrs. W. F. Browder)*

The above view shows over-all facilities at the mine and mill. To run this 200-ton cyanide plant, electric power was brought in from Bishop, California; the transmission line was said to have been the nation's largest at that time. Piped water came from Dead Horse Creek, ten miles away.

In December 1919 the company ceased operations, after having paid to its fortunate stockholders over $1.5 million in dividends. In 1924 equipment and structures were razed and machinery sold. (*Two photos, opposite page: Mrs. W. F. Browder; above: U. S. Geological Survey*)

Surface operations at the main shaft of the Nevada Wonder mine are shown at the top left. Muck was hoisted in cars on the cages in the three-compartment shaft. At the top, waste cars were pushed to the dump on either side. Ore was dumped into the bin in front where wagons hauled it to the mill. The underground picture is of the station on the lowest level of the mine. The hoist here handles a bucket in the third compartment which is used to deepen the shaft without interfering with the regular operations of the mine. A load of miners can be seen standing on the cage, waiting to be hoisted to the surface.

HERCULES, 2 miles north of Wonder.

This silver camp existed as an adjunct of Wonder during 1906-07 and the accepted mining camp enterprises were on hand, including the weekly *Miner* as well as a post office beginning in December 1906. The camp's largest structure was the wood-frame St. Francis Hotel which burned to the ground in the spring of 1907. The post office officially closed in October 1908, indicating that the camp went "poof" earlier that year.

VICTOR, 3½ miles southeast of Dixie Valley road at a point 16 miles north of its junction with US 50.

Several parts of the Wonder district were prospected in the spring of 1907, and on its western edge the camp of Victor sprang up. It soon embraced a couple of saloons, a boarding house, post office, and several tent habitations, and at least four gold-producing mines were active nearby. Probably not more than sixty men worked claims in 1907, and only three women lived here, all married. Water came from Dead Horse Creek in Dixie Valley, and the camp's hauler charged five dollars a barrel. By the fall of 1908 most work stopped and the post office was soon removed. Rock foundations are left.

SILVER HILL, 2 miles by road and trail west of the Dixie Valley road at a point 28 miles north of its junction with US 50.

A band of prospectors discovered silver ledges on the east flank of the Stillwater Range in 1860, and when assays reportedly ran as high as $1800 a ton locators boasted that they had found another Comstock. In the spring of 1861 a townsite was laid out which within a month had 200 inhabitants and an express stage line to Virginia City.

When Dan De Quille of the Virginia City *Territorial Enterprise* visited the district in June he found the new camp virtually deserted. He supposed that richer ledges had been found elsewhere and that everyone had rushed to new strikes. Probably very few miners returned to work claims; Silver Hill had become another example of the rainbow chasers finding the wrong end of the rainbow.

After rediscovery of ore in 1878, the I. X. L. district was organized, and in 1880 the camp had a boarding house, two blacksmiths and twenty

miners. That effort died out in the early 1880s but the canyon was active again in 1906-07. An earthquake in 1954 jolted the ghosts of Silver Hill and large cracks remain.

DIXIE VALLEY, 6 miles north and east of the Dixie Valley road at a point 28 miles north of its junction with US 50.

This 20th century ranching community grew in the middle of the valley of the same name. Perhaps as many as fifty people were here at one time, and a post office was maintained between March 1918 and December 1933. A few families remain.

BERNICE, 20 miles northeast of the settlement of Dixie Valley, via desert roads.

As early as 1863 silver mining was started on the west flank of the Clan Alpine Range, but the Bernice mines did not have a camp until about 1882 when a post office was opened and named Casket. The more cheerful name of Bernice was given to the post office the following summer, and two years later the camp had a ten-stamp mill, 50 miners, and tri-weekly mail service from Lovelocks. The mill crushed ore until the mines closed about 1894 after producing over $300,000. Foundations of several buildings remain.

DIXIE, west side Dixie Valley road at a point 45 miles north of its junction with US 50.

Two prospectors drove their burros into Wonder early in May 1907 and confided in friends about rich silver they had found. These friends told others in "strictest confidence" and soon the entire atmosphere of Wonder was charged with the news. Men slipped around to Wonder's livery stable and rented horses, wagons, or any type of conveyance that would carry them to the scene of the new strike.

Two weeks later the camp of Dixie was born. Surveyors laid out a townsite and eager buyers spent $6000 for lots the first week. Dixie soon contained five saloons, two restaurants, two general stores, a hotel, assay office, bakery, and "all else which lended comfort and amusement to a new camp." In June Dixie had 200 people but the town folded by the end of summer. A United States Geological Survey map published during the next year designated Dixie as "abandoned."

BOLIVIA, later Nickel, 4 miles northwest of the Dixie Valley road by road and trail at a point 57 miles north of its junction with US 50.

Wagon trains hauled copper ore to Sacramento after discoveries in the early 1860s, and a local arrastra worked less important gold deposits. During the 1870s Bolivia emerged after Unionville interests began working silver veins, but the long distance to the railroad hindered extended development. Nickel and cobalt were discovered in 1880, and some ore was said to have been shipped to Swansea, Wales. Later in the decade an English company built a $50,000 leaching plant which ran unsuccessfully because an Italian chemist miscalculated the true composition of the nickel-cobalt ores. A furnace was then built which treated less than 100 tons of ore, and a smaller five-ton furnace blew up a short time after being placed in operation.

Mining continued until litigation forced a temporary closing of the mines around 1890. A post office known as Nickel served the district from 1890 to 1895, and most activity ceased by 1907.

The Nickel mine at Bolivia was situated in picturesque Cottonwood Canyon. (*Mrs. R. R. Purdy Collection*)

At the top is shown a ten-horse team on the road to the Nickel mine at Bolivia, around 1905. The mine's boarding house is pictured at center.

(*Both photos: Mrs. R. R. Purdy Collection*)

The Cold Springs Overland Station had been reduced to these walls which over a hundred years ago housed facilities for overnight lodging, a blacksmith shop, and stables. Nearly a mile north of here are the rock ruins of a contemporary telegraph station.

110

EASTGATE, 4 miles southeast of SR 2 at a point 2¾ miles east of its junction with US 50 (47 miles east of Fallon).

Gold strikes in the hills southeast of the Eastgate ranch early in May 1906 sent dozens of prospectors whirring to the new find, and thereafter the trend was toward the Eastgate country. By the middle of the month a townsite had graded streets and all lots were reported sold on the first day of sales. A hotel threw open its doors, followed by a stable, feed yard and other businesses. After water supplies were tapped, it was thought that sources were sufficient for a city of 20,000 inhabitants.

During June a few hundred individuals lived in the Eastgate district. Townsite lots rose in value to $300 each and at least 15 businesses were open. After additional discoveries a promoter tried to get the rival townsite of Cripple Creek started. He offered free lots and other inducements to the first person to establish a newspaper, and one enthusiastic lady offered to board an editor and his family free for two months, provided that he had no more than six children who ate solids! None of the mines shipped any ore, and when rich veins were not tapped both camps folded by the end of the summer.

EASTGATE STATION, on SR 2 at a point 4½ miles east of its junction with US 50.

Eastgate's welcome location beside a stream at the mouth of a narrow canyon on the west flank of the Desatoya Mountains was an Indian campground in the middle of the last century, and sometime around 1870 a small vegetable farm and station was maintained. A blockhouse was built of tufa quarried four miles west. Eastgate was a noted landmark for travelers early in this century, and a service station and restaurant were added with the coming of autos. Those facilities remained in use through the late 1960s.

COLD SPRINGS (Overland Station) on west side of US 50, 12 miles northeast of its junction with SR 2 (53 miles east of Fallon).

Three stations known as Cold Springs existed in this vicinity early in the 1860s. When the Pony Express began running in the spring of 1860, its station was located east of this site as a change

point where fresh ponies were saddled and readied for an incoming rider. An 1860 traveler noted that it was a wretched place, rudely built and roofless, and maintained by four rough-looking boys.

The next year the Overland stage and mail line established a station in the middle of Edwards Creek Valley, as its route ran through New Pass, north of the Pony Express trail. Later in 1861 the transcontinental telegraph line was built and its station was erected northwest of the Pony Express, which was discontinued when messages began passing on the wires. The stage line abandoned its Cold Springs station in 1869. Walls of this building and of the nearby telegraph station remain.

CLAN ALPINE, 7 miles north of US 50 at a point 17 miles north of its junction with SR·2 (50 miles east of Fallon).

As early as January 1864 this district was organized on the east flank of the Clan Alpine Mountains, and many claims were staked and shafts sunk. By 1866, at the mouth of Cherry Creek, a camp was in being with post office, rock cabins and the ten-stamp mill and office of the Silver Lode Mining Co. Returns were small and the mines were abandoned two years later, to see little action in ensuing years. Mill machinery was moved to White Pine by 1869.

There was a small agricultural settlement here in the 1870s when the mill shell was used as a barn, and early in this century a ranching community of about fifty supported a store, post office, physician and stage service to Stillwater. Rock ruins remain.

LEETE, earlier Eagle Salt Works, 4½ miles southwest of I-80 at Hot Springs exit (24 miles northwest of Fallon).

Extensive salt deposits on a marsh here were discovered in 1869 by B. F. Leete, who began operations at the Eagle Salt Works the next year. The Central Pacific which ran just west of the marsh expeditiously shipped the product to the great Comstock silver mills as well as mills in Humboldt County. The works acquired a post office in 1877.

Vats covered several acres and each was fifty feet wide and about 100 feet long. The salt solu-

Massive mill walls of native rock remain at Clan Alpine, now located on property owned by the Clan Alpine Ranch.

The salt works at Leete is shown in 1916 after its abandonment.
(William A. Kornmayer Collection)

This early view of Jessup shows a street taking shape. When these tents appeared, the press described the district as "forging ahead." The gold veins found here were believed to be a continuation of the mineralized zone from Seven Troughs in Pershing County.
(Mrs. R. R. Purdy Collection)

tion crystallized on the sides and bottoms of the vats and on evaporation a thick layer of salt formed which was hoed into piles and shipped without refining. During the summer months an acre of vats produced about ten tons of salt daily. In later years salt was refined elsewhere for dairy and domestic use. After large outputs from 1879 to 1884, production drastically declined.

The Southern Pacific shipped salt to markets until 1903, but after that date the tracks were realigned to the east of Leete, leaving the camp desolate. The works immediately built a railroad over the old grade, connecting with the main line near Wadsworth. Production nevertheless declined and operations ceased after 1915 because of salt discoveries in southern California. Several old evaporators and numerous foundations mark the site.

NIGHTINGALE (Pershing County), 21 miles north of I-80 at Hot Springs exit (41 miles southwest of Lovelock).

Tungsten deposits were discovered on the east slope of the Nightingale Range in 1917, and the mill at Toulon, thirty miles east, treated ore for two years. The Gold-Silver-Tungsten Mining Co. acquired the principal properties in 1929 and built a 100-ton concentrator at the camp but it made only a few short runs. Mill foundations mark the site at Nightingale; at Toulon is the large shell of the mill.

JESSUP, 4 miles northwest of I-80 at the Jessup exit (34 miles north of Fallon).

After initial claims were located in February 1908, carloads of ore averaging over $100 per ton were shipped a few months later. Several small companies began extensive development, according to a New York mining paper, and during the next year Jessup's 300 residents supported three grocery stores, two lumber yards, seven saloons, and a meat market. A daily stage from Huxley on the Southern Pacific met the train and brought in additional settlers.

The initial boom apparently died out by the end of 1909, but during the next decade leasers made intermittent shipments of gold and silver. Wooden buildings remain, but no permanent residents.

WHITE PLAINS, half mile south of I-80 at Jessup exit (30 miles northwest of Fallon).

Mining on this arid, dreary timberless plain began about 1864 when a five-stamp mill was built to recover silver for the Desert Queen and other mines. The mill operated only a short time, failing because of difficulties in obtaining fuel and water. The district's real importance began after salt deposits were located in 1870, the county's second significant salt discovery in a year's time, the first being Leete.

Early in the 1870s the Desert Crystal Salt Co. built a series of vats to recover the product by solar evaporation. Each was a simple shallow excavation, enclosed by low embankments, into which brine was run. Vats 58 feet in width aggregated 4200 feet in length. Annual shipments during the 1870s approximated 200 tons of salt, most of which went to silver districts in eastern Nevada. The salt was so pure that it won awards in fairs. In 1877 a new series of vats was built a mile-and-a-half south near natural springs.

White Plains got a post office in 1879, as well as a telegraph office, and in 1888 the weekly Churchill *News* was published, claiming the largest circulation in the county. Actually it was the *only* paper published in this sparsely populated county until after the turn of the century! This publication did not overtax the capacity of paper mills, and it ran only a few issues.

Salt production declined during the 1890s, but as late as 1912 shipments were made. Acres of broken glass and the old Central Pacific grade mark the site.

The top view shows Vernon, looking south, about 1908. The camp even boasted board sidewalks (center) on part of its business street. Brokerage houses working out of a modest building often made small fortunes by selling mining locations and town lots, as well as listed and unlisted mining stocks. The stage to Farrell (below), five miles away, is ready to leave the Northern saloon. *(Top two photos: Trenchard Collection, Nevada Historical Society; bottom: Mrs. R. R. Purdy Collection)*

PERSHING COUNTY

Pershing County (the southern half of Humboldt County until 1919) has three distinct sections, each with a different history. The dry barren western half was exploited early in this century and gave birth to almost a dozen mining districts. The central valley cut by the Humboldt River sustained mining and milling communities during the last century. The eastern portion known as the Humboldt Region was extensively mined for silver during the 1860s and 1870s.

The Comstock boom after 1860 stimulated prospecting in north-central Nevada. Important early camps were Humboldt City, Dun Glen, Unionville and Star City, but by the mid-1860s exhaustion of high-grade ores, milling difficulties, and inadequate transportation facilities to and from California forced many mines and mills to shut down. Though the Central Pacific began running through this region in 1868, extensive new prospecting and development did not resume except at Unionville between 1869 and 1873. Oreana was the principal milling town. The American Canyon, Spring Valley and Kennedy districts were also active before 1900.

The 20th century statewide boom brought mining activity to the Seven Troughs district, Rochester, Chafey (Dun Glen) and smaller districts. Production began at Tungsten after World War I to continue until 1958. Rochester made its best showing in the 1920s and Scossa and Rabbithole made theirs in the 1930s. Only the Eagle Pitcher mine and several smaller efforts have been active since World War II.

TRINITY, by desert roads 10 miles north of Lovelock.

The Trinity district was organized in June 1863, four years after George Lovelock made initial silver discoveries on the east flank of the Trinity Range. Crude smelters were built, and near the principal mine, the Evening Star, a small stamp mill crushed ore after the fall of 1864. The original discoverer operated a hotel, and amid the rock huts a couple of other businesses were open. One of these was the Trinity Market, whose proprietor proudly advertised the best beef ever offered to a civilized community. "No superannuated milk cows are brought to this shop to rest their weary limbs; no disabled work cattle come here to pull their last breath; here no veal is served up to a wicked world before its time. I kill the fatted calf and serve up the unctuous loins of round-bodied bullocks."

Trinity made several shipments of bullion before 1870, when the mines were abandoned. Stone houses and mine dumps remain, accessible by high-axle cars only.

HALFWAY HOUSE, north side of SR 48 at a point 13 miles northwest of Lovelock.

Situated at the north end of Trinity Pass, this change station, with a station house and corral, served the Lovelock-Seven Trough stages for several years beginning in 1906. Only depressions remain where buildings once stood.

VERNON, on SR 48 at a point 26 miles northwest of Lovelock.

The opening of gold mines in the Seven Troughs district in 1905 led to the platting of Vernon townsite on a broad flat near the foothills of the Seven Troughs Range. Several lots initially sold for $75 each, buildings rose from the sage and a post office soon opened. Unclean water was hauled from Seven Troughs Canyon at a cost of six dollars a barrel, with no charge for dead bugs which the miners strained out with their teeth. When things were more orderly after the spring of 1907, the Vernon Water, Light & Power Co. began serving the town.

For a little over a year thereafter, Vernon was the chief commercial center of the district with about 300 inhabitants, a miners' union, weekly newspapers, hotel, restaurants, post office, bank, stock exchange and doctor's office. Incoming stages were loaded with investors. The local *Miner* admonished people to buy a one-way ticket or tear up the return check of a round-trip ticket — "Come to stay!"

Vernon's happy days were over by 1910 when mining subsided, though the post office remained until 1918. During the 1920s most buildings were hauled away to Tunnel (see below). Only one homely building is left — a two-cell stone jail that held Vernon's rowdy revelers and perhaps an occasional criminal.

TUNNEL, or New Seven Troughs, 2 miles northeast of Vernon.

Hopeful Canadians and Americans organized the Nevada State Mining Co. in 1927 to build a 100-ton cyanide mill and drive a tunnel into rock workings of the old Seven Troughs mines. The tunnel was to eliminate the drainage and haulage problems that overwhelmed its predecessor, the Seven Troughs Coalition Mining Co. in 1917-18.

The company camp contained about thirty structures, including store, bunkhouse, bathhouse, powerhouse and superintendent's home. The 2¼-mile-long tunnel cut into several promising gold veins, but when wet ground was encountered costs soared and all work ceased in 1934. Some mining was performed later in the decade and again in the 1950s. Occupied houses and mill ruins remain.

MAZUMA, 3½ miles northeast of Vernon (24 miles northwest of Lovelock).

Death rode downhill on a flash flood into the prosperous mining camp of Mazuma on July 29, 1912, when a heavy summer cloudburst at the head of Seven Troughs Canyon sent destructive waters roaring past steep rocky crags to the innocent settlement at the mouth of the canyon. About a dozen lives were lost, including five children from one family, and the water's powerful thrust carried wooden buildings and tent dwellings downhill for over two miles from their foundations. A bank vault was washed two miles to the flat below.

Mazuma was founded in 1907 when the Seven Troughs district was attracting other than local attention. The success of the Mazuma Hills gold mine reflected the optimism of its name and the camp grew rapidly. By the summer of 1908 Mazuma was the district's largest camp. In August it had a post office, the Seven Troughs *District News*, a two-story bank, three-story hotel, several stores, offices for professional people, stage service to Lovelock, a board of trade and a fire department. Discoveries by leasers led to organization of over forty mining companies and the building of two mills.

The ten-stamp Darby mill began running in 1909 and the town prospered until the flash flood washed away its hopes and enthusiasm three years later. The Darby mill was the only large building to survive the flood, and less than two weeks later a fire destroyed it too. The mill was reconstructed by the end of the year and it saw service until 1918.

SEVEN TROUGHS, 1½ mi. northwest of Mazuma.

Gold discoveries in the upper part of Seven Troughs Canyon during the fall of 1905 led to the founding of a district the next year, and in 1907 a rush developed when fantastic discoveries reportedly worth $100,000 a ton lured many miners, especially from Tonopah and Goldfield. A townsite platted in February 1907 was soon populated with tents. Seven Troughs Canyon was taken up with claims along its whole length and mining operations began at once. Trains of freight wagons hauled supplies thirty miles from the railroad at Lovelock, and a daily auto stage made runs to neighboring Vernon. The district's most important

Built in a vulnerable position at the mouth of Seven Troughs Canyon, Mazuma never-theless flourished because of its central location to the district's mines. Mazuma was prospering in June 1908, and continued to thrive until its economy was washed out of existence four years later.

Auto stages prepare to strike out for Lovelock, while burros burdened with bulky sup-plies linger on the main street. Behind the animals is the road to Seven Troughs Canyon, where the district's most important mines were located. (*Two photos: Mrs. R. R. Purdy*)

The destructive force of a flash flood is shown in the top two photos. A store has been torn from its foundation, and other buildings have been washed away. Though the Mazuma (or Darby) mill escaped the flood, it succumbed to flames less than a month later. The camp did not survive its baptism of fire and water and was only partially rebuilt.

At sunrise the camp's water hauler began making several trips from nearby springs to the camp, where he drew water from his barrels to fill buckets and small containers.
(Three photos: Mrs. R. R. Purdy Collection)

118

The center of Seven Troughs (above) shows typical mining camp businesses. In the general view of the camp (below), looking west and down the canyon, the ten-stamp Kindergarten mill, a fifty-ton cyanide plant built in 1911, appears at the extreme left. The business district is dominated by the Seven Troughs Hotel. At the right (facing camera) is a wooden building which contained the general store. The elaborate frame foundation of the Owl Club in the center of the picture shows how steep was the slope. *(Both photos: Mrs. R. R. Purdy Collection)*

Here the steepness of Seven Troughs Canyon is dramatically shown.
(Mrs. Gloria Oberg Collection)

A gully now bisects the canyon, worn deep by numerous flash floods through this century. Mill ruins, extensive mine dumps, and wood and rock dwellings remain.

mines opened nearby, and selected ore from the rich Wihuja mine did yield nearly $100,000 a ton.

Beginning in 1907, Seven Troughs had its own post office, saloons, stores, and a population of 350. At the height of speculation in 1907, some talked of building a railroad from the Southern Pacific at Lovelock through Vernon to the Seven Troughs mines. A water system and a school district were organized in 1908 and the camp continued through World War I on the strength of production from the Kindergarten mine and mill. By 1918 the post office closed and only leasers were active thereafter.

FARRELL, 5 miles north-northeast of Mazuma (27 miles northwest of Lovelock).

Although gold had been discovered in Stonehouse Canyon as early as 1863, mining did not begin until new locations were made in the spring of 1906. Streets were laid out and Farrell was thrown up in a week's time. There was also a smaller camp near the mines called Stone House. Above it was an old rock structure that dated from the 1860s.

At the height of the boom in the summer of 1907, Farrell had 75 tents, two restaurants, two rooming houses, two stables, several saloons and a lumberyard. Town lots sold for as high as $500. To show that their camp had come of age, Farrell's citizens celebrated the Fourth of July that year in true big-camp style, and people from Vernon and Seven Troughs joined the festivities. Speeches were followed by a baseball game that lasted until early morning drinking caught up with the players, and then everyone staggered over to a makeshift ring to watch the boxing matches. Less than a month later a post office opened, but no permanent veins were found and the camp probably survived no later than 1908 or 1909, although the post office officially closed in 1911.

Later, in 1935, a five-stamp mill was built, but milling was handicapped by a lack of water. Cellars and acres of broken glass mark the site.

PLACERITES or Placeritos, 1½ miles west of Lovelock-Scossa road at a point 41 miles north of Lovelock.
The spelling "Placeritas" found on some maps cannot be justified historically or linguistically.

In the low hills on the east slopes of Kamma Mountain early in the 1870s four men led by Ma-

hogany Jack recovered gold worth $30,000 in limited placer operations. After 1880 various individuals tried to work the ground, bringing gravel to rockers at Rabbithole Springs until water was brought into the district from Cow Creek in 1890.

In 1929 the Newmont Mining Co. acquired 4000 acres and began sophisticated large-scale operations which included building a large reservoir, tanks and a dragline scraper to mine the gravel. The camp of Placerites then formed with a store and a speakeasy, but all work ceased by 1942. Wooden buildings remain.

SCOSSA, ½ mile east of the Lovelock-Scossa road at a point 46 miles north of Lovelock.

Born in March 1907 when a platted townsite rose near discoveries of jewelry rock on the west fringe of the Antelope Range, Scossa was active awhile but faded months later, after limited mining development. Little was heard of this camp until a strike in December 1930 by Charles and James Scossa, longtime workers in the district, sent several prospectors to stake claims. Hoping for a stimulant to combat the depression, the *Saturday Evening Post* told of the discovery in a feature article. The county graded a road to Scossa and a town was laid out.

Large gold production began in 1931, and in 1932 newspaperman C. B. Glasscock described Scossa as the only camp of immediate promise on the Nevada desert. For the next five years Scossa helped Nevada regain its former mining vigor, and the local developments were among the state's largest gold producers of the 1930s. But when the veins played out in 1937, the camp declined and quietly passed into the limbo of ghost towns. A woodframe saloon and other shacks remain.

ROSEBUD, 7 miles north and west of Scossa (45 miles north-northwest of Lovelock).

Silver discoveries in 1906 sparked the founding of a platted town north of Rosebud Canyon in December 1906. Soon there were graded streets, a hotel and a bank erected by the Rosebud Development Co., promoters of the town. In Rosebud Canyon itself the rival townsite of Goldbud was platted near some springs. A boom quickly got under way and as usual folly played eagerly into the hands of fraud — the towns had been established before sus-

Among the last of Nevada's old-time camps was Scossa, a boom of the 1930s. In March 1931 the camp began to emerge (above) and weeks later a few businesses had opened up (below), including a lumberyard that sold all types of building supplies. Note the underwear drying on the bushes in front of the tents at the left.

(Two photos: Ernest Baumann Collection)

taining ore bodies had been found. A post office opened at Rosebud in January 1907 and during the next month the Rosebud *Mining News* was distributed.

Goldbud's principal feature was a general store which was reportedly "doing a business considered good in a town of 5000 inhabitants." In March the district had 800 inhabitants. A weekly stage to Humboldt House on the railroad was in operation at various times until the fall of 1908, when Rosebud wilted, and many of the town's pretentious buildings were abandoned before completion. Except for a few buildings of later construction, not a bloomin' thing is left.

RABBITHOLE SPRINGS, 5 miles west-southwest of Rosebud.

Emigrants in the mid-19th century stopped at Rabbithole Springs for water before crossing the Black Rock Desert to the west. Some emigrants investigated placer deposits in the 1850s, but not until this century was mining here carried out on a sustained basis.

In 1916 two brothers took out gold worth about $3000. A company installed a washing plant at the springs in the fall of 1932 and built a 3½-mile road to the placers for its first fleet of five trucks. By the middle of the decade about 150 individuals were placering in the district, with dry washers and rockers. The Rio Seco Mining Co. in 1939 treated several hundred yards of gravel a day, and a camp 3½ miles east of the springs contained 28 families and 100 men. Until the 1960s the Double-O Mining Co. and smaller operators continued placering in the area. Three large springs and wooden ruins mark the site of Rabbithole Springs; at the placer camp about five buildings and immense piles of tailings are left.

WILLARD, later Loring, about 3 miles east of US 40 (I-80) at a point 6½ miles northeast of Lovelock.

Gold discoveries in the spring of 1915 sparked a little boom, and the small camp of tents and wooden structures was named for the boxing champion who defeated Jack Johnson. Several hundred people were in the Loring district that summer, and a thirty-ton mill, built nearby at Kodak siding, ran only a few months before shutting down. Another mine was active in 1921 but the district was never a sustaining producer.

Willard, shown here around World War I, was never known as a fighting camp.
(William A. Kornmayer Collection)

The Montezuma Smelting Works (top) at Oreana is shown in 1867, with the Humboldt River in the background. Beginning late the previous year, bullion in commercial quantities was produced, three years before smelters began treating similar ores at Eureka. Its superintendent A. W. Nason displayed unusual courage in building eight furnaces in a region destitute of fuel. (*Library of Congress*)

Oreana Station came to life after the rebirth of the Rochester district. A townsite was laid out in February 1913, and promoters claimed that lots in a short time "should show 300, 500 or even 1000 per cent profit." It was anticipated that the station would also be the shipping point for agricultural products from throughout Humboldt Valley. (*Ed A. Smith Collection*)

Dad Lee's first site at Oreana Station (bottom), during 1924-1929, was a few hundred yards east of the present location. He called himself "King of the Desert."

(*Willie Capucci Collection*)

OREANA, 3¼ miles north of US 40 (I-80) at Woolsey (11 miles northeast of Lovelock).

Not to be confused with Oreana Station (which see) on the Southern Pacific, 3 miles northeast.

After a five-stamp mill was moved from Trinity in October 1865 and relocated here in the east bank of the Humboldt River, a camp which took the name Oreana sprang up on an overlooking bluff. This mill crushed ore from the Montezuma mine at Arabia and was joined by a second mill in the summer of 1866 when A. W. Nason became superintendent of the Trinity & Sacramento Co., part owners of the Montezuma. Nason at once began building a huge smelting works to treat Montezuma ores and proceeded to secure the entire Montezuma claim. In all, he spent $300,000 and the smelter began to produce bullion late in 1866.

In November 1866 a toll bridge was opened, and in a horseshoe bend in the Humboldt the town of Oreana was relocated at a site central to the milling activity. It grew rapidly and acquired a post office in February 1867 as well as hotel, general store, boarding houses, restaurant, meat market, blacksmith shop, livery stable and saloons. Its population of 200 or 300 made it the largest town in the Humboldt Valley.

The furnaces operated at full blast both day and night producing silver, and its five chimneys belched dark clouds of smoke and antimonial vapors over the town. By 1868 more bullion was being shipped from Oreana than from any other place in Nevada; the works were acclaimed the most complete in the state, producing $45,000 monthly.

Beginning that May the Oreana Jockey Club began sponsoring seasonal horse races. It was said that if a man wanted to collect money from old debts, his best chance to catch an elusive debtor would be at the races.

In spite of its apparent success, the operation got into financial distress. Mounting debts and tax delinquency forced a shutdown in 1869, and the same fate befell new owners who reactivated the smelter during 1870-71. After intermittent work during the 1870s the Montezuma smelter was destroyed by fire. Traces of its foundations and slag piles remain, and caved-in cellars mark the Oreana townsite.

ARABIA, 6 miles north of US 40 (I-80) at Woolsey (14 miles north-northeast of Lovelock).

During the late 1860s the county's most notable event other than the completion of the Central Pacific was the exploitation of the rich Montezuma mine at Arabia in the Trinity district. Its superintendent, A. W. Nason, built furnaces for smelting at Oreana (which see), making both mine and mill highly lucrative.

When the Montezuma became northern Nevada's leading silver mine in 1868, the county assessor gave the optimistic opinion that Arabia's mines would produce more bullion than any other of like size. Selected Montezuma ore was so rich that each ton produced nearly a half ton of lead, antimony and silver. That mine gave forth $455,000 in silver and 3150 tons of lead by 1875, but thereafter Arabia declined. Headframes and stone walls mark the site.

POKER BROWN, 15 miles northwest of US 40 (I-80) at Woolsey (16 miles northwest of Lovelock).

Early in the 1870s silver was initially discovered in the San Jacinto district, but not until early in this century did a camp form when the district was briefly prospected. Nothing of interest remains.

TORREYTOWN, 6 miles north of US 40 (I-80) at Woolsey, by road and trail.

This milling settlement was founded on the west bank of the Humboldt River at Torrey's 12-ton smelting works which treated lead-silver ore from Arabia during the spring of 1867. In April, forty hands were at work receiving "good wages and good grub." Before closing later that year, the smelter led a spasmodic life: sometimes it glowed with melting ores, sometimes it took a long hopeless sleep. Only faint foundations remain.

OREANA STATION, west of I-80 at Oreana exit.

Not to be confused with the milling settlement of the same name, this newer Oreana was a mere sidetrack and section house for Southern Pacific overland trains from the 1880s until late in 1912, when rich mines opened up in the Rochester district, nine miles east. A community developed around the section house and Oreana became the jumping-off place for the new boom. Early in 1913 stores, saloons, post office, depot and restaurants were in operation, as well as the commodious Nenzel hotel which accommodated fifty guests. Later that year the Nevada Short Line Railway was built eastward toward Rochester, and shops for that line were built here. When activity on the new short line lessened after 1917, Oreana declined. After 1924 a one-store community known as Dad Lee's was situated east of the interstate highway. Only foundations remain at Oreana Station; Dad Lee's business house remains occupied.

ETNA, or Aetnaville, 2 miles north-northwest of I-80 at Oreana exit, by road and trail.

This milling settlement rose on the east bank of the Humboldt River in 1865 when the local mill began treating silver ore from mines at Arabia, the Black Rock Desert country, Prince Royal, Lima and Dun Glen. During the next year at Etna there were two mills, a general store, livery stable, surveyor's office, post office and a ferry service across the Humboldt. This camp was regarded as one of the busiest in the county, but by the end of 1866 one mill had been dismantled and moved to Oreana and the other was temporarily idle. Etna "caved" and the post office closed.

HO, YE THAT HUNGER AFTER THE FLESH---OF FAT BULLOCKS!

A. M. SADORUS

SENDS GREETING—to the miners in Arabia, and in Sacramento; also, to the ranchmen along the river; and especially to the citizens of Etna.

I have fitted up a

MEAT MARKET

IN ETNA,

 where the public will at all times find a display of fresh

FAT BEEF,

equal to any sold in the State. Orders from a distance promptly attended to.

☞ Best of Corned Beef always on hand.

A. M. SADORUS.

Etna, Nev., Sept. 23, 1865.   22tf

For the rest of the decade limited milling produced only a small amount of bullion, then in 1870 Median Torrey repaired the mill and powered it with an undershot waterwheel on the river. This attempt to revitalize milling operations failed because millhands became sick from antimonial fumes and inadequate ventilation. By 1872 Etna was abandoned forever.

ROCHESTER, 10 miles southeast of I-80 at Oreana exit via SR 50.

Migrants from Rochester, New York found gold in Rochester Canyon in the early 1860s, but the district's importance was not realized until Joseph Nenzel uncovered rich silver ore in June 1912. The first ore shipment was made in August and by November a wild rush was on. During that winter hundreds of people swarmed there. Strings of freight wagons, autos and trucks lined the road from Oreana Station.

When 1913 arrived about 2200 men were established in the camps of Rochester and Lower Rochester along a two-and-a-half-mile-long main street which extended from Lincoln Hill to the base of Nenzel Hill. Streets were laid out in four townsites, and many frame buildings poked up among the tents. In February Upper Rochester had the rival *Miner* and *Journal,* substantial stone buildings, hotels, office buildings "built to stay," and saloons and dance halls were in full blast. Near the base of Nenzel Mountain, the camp of Rochester Heights boasted the highest saloon in the district; its liquors and cigars were advertised as being "on top" in quality as well as in location.

By March Rochester had its post office and was the district's leading camp. The Rochester Philharmonic Orchestra, composed of a mando-cellist, flautist, guitarist, mandolin artist and vocalist, provided culture and refinement playing such selections as "The Poet and the Peasant." Freight service was provided by twenty automobiles, two trucks and about 15 horse-and-mule outfits. During the rest of 1913 Rochester's fame grew and leasers accounted for most of that year's $500,000 recorded output.

In 1914 the Nevada Short Line Railway, which had been built from Oreana to nearby Limerick Canyon during the previous year, was extended to Lower Rochester better to serve the district. At the same time the Rochester Mines Co. built a new 100-ton mill to eliminate expensive hauling of ores. By February 1915 when both mill and new railroad line were completed, Lower Rochester with its post office and businesses was the district's largest camp. After September 1915 another railroad extension eastward to the mines made it possible to transport ore directly to the mill. Its service was

Lower Rochester in 1913 had an assortment of businesses. On the left a miner's "beauty shop" vies for attention with a popular bar. More than half of the businesses in this picture are saloons.
(*Nevada Historical Society*)

House moving was never a problem in Rochester. Find a few idle hands, buy them drinks, and have them carry your tent to the desired site. (Las Vegas *Review-Journal*)

Home was never like this. Coffee on the stove, a few newspapers, and a large bunk in a Rochester lodging house.
(*History Room, Wells Fargo Bank*)

This picture of Upper Rochester at the top of the page shows the camp during World War I when it was smaller than in the boom of 1912-14. From the bins at the left, ore was transported by an aerial tramway over the hills to the mill at Lower Rochester (center). This custom mill could process 100 tons of ore daily. Several hundred yards above the mill was the saloon district at Lower Rochester. (*Top: David F. Myrick Collection; center: Nina Hood Collection; bottom: Ed A. Smith Collection*)

undependable and in 1917 the company built a new tramway to replace the foreign-owned railroad which was abandoned a year later.

The district's mines made their best showing during the 1920s, but by 1942 most operations ceased after more than $9 million was produced. Smaller efforts after World War II continue to the present time. Lower Rochester contains several wooden buildings and mill foundations, while the upper camp also has a few wooden ruins.

PACKARD, 8 miles southeast of SR 50 at a point 2½ miles east of I-80 at Oreana exit.

The Packard mine was discovered 2½ miles south of Rochester in December 1912, and the Nevada Packard Mining Co. completed a 100-ton cyanide plant by December 1915 to work the ore for gold. The mill was built below the portals of the Packard mine's two working tunnels, thus placing the mill in an advantageous position to handle ore directly from its source. Water for milling was piped in from a spring three miles away, and a power substation in Rochester Canyon sup-

plied electricity. During periods of peak operation, up to 150 people were here. Mine and mill lasted until 1923, producing about $5 million.

LIMA, 2 miles east of SR 50 at a point 2½ miles east of I-80 at Oreana exit.

Briefly known as Williamsburg when founded in the summer of 1865, this thriving little village near the mouth of Sacramento Canyon had by the fall of the year a meat market, restaurant, saloon, grocery store, telegraph office, and several stone houses. The lead-silver Humboldt Queen was the principal mine. Lima remained active throughout the mid-1860s and had a post office for 12 months during 1866-67. Stone ruins mark the site.

PANAMA, 1½ miles east of SR 50 at a point 8 miles east of I-80 at Oreana exit.

This tent camp housed about fifty inhabitants briefly early in 1913, but mining in this part of the Rochester district was a losing fight from the start and the camp folded by midyear. One cellar remains.

The camp of Packard was built in the flat below the mine. Among the neat cottages a few businesses were opened. Unlike Rochester and other nearby camps, Packard was peaceful and orderly. *(Nina Hood Collection)*

AMERICAN CANYON, 6 miles east of SR 50 at a point 8 miles east of its junction with I-80 at Oreana exit.

A colorful era of Chinese placering began in 1884, three years after the Americans had come and gone, and as many as 3000 Orientals washed gravel during active periods. A large settlement developed, and most structures were built of native rock. Chinese regularly came to bow to a mysterious idol inside a gaily decorated joss temple which was painted with bright colors and embellished with dragons and devils. Diversions included gambling and smoking opium in the evening after a meal of dried fish and rice. Before the Chinese stopped work in 1895, between $5 and $10 million in gold was recovered — the largest placer output in the state during any period. Extensive stone ruins are left.

SPRING VALLEY, later Fitting, on SR 50, 13 miles east of I-80 at Oreana exit.

This locality twice experienced large-scale placer mining. Chinese were the first to work the Spring Valley deposits after 1881. In 1905 a post office named Fitting was opened here; six years later a 2000-cubic-yard dredge thoroughly worked the gravel near a large pond. Below the camp a 15-stamp amalgamation and concentrating mill operated without success. Fitting was connected with Lovelock, 29 miles southwest, by a semi-weekly stage with a three dollar fare. The post office closed in 1915. Placer dumps and mill ruins mark the site.

RYE PATCH, ¾ mile west of I-80 at Rye Patch exit (22 miles north-northeast of Lovelock).

Mining began after 1863 discoveries in Rye Patch Canyon, Echo district, and rich silver lodes were found the next year at the Rye Patch mine. A small camp was near these operations until about 1865. Four years later the English-owned Rye Patch Milling & Mining Co. purchased the mines, increased operations and built a ten-stamp mill on the east side of the Humboldt River in 1870 to eliminate hauling ore to the Auburn mill near Reno.

The new mill burned in 1871 but a replacement began work the following year and ran for another six years. In 1872 Rye Patch had a post office,

school, store, saloon and freight house. Before operations ceased late in the 1880s, the district had produced more than $1 million in silver. Later, in 1914 and 1923, small attempts to cyanide the tailings were made. Mill foundations remain.

HUMBOLDT HOUSE, west side of I-80 at Humboldt exit (32 miles northeast of Lovelock).

The Central Pacific Railroad founded Humboldt House in 1868 as an eating station. While travelers dined, train engines were serviced or changed. Contemporary travel guides described this place as an oasis in the desert, a stunning contrast to the barren desolation which a traveler had to endure for hundreds of miles across northern Nevada. Some passengers rested for a few days before resuming the suffocating ride.

Dining cars were added to trains in the 1890s, eliminating the meal stops and thereafter Humboldt House served as an inn for stage travelers. Trains stopped only for mail, freight and occasional passengers, and then toward mid-century no longer stopped here at all. The post office which had opened here in 1872 finally closed in May 1919.

HUMBOLDT CITY, 4½ miles southeast of I-80 at Humboldt exit.

As an outgrowth of the Comstock excitement, a French trader on the Humboldt River discovered silver in the rocky gorges of the Humboldt Range in the spring of 1860. Initial specimens carried to the Comstock assayed $400 to $2700 per ton and soon a prospecting party rushed to the Humboldt, made a peace treaty with the Paiutes, and established a settlement by the end of 1860, the first in the region. Living expenses were high and the Indians hostile, so these few prospectors left early in 1861, but a late spring rush brought 200 people by August and the founding of Humboldt City.

The growth continued and the camp contained almost 500 people in 1863. A contemporary described Humboldt City that year as a picturesque village of 200 buildings including substantial stores and well-built houses constructed without mortar, with a babbling stream running through every street, and possessing many beautiful gardens which attested to the taste of the inhabitants. The town had two hotels, a post office, and two saloons

At Spring Valley the stamp mill operated in the gulch just east of the camp. It was unsuccessful from the start. This wooden gold dredge (middle) of the Federal Mines Co. was active between 1910 and 1914. Water was piped and flumed in from Indian Creek, five miles north. It was difficult to keep the dredge afloat because older underground workings continually drained the dredge pond. The bottom view shows Spring Valley in 1968, with Buena Vista Valley in the distance. (*Top and middle: William A. Kornmayer Collection; bottom: Gary Allen photo*)

The railroad station at Humboldt House had a sparkling fountain, which, together with surrounding trees formed a pleasing picture. Irrigation made green fields, fruit orchards and flower gardens possible in this area.
(Northeastern Nevada Museum)

In the dining room at Humboldt House, glasses and water pitchers stand ready to quench the traveler's thirst, and a bar was provided for stronger refreshment. This station had a reputation for serving the best meals on the line; they cost 75¢ in coin or $1 in paper. *(Nevada Historical Society)*

The Humboldt Range in the background dwarfs the ruins at the city of the same name, a few miles from Humboldt House.
(Ed A. Smith Collection)

one of which was run by two partners who were always ready to argue or fight politics or deal out redeye to thirsty customers. Reconstruction and Negro suffrage were favorite topics for debate; very little was said on religion. Two men ran the blacksmith shop, and at any moment they would stop shoeing a refractory horse to spin a yarn. A few families also lived here, as well as enough children, chickens, pigs and dogs to give Humboldt City a lively appearance.

Local prospectors made strikes in surrounding canyons. On the basis of over 1000 silver discoveries in the canyon, a joint stock company was formed by 16 San Franciscans, to build a 61-mile ditch from the Humboldt River to the foot of the canyon. Surveys were made to divert the entire river to create a 250-foot fall for milling purposes, but that plan died. The Atlantic & Pacific Mining Co. carried on extensive operations during 1863-64 but thereafter production slowed despite diligent prospecting, and by 1869 Humboldt City became one of the "places that were," with removal of the post office. Stone ruins survive nearly a century of desertion.

IMLAY, off I-80 at Imlay exit. (38 miles northeast of Lovelock).

After the Southern Pacific realigned railroad districts in 1904, Imlay was founded four years later at a new terminal where roundhouse and other facilities were built. A post office opened that October, and within another three or four years the community had three saloons, restaurant, hotel, physician, church, boarding house, livery stable, mercantile company, and a few hundred people. The station served the Imlay mine to the south where a ten-stamp mill had been built, and four other mining companies were headquartered here. In late years when the railroad removed shop facilities, Imlay declined and now only about sixty people make their home here.

PRINCE ROYAL, 5 miles south of Imlay.

This small camp grew near mines at the north end of the Humboldt Range around 1864-65, but was abandoned in the general decline of mining in the Humboldt region in the mid-1860s.

MILL CITY, north of I-80 at Mill City exit (41 miles north-northeast of Lovelock).

This town was born in 1862 with great promise. It was to be the silver reduction center for most of Humboldt County, with mills powered by water from the Humboldt Canal, a project promoted by a San Francisco firm. A ditch was planned 90 miles long, 15 feet wide and 3 feet deep, constructed from a point east of Winnemucca to irrigate land along the canal route, and with a 113-foot fall to the southern terminus at Mill City on the Humboldt River, there was enough power for a few score mills with an aggregate of 900 stamps! The sum of $1000 per mile was allocated to the project, but $100,000 was spent in constructing the first 28 miles and all digging stopped in 1863 at a point near modern Winnemucca. Vestiges of the canal may still be seen a mile east of that city.

In the fall of 1868 Mill City became a station on the newly completed Central Pacific and thereafter served as railhead for Dun Glen, Unionville and other localities. Mill City soon had a hotel, post office, saloons, store, livery stables, telegraph office, several dwellings and a stamp mill. After the spring of 1875 a new foundry repaired mining machinery and manufactured castings and other metal parts for mills and furnaces in northern Nevada as far away as Cornucopia in Elko County. By 1880 Mill City had declined to fifty residents supporting eight businesses, and it expired early in this century after Imlay became a railroad division point.

Tungsten mining began eight miles to the west during World War I and Mill City reawoke as a freight station for that district. Wood and stone ruins remain near modern businesses.

LANCASTER, 2 miles northwest of I-80 at Mill City exit, by unimproved road.

Mining in the Central district to the north led to the settlement of Lancaster, which was expected to be an important silver milling center after plans were announced for building a forty-stamp mill. By May 1863 the place was beginning to flourish as a suburb of Mill City and streets were surveyed. By August 100 lots had been sold and stores, saloons and a lumberyard were in business. The camp then had about 200 inhabitants living in

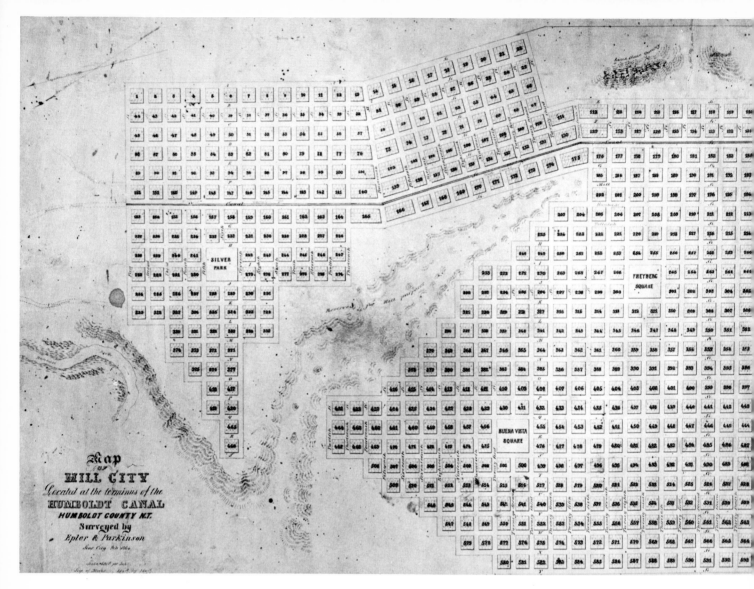

Map of MILL CITY
Located at the terminus of the
HUMBOLDT CANAL
HUMBOLDT COUNTY N.T.
Surveyed by
Epler & Parkinson

This optimistic plat of Mill City is the largest survey of a proposed town in the state. The grid shows 593 blocks with highest numbered streets extending to Y and 35th. Top of the map is east; proposed route of the Humboldt Canal enters from left and passes above gulch in center of the picture, where a series of stamp mills was to be built. The grandiose plan for this metropolis died when the canal scheme failed. (*E. W. Darrah Collection*)

The orderly company camp such as at Tungsten (below) in the 1930s replaced the helter-skelter assemblage of tents and wooden buildings that sprang up near most earlier discoveries. During peak periods of production the company employed up to 250 men. Buildings, left to right: boarding house (with old mill against the hillside), office building, store, school, post office, and about 85 cabins. Miners' apartments are at right. (*E. W. Darrah Collection*)

crude brush huts, canvas-walled dwellings and adobe structures. North and south of the camp a mile-long, 15-foot-wide canal was projected to create a 16-foot fall, affording driving power for several hundred stamps; work actually started at both ends, but the canal was never completed and nearby mining operations ceased in favor of more promising prospects elsewhere in the county. At the end of 1863 Lancaster was completely abandoned. Crumbling adobe walls mark the site.

ST. MARYS, 6 miles west of I-80 at Mill City exit by unimproved road.

Early in the summer of 1863 a half-mile-square townsite was surveyed on the north side of the Humboldt River as a prospective milling town for nearby silver mines, and by the end of August, St. Marys consisted of two hotels, store, butcher shop, and several houses of cement and adobe construction. A ferry also operated across the Humboldt. Elaborate plans were drawn up to construct the "St. Mary's ditch" with an eight-foot fall sufficient to power several mills, but when the project was abandoned that fall hopes of establishing a permanent town ended.

TUNGSTEN, 8 miles north of I-80 at Mill City exit.

Silver was found at the south end of the Eugene mountains as early as 1856; the Central district was organized five years later, and by 1872 two small mills began treating ore. This early silver mining never developed to any extent.

Tungsten ore was discovered in 1916; work started the next year and by 1919 competing companies had each built a mill and the camp of Tungsten was founded. The Nevada-Massachusetts Co. acquired some choice properties in 1926 and increased mining operations three years later. In 1930 the main mill's capacity was increased and for several years the company produced most of the nation's tungsten. For nearly three decades the company consistently shipped ore and experienced only occasional shutdowns until 1958, when the federal government stopped buying tungsten. All surface equipment and houses were sold in 1962 and only foundations are left.

SANTA CLARA, 4½ miles by road and trail west of SR 50 at a point 7 miles south of I-80 at Mill City exit.

Tucked away in narrow Santa Clara Canyon on the east flank of the Humboldt Range, the little camp of Santa Clara at the north end of the Star mining district was founded about 1862 around silver mines. A cluster of rock dwellings for almost 200 individuals had been built by 1864, and a twice-a-week mail run from neighboring Star City brought in freight and outside news.

A unique feature of this lively camp was the friendly rivalry between the "Santa Clara Roughs" and the "Amazon Maids," with the latter usually getting the best of it. The Roughs would invite leap year proposals from the Amazons, stating time, terms, etc., which invitations the Amazons indignantly repelled "because of lack of thoroughbred blood in the town and . . . Amazons did not mate with scrubs!" The two parties had a set-to now and then, and the Amazons won most confrontations because they "could talk louder, roll their sleeves higher without injury to muscle, spread themselves to better advantage, slam around more promiscuously, and were more generally on the rampage anyhow!" Another amusement was the "tinpandemonium" in which the town's juveniles assembled about three times a week, armed with milk pans and sticks, and beat the devil's tattoo with infernal gusto, especially around any of the Roughs who had been caught napping by the Amazons.

A sale of stock by the Union Tunneling Co. for delinquent payment of assessments, during the summer of 1864, was proof enough that the mines could not sustain a long production, and a year or two later Santa Clara turned in. About ten stone structures mark the site.

STAR CITY, 4½ miles west of SR 50 at a point 10 miles south of its junction with I-80 at Mill City exit.

Discoveries of rich silver in this deep canyon in 1861 set miners agog and by the next year the place was booming. Within two years Star City with 1200 residents was the county's largest town and a place of busy enterprise with two hotels, one costing $40,000, saloons, stores, Wells Fargo office, livery stables, post office, school, Sunday school with services conducted every other week by the Methodist minister, and a telegraph office with a special line to Virginia City. Most businesses faced a large park-plaza, a not-uncommon feature of mining towns in Nevada's early days.

Alex Wise's Telegraph Saloon was a representative establishment. It assured the thirsty that its liquors were as good as those in San Francisco and invited smokers to enjoy prime Havana — "so soothing when it has been bought with the last quarter, and a fellow's busted." Its marble-bed billiard tables promised improvement for body and mind; the game "employs the mind, while interest in your loaned money keeps counting up. Exercises your legs, by sending you around the table to get your ball out of the pocket. Gives grace to the body, by introducing that elegant posture, one leg in the air, hat for a bridge, and cue harpoon style. Exercises the lungs, by the large amounts of whistling after bad shots."

At the mouth of the canyon the Sheba Company's ten-stamp mill banged away. Star City shone brightest in 1864-65, when seven large mining companies conducted operations, and the town enjoyed such an amenity as a literary society known as the Gander Club, besides the usual pastimes and problems. It continued to be the scene of enthusiastic and productive mining and lively prospecting until 1868, but a swift turn from hope and prosperity to abandonment and despair resulted when ore at the Sheba mine ran out. The stamp mill shut down and was moved to Unionville. In 1871 only 78 people were left and by 1880 Star City was totally eclipsed.

UNIONVILLE, 5 miles west of SR 50 at a point 13 miles south of I-80 at Mill City exit.

In the spring of 1861 Indians came to Virginia City bearing rich ore from Buena Vista Canyon. Impressed with assay reports two men traveled across deserts with supply-laden donkeys and Paiute guides to the place, arriving early in May. Ten days later a mining district was organized at Buena Vista and soon the cry was "Humboldt! Humboldt!" In the upper part of the canyon a townsite was laid out and briefly called Dixie until federal partisans won a local political fight and named the camp Unionville. In November it was selected as seat of newly created Humboldt County.

Others came to share in the fortunes which were to be made. A Humboldter wrote with calm hand to the *Territorial Enterprise* late in 1861: "I shall be candid with you . . . Humboldt County is the richest mineral region upon God's footstool. Each mountain is gorged with the precious ores." Reporting assays of $4000 per ton, he added, "Have no fear of the mineral resources of Humboldt. They are immense, incalculable."

Such delirious words led Mark Twain to strike out with companions for Humboldt to pick up, as he said, "masses of silver lying all about the ground glittering in the sun on the mountain summits." They located a claim but abandoned it after sinking a 12-foot shaft. They drove a tunnel into a mountainside and forsook it 900 feet short of finding a rich vein. Mark Twain and friends then took up new claims, gave them grandiloquent names, and began "trading feet" of ledges until they all wound up with thousands of "feet" in undeveloped mines. After three weeks in Unionville, Mark Twain left this camp of "bloated millionaires."

In 1862 a rival townsite started in the lower part of the canyon, boasting over 200 houses within a year. In the summer of 1863 Unionville had almost 1000 people and served as the county distribution point for supplies and machinery shipped overland from California. The camp had ten stores, nine saloons, six hotels, four livery stables, drug stores, express houses, a brewery, assays, a jeweler, watchmaker, notaries, lawyers and a lively weekly, the *Humboldt Register*. An omnibus line made hourly trips along the tri-sectioned town which extended for two miles.

The two-year-old camp consisted of imported adobe and lumber structures. According to the *Register*, about half of the poor quality shipped-in lumber was "just what it was cracked up to be" and the other half was "knot." The building that housed county offices was so poorly built that once a visitor who called on the county clerk during a rainstorm found him and his records in a corner of the room "where the rain didn't come any thicker than it did outside."

Almost three dozen wildcat companies were formed during 1863-64; scores of claims were made, many tunnels were in development, and speculation and trading of "feet" took place at a brisk pace. The peak year 1864 was followed by

This view of Unionville in 1871 looks westward up Buena Vista Canyon, where the Arizona and other important mines were located. Unionville was the center of rich mining and considerable prospecting during 1861-1865, and by the early 1870s three mills had been built in the lower part of town. One mill with stack is shown at center left. *(Nevada Historical Society)*

The Hidden Treasure stage carrying mail and passengers to Unionville pulls up beside businesses on the main street. Large leather straps extending below the body of the coach ease the severe bumps and sway of the ride. *(Mrs. A. S. Davidson Collection)*

Early in the 1870s Unionville's Wells Fargo & Co. was housed in a fine frame building which also contained the office of the county treasurer. The panorama of Buena Vista Canyon (below) shows the small farms in the area around 1905, long after most mining had ceased. *(Top: Nevada Historical Society; bottom: Ed A. Smith Collection)*

three years of decline which were finally broken up by increased development at the Arizona mine in 1868. Before the coming of the railroad to the county that same year, prices were high. A dozen eggs cost a dollar; a box of candles was $8.50 and kerosene was $4 a gallon.

Early in the 1870s, three ten-stamp mills treated low-grade ores and the Arizona mine poured forth immense treasures, but a $30,000 fire in August 1872 and a general mining decline in the Humboldt Range hastened the removal of the county seat to Winnemucca in the spring of 1873. Loss of political supremacy struck hard at Unionville's prosperity. The town's last newspaper the *Silver State* followed the courthouse during the next year, and by 1880 Unionville had only 200 inhabitants. Recorded production to that year amounted to nearly $2.7 million, and during the next fifty years only small operators were active. In this century irrigation has made possible the maintenance of a few attractive farms and orchards. Stone ruins are to be found for a three-mile distance in deep Buena Vista Canyon amid occupied homes. A cemetery and mill ruins remain near the mouth of the canyon.

JACOB'S WELL, 6 miles north and east of SR 50 at a point 3½ miles south of its junction with I-80 at Mill City exit.

This was the water and whiskey stop on the Star City-Dun Glen road in the 1860s. The station keeper extended a welcome to all travelers but having no desire to be victimized by freeloaders, he posted the following notice: "Travelers are not obliged to patronize our bar, but if they don't, they are not our guests, and people who are not our guests must pay 12½ cents for each of the animals they water here." Another sign read:

To Jacob's Well the traveler comes,
His drooping heart to cheer;
We've whiskey, brandy, gin, and rum,
Likewise good lager beer!

DUN GLEN, later Chafey, 9 miles northeast of Mill City by graded road.

Soon after silver discoveries in the Sierra district in 1862, Dun Glen was founded. Within a year this camp became the commercial center for 250 people — the second largest district in northern Nevada — and mining was brisk and systematic in every direction. A mill began running at the Auld Lang Syne mine in December 1863, and by that time Dun Glen possessed hotels, "temples of the gods," and stores selling powder and fuse, wine and liquors, California butter and meats. A post office, school and meeting hall were also built.

A visitor in 1864 noted that his hotel was as good as could be expected. The bar room temperature was maintained at 90°F; his room was dry until it started to thaw and then it became damp but warm; the beef, bread, and tea were good; the potatoes as fine as he ever tasted; and plenty of milk was on hand until the cow went off to pay a visit to some of the neighbors. He added that the outhouses were large and very *airy*. The principal amusement was playing freeze-out poker for shots of whiskey, which impecunious losers paid off with "jawbone" promises. An occasional dogfight also furnished diversion.

To keep the Indians in check, a company of regulars was garrisoned here in 1863 and again in 1865. They maintained a small military post. The

TELEGRAPH SALOON!

DUN GLEN, NEV.

ALEX. WISE hereby gives notice to all whom these presents may come, that he has erected a magnificent building in Dun Glen, and dedicated it to Bacchus, and the name thereof shall be known as the Telegraph Saloon; and the arrangements of this retreat of leisure have been perfected so as to meet the views of his most fastidious customers.

It isn't every man who knows how to keep a saloon; but I think I have discovered the merits of the secret, and am determined that the Telegraph shall have no superior in the proper delivery of fluviatic stimulants, and from my bar will be dispensed to the public as well as to my particular friends the choicest selection of

Wines, Liquors and Cigars,

such as the gods, looking down from their etherial adobes must envy—and all for two bits a single chance!

"Man being reasonable, must get drunk;
The best of life is but intoxication;
Glory, the grape, love, gold—in these are sunk
The hopes of all men and of every nation."

BILLIARDS.

Two of Phelan's best marble-bed, combination-cushioned tables, in excellent running order. It is a conceded point that a man saves money by playing much at billiards; for the more practice he has the less he will lose when he happens into a pool game.

Come around anyhow, and see us; we're in the habit of treating, and one man's show is as good as another's —if not better. At all events, you can take a chair and put your feet upon the card tables, and tell a pretty story about the money you once had when stocks were up; and how much better your ledge gets as you widen down where it pinches out. All that sort of talk gives tone to a well regulated saloon, and pays license. He will not be an unwise man who calls upon

A. WISE.

Dun Glen, May 10, 1867. 3-ty

The above picture of Dun Glen around 1880 shows a horse-powered arrastra grinding ore from rich surface veins. A buckboard in the rear is ready to travel, but the miner at the right has brought his equipment into camp: water bucket, shovel and explosives.
(Nevada State Museum)

In 1908 Dun Glen leaped from lethargy and was renamed Chafey. Many new buildings were built and a contemporary paper wrote that stores were not outnumbered by saloons in this industrious burg. *(E. W. Darrah Collection)*

ten-stamp Essex mill erected below town in 1867 was followed eight years later by the building of a third mill which carried production through the late 1870s. Dun Glen had dwindled to about fifty miners by 1880, and stock raising took over as mining declined. Chinese invaded nearby canyons during the 1880s and conducted placer operations, but even before the post office closed in 1894 both mining and ranching had become insignificant.

In the summer of 1908 the camp of Chafey rose on the site of old Dun Glen and soon had a newspaper, over 1000 hustling inhabitants, post office, as well as saloons and stores. For a few months buildings rose on all sides, and dusty freighters and four daily stages plied to Mill City on the Southern Pacific. Until operations ceased about 1913 the camp used both names with the older name more popular. Adobe walls and mill foundations remain.

GOLDBANKS, ½ mile west of the Winnemucca-Dixie Valley road, at a point 39 miles south of Winnemucca.

Gold and quicksilver discoveries sparked a mild rush early in 1907, but leasers worked the veins with only limited success. A few men stayed until 1908 but after that date only quicksilver was found from time to time. Mine dumps indicate the site.

KENNEDY, 5 miles west of the Winnemucca-Dixie Valley road at a point 51 miles south of Winnemucca.

A perceptive hospital manager believed that a gold belt connected the gold mines at Spring Valley with those at Golconda. To prove his theory he secured the aid of an old Esmeralda County prospector named Kennedy and furnished him with an outfit and a year's pay to prospect the east base of the Granite Range between the two points. Kennedy started from Winnemucca in 1891 with two horses and a buckboard loaded with supplies. After two months he discovered the gold-bearing veins that became the Cricket and Imperial mines, and continued explorations. In the spring of 1892 the grubstaker resigned from the hospital and joined Kennedy in the desert.

Rumors of discoveries brough an influx of one-blanket, jackass prospectors during the rest of 1892 and 1893. By 1894 a lively camp of 500 had formed with post office, the weekly *New Era*, saloons and stores. The Imperial mine built a twenty-stamp mill in 1895, and two smaller stamp mills were active. The big Imperial mill added a leaching plant in 1901, but the district soon declined and made only irregular shipments thereafter.

The post office at Kennedy, around 1900, was in a private residence. After this building was torn down in the 1960s, no structures remained at the townsite.

(*E. W. Darrah Collection*)

Bridge Street in Paradise Valley just before the turn of the century shows pioneer business establishments. At left the large adobe building with balcony contained a store and saloon, with theatre and dance hall upstairs. Adjacent was the town's first hotel and stage station. Farther down the street were a butcher shop, blacksmith, and wagon maker's shop. The building with flagpole at right was a store; the IOOF held meetings on the second story. It still stands. *(Fritz Buckingham Collection)*

An early 20th century Paradise Valley landmark was the Auditorium Hotel, on Main Street. Here was the valley's gathering place for dances and parties. Traveling salesmen arriving by stage found accommodations as good as in Winnemucca; room and board were on the American plan. Fire destroyed it in the mid-1930s.

(Fritz Buckingham Collection)

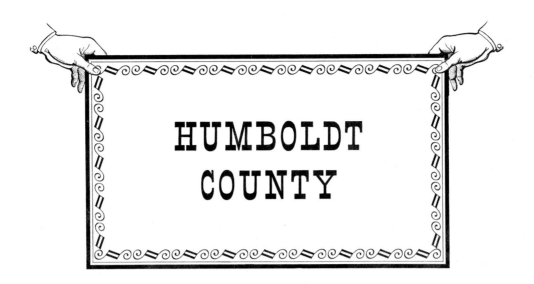

HUMBOLDT COUNTY

The first mining district organized in the present area of the county was Vicksburg in 1863 and the Pueblo district in adjacent Oregon was at that time thought to be in Nevada. These and other districts of the 1860s remained small because of remoteness, poor transportation facilities and harassment by nomadic Bannocks. After three army camps were established the Indians were brought under control, then ranching developed at Paradise City and mining at Spring City. The latter remained active in the 1880s, and in 1897 the Golconda-Gold Run area, which had been active in the late 1860s, reawoke for a decade.

A rich district was National, noted after 1907 for its bonanza ore. Smaller camps were active until World War I, but then mining was quiet until the Jumbo boom of the mid-1930s revived surrounding districts. The Getchell mine, Humboldt County's most productive, was in operation after 1940 until its closing in 1967.

DUTCH FLAT, 11 miles via desert road east of US 95 at a point 13 miles north of Winnemucca.

Placer gold was discovered on the west slope of the Hot Springs Range in 1898, and for many years several men used rockers to wash gravel, but operations were difficult because water had to be hauled by wagon from a source a mile away. The Dutch Flat Gold Mining Co. began extensive systematic placering in 1904 using modern equipment including a dragline scraper and washing plant, but the inadequate water supply hindered profitable oper-

ations and the company gave up after a few years. In 1909-10 Chinese began extensive operations, burrowing for rich pockets of ore and recovering gold with water carried to the placers by a line of Chinese water boys. In later years work by leasers pushed district production past $200,000. Extensive dumps remain.

WILLOW POINT, 4 miles southeast of SR 8B at a point 1½ miles northeast of its junction with US 95.

This station served travelers on the Winnemucca-Paradise Valley road during the last part of the 19th century and by 1910 it had a hotel, saloon, and livery stable. A post office was open in 1868 and during 1878-1910. No buildings remain.

PARADISE VALLEY, at end of SR 8B, 18 miles northeast of US 95 at a point 22 miles north of Winnemucca.

A four-man prospecting party from Star City ventured onto a beautiful plain now known as Paradise Valley in the summer of 1863 to seek minerals in the surrounding hills. While nothing of value was found, they were impressed by the valley's fertile acres. One man abandoned his pick and tools and returned within a few weeks with horses, wagons, mower, haypress and blacksmith tools to begin a hay ranch. By the end of the next year about twenty ranchers had started work, but Indian raids were so numerous that Camp Scott was established nearby to insure the safety of the ranch-

143

The Fourth of July celebration at Paradise Valley consisted of foot races, horse races, tug-of-war and other games. To augment the popping noise of firecrackers, anvils placed face to face and charged with explosives were "shot off," resulting in a boom that sounded like a cannon. The shooting of the anvils often took place as early as four in the morning to awaken everyone. *(Fritz Buckingham Collection)*

Buckaroos are herding cattle from the range in Paradise Valley down to the railroad station at Winnemucca.
(Les Stewart Collection)

Six miles north of Paradise Valley is the famous water-powered Silver State Flour Mill. Built in 1869, it was the first Mill in Nevada which regularly shipped flour to commercial markets. Northern Nevada railroad and mining towns were the chief users.

(Las Vegas *Review-Journal*)

Among the buildings still standing at Camp Winfield Scott is the enlisted men's barracks (right).

Early in this century the Spring City district revived, and a camp was located above the new mill shown at center.
(Fritz Buckingham Collection)

An ox team in Winnemucca (bottom) prepares to deliver boiler parts to the Spring City district, sometime late in the last century.
(Les Stewart Collection)

ers. Late in the 1860s the village of Paradise City was begun, and by 1879 it had the Paradise Valley post office, the *Reporter*, a score of other businesses and a population of 100.

Though Paradise City was never a mining town, one of the locals working nearby must have been quite a character. Wells Drury of the Gold Hill *News* once saw a miner from Paradise walk into a Virginia City saloon, and pounding on the bar with his six-shooter until the glasses danced, announced: "I'm a roarin' ripsnorter from hoo-rah camp, an' I can't be stepped on. I'm an angel from Paradise Valley and when I flop my wings there's a tornado loose . . . Give me some of your meanest whiskey, a whole lot of it, that tastes like bumblebee stings pickled in vitriol. I swallered a cyclone for breakfast, a powder-mill for lunch, and haven't begin to cough yet. Don't crowd me." Drury further related that one by one the saloon patrons quietly left, and when the bad man turned around, the place was empty!

Paradise Valley, which long ago dropped the word City from its name, continued through the mid-20th century as a quiet ranching community with hotels, stores, saloons and Methodist and Catholic churches. Hitching posts, old sidewalks, frame buildings of a bygone era (many uninhabited) and dirt streets make this town an interesting place to visit.

CAMP WINFIELD SCOTT, 4½ miles northwest of the town of Paradise Valley.

For five years after December 1866 this army camp protected Humboldt County settlers and travelers from Indian depredations, such as theft of stock and slaughter of men and women. During the winter of 1866-67 officers' quarters and a large adobe brick barracks were constructed, as well as hospital, guardhouse, trading post and stables.

Attacks on travelers and theft of livestock greatly diminished by 1869 and the camp was abandoned in February 1871, after it had lived out its usefulness. Several original structures are now used by the Buckingham Ranch. Ask permission to visit.

SPRING CITY, by unimproved road, 2 miles east, 6 miles north, then 1 mile east of the town of Paradise Valley.

After initial discoveries in 1868 a district was organized in 1873 and soon Spring City was a lively burg containing an express office, seven saloons, stores, two hotels, restaurant, brewery, bookstore and daily stage service to Winnemucca via Paradise City. Local ores were treated at nearby Queen City. Siskron post office was opened here in November 1878, but the name was soon changed to Spring City. Eighty townspeople voted in the 1880 election, suggesting a population of perhaps 150.

The peak years came in the 1880s when over $1 million in silver and gold were recovered at a local ten-stamp mill, but with the fast decline after 1890 there was little further reason for Spring City's existence and the post office closed in 1895.

Revivals in 1907-15 and 1931-35 netted limited amounts of silver and brought the district's production to $1.5 million — although generous estimates double that figure. Old buildings remain from 20th century operations and stone and mud walls from older structures are also found here.

QUEEN CITY, by graded road, 8 miles east and north of the town of Paradise Valley.

Queen City was founded as a milling town for Spring City gold mines, seven miles west, in 1874 when two mills were built on Martin Creek to take advantage of its water power. The camp grew steadily to a peak population of about 100 in 1879, rivalling nearby Paradise City, now Paradise Valley, but because of Queen City's poor location at the mouth of a canyon its competitor became the area's chief town. By the next year Queen City had been deposed, and all stores soon closed. During its short five-year life milling production of $235,-000 was recorded. Only block foundations mark the site, located just a few yards north of the Martin Creek county park and swimming pool.

PARADISE WELL, or Flynn, east side of US 95 at a point 1 mile north of its junction with SR 8B (25 miles north of Winnemucca).

This stage station with store, hotel, and livery stable early in this century had its origin during the early statehood days. A windmill marks the site.

The mill hands at Queen City gather to show off their ten-stamp mill. It had a roasting oven, and treated ores from the Spring City district. *(Fritz Buckingham Collection)*

A buggy, a wagon and a couple of freight wagons are seen around the corrals and station house at Paradise Well, about 1885. These were typical rigs which might be found at a stage station during the days when animals furnished power for movement across the desert. *(Fritz Buckingham Collection)*

CANE SPRINGS, one mile southeast of SR 140 at a point 2¼ miles west of its junction with US 95 (23 miles north of Winnemucca).

For many years around the turn of the century, this stage station, consisting of hotel, saloon and livery stable, served travelers passing through this part of the Santa Rosa Range. Amos post office was open here in 1889-90 and from 1898 to 1926.

JUMBO, via desert roads 12 miles west-southwest of SR 140 at a point 2¼ miles west of its junction with US 95.

Mining activity began about 1910 after the discovery of the Alabama and other mines, and during the next year on the east slope of the Slumbering Hills arose a small camp called Awakening which briefly contained a saloon, store and other buildings. The district proved itself in 1912 when gold was shipped out, and with increased mining, three different mills came into operation by the end of the decade, including an amalgamation mill at nearby Daveytown.

Nothing eventful happened after 1918 until the discovery of the Jumbo mine in the Slumbering Hills in February 1935 created considerable excitement and several claims were located that spring. The mine was sold later in the year, and in 1936 the new owners equipped the property with a thirty-ton mill paid for out of proceeds from the mine. Following Herbert Hoover's visit in the summer of 1936 and his favorable mention of the Jumbo mine it received nationwide publicity.

The west coast mining community believed that another great gold discovery had been made and a rush quickly populated the district with prospectors, agents for mining companies, engineers and others. San Francisco papers covered the story in detail and "The March of Time" radio program beamed the news to the world. A number of small mining companies began work but only the Jumbo sustained production and the boom died out. In May 1937 H. L. Hunt and other Texas oil operators secured a 35-year lease on the Jumbo mine for a cash down-payment of $250,000 with royalty payments of ten to fifteen per cent of extracted ore. An option of buying the mine for $10 million at any time within twenty years was also purchased.

But Hunt did not follow through with large development because of extensive litigation and the mine reverted to its original owners. Significant production took place until 1941 and again in 1948 until 1951. The district is now generally idle. Only mill foundations remain at the Awakening site; a mill and several buildings are left at Daveytown; and below the Jumbo mine lie the ruins of a dance hall and saloon.

SOD HOUSE, north side of SR 140 at a point 14 miles west of its junction with US 95.

This primitive station house, built entirely of sod, has been a landmark and part of a ranch for decades since about 1880. Authorities do not agree on its origin.

VARYVILLE, or Columbia, 30 miles west of SR 140 at a point 38 miles west of its junction with US 95 (70 miles northwest of Winnemucca).

Five years after discoveries near Bartlett Creek, the Columbia district was organized in 1875 and a camp started here. Ore was initially worked in an arrastra, but in the late 1870s two five-stamp mills were running. The district never gained prominence and in the 1880s it was forgotten.

Modern developments began in 1931 in the middle of the Depression by the Leonard Creek Placers, Ltd., which ceased operations before 1935. Some buildings are left.

PUEBLO (Oregon), approximately 5 miles north of Denio on SR 140.

Late in the summer of 1863 a Major Harmon discovered silver on the east flank of the Pueblo Mountains in an area then thought to be in Nevada. By the following summer a small mill was installed, but Indians burned it down in 1865 and drove the settlers out of the district. For the next few years mining continued to be harassed by Paiutes and Bannocks who had "an ugly and disagreeable way of giving little surprises for the boys working there." By February 1867 things were more orderly and a post office was established, which suggests that a small community may have formed. The district declined later in the year, the post office closed in August and little has since been heard of Pueblo.

VICKSBURG, later Ashdown, 5 miles southeast of SR 140 at a point 11 miles southwest of Denio (78 miles northwest of Winnemucca).

Although locations were made in the Vicksburg district in the summer of 1863, Indian troubles retarded early development of silver mines. The Pine Forest Gold Mining Co. began developing gold deposits about 1904. A post office was opened and production proceeded intermittently.

In 1919 the Ashdown Gold Mining Co. installed a new mill and the mines continued irregular operations for several years. The Ashdown mine had produced about $400,000 by 1950 and was being worked in the 1960s.

CAMP McGARRY, 36 miles southwest of SR 140 at a point 11 miles southwest of Denio.

The army established this camp in November 1865 to protect travelers using trails in northwestern Nevada and southern Oregon. Its several stone buildings included a large storage barn, mess hall and barracks with walls two feet thick. The camp and reservation were abandoned after three years of use and troops were sent elsewhere. The grounds eventually became part of the Summit Lake Indian Reservation, and in later years Indians came in the summer to graze stock.

REBEL CREEK, ¾ mile east of US 95 at a point 14 miles north of its junction with SR 140 (44 miles north of Winnemucca).

Both placer and vein deposits were worked at this point on the west slope of the Santa Rosa Range as early as the 1870s, and scores of prospectors returned in June 1907 after "remarkable" finds were reported. The district has never yielded gold in paying quantities, though some work was done in the 1930s.

WILLOW CREEK, later Platora, 1 mile north-northeast of US 95 at a point 18 miles north of its junction with SR 140.

A stage station functioned at this point on the Winnemucca-Idaho line in Nevada's early years. A winter traveler in 1864 described Willow Creek as a good inn, managed by hospitable people who maintained a bounteous table, clean beds and a bar offering merchandise from San Francisco. To the east, Willow Creek Canyon's small gold and silver mines fed a local five-stamp mill, and a boarding house and assay office were built at the head of the canyon.

In this century the station was known as Platora, and a post office operated from 1909 until 1925. At that time placering was under way nearby in an area which had previously been worked by Chinese, probably as early as the 1870s.

NATIONAL, 10 miles east of US 95 at a point 29 miles north of its junction with SR 140 (62 miles north of Winnemucca).

This camp is noted for its bonanza gold ore, probably the richest ever mined in Nevada. Two prospectors made initial discoveries in June 1907 and quickly located all the choice properties in the vicinity. They entered the district by car and named the prominent elevations around their 34 claims after parts of their National automobile — Radiator Hill and Auto Hill, for example. Large leasing blocks several hundred feet square were drawn up during 1908, and leases were let on them for one-year or 15-month periods based on a sliding scale of royalty payments.

Early in 1909 certain leasers found an extraordinarily rich ore shoot in their shaft, and the initial shipment from it averaged almost $30 per pound of ore! After news of the high grade broke out in the mining press, all sorts of adventurers, miners, and gamblers flocked here, swelling the camp to 1800 or 2000. For several months during 1909-1910 that lease produced $250,000 to $275,000 per month, and selected ore up to $100,000 a ton was shipped. In September 1910 the National Mining Co. purchased the lease and stepped up operations. Total production from that narrow shoot was said to have reached $4 million by 1911.

The rich rock encouraged high-grading and stealing, and on two occasions armed men broke into the mine and removed several sacks of ore. After these incidents the owners hired guards to keep watch around the clock. On a steel tower was installed a large searchlight; its rays played upon the mine entrance throughout the night.

In 1911-1912 National had several stores, saloons, a two-story hotel, post office, the weekly *Miner*, offices for professional people including doctor and dentist, stage lines running north and south, and other businesses, legitimate and other-

This view of National, taken from Radiator Hill at the west end of the camp, dramatizes the narrowness of the sagebrush basin along which the camp straggled for over a half mile. Businesses occupied the center area, and over fifty frame houses and a hundred tent dwellings clung to the hillsides. Up the canyon a few miles the National and other mines boomed. *(Mrs. R. R. Purdy Collection)*

By the 1960s most structures had been removed (below), and except for the topographic features, the location of the camp is not identifiable. *(E. W. Darrah Collection)*

wise. This spirited town with streets "paved with gold" was hit by apex litigation in June 1912, when the National brought suit against two adjacent mines for trespassing. In a notable trial before the U. S. Circuit Court at Carson City the following October, the National emerged victorious. That mine continued operations a while longer, but by 1915 the camp expired after producing about $7 million. The mill shell, assay office and a few other wooden buildings remain.

BUCKSKIN, by unimproved road, 12 miles east of US 95 at a point 29 miles north of its junction with SR 140.

Two Winnemucca prospectors located the Buckskin mine on the northeast slope of the Buckskin Mountains in 1906, and when mines boomed at National, four miles to the northwest, several more people prospected this vicinity. The Buckskin National Gold Mining Co. built a 100-ton flotation mill, but that process proved unsuitable for the ores. The company and various leasers operated the mine intermittently for two decades until the Nevada Lucky Tiger Co. took over the property about 1930 and erected another mill. Even

that effort was short-lived, and operations were halted when the mill burned during the Depression.

FORT McDERMITT, 5 miles east of US 95 at a point 40 miles north of its junction with SR 140 (69 miles north of Winnemucca).

This place is not to be confused with the community of McDermitt on US 95, 5 miles to the west.

Lieutenant Colonel Charles F. McDermitt (also spelled McDermit), commander of the Nevada military district, ordered establishment of a camp at Quinn River Station on the north bank of the East Fork of the Quinn River during the summer of 1865 to protect travelers passing between Boise, Star City and Virginia City. That same summer Colonel McDermitt was ambushed and killed by Indians while riding in Quinn River Valley, and by 1867 the camp renamed in his honor had stone and adobe buildings which housed the usual army facilities. About a decade later frame buildings were added, and in 1879 Camp McDermitt became Fort McDermitt, but the need for military presence in the area was diminishing, and a decade later the fort, Nevada's last cavalry post was abandoned. The buildings became part of the Fort McDermitt Indian Reservation, and some of them still stand.

Long after the last bugle toot at Fort McDermitt, the buildings remained in use by local Indian reservation of the same name. (*Ida Le Nord Collection*)

151

LAUREL, 4½ miles north of SR 49 at a point 6 miles west of Winnemucca via graded roads.

Two companies began to mine silver in 1910-11 and the camp of Laurel formed. The post office opened in June 1911, but the boom was cut short when the townspeople learned that they had settled on patented railroad land. Late in 1912 a new corporation bought the railroad section on which the mines were located and began development, but the veins were shallow and the camp was soon abandoned. The post office closed in July 1913. A cluster of wooden buildings remain of Laurel, now known as the Ten Mile District.

JUNGO, on SR 49 at a point 36 miles west of Winnemucca.

The newly completed Western Pacific Railway in 1910 established Jungo as a station which gained initial importance as a stock shipping point for ranches as far north as Denio and the Quinn River country. Jungo acquired a saloon, post office, blacksmith shop, warehouse, school, feed lot, loading corrals, and a hotel and store of general merchandise run by G. B. Austin, who maintained it

for over forty years. Auto stages ran to Burns, Oregon, and prospectors from nearby districts hung out at this town of forty people.

A Bay Area promoter organized a corporation in 1923 and sold desert lots near Jungo for dry farms. Several were started, but alkali prevented crops from growing. The gold discovered at nearby Jumbo in 1935 briefly increased activity, but by the end of World War II Jungo had only a single family and in 1952 lost its post office.

RED BUTTE, 15 miles northwest of SR 49 at a point 5 miles west of Jungo.

The Jackson Mountains were first prospected for gold on their western flank in the spring of 1907 and the camp of Red Butte emerged. By September 1908 it contained thirty tents and businesses. Gold ore was freighted to Humboldt House on the Southern Pacific for awhile, and a three-seater stage ran between the two points in 18 hours' time. After completion of the Western Pacific nearby in 1910 copper ore was shipped, especially during World War I. Some buildings still remain but low-axle cars cannot reach the camp.

The Jungo Hotel was the principal building of the railroad community which served as a depot for much of Humboldt County. While he was en route to the Jumbo mine in 1935, Herbert Hoover stayed overnight in this building *(Theron Fox photo)*

SULPHUR, on SR 49 at a point 58 miles west of Winnemucca.

A lone Paiute discovered native sulphur deposits on the western base of the Kamma Mountains about 1869 and then directed prospectors to little mounds of the yellow rocks in exchange for the promise of a bronco, saddle and blankets which he never received. Some sulphur was mined in 1874, and during the early 1880s six tons were produced daily.

The Nevada Sulphur Co. gained control of the deposits in August 1899 and began extensive operations. The Western Pacific Railway laid lines through here in 1909 and named the station Sulphur. A settlement which included a post office then formed, and the station was receiving point for the mined sulphur, which reached 12 tons a day in the early 1920s. The automobile age eliminated the need for a local store, and by 1953 the post office was finally closed. Sulphur mining continues.

HARDIN CITY, by graded and unimproved roads, approximately 32 miles northeast of SR 34 at a point 12 miles north of Gerlach. Inquire locally about road conditions.

While traveling across the Black Rock Desert with a California-bound emigrant train early in 1849, James Hardin was sent out with others to hunt game to replenish the depleted larders of the camp wagons. In the Black Rock Range they found what they thought was silver, enough of it they said to fill all of the 14 wagons of the emigrant train. Hardin's find was cause for rejoicing, but because California was in sight and hostile Indians lurked in the vicinity, the wagons continued to roll westward. Many of the men planned to return some day and begin mining here, but after establishing comfortable homes in California, almost all reconsidered the idea of retrieving the treasure when they remembered the heat, waterless distances and other hardships, to say nothing of the possibility of slaughter by nomadic Bannocks.

Finally in 1858 Hardin conducted a search party to Black Rock to find the "rich slabs of silver" they had seen in a "strange ash deposit" almost a decade earlier. The party searched up and down, retracing their steps again and again without finding any silver. In 1859 Hardin made a final unsuccessful search, yet the mystery of the silver locked up in the Black Rock Range persisted in tantalizing the imagination of the adventurous.

Beginning about 1862 several persistent individuals worked the black-looking rock "with all the patience and hope of the old alchemists seeking the philosopher's stone." Ore specimens were sent to experienced assayers in California and even to New York, but all verdicts were against the area containing silver in paying quantities.

Nevertheless, in the mid-1860s, Charles Isenbeck labored at the Dall mill in Franktown, Washoe County, to find ways to work the soft black rock, using a peculiar reducing agent or flux that contained a compound of silver, thereby assuring at least that much silver in the product.

An initial rush in the spring of 1866 led to the building of an adobe settlement know as Hardin City and another at Double Hot Springs, four miles south. The Humboldt Register wrote, "Black Rock is all the go now. When you see a man sitting in front of a roll of blankets and behind a Henry rifle, you need not ask him where he is going. He is going to 'Black Rock or burst.'"

In the summer of 1867, 13 tons of selected ore were hauled the 140-mile distance from Black Rock to the mill at Franktown where it was treated, perhaps under Mr. Isenbeck's direction. News that the ore yielded from $70 to $565 a ton made the miners at Black Rock go wild. Large sums of money were raised at once to build a four-

This mill ruin is the outstanding remnant of the Hardin City fiasco of the late 1860s.

stamp mill at Hardin City to be managed by Isenbeck, and machinery for two other small steam-powered mills was hauled to the district. Another group planned to initiate steamboat service across Pyramid Lake. The price per foot of ledges went up and excitement over the richness of the silver pervaded both Nevada and California.

Because Isenbeck could not afford to use his expensive flux on a large scale, he skipped out of Nevada and left the people at Hardin City holding the bag. The boom collapsed and miners abandoned their houses in despair. Contemporary scientific men declared that Black Rock was a swindle, and thus on the word of a single pretender several hundred thousand dollars had been expended by ordinary men, especially Californians. By the summer of 1868 Hardin City was completely emptied, and for years even thieves would not go there to steal the abandoned property. Remaining today are foundations of three mills, an arrastra and other rock ruins.

LEADVILLE (Washoe County), 1 mile west of SR 34 at a point 37 miles north of Gerlach.

Development work began after lead-silver discoveries in 1909, and the district produced modestly until as late as 1940 or 1941. Peak years were 1924 and 1925. Still remaining are the blacksmith shop and other wooden buildings, mine track and tunnel.

BUFFALO MEADOWS (Washoe County), by graded and unimproved road 18 miles southwest of SR 81 at a point 9 miles northwest of Gerlach.

Originally settled in 1865, Buffalo Meadows was in the center of a stock-raising district. A salt works was active nearby. The settlement had a school and two hotels and the post office was open from 1879 to 1913.

GOLCONDA, north of I-80 at Golconda exit, 16 miles east of Winnemucca.

Golconda's eight or ten hot springs were a noted landmark for westbound travelers years before Nevada was born, and during the territorial days it was a minor spa and resort. When the Gold Run district, 12 miles to the south, was organized in 1866 and the Central Pacific was laid through here two years later, the village of Golconda

formed and soon became an important freight and telegraph station. Transcontinental train riders swam in the warm springs, and nearby farmers scalded their swine in one spring which was said to be so hot that it could boil an egg in a minute.

The community didn't grow in the 1870s, but struggled on until 1897, when a townsite was laid out by Scottish interests who organized the Adelaide Star Mines Ltd. as a subsidiary to their nationwide firm to work the Adelaide and other newly acquired copper mines in the Gold Run district. The parent Glasgow & Western Exploration Co. constructed the 12-mile-long Golconda & Adelaide narrow gauge between their large ninety-ton smelter and concentration plant half a mile north of Golconda and the mines.

Within months Golconda grew to 500 inhabitants, with six hotels, post office and the weekly *News*. The town's slogan was "What Anaconda has been to Montana, Golconda promises to be for Nevada" and the most optimistic envisioned this town as soon having 10,000 people. Unsatisfactory milling returns led to a shutdown by the spring of 1900, but some irregular activity continued until 1905. Two years later the mill reopened with additions, and mines and railroad were again operating; but the Scottish interests suspended all work in 1910 after incurring additional losses.

The Nevada Massachusetts Co. built a 100-ton chemical plant in 1939 to treat ores from mines four miles east, but that operation shut down after World War II because of losses. Sleepy Golconda contains several old buildings and foundations of the two mills remain.

GOLD RUN, later Adelaide, by graded road 11 miles south of I-80 at the Golconda exit (15 miles southeast of Winnemucca).

After formation of a district in October 1866 several gold and silver mines were opened. In the spring of 1867 the Humboldt *Register* reported in glowing terms that thousands of tons of ore in sight were worth nearly $100 per ton. A townsite platted that fall on an elevated site on Gold Run Creek soon had a few businesses around a plaza, including a commodious hotel which claimed to have the best of liquors and cigars at the bar at all times. Gold Run, then also known as Cumberland, had a population of sixty including a few families at the

Around the turn of the century, the Hot Springs Hotel at Golconda was a fashionable spa. It had doctors in residence and French waitresses. Miners crippled with rheumatism took baths here. In 1908 when this picture was taken, the camp of Gold Circle (Midas) was booming in Elko County; sign at the left directs the traveler to the stage office. *(Robear Newman Collection)*

In 1897 the Glasgow & Western Exploration Co. erected this concentrating plant and smelter to work ores from the Adelaide and Battle Mountain districts. Note the engine and cars of the Golconda & Adelaide short line leaving from the left. The mill operated irregularly for less than five years before it was scrapped in 1911. Only foundations remain. *(Ed A. Smith Collection)*

155

Four members of the Golconda brass band pause during a Fourth of July celebration to enjoy liquid refreshment in the welcome shade. These amateur musicians played at town dances, at funerals and during holiday festivities. *(Ed A. Smith Collection)*

The Nevada Massachusetts Co. built this chemical plant at Golconda in 1940 to treat manganese-tungsten ore found east of town. A costly reducing process led to cessation of operations at the end of World War II. In 1952 the plant was dismantled and sold. Foundations are left. *(E. W. Darrah Collection)*

end of 1867, and during the next year the eight-stamp Golconda mill three miles south of Golconda worked ore from the Hope and Golconda mines. For fuel the mill used sagebrush, collected by Indians at a cost of $4 a day. But a sustained boom did not develop and the camp probably expired by the spring of 1871, when the Golconda mine closed.

Scottish interests renewed mining with vigor for a decade after 1897 (see Golconda), and the Adelaide mine was the principal producer. In the summer of 1907 the town of Adelaide was laid out below the mines, but the district was only intermittently active thereafter with leasers producing almost $200,000. During World War I the mines sustained a lengthy development. By the 1930s the camp of Adelaide had moved a mile and a half west where a new mill had been built. A few 20th century wooden buildings mark the site of Gold Run, while Adelaide has mill foundations and a few shacks.

GETCHELL MINE, 10 miles north of SR 18 at a point 16 miles northeast of I-80 at Golconda exit.

Though the northeast slopes of the Osgood Mountains were prospected as early as the 1880s for copper and silver, the first important discoveries were made in 1933 when two Winnemucca prospectors found gold. Mining tycoon Noble Getchell purchased the ground during the next year and formed a company to begin exploration. Ground was broken for a 400-ton cyanide mill in June 1937, and after a power line was extended from Golconda an era of intensive gold mining followed. A company camp was built around the operation, with ninety cottages, a store of general merchandise, boarding house, bunkhouses and recreation hall.

The federal government allowed the Getchell to operate during World War II because of the badly needed arsenic that was found with the gold. Of the latter, about $8 million was recovered by 1949. From 1950 until 1957 the Getchell became a profitable tungsten producer, and almost $30 million in that metal was recovered in six years of operation. The mill could recover tungsten from 1000 tons of ore daily when running at full capacity.

During the 1950s much gold had been blocked out, and so the mine was reopened in 1961 to work the gold veins for six years. Finally in 1967 the Getchell mill was dismantled, leaving walls and foundations.

In 1941 the three-year-old Getchell mill was already a ranking gold producer. The building contained the mill and crushing plant; to the right was the roaster; and off to the left the miners' cottages. Not shown farther left is the rest of the camp.
(Roy A. Hardy Collection)

These cabins built around World War I remain at Copper Basin near mines worked in the late 1960s. *(Gary Allen)*

Galena in 1966 still enjoyed its attractive setting. In addition to these cabins, mill ruins and cemetery in fair condition are left. *(Gary Allen)*

LANDER COUNTY

The area was first settled in 1862-63 during the rush to Reese River, a mining area embracing the southern part of the present county. Initially, over a dozen camps were active in Reese River including Jacobsville, Clifton, Geneva, Kingston, and Austin, but only the latter two survived past the mid-1860s. Other camps established in the 1860s and 1870s were Cortez, Galena, Copper Canyon and Lewis. Though the Nevada Central Railway began running in 1880, no new discoveries were made and by 1887 Austin ended its prosperous era.

Early in this century Galena reawoke and Skookum and Tenabo boomed. Mining began at Hilltop before World War I, and the Betty O'Neal mine in the Lewis district was the premier producer of the 1920s. Smaller operators were active in various districts in the 1930s. Production was significant after World War II at Galena and in the late 1960s in the Cortez district.

COPPER BASIN, 3 miles northwest of SR 8A at a point 5 miles southwest of Battle Mountain.

The Battle Mountain district was organized two years after discoveries in 1864, and the Little Giant mine was the first steady producer, yielding over $1 million during its first two decades of operation. The district was idle after 1885 until 1897 when the Glasgow & Western Co.'s renewed operations started the small camp of Copper Basin. In addition to some turquoise, several kinds of ore have been mined here, including gold, silver and lead, but low-grade copper has been the principal metal. Mining activity reached its peak during World War I and since then the district has been worked only sporadically, chiefly by leasers. Dilapidated wooden buildings are left.

Old BATTLE MOUNTAIN, ½ mile south of Copper Basin.

Mining in the Battle Mountain district increased in 1868 when Central Pacific trains began running nearby, and the camp of Battle Mountain formed on Licking Creek. It had a post office from June 1870 until October 1872 during the peak of mining activity. To avoid confusion with the rising town of Battle Mountain Station (Argenta post office, during 1871-74), the name of this camp was changed to Safford, but that name did not stick. Little evidence of old Battle Mountain remains.

GALENA, 5 miles west of SR 8A at a point 10 miles southwest of Battle Mountain.

Silver was discovered in 1863 at the head of Galena Canyon; a camp emerged by 1866 and three years later Galena had a platted townsite with park-plaza and water system. Wide graded streets were flanked by numerous stores, as well as a large public hall, school and post office, and local businessmen were described as thoroughgoing and wide-awake. Many large trees and a creek amid the wooden buildings made this camp one of the prettiest in the state.

The year 1870 saw the district growing monthly, and the daily stage from rail connections at Battle Mountain Station brought in supplies and additional settlers. With development of several large mines, two smelters and a mill in full blast, the

In their rakish headgear, these men are panning gold at Bannock, probably about 1912. Even the deputy sheriff took time off from official duties to look over the promising finds on the high ridges of Philadelphia Canyon. *(Nevada Historical Society)*

Below is a dramatic view of Copper Canyon with mill ruins in the foreground and the placer camp of Natomas at the canyon's mouth. *(Bob Stewart Collection)*

district was active all hours of the day and night making significant productions of silver, gold and lead from the ore for which the camp was named. Galena had a population of several hundred in 1872 and was in serious contention with Winnemucca for the Humboldt County seat; but when the Galena Range area was ceded to Lander County in 1874, the courthouse dreams were shelved, as it was then in the same county as Austin.

Galena's production slowed after 1875, and the condition of its school reflected the loss of prosperity. A visitor in 1877 noted that one tattered map adorned the wall, a rough box served as a receptacle for books, and the children were insecurely seated in old desks.

In 1886 work was practically suspended after a French mining company took over the largest claims and did not continue development. In this century the district was active during World War I, through most of the 1920s, just before World War II and in the late 1960s. Production is estimated at about $5 million.

BANNOCK, 2 miles northwest of SR 8A at a point 12 miles south of Battle Mountain.

The discovery of a rich gold vein early in 1909 brought mild excitement to Philadelphia Canyon, and prospectors turned up several interesting leads. By October a townsite was platted on a steep hillside where an assay office, blacksmith shop, garage and stores in substantial frame buildings soon appeared, and in November a post office. But the boom was short lived, as the mines could not sustain the camp, and the post office closed eight months after its opening.

Within a few years mining of placer gold was started, and operations continued intermittently until the late 1930s. Bannock was the talk of the county early that decade when the placers gave forth one nugget worth $150 and several other specimens each weighing over an ounce. Only placer tailings mark the site.

COPPER CANYON, 5 miles northwest of SR 8A at a point 12 miles south of Battle Mountain.

Mining started as early as 1871 and over the next several years an English mining company shipped over 40,000 tons of hand-sorted ore via windjammers around Cape Horn to smelters at Swansea, Wales. The ore was carried as ship's ballast, and total cost of freight from mine to mill over 20,000 miles away was a mere $45 per ton. A concentrator erected in 1875 on Willow Creek, three miles away, handled low-grade.

After 1885 the mines stood silent until 1897, when the Glasgow & Western Co. acquired the mines and resumed large-scale work. When placer gold was unearthed at the mouth of Copper Canyon in 1909 the camp took the name Natomas, and with large- and small-scale placer operations, district production continued into the late 1930s. Mill ruins and extensive placer dumps remain.

JERSEY CITY (Pershing County), 36 miles southwest of SR 8A at a point 12 miles south of Battle Mountain.

The Jersey district was organized in 1874 after discoveries were made in Jersey Canyon, and during the following year 500 tons of silver-lead ore were shipped to a smelter at Oreana. Early in 1876 the camp contained about fifty dwellings and a post office which was discontinued the following year. Small annual shipments were made for at least three decades but the camp never revived. Small furnaces erected in the district were never successful in treating or concentrating the ore, and Jersey never bounced to fame.

Mc COY, 11 miles southwest of SR 8A at a point 22 miles south of Battle Mountain.

After gold discoveries in 1914 several claims were staked. For a number of years prospecting was desultory and no shipment of ore was made until 1928, when the discovery of high-grade gold sparked a small boom. McCoy had about 75 people in 1930-31, but activity subsided and the camp died. In all the district produced about $35,000. Houses remain.

ARGENTA, north side of I-80 at a point 13 miles east of Battle Mountain.

After silver was discovered about 1866-67 and mines opened, a small but thriving community grew near the north base of the Shoshone Range. A post office opened in December 1868, less than a month after the Central Pacific Railroad had been completed to this point in its eastward progression

In the early 1880s Lewis ranked among Nevada's most important mining camps. Looking east up Lewis Canyon (center), the mills at the mouth of the canyon are the Starr Grove on the left and the Highland Chief on the opposite side. The Battle Mountain & Lewis Railroad engine house is the long shed at the left; that line ran to the Starr Grove mine at Dean, three miles up the canyon. On the far left is the business district and more houses. Off the picture to the right was the Betty O'Neal mine. Its camp and mill (below) is shown as it was in the late 1920s. *(Top: Las Vegas Review-Journal; middle: E. W. Darrah Collection; bottom: Dale Malmgrem Collection)*

across Nevada. The railroad established an eating station and freight wagons began a line to Austin. It was expected that Argenta might become a major station to serve as Austin's permanent railhead, but Battle Mountain gained the distinction, for it was closer to Reese River and to the promising Galena mines. Argenta declined during 1869 and the town migrated bodily, buildings and all, in the winter of 1870 to the site of Battle Mountain Station. Argenta thereafter was a mere siding until the 1930s when nearby mines were reworked with modern methods.

LEWIS, 14 miles south of Battle Mountain via graded roads.

Silver deposits in the summer of 1874 led to the founding of Lewis at the head of Lewis Canyon three years later. A ten-stamp mill with furnace was built at the canyon's entrance to handle ores from the Eagle, Starr Grove, and other mines in Lewis and Dean canyons. When the Nevada Central Railway was being laid in Reese River Valley below Lewis in 1880, plans were made to extend a short line from Galena siding on the N. C. into Lewis Canyon to open up additional deposits, and the new forty-stamp Eagle mill was built to handle the anticipated increase in mining operations.

The Battle Mountain & Lewis Railway became a reality in April 1881, and in that year thriving prosperous Lewis had 700 people who supported saloons, many stores, hotels, a dance hall, boarding house, lumberyard, jail, post office, weekly newspaper and school. The camp was called a great place for opium smokers, and dozens of Chinese pre-empted most of the available shady spots where they reclined and enjoyed their pipes. In Dean Canyon the camp of Dean, or Upper Lewis, was built near the Starr Grove mine, with houses and a boarding house.

The short-line B. M. & L. operated only eight months before mounting debts forced it to suspend. A fire swept through the Lewis business district in December 1881, and enthusiasm fell the next year with the coming of labor troubles. A serious boiler explosion demolished mill machinery and buildings at the nearby Betty O'Neal mine, but even subsequent rebuilding of the mill did not revive the camp. In 1882-83 the short line saw only limited action — one time a train ran into the canyon and retrieved a dismantled mill — and after 1883 most of Lewis' businesses including the newspaper had closed shop. Some mining in Dean Canyon continued and Lewis' post office was moved in 1894 to Dean, where it remained with that name until 1905.

After its closing in 1885, the Betty O'Neal mine lay dormant until about 1922 when mining giant Noble Getchell reopened it and installed a modern mill. The renewed operations gave rise to the company town of Betty O'Neal with newspaper — the *Concentrator*, a baseball team, and a post office beginning in 1925. A business district did not develop because modern transportation allowed the miners to shop or make their home in Battle Mountain. The Betty O'Neal produced over $2 million in silver and gold during the next seven years with peak of activity coming in 1928-29. Thereafter the mine was worked intermittently, principally by leasers, and the post office closed in 1932.

Jail foundations, cemetery, and mill ruins are left at Lewis; rock ruins identify the site of Dean; and an abandoned mill remains at Betty O'Neal.

HILLTOP, or Kimberly, 1¾ miles southeast of Hilltop road at a point 17 miles southeast of Battle Mountain.

Before organization of the Hilltop district in 1906, a small mining camp known as Marble City also served travelers of the 1860s at this convenient watering place. Prospectors found gold 100 yards from the old workings in 1907, and after other discoveries in Hilltop Canyon, scores of individuals came and a camp formed. By 1910 Hilltop sprawled along the intersection of two gulches and contained a hotel, saloons and stores in frame buildings, office of the weekly Kimberly *News*, post office and numerous cottages and tents.

A ten-stamp amalgamation mill in 1912 began making small annual production. Hilltop's businesses thrived, but the auto age came and most of the stores moved to Battle Mountain, the last one in 1923. In the early 1920s the Hilltop Nevada Mining Co. reorganized the properties, built a new mill and made large productions for about three years. The post office was removed in 1931. Mine buildings and wooden houses remain.

PITTSBURG, west side of Hilltop road at a point 19 miles southeast of Battle Mountain.

During the height of the boom in the early 1880s at nearby Lewis and Dean canyons, two miles west, prospectors searched the vicinity and found gold in Maysville Canyon in 1882. The English-owned Pittsburg Mining Co. began gold mining operations, a townsite was laid out in Crums Canyon and a mill was built east of the mines, connecting with them by a tramway. Mining increased after 1887, and mines and mill operated intermittently until this century. The years in which the post office was open probably indicate the camp's most active periods: 1888-1893 and 1897-1900. Mine ruins remain.

LANDER, 6 miles southwest then west of SR 21 at a point 24 miles southwest of I-80 at Beowawe exit. (24 miles southeast of Battle Mountain).

Discovery of the Bullion district dates to sometime in the early 1870s, and during irregular periods through the 1880s Lander was a small but active camp. Two smelters were built and an average of fifty prospectors and miners worked during the early activity. The district revived in 1906 after silver mines opened up south of Indian Creek, and the camp had a saloon, boarding house and post office. The rival townsite of Bullion was platted a half-mile east on Indian Creek and several buildings were thrown up but it quickly died. Height of activity came in 1907 but when the mines declined the post office was removed in 1909. Stone buildings and dugouts mark the site of Lander; nothing remains at Bullion.

TENABO, 5 miles southwest of SR 21 at a point 24 miles south of I-80 at Beowawe exit (24 miles southwest of Battle Mountain).

After silver deposits were located in the Bullion mining district in 1907, a large rush took place and Tenabo was founded on the eastern slope of the Shoshone Range. A townsite was platted east of the mines; several substantial wooden buildings were erected and within a few months Tenabo had 1000 people to support a hotel, restaurant, assay office, lumberyard, grocery store, school, post office, saloons and sporting houses. A tri-weekly stage ran to Beowawe on the Southern Pacific, and for a time automobiles and a steam traction line also made the trip.

During the next three years several active mines kept a mill running in Mill Gulch, but after 1910-11 expenses, including hauling water from a distance, did not justify continuing operations. Tenabo soon folded and lost its post office in 1912. Four years later A. E. Raleigh found placer gold in Mill Gulch, where rose a camp named for him, and placering continued in all the nearby ravines for over two decades. A floating dredge operated in the late 1930s, making a significant showing. Wooden buildings are left.

GOLD ACRES, 9 miles southwest of SR 21 at a point 24 miles south of I-80 at Beowawe exit.

Initial development on the east side of the Shoshone Mountains began in 1936 and a half-mile southeast of the camp a mill was built. It is said to have produced about $250,000 in gold before the London Extension Co.'s modern 400-ton cyanide

Heavy wagons requiring large teams hauled ore from the Little Gem mine at Tenabo to the railhead at Beowawe, 25 miles north. (*N. A. Lamb Collection*)

164

plant opened in March 1942. Both the mine and the new mill operated throughout the decade, one of the very few gold mines in the nation that did not close during the war. About 100 men were employed during peak periods, and a modern company camp of 300 consisted of a bunkhouse, 32 dwellings, store, post office and elementary school.

Living conditions at Gold Acres were modest yet satisfactory. The mine was a steady producer, the climate agreeable and for diversion the local residents went to Battle Mountain, Carlin and Elko. Operations ceased in June 1961, and after an auction that December the camp was completely wiped off the face of the earth. Only a large pit and extensive foundations mark the site of this operation which produced about $10 million in slightly under two decades of effort.

MILL CANYON (Eureka County), 3½ miles east of SR 21 at a point 34 miles south of I-80 at Beowawe exit. (38 miles southeast of Battle Mountain).

After nearby Cortez was discovered, an eight-stamp mill was erected here in June 1864 to treat its silver ores. Mule pack trains carried the ore over the narrow trail eight miles between mine and mill; ore wagons used a longer route. The mill's capacity was doubled in 1869, and during the next decade the canyon itself was thoroughly prospected without success. The mill operated until 1886 when a new mill was built at Cortez below the mines.

The canyon was virtually forgotten until 1909 when a mild boom took place because of interest displayed by Patsy Clark, a prominent mining man who helped promote Greenwater in Southern California. Gold properties were then worked briefly. In the 1930s the Roberts Milling Co. built a mill in the lower end of the canyon. Ruins of that mill remain, as well as older stone walls.

CORTEZ (pronounced Cor'-tus), 1 mile east of SR 21 at a point 41 miles south of I-80 at Beowawe exit (39 miles southeast of Battle Mountain).

Located in the shadow of Mount Tenabo (Indian for "lookout mountain," because from its peak distant ranges throughout Nevada can be seen), the Cortez mines have been active for over a century. At first Mexicans shipped some rich silver ore to mills in Austin in 1862, and the next spring an

Patriarch of Cortez was Simeon Wenban, whose mansion had 22-foot ceilings and piped-in water. After three decades of mining, he sold out in 1893; at his death in 1901 he left an estate worth $567,-000. (*Mrs. Jean Bradish Collection*)

eight-man prospecting party from Austin found Indians gathering silver in gulches southwest of the mountain. By tracing the float to cliffs above, large silver ledges were located in March 1863, which led to organization of a district and the formation of the Cortez Co.

Buildings and roads were constructed that summer and machinery for an eight-stamp mill was dragged into the district by bull teams from California. In 1864 Simeon Wenban, one of the original locators, and George Hearst, father of the newspaper tycoon, became partners. That same summer the mill began running nearby (see Mill Canyon), but because it had trouble at first in reducing the ore, shipments to Austin continued by mule train for another year. Impatient with the Cortez operations, Hearst sold out his interest in 1867 to Wenban, making little if anything.

In 1868 Cortez got a post office which was discontinued a year later. By 1870 Wenban had enlarged the mill; there he employed Chinese miners and millhands, available at lower cost than Americans or Mexicans. For the next two decades the district shipped bullion most years. An efficient fifty-ton leaching plant was built in 1886 at the Garrison mine; it saw constant service until the mid-1890s, bringing production to about $3 million. Leasers then worked the ground on a small scale until 1919 when the Consolidated Cortez Silver Mines Co. purchased the mines and four years later built a 125-ton cyanide plant, which in 1927 was converted to the flotation process. Cortez prospered until the 1930s when the depression price of silver made operations unprofitable.

Gold mining commenced at Cortez in 1969, producing 400 ounces of gold daily, and giving promise of outstanding future production.

AUSTIN, at intersection of SR 8A and US 50, 84 miles south of Battle Mountain and 179 miles east of Reno.

Until the spring of 1862 the sage wastes and uninviting mountains of central and eastern Nevada were practically unknown to anyone except Pony Express riders and Overland Mail personnel. Maps designated it as "unexplored"; western Nevadans called it the "Great East," and because of nomadic Indians, only a few daring prospectors sought minerals there. But an important silver discovery in Pony Canyon early in May 1862 changed all this within a few months' time.

While wandering up that canyon in search of horses that had strayed, William Talcott, an employee of the stage station at Jacobs' Spring, stumbled onto a quartz-bearing vein. Samples were eventually sent to Virginia City for assay, and the results showed the ledge to be rich in silver. This news spread rapidly throughout western Nevada. The Reese River district was organized in July, and for the rest of the year scores of prospectors flocked to this region. At year's end news of extraordinary ore assaying $6000 to $7000 a ton in Virginia City spread rapidly throughout the far West.

In January 1863 a great rush developed — the Comstock excitement all over again — and the beckoning cry of "Ho for the Reese River!" lured all kinds of miners, adventurers and homeseekers who swarmed the steep frozen sides of Pony Canyon to stake thousands of claims. The camps of Clifton and Austin emerged around the activity. All roads from the west were crowded with people rushing wildly to the land of promise, mecca of fortune's devotees.

Situated on the line of the telegraph and Overland Stage, Reese River was relatively easy to reach. A local correspondent to a leading California journal had advice for any reader planning to come to Austin. He should "purchase himself a plug for $40 to $75 at Sacramento, Carson City or Virginia City, array himself in homely apparel, hang a bag of lunch, a six-shooter and a canteen on the horn of the saddle, and tie carefully behind the same two substantial California blankets. You may then establish yourself in the saddle and wheel off." His final word of caution was that the horse had better not be a mare.

The rush continued through the spring of 1863; the arrivals at the new camp of Austin lived in stone huts with cloth or canvas roofs, tents and a sprinkling of log houses. Even the camp's founder, David Buel slept in an open tent. Great freight wagons from the west carrying high-priced whiskey, food and clothing deposited their cargo at nearby Clifton (which see), the steep trail up Pony Canyon being too narrow for anyone except horsemen and footpackers. Claims riddled the hillside and speculation over feet of ledges reached a high pitch of trading and extravagance, though very little work had been done on the ledges.

By summer mining companies organized for development work were incorporating on the average of ten per day, and many days saw six times that many. Heavy traffic continued from both east and west; one observer on a trip between Austin and Virginia City counted 274 freight teams, 19 passenger wagons, three pack trains, 69 horsemen and 31 footpackers, all heading east. To serve a population of over 2000, stores of every description had opened up including bakeries and barber shops, breweries and a hotel with a splendid bar. Board there was $15 a week; lodging was 75 cents. Two mills were running in June and another was under construction.

From Austin silver seekers prospected the huge faces of the Toiyabe Range both north and south, founding a dozen satellite camps. The Reese River *Reveille*, Austin's weekly which had begun publication in May, gave extensive coverage to Austin's mines and to developments in the surrounding districts. Austin quickly developed into a center of commerce for those and other camps as far away as northern Nye County. In a September election Austin won a three-way fight for the county seat, capturing about half the vote, and that fall the permanent and transient population numbered about 7000 when the frenzied Reese River boom hit its peak.

Austin began its 17-year career as a city by being incorporated in January 1864 and after April elections had a mayor and board of aldermen, police force and hook-and-ladder company. A wager on the mayoral race obliged the loser Gridley to carry a sack of flour up Main Street where it was auctioned. The sack was offered for sale again and again, and subsequent auctions in western Nevada and across the nation raised money for the Civil War Sanitary Fund, forerunner to the modern Red Cross.

Eventually Austin had other features of a city including a national bank, other banks, costly brick churches, public and private schools, public lecture halls, comfortable private dwellings, gas works for lighting the city, competing newspapers and the Sazerac Lying Club. Beginning in 1864 the Reese River *Reveille* was issued daily, and during the next year systematic development of mining was begun when the Manhattan Silver Mining Co. consolidated many important holdings and built a mill.

Austin was then considered the home of the prospector, for from here men fanned eastern Nevada during the mid-1860s, founding at least sixty mining districts and opening up over 20,000 claims from Pahranagat to Tuscarora. When the White Pine excitement swept the area during 1869, mining briefly slumped at Austin, but by 1871 the Manhattan company controlled nearly all the mines and settled into a relatively stable period of production which lasted until operations ceased in 1887, producing $19.2 million in silver.

Thereafter several unsuccessful attempts were made to rehabilitate the mines. For a decade beginning in 1894 the J. Phelps Stokes interests of New York worked the mines, driving the Clifton tunnel, a 6000-foot crosscut which had its mouth in lower Pony Canyon. Smaller operators have been active at various times in this century to bring the district production to an estimated $28 million.

To the present time Austin has remained a sleepy county seat and small regional center, retaining enough strength to withstand several attempts by Battle Mountain to take away the courthouse. Points of interest include the Gridley store, churches, courthouse (built in 1871), Masonic and Odd Fellows halls, residence of 19th century opera star Emma Nevada and the engine house of the Austin City Railway. The commercialism of Virginia City is conspicuously absent, making Austin one of the most delightful towns in the state.

After its founding in 1863, Austin grew quickly and by the late 1860s had become quite a respectable city when government photographer Timothy O'Sullivan took this picture. The view looks northwest, with Reese River Valley appearing over the hill to the left. *(Bancroft Library)*

The west end of Austin in the mid-1880s was a busy place. The Austin City Railway engine, Mules' Relief, chuffs its way up Pony Canyon to Lander Hill, hauling wood for the mines. In 1882 the locomotive ran off the track in back of the Citizens custom silver mill, shown at right. The lower end of Pony Canyon (background left) shows the early trail from Clifton into Austin.

By the early 1880s Austin had acquired its principal buildings. From the left are the Catholic, Methodist and Episcopal churches. The small white frame building immediately below the trees next to the Catholic church is the first Lander County courthouse. In front of the Episcopal church is the present courthouse built in 1871.

(Two photos: Nevada State Museum)

Lander Hill, the productive part of the district, and Mt. Prometheus (above) are shown in back of the Manhattan mill in center of picture. That facility was the town's mainstay for over twenty years. In the foreground is the Boston Co. mill. *(Bancroft Library)*

Several of the houses (below) still stand, but only foundations are left to indicate the site of the Manhattan mill, shown at the extreme right. Modern U. S. 50 has been built through the residential area in the foreground.

(Las Vegas *Review-Journal*)

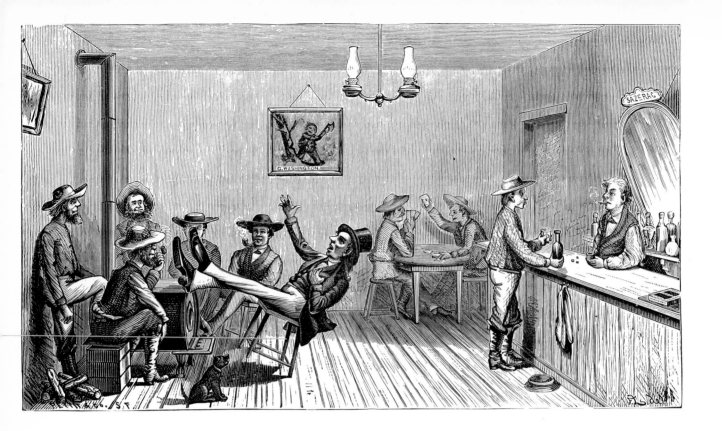

Along with hoaxes and practical joking, an essential part of early western humor was the tall tale. These fanciful lies found their way into local newspapers and were picked up by journalists throughout the nation, giving exaggerated impressions of conditions on the mining frontier. The Sazerac Lying Club (above) is in session; there the imaginative swapped their tales without harm. (From the book *Sazerac Lying Club*)

The bottom picture shows the metallurgical works at one of Austin's smaller mines.
(*Don Cirac Collection*)

After the turn of the century, lower Main Street in Austin did not pulsate with activity; other booms to the south drew people away. Many of the buildings shown are still standing. *(Theron Fox Collection)*

The International Hotel, first erected in Virginia City, was moved to Austin by wagon in the fall of 1862. It burned about 1958. *(Mrs. Ida Le Nord Collection)*

Though Clifton by 1908 was no longer a town, it was the scene of considerable activity. Austinites often came to play baseball and other sports, since they had no level ground in their city. Against the hill is the Austin Silver Mining Co.'s mill, built by Anson P. Stokes around the turn of the century. It used the machinery of the Manhattan mill which had ceased operations in the early 1890s. In foreground and center are the engine house, turntable and station of the Nevada Central Railway. Here was its southern terminus. The MULES' RELIEF of the Austin City Railway is waiting to get a load of passengers or freight for the last leg of the journey to Austin.

(Top: Mrs. R. R. Purdy Collection; bottom: Don Cirac Collection)

CLIFTON, ¼ mile south of junction of US 50 and SR 8A (1 mile west of Austin).

After the discovery of silver in Pony Canyon in May 1862 and organization of the Reese River mining district, the camp of Clifton formed at the foot of the canyon below the new claims. By early 1863 it had become a town of respectable dimensions with a post office, Wells Fargo office, hotels, restaurants, meat markets, shoe stores, a tailor, bakeries, stationery, hardware and sugar merchants, a drug store, blacksmith shops, lumber and hay yards, an assay office, recorder's office, justice of the peace, lawyers, physicians and about 500 citizens.

Clifton was pleasantly situated with wide streets and its prosperity seemed assured, but when Austin was laid out in the middle of Pony Canyon, the two camps soon engaged in a wild race for supremacy. While Clifton had the advantage of a level site, Austin offered free business lots to merchants who would help build a road from Austin westward to the floor of the Reese River Valley. Before that road's completion both towns were growing rapidly in population with Clifton ahead by a margin of fifty in May and having eight saloons to Austin's five. But when Clifton was bypassed by the magnificent new grade up the canyon to Austin, the latter became the terminus of the many stages and wagons carrying passengers and freight to Reese River.

Another reason for Clifton's decline was the excessive price for town lots, beyond anything most newcomers were willing to pay. When Clifton failed to win the county seat in the fall of 1863 the camp died a sudden death. Within months its Montgomery Street, named after San Francisco's proud thoroughfare, lay deserted and flanked by the wrecks of many frame shanties. The post office was officially removed in February 1864. Clifton saw new activity in 1880 when it became the terminus of the Nevada Central and Austin City railways. An abandoned ranch now indicates the site.

YANKEE BLADE, or Yandleville, 2¾ miles north and east by foothill road from Austin.

Another member of the Reese River class of '63, this mining suburb of Austin on the west flank of the Toiyabe Range rapidly came to the front with development of silver mines in Emigrant and

Southwest of Austin is Stokes Castle, built in 1897 as a summer residence for Anson P. Stokes. Balconies, fireplaces, and a sun deck were built, but it was used only briefly in the summer of 1897 and only intermittently for several years thereafter. This architectural curiosity still stands. *(Fred Minoletti Collection)*

Yankee Blade canyons. A camp was founded amid several springs and a brook, and a stage company initiated twice-a-day service to Austin, though many people regularly walked the three-mile distance. At the end of 1863 Austin's *Reveille* announced that Yankee Blade's mines had a promising future and that two mills would soon be erected.

During 1864 the steep mountainsides around the camp were defaced at countless spots in the search for rich silver veins; and with a collection of over thirty adobe and stone structures and a stockade, the camp had a lively appearance. Humorist Artemus Ward is thought to have lectured here early in 1864 on "Babes in the Woods" after performances in Austin and Canyon City. When water was inadvertently struck at the mines in 1866-67 operations came to a halt and there has been no revival since. Mill walls still stand.

AMADOR, 5 miles north of Austin by foothill road.

Following silver discoveries in Amador Canyon, during the great Reese River stampede in the spring of 1863, a camp sprang up in the foothills overlooking Reese River Valley. Within a few weeks Amador became a prosperous village because many thought that its mines had more promise than those in adjacent districts. Its population reached several hundred by the fall of 1863, including those living at adjacent Coral City, but contrary to general belief Amador was not considered for selection as county seat. The camp is credited with 700 votes in the regular election of 1864 but these were rejected because of fraud.

Amador's best years were 1864-65 when it had a post office and the usual establishments, diversions and problems. The district had an ore crusher which was described in a contemporary report as an "exploded humbug which could not crush potatoes, much less quartz." Though large sums had been spent in development, the much-discussed ledges gave out and the camp died by 1866 without getting within a rifleshot of permanence.

RAVENSWOOD, about 6 miles northwest of SR 8A at a point 17 miles north of Austin via US 50 and SR 8A (22 miles northwest of Austin).

Austin prospectors looking for silver found ore on the east slope of the Shoshone Range in 1863, but the veins had only copper values and were soon abandoned. The district was explored intermittently thereafter until 1906-07 when Tasker Oddie of Tonopah acquired the principal properties and inaugurated a short-lived boom. But production was never significant.

LEDLIE, by unimproved road, 4 miles southwest of SR 8A at a point 6 miles northwest of Austin.

After the Nevada Central Railway was completed through here in 1880, Ledlie became the station for fast freight teams which carried cargo destined to several points in central and southwestern Nevada including Ione, Grantsville, Silver Peak and Jefferson. To accommodate the traffic, as many as 250 mules and 60 wagons were employed at peak times, and in 1880 an eighty-mile narrow gauge was planned to extend from here to Cloverdale in Nye County. Early in this century Ledlie was a busy railroad station for the adjacent

Amador's several stone ruins are the epitome of desolation. This former saloon served its last drink over a century ago.

Skookum mines, two miles northwest. One small building remains.

SKOOKUM, by unimproved road 5 miles west of SR 8A at a point 6 miles northwest of Austin.

Early in 1906 an Indian recognized quartz fragments unearthed by a badger as being rich silver-gold float and sold his discovery to others who began development work the next year. After a rich hornsilver discovery in March 1908, hundreds of individuals furiously prospected the south end of the low hills on the west side of Reese River Valley, and each train of the Nevada Central Railway added to the horde at nearby Ledlie.

The tent towns of Gweenah and Skookum sprang up and attained a combined population of 200. The latter camp had stores and a newspaper, the *Times*. With proximity of the railroad, unlimited water supply and rich surface ores, the district had every indication of becoming prosperous, but the boom subsided that fall, though the Gweenah mine produced ore for several years afterward. Only one frame structure and a shaft remain at Skookum; open cuts indicate the site of Gweenah.

JACOBSVILLE, earlier Jacobs' Spring, by unimproved road 5 miles southwest of SR 8A at a point 6 miles northwest of Austin.

The Pony Express maintained Reese River Station on the western bank of that stream during 1860-61. In July 1861 the Overland Mail & Stage Co. established its base across the river a mile to

Reese River Station, one mile west of Jacobsville and on the west bank of the Reese River, is identified by these rock ruins of the former Overland station.

the east at Jacobs' Spring, named for the company's division agent. That fall the transcontinental telegraph reached this vicinity and a maintenance station was built here.

When Lander County was created in December 1862, Jacobs' Spring, renamed Jacobsville, was selected as the provisional county seat, and early the next month a townsite was laid out on speculation. During the first half of 1863 Jacobsville shared in the excitement over mines in Reese River and many people made their homes here, the only place in the region where whiskey could be obtained in quantity. This enterprising town had two hotels, three stores, a post office, telegraph office, a wood-framed courthouse that cost $8400, a mill and a population of 300 to 400. Its other principal feature was a fine spring, a notable attraction in this dry country.

As 1863 progressed, Jacobsville did not maintain its lead as the area's largest town; and with election time approaching for the selection of the permanent county seat that September, something had to be done about the steady defection of business to Clifton and Austin. As an inducement to come to Jacobsville, a letter signed "Tortio, Jr.," the name of a local Shoshone chief, was sent to Austin's *Reveille* which read, "How do you do way up in Austin there? . . . If you will come down and make us a visit here, I will take you around and show you some of the prettiest ladies on the Pacific Coast. There is the beautiful Miss J. and Miss K., then there is pretty little Miss S., with her nice curls, then there is the gold widow L. of the L. Hotel, then there is the dashing little black-eyed widow St. C., who is going to California in a day or two — but to return again. Then if you aren't satisfied, I will see that you become acquainted with some of our fine-looking married women. You fellows can brag of your rich mines and mountain fever up at Clifton and Austin, but they are nothing to be compared with our pretty women at Jacobsville."

The invitation went unnoticed. Jacobsville lost the election to Austin, then went into a decline and in a year almost everyone had moved away except for a few mill hands. Within a decade the once-proud camp was reduced to a ranch. The few faint rock foundations now remaining at the site deform such a minute part of the desert that their intrusion is practically unnoticed unless one knows exactly where to look.

CANYON CITY, or Big Creek, 14 miles southwest of Austin via the Big Creek road.

Founding of the Big Creek district in 1863 gave rise to Canyon City at a point in the Toiyabe foothills where the sagebrush meets the stunted piñons. The camp soon gained several hundred inhabitants and within a year contained express and telegraph offices connected by wire with the transcontinental line at Austin, schools, municipal court, mills and a post office. Attractive farms and gardens were maintained, and the canyon was a pleasant place to live. Besides numerous rock dwellings, mud and willow houses with brush roofs were thickly studded not only at Canyon City but along Big Creek in four other villages, pretentiously known as Montrose, Mineral City, Watertown, and Lander City, the latter located at the mouth of Big Creek Canyon and incorrectly thought to have had several hundred inhabitants. All were deserted when Austin became prosperous.

The famous lecturer-humorist Artemus Ward visited the camp while on a western lecture tour. He spoke at the Young America saloon which had a dirt floor and sagebrush roof. A blazing wood fire and half a dozen tallow candles provided lighting. Ward spoke from behind a bar which had a row of decanters behind him, and pictures of race horses and prize fighters hung from near the ceiling. At the close of every point which Ward made, the barkeeper pounded the counter with a vigorous fist and exclaimed, "Good boy from the New England States! Listen to William W. Shakespeare!" Likely the bar remained open during the lecture for the benefit of 150 thirsty miners who paid two dollars each to hear him.

Canyon City prospered until 1866 when ore veins grew thinner and less valuable. The main mill, the Pioneer, had been abandoned as an abortion shortly after it was built. The copper-filled silver veins proved difficult to reduce, and interest withered away. Big Creek Forest Camp has obliterated the site of Canyon City; at Lander City stone ruins remain.

WASHINGTON (Nye County), 7 miles southeast of SR 21 at a point 29 miles southwest of Austin via US 50, SR 2 and SR 21.

Many locations were made in Washington Canyon in 1862-63, and for the next few years the area had its share of turmoil, scrambling for feet of silver ledges, jumping of town lots and fighting for wood ranches, but most of the crowd which swept over the district eventually left for greener fields. A $40,000 ten-stamp mill built in the summer of 1863 lay idle for lack of ore, as local miners did not immediately develop their properties, waiting for capitalists to come in and spend money. The few mines worthy of notice were worked and managed by Spaniards.

That year the picturesque village below the mines had saloons, bakery, store, livery stable and a billiard hall said to be Nye County's first. After 1865 the inhabitants abandoned their picks and tunnels and employed themselves to better advantage in raising turnips and cabbage. The stamp mill was converted into a sawmill which produced large quantities of lumber from the white pines poised above the canyon.

A post office was established in 1870 but lasted only two years when activity declined. Very little mining took place thereafter until 1918-19 and the mid-1930s, when renewed silver operations began after a mill and tram were constructed. In 1956 some tungsten was mined. Mill foundations and other stone remnants mark the site.

SAN JUAN (Nye County), 7 miles southeast of SR 21 at a point 29 miles southwest of Austin via US 50, SR 2 and SR 21.

After silver discoveries in 1862-63 in the upper part of San Juan creek, mining was started and a camp formed. But the small veins could not be mined profitably and San Juan was abandoned weeks after its founding. A large stone building of later origin marks the site.

GOLD PARK, by road and trail, 8 miles south of SR 2 at a point 32 miles west of Austin via US 50 and SR 2 (36 miles southwest of Austin).

A lone prospector found gold in 1864. After it was rediscovered in 1880 the area attracted some attention, but mining did not get under way until 1893 when the Nevada Mines Co. built a mill and opened up several locations. Irregular production carried the district until litigation arose in 1911, and very little gold was produced thereafter until the 1920s. District production was over $500,000, most of which probably came during 1897-99 and 1921-25, when Gold Park had a post office.

CARROLL, south side of SR 2 at a point 45 miles west of Austin via US 50 and SR 2.

An overpublicized gold discovery in the fall of 1911 brought a rush and led to the platting of Carroll townsite in a sagebrush meadow opposite a small cave on the stage road over Carroll Summit. The camp soon had a saloon, store, hotel and post office which opened in December 1911. But shallow veins did not sustain production and Carroll sank out of sight in 1912.

MOUNT AIRY, north side of US 50 at a point 17 miles west of Austin.

An Overland Mail stage station was maintained here from 1861 until 1869 and the station remained open during the 1870s, probably not closing until the 1890s. Walls and foundations and a solitary grave mark the site.

NEW PASS, 4½ miles north of US 50 at a point 25 miles west of Austin.

An Indian showed rich gold specimens to some Reese River miners, and a district was organized in the spring of 1864. On the basis of favorable reports a five-stamp mill was moved from Austin in 1868 and set up at nearby Warm Springs. The mill operated several years, treating 12,000 tons of ore before shutting down. Mining again resumed around the turn of the century and a post office was open between 1900 and 1904. During World War I copper mining kept a 75-ton cyanide mill running, but operation became unprofitable and all work ceased by 1920.

NEW PASS STATION (Churchill County), quarter-mile north of US 50 at a point 28 miles west of Austin.

An Overland Mail stage station was built at this point in the 1860s below a spring on the west side of New Pass Range; foundations mark its site. Another station known as New Pass was active on the east end of the range during Nevada's early statehood days and may also have been built by the Overland Mail Co. That station was used by travelers of the 1870s and in later years. Massive walls still stand.

SIMPSON PARK, 2 miles southeast of SR 21 at a point 4 miles north of US 50 at a point 6 miles east of Austin.

After functioning as a Pony Express station during 1860-61, Simpson Park became a ranch and stage station with two or three log houses and a blacksmith shop. Massive stone foundations remain in a private field.

GENEVA, 2½ miles west of SR 8A at a point 15 miles south of Austin via US 50 and SR 8A.

Charles C. Breyfogle and six others uncovered rich silver ore on the east flank of the Toiyabe Range in March 1863, a year distinguished for discoveries in central Nevada, and by June a settlement had developed at the mouth of Birch Creek Canyon with a floating population of a few hundred. A blacksmith shop, meat market, saloon and store all opened, as well as a hotel run by Breyfogle, a true prospector, who soon gave up renting rooms and headed south into the undeveloped wilds. On this journey which ended in the Death Valley country, he uncovered a rich ore ledge which became known as the "Lost Breyfogle," and the story of his fabulous discovery circulated swiftly and widely. But the discoverer could not retrace his steps to the phantom ledge before he died in 1870. For several decades thereafter, even in this century, prospectors have searched in vain for that lost ledge.

The buildings at Carroll in the winter of 1911 include a Northern Saloon, a store, a hotel, and a post office which was officially removed three years later.
(Mrs. Myrtle Myles Collection)

The townsite of Geneva was platted in November 1863, and a rich strike in the spring of 1864 drew several hundred people who built dozens of stone, log and tent houses. Many promising ledges were being developed, but the district had no mill for ore reduction. Birch Creek ran to no other music than its own babbling, but when the Big Smoky Mining Co. of New York began acquiring property in 1864-65, the Genevans anticipated that the steam whistle and the pounding of stamps would soon play a more boisterous tune just below town. About 1866 the company built a twenty-stamp mill which ran but a few days before shutting down because the ore was worth only $10 to $12 a ton. Geneva was deserted by 1867 and everything was removed, leaving empty stone buildings in the wilderness.

John Muir described the fate of an abandoned mill, possibly Geneva's, when he traveled through Reese River early in the 1870s: "I noticed a tall and imposing column, rising like a lone pine out of the sagebrush on the edge of a dry gulch. This proved to be a smokestack of solid masonry. It seemed strangely out of place in the desert, as if it had been transported entire from the heart of some noisy manufacturing town and left here by mistake. [It was] built by a New York company to smelt ore that was never found. The tools of the workmen are still lying in place beside the furnaces, as if dropped in some sudden Indian or earthquake panic and never afterwards handled. These imposing ruins . . . present a most vivid picture of wasted effort."

Several stone structures are left.

177

Kingston in the mid-1880s thrived both as a mining and ranching area. Beyond the small farms in lower Kingston Canyon (below), the Victorine mill handled ore from revived mines on the east flank of the Toiyabe Range, especially at Kingston. Closeup of the massive mill (above) shows its rock walls, remnants of which can be seen today.
(Top: Mrs. Myrtle Myles Collection; below: Don Cirac Collection)

CLINTON, ¼ mile west of Geneva.

After promising silver mines opened up in 1863, a camp rose on a platted townsite with park-plaza early in 1864. Several stores and a post office were here most of that year and Clinton served as a small distribution point for mines in upper Birch Creek Canyon. A sawmill began operating and in 1865 a four-stamp quartz mill handled local ores, but that mill according to one report did not successfully reduce anything except the hopes of the miner who carried his rock there. Clinton's brief career ended about 1866, never to be revitalized.

GUADALAJARA or Santa Fe, 2 miles west of SR 8A at a point 24 miles south of Austin via US 50 and SR 8A.

At the mouth of deep rocky Santa Fe Canyon, the camp of Guadalajara emerged after Mexicans discovered silver early in the 1860s. By 1863 American prospectors organized the Santa Fe district and made over 3000 locations. It was said that enough silver lay in the canyon's untapped ledges to build a city of solid silver bricks! A mill was installed in Kingston Canyon, and the Mother Lode mine owned by the Centenary Company began operations. A nearby sawmill furnished excellent lumber. Guadalajara was laid out as a city in 1864, but the anticipated influx never materialized and the district was abandoned about 1867 when ore values continued to yield less than milling expenses. The mill was moved to Newark in White Pine County and the mines closed. Ask owner's permission to visit.

KINGSTON, 4 miles west of SR 8A at a point 27 miles south of Austin via US 50 and 8A.

Of all the camps in the Reese River country, Austin excepted, Kingston endured the longest. Mining began in Kingston Canyon when valuable gold and silver croppings were uncovered in 1863. The small camp of Bunker Hill appeared, its settlers drawn by minerals, a cold sparkling stream, an abundance of wood and availability of sites for buildings and gardens. During its short two-year existence, Bunker Hill consisted of a collection of rock cabins, but no fortunes were made in the sale of town lots because there was never a great rush.

Bunker Hill thrived until early in 1864, when the town of Kingston with mill sites and vineyards was laid out two miles lower in the canyon closer to new discoveries. In February 1864 the *Reveille* in Austin reported that at Kingston many improvements were under way in building, fencing and mining. Prosperity seemed assured because of such benefits as unlimited water power for milling and "inexhaustible rich quartz ledges" — it couldn't miss. Flush times prevailed for a few years; two water-powered mills each with twenty stamps were erected in 1865-66 as well as two smaller mills; and Kingston, with its own post office, flourished.

After 1866 the mines did not meet expectations, and as milling declined the machinery of the twenty-stamp Big Smoky mill at the canyon entrance was moved to booming White Pine in 1869. The mines were worked only intermittently until the mid-1880s when increased operations revived Kingston town and its businesses, post office and school. Another revival between 1906 and 1911 was inconsequential. Mill walls remain as well as other stone remnants concealed in thick brush. Camp facilities are available.

DRY CREEK STATION, 6 miles north of US 50 at a point 27 miles east of Austin.

This Pony Express station was the scene of the Dry Creek fight of May 1860, in which two men (one was the stationmaster) were killed in an Indian raid. Two other men and a squaw managed to escape by outrunning the attacking Indians.

Thick walls of several miners' cabins are left at Guadalajara, an outlying district in Reese River.

179

After Eureka became the railhead for eastern Nevada in 1875, merchandise of all kinds and a considerable amount of whiskey were teamed to Hamilton and other points by canvas-topped schooners (above), with their high sides. During the slow journey the skinner (shown here on one of the "wheelers") battled poor roads, monotonous distances, and the elements to get through. Every animal had a name, and teamsters continually talked to the animals as a pastime. On the return trip to Eureka, ore was hauled for rail shipment to distant mills. *(Stanley Fine Collection)* Eureka around 1885 was an imposing city with courthouse and buildings of fine masonry. The Eureka Consolidated smelter is situated on the ridge at the north end of town. *(Morgan North Collection)*

EUREKA COUNTY

Nevada's second largest mineral producer during the 19th century was Eureka, the nation's first important lead-silver district. Discoveries date from 1864 but no mining got under way until 1870. Palisade was founded in 1868 on the Central Pacific, and Mineral Hill boomed in the early 1870s. The Eureka district prospered through the 1870s, and beginning in 1875 the Eureka & Palisade Railroad began running between the two towns of its corporate name. Best years of mining at Eureka were 1878-85, but thereafter the district joined the rest of the state in depression.

Eureka revived early in this century but declined again before World War I when Buckhorn made a showing. Since 1920 the county's mines have been silent except for some efforts in the Eureka district, Buckhorn and developments at the new Carlin mine, today the second largest gold mine in the United States.

EUREKA, on US 50, 69 miles east of Austin.

A five-man prospecting party from Austin discovered silver here in September 1864. These deposits later proved to be the first important lead-silver discovery in America, but attempts at separating the two metals at mills in Austin and at locally built smelters in 1865-66 failed because of the ore's high lead content. Interest languished for three years until the installation of new furnaces in 1869 showed that the ore could be treated successfully. During the next year hundreds of former White Piners turned their attention toward Eureka.

In 1870 Eureka grew rapidly in a canyon between the Diamond and Prospect mountains north-east of the mines. The influential Eureka *Sentinel* began publication in July 1870. Stages began arriving more frequently from both east and west, and a fast freight line was established to Palisade on the Central Pacific. Slower oxen hauled ore to the railroad at a cost of $20 per ton. Further improvements in smelting techniques and the construction of additional furnaces started Eureka on 14 years of prosperity during which $64 million in silver and gold was recovered in addition to over 225,000 tons of lead. Two large mining companies, the Richmond Consolidated and Eureka Consolidated, accounted for most of the production.

After the completion of the Eureka & Palisade Railroad in October 1875, Eureka became the center of wagon and stage transportation for most camps in eastern Nevada including Austin, Belmont, Tybo, Ward, Hamilton and Pioche. Eureka now had become Nevada's second largest city with about 9000 residents in 1878, the peak year when $5.2 million was produced. Eureka supported over 100 saloons, a few dozen gambling palaces, many theaters, competing newspapers, luxurious hotels, churches, boarding houses, stores and restaurants, opera house, five fire companies, brass band and two militia units. On the outskirts of town 16 smelters with a daily capacity of 745 tons treated ore from over fifty producing mines. Furnaces poured forth dense clouds of black smoke which constantly rolled over the town and deposited soot, scales and black dust everywhere, giving the town a somewhat somber aspect and killing vegetation. The "Pittsburgh of the West," Eureka was indeed the foremost smelting district in the entire West.

After the days of large-scale mining in Eureka, ore was shipped to distant smelters on Eureka & Palisade flatcars. Governor Sadler, from Eureka County, stands third from the right.

Hauling bags of charcoal to the smelters by 14-mule team was a big job in 1882. The teamster, or skinner (on the horse and manning the jerkline) started out at daybreak from Antelope Valley, 30 miles west of Eureka, and arrived about dusk the next day. The wagon train made at most two miles an hour while carrying about 16 tons of charcoal in sacks. If the train got stuck en route, one or two wagons had to be dropped for later pickup. As many as 800 *carbonari*, all of whom lived in satellite charcoal camps, gathered wood and made charcoal.

(*Both photos: Stanley Fine Collection*)

Both of the Eureka district's two large mining companies erected costly smelters. At the Eureka Consolidated works, lead fumes were diverted from the workers and discharged from the elongated stack on the ridge in the distance. As early as 1869 small smelters were in operation, and by the mid-1870s 19 furnaces, each with varying capacities of 40 to 60 tons had been built. Operators soon realized that larger facilities resulted in lower costs, and by the end of the 1870s virtually all smelting was done by the two major companies which by 1881 processed 750 tons a day. To smelt a ton of ore, 25 to 35 bushels of charcoal were required, and in 1880 at the height of smelting activity, 1¼ million bushels were consumed per year.

The Richmond Consolidated smelter (bottom) was at the south end of the town of Eureka. Ore cars of the Ruby Hill Railroad in center of picture brought ore from the mines to the west. *(Both photos: Stanley Fine Collection)*

183

This precariously loaded wagon made deliveries in Eureka, around 1905.
(Fred Minoletti Collection)

Early in this century the town of Eureka still presented an imposing appearance. Behind Cariboo Hill to the right were the district's rich mines at Ruby Hill.
(John Dewar Collection)

A lengthy strike took place in the summer of 1879 when the Charcoal Burners' Association stopped delivery of their indispensable product to the smelters for several weeks in protest against a unilateral price reduction for charcoal from the 30 cents they asked to 27½ cents. After the burners threatened taking possession of the town and destroying property, the county sheriff and an augmented posse descended on the camp of Fish Creek where in an ambush five charcoal burners were slaughtered and at least an equal number were severely wounded resisting arrest. Despite the strike and a million-dollar fire in April, production that year almost equalled the previous year's effort, and the Eureka mines were still an important factor in the price structure of lead. The population of Eureka and Ruby Hill dipped to about 6300 in 1880.

The West's first apex case occurred in 1877-81, forerunner of many similar suits, when the district's two mining giants locked horns in a fierce dispute over a bonanza ore body known as Potts Chamber. Protracted lawsuits between the Richmond and Eureka companies had started as early as 1871, and hard feelings always existed between them. During the mid-1870s the Richmond company had worked downward from one of its claims to an ore shoot which terminated in Potts Chamber, also claimed by the Eureka company. To reach that chamber, the Richmond crossed over a compromise plane established in a previous suit, but nevertheless claimed the right to follow the ore body because the Potts lode apexed on its property.

But the same ore body also apexed on the Eureka ground. That company then proved that it possessed a lode according to existing mining law, and because of the earlier compromise it emerged from court victorious over the Richmond. The U. S. Supreme Court affirmed the lower court's decision, according to which it was estimated that the Richmond company had mined $2 million worth of Eureka company ore.

Also during 1881 mines of the Eureka Consolidated encountered water, and thereafter expensive pumping was required to work lower levels. Despite this the Eureka district led the state in mineral production. Bonanza ore bodies were exhausted by 1885, and thereafter mining passed into the hands of leasers. In the late 1880s the price of

silver fell; in 1890, the Richmond smelter closed down and the Eureka smelter followed a year later.

A five-year revival began in 1906 when the district's two large companies merged to form the Richmond-Eureka Consolidated. But in 1910 the Ruby Hill Railroad to the mine was washed out and the Eureka & Palisade was rendered useless by disastrous flash floods. Leasers then again made a living by working some of the mines. Best years of production in later years were 1923, 1926-29 and 1938-40, principally by newly formed companies. Total production in a century of effort has been about $110 million.

Commercialism has not ruined this old camp, and the fine mountain scenery and numerous aged buildings make Eureka an attractive place to visit. Points of interest include the courthouse, office of the *Sentinel*, churches, old homes, and nine cemeteries.

RUBY HILL, 2 miles west of Eureka.

When mining activity in the Eureka district rapidly increased after 1871, many miners chose to live near the mines. The town of Ruby Hill formed and by 1873 possessed businesses and a post office. Further increases in mining operations encouraged the building of the narrow gauge Eureka & Ruby Hill Railroad from the mines around Ruby Hill to the smelters at Eureka in 1875. At the height of mining activity in 1878 Ruby Hill boasted a population of over 2500, including over 900 miners with families.

Many fine buildings on wide streets housed stores and shops, schools, theater, miners' union, Methodist, Episcopal and Catholic churches, a brewery, and printing shop of the weekly *Mining Report*, later replaced by the *Mining News*. The extensive shaft houses and mining works of the famous Eureka Consolidated and Richmond Consolidated mining companies enhanced the camp's appearance of prosperity. The 1880 census showed a population of 2165, and though the district declined after 1885 around 700 people continued to make homes here until the end of the century. Family men leased certain areas in the old workings and mining continued when a vein of paying ore was found.

Only three businesses were left early in this century, and after the local railroads were washed

Empty cars of the Ruby Hill Railroad approach the Eureka Consolidated mine to carry ore to its smelter. The date is sometimes in the early 1880s. On the incline at right a cable elevated small cars (not shown) loaded with wood which was used in the shaft house, the large building in the center of the picture. To its left are the blacksmith shop and residences. *(Fred Minoletti Collection)*

The Richmond mine is shown from the town of Ruby Hill. In the foreground is a trestle of the Ruby Hill Railroad. *(Stanley Fine Collection)*

The Albion mine and its 100-ton smelter located about a mile west of Ruby Hill began operations around 1885. A few years later the Richmond Co. sued the Albion for trespassing, and after the Richmond won the lawsuit, the Albion closed down around 1895.
(Stanley Fine Collection)

The bottom view shows Ruby Hill in 1908, the Ruby Hill Railroad, and the recently completed Richmond-Eureka Consolidated works with its four tall stacks.
(Library of Congress)

out (see Eureka) major mining operations ceased and many people moved away. Periodic revivals have kept the mines in operation, and large interests now hold the ground waiting for an opportune time to develop the district's mineral potential. Several buildings at Ruby Hill remain, but only one dates to the 19th century.

COLUMBIA, about 12 miles southwest of Eureka via Spring Valley Canyon road.

Discoveries of silver in the spring of 1869 led to the formation of a mining district in Spring Valley that June, and soon the camp had fifty or sixty miners, store, unofficial post office, and several cabins. Some ore shipments were made to Austin, but most left by year's end in favor of Eureka.

PROSPECT, 5 miles south of Eureka via US 50 and Secret Canyon road.

Initially settled about 1885, Prospect early in this century had a saloon, school, post office, tri-weekly stage to Eureka, and about 100 people. All supplies were hauled from Eureka. The post office was closed in 1918 after silver mining had virtually stopped.

VANDERBILT, 8 miles south of Eureka via US 50 and Secret Canyon road.

Early in the 1870s Vanderbilt was founded among silver-lead mines in Secret Canyon and contained three stores, two boarding houses, a post office for two years beginning in August 1871, blacksmith, and 125 inhabitants. It died when Eureka grew and the township was abolished in 1876. When the Geddes mine and mill were operating here in the next decade, the post office (1882-85) took the name Geddes. Mine ruins remain.

DIAMOND CITY, 12 miles northeast of SR 51 at a point 11 miles north of Eureka.

Though silver was initially found on the west side of the Diamond Mountains in May 1864, serious mining efforts did not begin until 1866 when $150-a-ton ore was shipped to Austin for reduction. A smelter erected below the Champion mine in 1873 produced limited amounts of bullion, but ineffectual attempts at large-scale mining ultimately led to abandonment by the mid-1870s. A post office known as Diamond was open some-where in the area from 1874 until 1883. Mill foundations mark the site.

ALPHA, west side of SR 51 at a point 38 miles north of Eureka.

Here was the most important station on the Eureka & Palisade Railroad because southward construction of the railroad from Palisade toward Eureka stopped at this point in the fall of 1874. With Alpha as winter terminus, a town formed with railroad shops, saloons and stores, a large depot, freight barns, and a hotel large enough to accommodate 75 guests. Stages took train passengers into Eureka, covering the distance in about six hours.

Early in 1875 W. L. Pritchard, nicknamed "Nick of the Woods" and a partner in the building of the E. & P., platted a huge townsite with intersecting streets and enormous stable areas for horses and wagons, intending to terminate the line here and not continue to build further south. Pritchard owned a vast freighting empire and monopolized the Eureka and Hamilton shipping trade by routing traffic from the transcontinental Central Pacific to Alpha via the Eureka & Palisade and then to Eureka with his fast stages and wagons, employing more than 500 wagons and 2000 animals in hauling supplies into Eureka.

Pritchard's partner killed the lucrative trade by insisting on finishing the railroad into Eureka in the fall of 1875. Thereafter Alpha declined and soon lost its hotel; the railroad shops were relocated at Palisade; and the eating stop was moved down the line to Mineral station. By 1880 Alpha had only 25 residents and a small post office which finally closed in 1886. Only cellars remain at the site.

BUCKHORN, 18 miles west of SR 51 at a point 38 miles north of Eureka.

Gold ledges discovered on the east side of the Cortez mountains in the winter of 1908-09 were acquired the next year by financier George Wingfield, who erected an 800-horse power electric power plant at Beowawe to supply power for a 300-ton cyanide plant built in 1914. That year the camp's 300 citizens supported saloons, stores, a post office, restaurant, hotel, barber, livery stable and daily stage to Blackburn on the Eureka & Pali-

Lingering snow is visible on the hills surrounding Prospect in 1908, indicating that this general view was taken in early spring.
(U. S. Geological Survey)

The Buckhorn auto stage met the train at Palisade and took its load forty bumpy miles to Buckhorn. The tiring trip over rutted roads and dust pockets took about two hours and the one-way fare was ten dollars. Auto stages were well established in most parts of Nevada when this picture was taken, about 1913.
(Nevada Historical Society)

The camp of the Buckhorn mine is shown after its second failure, in the 1930s.
(Mrs. Ida Le Nord Collection)

sade Railroad. But after the vein pinched out in 1916, the mill was dismantled. A revival at the Buckhorn mine two decades later followed building of another mill, but that effort lasted only until the end of 1937. District production was $1.1 million.

BLACKBURN, west side SR 51 at a point 53 miles north of Eureka and 37 miles south of Carlin.

This station on the Eureka & Palisade Railroad thrived in 1910 as the shipping point for Buckhorn. A hotel, saloon and livery stable were in operation until the end of mining at Buckhorn, but all buildings have been removed.

MINERAL HILL, 11 miles south of SR 51 at a point 32 miles south of Carlin.

Reese River prospectors seeking a stray horse on the west flank of the Piñon Range in the spring of 1869 found silver float. That summer fifty tons of ore were hauled to Austin, where they yielded $200 to $400 a ton. A new camp started here, taking its name from the isolated 500-foot hill where mining operations centered. The next spring a ten-stamp mill was erected and soon enlarged to 15 stamps. A rush in the latter half of 1870 populated the district with 400 to 500 people, and within a year the camp built up rapidly with ten saloons, restaurants, stores, a meat market, bakery, brickyard, school, post office and a stage line to Palisade on the Central Pacific. Many buildings were built of dressed lumber.

The big boom was stimulated in part by the London-based California Mining Co. Mastermind of this so-called company was Albert Grant, whose employees were directors and shareholders; it purchased mines and mill for $1,150,000 in May 1871, then sold them in June to another Grant-owned company for $2.5 million, half in cash and half in paid-up shares. The shares of the new company were dumped on the market at a price of $3 million to finance the Mineral Hill operation. This well-heeled company then exploited the mines at a furious pace, and in the fall of 1871 built a twenty-stamp mill with furnaces. By the end of that year Wells Fargo had carried away over $700,000 in bullion, a figure nearly equalled in 1872. But by the middle of 1872 the main deposits were worked out and the camp declined to a mere handful of people.

During 1873 new ground was sought to work in hope of saving the big investment, and the mines operated a few months for debenture holders, but results were unsatisfactory. Smelting furnaces were abandoned and an amalgamation process, substituted in 1874, fared no better. At the close of the year the company reported its third straight losing year. Unable to pay its bills, the discouraged English company went into bankruptcy that year without ever having paid a dividend. The big mill was sold and removed and the high court of England ordered the mines sold to the highest bidder. Finally in 1880 Americans acquired ownership and began intermittent operations for small recoveries until 1887.

Leasers were then active until 1910, when the Mineral Hill Consolidated Co. was formed. Its cyanide plant, built in 1911 to work the dumps, ran only two years before operations suspended, and leasers again carried on small-scale work until World War II. Vast mill foundations and a few buildings remain.

UNION, 11 miles southeast of SR 51 at a point 32 miles south of Carlin.

Though lead-silver was found in 1880, mining finally started in 1887 when a local smelter ran for several months. In 1915 the Union Mines Co. rehabilitated the district and built a small company town consisting of a two-story bunkhouse, boarding house, dwellings, mine buildings and post office. Lead-silver ore was regularly shipped to smelters at Midvale, Utah, but operations declined in 1918. Two shacks remain.

PALISADE, 1½ miles west of SR 51 at a point 10 miles south of Carlin.

This community was founded in 1868 as a station on the Central Pacific and it immediately became a jumping-off point for Mineral Hill, Hamilton, Eureka and many other eastern Nevada camps. When construction of the Eureka & Palisade Railroad started from here southward in 1874, Palisade assumed additional importance. To meet the need for the increased activity and traffic through town, an array of stores, hotels, saloons and other businesses were opened for travelers and the local population of 600.

A school was started, the Catholic and Episcopal churches established missions, and the I.O.O.F.

These views of Mineral Hill around the turn of the century show most features of the camp. The Mineral Hill district's most important lodes were located on the hill of the same name (above), situated immediately east of the camp. Mills of 15 and 20 stamps were in the gulch to the north. Until 1873 these mills paid taxes in Elko County, but during that year Eureka County acquired the Mineral Hill section in exchange for the cooperation of its legislative delegation in voting to locate the state university at Elko. By 1902 the mill on the left had long since been dismantled, although the Atwood mill on right was still used (below). *(Mrs. Ida Le Nord Collection)*

Palisade, shown here in the 1870s, was a busy railroad town. Two separate ox teams rest in the street before hauling lumber and bulky supplies to nearby mining camps on regularly scheduled runs which met the Central Pacific on arrival. A portion of the business district is shown. *(John Zalac Collection)*

After 1880 Palisade settled down to be a small community. In this view the tracks of the Central Pacific are shown as well as its two-story station. A train heads east toward Palisade Canyon and Elko. The sheer cliffs whose walls rise more than a thousand feet took their name from a similar formation on the Hudson River in New York.

(Marion Schendel Collection)

and Masons organized lodges. After the E. & P. finished construction, that line built machine repair shops in Palisade which also manufactured boxcars and flatcars for the line. Immense piles of Eureka bullion on railroad platforms awaiting transshipment between lines caught the curiosity of transcontinental travelers. By 1882 a new station house with telegraph office was constructed. Said to be the state's finest on completion, the new facility was used jointly by the two railroads.

When the Eureka mines declined after 1885, activity on the E. & P. subsided, and the town of Palisade diminished in size and importance. A third railroad began running through here after 1908 when the Western Pacific built its line across northern Nevada, but in 1910 heavy floods destroyed much of the town and damaged all three lines. The town never regained its importance and after abandonment of the E. & P. in 1938 Palisade had no hope of recovery. Several dilapidated wooden buildings and stone ruins remain in a picturesque canyon setting.

SAFFORD, 7 miles southwest of Palisade by road and trail (14 miles southwest of Carlin).

Iron discoveries were made about 1869 probably by surveyors while mapping the route of the Central Pacific Railroad, but not until 1881 when silver veins were uncovered was a district formed. By the spring of 1883 the camp of Safford had both a post office and a newspaper, the *Express*, which was published at Palisade because the editor saw little hope of permanency for the district's mines. His hunch proved to be correct, as Safford never "panned" and did not even last out the year.

Between 1903 and 1918 the American Smelting & Refining Co. leased the Barth mine and produced $1.9 million in iron ore. After exploratory work beginning in 1954 revealed that the main ore body extended under the nearby Humboldt River, the channel was diverted and in 1960 the Nevada Barth Co. began making shipments which by 1964 had surpassed the earlier production.

Use of the Southern Pacific railroad station steadily diminished early in this century, when this picture was taken. *(Bob Stewart Collection)*

193

Early in this century both autos and horse-drawn stages stopped at Dinner Station, one of Nevada's most popular country inns of that era. Stages met the trains at Elko and whisked away Tuscarora-bound travelers, stopping here at the dinner hour to eat meals which cost fifty cents. *(Both photos: Tony Primeaux Collection)*

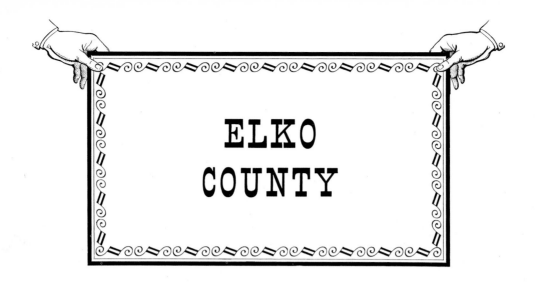

ELKO COUNTY

The early development of Elko County reads like a capsule history of the West. Explorers and fur trappers came and went between 1826 and 1844, and after 1848 emigrant trains bound for California passed through. Some homesteads were established in the early 1860s; Mormons started farms by the middle of the decade; itinerant prospectors organized a placer district at Tuscarora in 1867; the transcontinental Central Pacific began running across the county in 1868 and the following year the silver camp of Mountain City was founded. By then the newly settled area was protected by army units based at Fort Halleck.

During the 1870s Cornucopia and Bullion were also active, and Tuscarora dominated Elko County mining from 1875 until the beginning of this century. Edgemont was a significant discovery in the 1890s. The southern Nevada boom after 1900 gave new zest to prospecting and most old districts revived because of new mining practices and the availability of cheaper power and transportation. Jarbidge and Midas became significant new producers and in 1932 a copper boom at Rio Tinto began that lasted through World War II. Since then only smaller operators have been active.

DINNER STATION, west side of SR 51 at a point 23 miles north of Elko.

This famous stage station was established sometime in the early 1870s as a meal stop for the Tuscarora and Mountain City stage lines. Originally a frame structure accommodated the traffic, but when it burned down during the 1880s a fine two-

story stone station house was built along with other buildings and a corral. Initially the station was also known as Weilands but later the name was changed to Oldham's Station, denoting the change in ownership. After 1910 when autos became more common, the station saw less frequent use. The station house from the 1880s is a landmark in the area and people still live in it.

TUSCARORA, 52 miles northwest of Elko via SR 51, SR 11 and SR 18 (40 miles northwest of Elko).

Late in the spring of 1867 a Shoshone revealed gold to a trader on the Humboldt River. After the white man found the site, he went to Austin and induced six others, well armed for defense against Indians, to accompany him to the west side of Independence Valley. Early in July a district was organized, taking the name Tuscarora after a Union warship of the Civil War. Placer mining began and a camp formed on McCann Creek, two miles southwest of the present site of Tuscarora.

When news of the discovery reached Austin later that summer, nearly 300 miners rushed to the new gold fields. For protection against Indians a four-room adobe fort 68 by 14 feet was built in September, with portholes arranged to command the countryside. During the next year ore was found in lodes on Beard Hill and a four-stamp mill, dragged in from Austin, operated briefly without success. Meanwhile placering continued in the spring months when enough water was available.

After completion of the Central Pacific in 1869 the district attracted hundreds of discharged Chi-

Before spring came to Tuscarora (top), additional freight wagons brought immense loads of supplies to take care of the anticipated annual influx of miners. This picture of the northeast side of Weed Street shows a candy store, the post office, the Idaho Bar, and Primeaux' general merchandise store. (*Nevada State Museum*)

In this general view of Tuscarora from 76 Hill probably in the 1880s, the commercial district on Weed Street is shown extending from the middle of the picture to the background left. The camp is encircled by mines. At the left (east) end of town was the Grand Prize; to the south was the Dexter (worked in later years); and to the northwest was the Navajo and other mines. (*Mrs. Della Phillips Collection*)

The Independence mill on the north side of Tuscarora had a furnace to smelt ore when necessary. Sagebrush stacked in the foreground ran the steam plant. Barrels of water on the roof were for protection against fire. This was one of the district's early mills, a steady producer in the early 1880s. *(Mrs. Della Phillips Collection)*

At the west end of the camp at the foot of Mt. Blitzen was the North Belle Isle ore bin and hoisting works. Waste dumps are forming under the trestle.

(Tony Primeaux Collection)

Tuscarora's Weed Street in the early days had no trees in front of its business establishments. These potted pines were brought in before a celebration to decorate the street. Two popular saloons are plainly shown. Mt. Blitzen is in the background to the west.
(*George Nelson Collection*)

Just before the turn of the century, Tuscarora in decline (below) shows that almost all buildings were of wood; no solid brick fronts lined the streets as at rich camps such as Eureka or Austin. Against the base of the Independence Mountains in the distance were large cattle ranches whose personnel found the town a convenient market place.
(Las Vegas *Review-Journal*)

In the mid-1880s the children of Tuscarora's miners and merchants attended a typical school where grades one through eight were taught in the same room. Large and small students sat side by side in double desks. From the recitation bench in the mid-fore-ground, students gave readings and other exercises. The teacher taught from a raised platform beneath the clock. Colorful maps adorned the wall.

The Tuscarora company of the first infantry of the Nevada National Guard line up in full dress uniform, in the mid-1880s. *(Both photos: Mrs. Della Phillips Collection)*

Because wood was scarce (what was available cost up to $11 a cord), the sagebrush that covered hills and fields surrounding Tuscarora was put to use as an all-purpose fuel. Quite a trade developed in gathering sagebrush and hauling it into the camp to run the furnaces and hoists. At the Dexter mine (below), sage at $2.50 a cord is being delivered from a nearby ranch. During the boom the surrounding area was denuded of all sage and scrub pine.

(Top: Tony Primeaux Collection; bottom: William A. Kornmayer Collection)

Sagebrush fed into the boiler of the mill created steam to drive the machinery. The fast-burning brush produced a long hot flame which built steam faster than other available types of fuel. Smoking like a miniature Vesuvius, the hoist works of the Dexter (below), Tuscarora's third largest producer, is shown at the right opposite the assay office. Children often played near the mill, making deep tunnels in the vast sagebrush piles.

(Top: Mrs. Della Phillips Collection; bottom: Nevada State Museum)

nese laborers who gleaned placer tailings abandoned by whites. In 1870 Orientals were hired to build expensive water ditches so that placering could continue most months of the year. One six-mile-long ditch from Six Mile Canyon and another from upper McCann Creek brought water to the placer field near the camp.

When a disgusted placer miner named W. O. Weed found rich silver veins on the east side of Mount Blitzen in 1871 most of the whites left the gold gulches to the Chinese and scrambled to locate silver ledges. The present Tuscarora townsite was then platted below the new finds. Each year thereafter other lodes were uncovered, and after the Grand Prize bonanza was uncovered early in the summer of 1876, mining eyes were focused on the district. Ox teams loaded with mining machinery and supplies came, especially from Carlin, and miners, carpenters and even a few preachers rushed here.

In 1877 a dozen steam hoists had replaced the windlasses, ropes and buckets which had lifted ore from shafts as deep as 500 feet, and the extraordinary bullion yields that year placed Tuscarora in the front rank of mining districts. This camp of 3000 to 4000 supported many saloons, restaurants, post office, an array of stores, competing weeklies—the *Times* and *Review*, Methodist and Catholic churches, public school, and lodges of Masons, Odd Fellows and the Independent Order of Good Templers. Eventually ballet and ballroom dancing academies were opened, as well as a private elocution school.

Thickly congested Chinatown on McCann Creek consisted of many shacks, opium dens and gambling houses. The richly colored joss house was gaily decorated with red lacquer, peacock feathers, pictures of fiery dragons and devils, and it contained an idol. In January 1878 the papers merged into the daily *Times-Review* and Tuscarora dominated county politics. Much livestock was raised on surrounding ranches.

Carlin, Battle Mountain and Elko on the Central Pacific vied for Tuscarora's bullion and freight trade, and over 200 oxen were employed to haul wagons from Elko. Six mills with an aggregate of eighty stamps processed ore from the district's most productive mine, the Grand Prize, as well as from the Navajo, Independence and Argenta

mines. Over $1.2 million in bullion was shipped in 1878, but in 1880 production fell to half that of the peak year. The 1880 census showed 1400 Americans living here, as well as ten mines and three mills in operation. Mines were especially active from 1882-84, and Tuscarora weathered the storm of low silver prices which prevailed late in the 19th century, but the attractive new booms downstate after 1900 led to a decline of the camp.

In 1907 a new company took over the Dexter mine and mill as well as dozens of other claims, but financial difficulties snuffed out the renewed effort. Other individuals have since tried to work the mines, but without success. Estimates of total production range from the recorded $9.4 million to a hearsay figure of $40 million. In either case over half of Elko County's 19th century production was made here. Old buildings remain as well as mines and mill stack.

FALCON, 12 miles west and north of SR 18 at a point 2 miles south of Tuscarora.

At the height of the Tuscarora boom prospectors searched surrounding country for similar rich districts. After silver finds in 1876 the Rock Creek district was organized. Two years later the Falcon post office was open for eight months and during 1879-81 silver ore was shipped to a mill in Tuscarora. A local stamp mill under construction at Falcon in 1884 was never finished. During the 1920s some mining was attemped, but results were discouraging because of the hardness of the rock.

MIDAS, originally Gold Circle, on SR 18 at a point 42 miles west of Tuscarora by graded road (62 miles west-northwest of Elko).

Gold discoveries in the summer of 1907 brought about a stampede to the Gold Circle district early the next year. The yellow stuff was said to be abundant; in fact, so many discoveries were made that all surrounding canyons seemed to have been showered with golden drops when the legendary Midas sprinkled his mineral garden. The camp was first called Gold Circle, but when the post office was established in November 1907 it was named Midas, as government officials felt that too many Nevada towns already had names prefixed with "gold."

In 1907 Midas was called Gold Circle because the district's new mines encircled the camp. The first settlers erected their tents (above) down the gulch from the Bamberger mine, the site of the first discovery.
(E. W. Darrah Collection)

Midas soon rose on a platted townsite. In February 1908 its streets were crowded with hopefuls waiting for spring mining to begin. (Dr. James Herz Collection)

Later in the year the principal street was clearly defined. The route to the main mines leads off the picture in the foreground right. The promotional townsite of Summit, two miles south, is shown in mid-background. It had a post office for over a year beginning in February 1908. Over the next three decades the district weathered many storms, but Midas lost its touch at the beginning of World War II. A few permanent residents remain. (Mrs Della Phillips Collection)

By the summer of 1908 about 2000 people were established in tents and frame cabins. A chamber of commerce and the Gold Circle *News* boosted the town; on the main street were rooming houses and hotels, restaurants and saloons, laundry and stores. For awhile the Gold Circle Club provided entertainment by giving vaudeville performances.

After the fall of 1908 Midas' golden touch vanished; the town had developed far ahead of the mines, and only 250 miners remained through that winter. This first attempt at permanence failed because the low quality of the ore and high shipping costs via wagon justified shipment of only high-grade. A couple of small mills were built after 1909, and the camp gained its second wind in 1915 after a fifty-ton cyanide mill began running. Midas prospered for seven years until this mill burned down and mining activity ceased.

The Gold Circle Consolidated Mines constructed a 75-ton mill in 1926, began operations the following spring and continued until the fall of 1929. Other operators were active until 1942. The mines produced $4.3 million with over half of it made during the 1915-1922 era.

CORNUCOPIA, 6 miles west and south of SR 11 at a point 4 miles west of its junction with SR 11A at Deep Creek (57 miles northwest of Elko).

Silver discoveries at the Leopard mine in August 1872 were followed by a stampede and the founding of a camp. Numerous locations soon covered the mineral belt and by November of the next year the young town, optimistically named after the mythological horn of plenty, was big enough to have a post office. Considerable excitement arose when a vein of $1000-a-ton ore was tapped early in 1874, and during that summer around a thousand silver seekers lived in the district. In the election that fall, Cornucopia polled about 400 votes.

Mining activity peaked in 1874-75 when the camp had five stores with mammoth stocks supplying the district's physical wants, a bakery, chophouse, drugstore, saloons, a thirty-room hotel and other lodging houses all doing a brisk business. A stage line from Tuscarora and Elko brought in additional newcomers; outgoing stages took isolated Cornucopians to the race track and bistros at Tuscarora.

On the south side of Deep Creek, 2½ miles below the camp, the principal mine, The Leopard, built a ten-stamp mill that regularly sent coachloads of silver bricks from the district. Late in the summer of 1875 the mill burned and that catastrophe, coupled with a boom that same year at Tuscarora, led to Cornucopia's decline. A replacement mill of double capacity was built a year later but failed to reverse the camp's downward trend, and in 1880 this mill too succumbed to flames. Only 174 people were counted in that year's census and the camp turned in about 1882, after a decade of mining had produced over $1 million mostly from the Leopard and Panther mines.

No revival took place during the early years of this century. Mill ruins are left below the townsite, still marked by stone buildings and foundations.

GOOD HOPE, approximately 21 miles west of SR 11 at a point 4 miles west of its junction with SR 11A at Deep Creek.

Silver was discovered on Chino Creek in 1878, a district was organized, and a collection of cabins made up the settlement of Good Hope. By 1884 a post office was established which lasted less than three years, and over $100,000 worth of ore was run through a five-stamp mill located 1½ miles below the main group of mines. Later production has been insignificant.

EDGEMONT, ¾ mile east of SR 11 at a point 14 miles west and north of its junction with SR 11A at Deep Creek.

Elko County's stagnant mining industry was briefly revived in the early 1890s by gold discoveries on the west flank of the Bull Run Mountains. As the Montana Gold Mining Co. proceeded with development, a small but active camp grew on the steep slopes around the operations, and by October 1901 remote Edgemont got its post office. Activity increased during the next year after Alex Burrell purchased the district's principal claims and installed a twenty-stamp mill, capable of treating sixty tons of ore daily. When the rest of Elko County boomed after 1905, Edgemont's Lucky Girl mine was for four years the county's largest producer.

Despite an occasional avalanche which disrupted operations, mining continued until 1917

204

The camp of Edgemont, precariously perched on the steep slope of the Bull Run Mountains, is shown during a renewal of activity in the late 1930s. In the valley below are important ranches.

Early in this century, ore for the mill at Edgemont was brought from the Edgemont mine, a quarter-mile away and 1200 feet higher, by way of a small aerial tramway. The mill operated irregularly for 15 years before it was buried in an avalanche in 1917.

(Both photos: Mrs. Della Phillips Collection)

Mill at Edgemont; Aerial Tram in Background, Nev.

when an unusually severe snowslide demolished the mill and the camp's principal buildings. With no local mill, the low-grade ores did not warrant shipment to distant mills for reduction and mining ceased. The post office closed October 1918. When a revival came during 1935-1942, a new company town with attractive wooden houses was built. Total production was $978,000. Buildings remain.

WHITE ROCK, west side of SR 11 at a point 18 miles west and north of its junction with SR 11A at Deep Creek.

This settlement had its origins sometime after a post office was established for nearby settlers in June 1871, and later in the decade the Tuscarora-Mountain City daily stage stopped here. Early in this century a store and saloon were open for nearby ranches and the area population was about 100. The post office was finally closed at the end of 1925. The site is situated on a private ranch; only a few foundations remain.

NORTH FORK, on east side of SR 51 at a point 52 miles north of Elko.

This small community on the North Fork of the Humboldt River had a post office as early as 1889 and by about 1910 had developed into a small hamlet with hotel, saloon and stage station in the midst of a stock-raising area which had about 75 people. Later a school and grocery store were added and for awhile a service station. Dances were held here. After about 1930 local services were gradually curtailed; the post office was discontinued in 1944 and now the place is abandoned.

CHARLESTON, 28 miles east and north of SR 51 via graded road at a point 4 miles north of North Fork.

Discovery of placer gold on Seventy-Six Creek near the southwestern base of Copper Mountain in 1876 led to the founding of a camp that was briefly called Mardis, four miles south of the new finds. The camp grew quickly and soon had several stores, hotel, icehouse, saloons and school.

Charleston gained a reputation for lawlessness. One time the sheriff of Elko, returning from an extended search for a lawbreaker, rode back home and supposedly boasted, "I didn't get him, but

I rode plumb through Charleston without being shot at!"

Perhaps the camp's toughest character was its co-founder, George Washington Mardis, a Bible-quoting teamster who preached forceful Old Testament interpretations to his faithful burro, "Samson." Eventually he bought a ranch, married and settled down to a prosperous life. He made regular trips to Elko, and on one occasion carried gold there for a Chinese storekeeper. Word leaked out that Mardis was carrying money, and as he left Charleston he was pursued and killed by a certain "six-toed Chinaman" who left a peculiar track on the hub of the wagon. A vigilante group soon found the assailant and gave him a speedy trial before hanging him.

Most mining ceased by 1883 or 1884, and for the next two decades the district passed under a cloud. A brighter era dawned in 1905, when the mines produced enough to support a five-stamp mill. Charleston gained a school, saloon, store and post office, but production was small and the camp folded. Another revival took place during 1932-37, but the mines are now silent. Two buildings are left on a private ranch.

BRUNO CITY, approximately 12 miles north-northwest of Charleston by road and trail.

Placer gold and silver veins were discovered near the Bruneau River in the spring of 1869. A district was organized but that summer the miners scattered to White Pine and Mountain City where prospects seemed better. Many returned a few months later, and after discovery of veins on a hill dubbed Silver Mountain, the district was reorganized. Bruno City was laid out east of the river and soon had a modest business center and a population of 122 according to the 1870 census. Because the rock was turning out well, the Elko paper thought that this camp would soon be lively, but it apparently died that fall.

JARBIDGE, via graded but often steep road, 48 miles east and north of SR 51 at a point 4 miles north of North Fork.

Rumors spread after a discovery of gold in the latter part of 1909 and by October fifty men had arrived and a mining district was speedily organized. Inflated reports in newspapers of February

Jarbidge was a boom camp of the first magnitude in the spring of 1910. Prospectors crowded the streets, and enterprising individuals offering food and lodging had set up tents. At an altitude of over 6000 feet, Jarbidge in 1910 consisted of a long string of tents on the banks of the Jarbidge River. More substantial wooden buildings soon replaced the canvas dwellings.

(Both photos: Northeastern Nevada Museum)

The Ja-ha-bich restaurant was named for a furtive man-eating giant known as Tsawhawbitts, whom the area Shoshones believed lurked in the canyon. Like Paul Bunyan, he could step across the turbulent Jarbidge River while going about capturing unwary tribesmen. He then stuffed them in a basket tied to his broad back and carried them to his lair in the crest of a nearby ridge. The camp's name, Jarbidge, is a corrupted Anglicized spelling of the giant's name. At the post office, prospectors eagerly awaited the arrival of the mail in hopes that money for a grubstake might have arrived.

(Both photos: Northeastern Nevada Museum)

This Jarbidge street scene was taken about the time that telephone service was extended to the camp. The initial rush had ended in 1910 but thereafter mining began in earnest. From a vantage point south of town (below), the main street in 1917 had the appearance of permanency. Many buildings shown here still stood a half century later. The Jarbidge River flows northward into Idaho, past the canyon in the background.

(Both photos: Getchell Library, University of Nevada)

and March 1910, indicating that the Bourne mine had over $27 million of gold in sight, brought a stampede and Jarbidge swelled to 1500 in six weeks' time. About 500 tents extended for three miles along the Jarbidge River and prospectors tramping about on snowshoes staked out over 500 claims by mid-April in the ground covered with snow often to a depth of 15 to 18 feet. But the initial excitement was quickly extinguished when the local crowd learned of the grossly exaggerated reports of the Bourne property. A mass exodus took place in May, leaving just a few hundred in camp by early summer.

After the snow melted in June, many ore-bearing ledges were uncovered. Wooden structures rapidly replaced drafty tent shelters, and a mill was hastily built to handle ore. The commercial street was lined with rudimentary hotels, restaurants and other mining camp businesses. Stage service was initiated from Twin Falls, Idaho and autos made the trip in only one day but horses had to pull them the last six miles of steep slopes into the camp. Pack horses brought in supplies not provided by nearby ranches, and some items were said to be sent to Jarbidge by parcel post, as one alert Boise merchant discovered that he was within a mailing zone close enough to allow shipment of groceries and supplies to Jarbidge at a cent a pound, half the prevailing freight rate by stage!

At the end of summer most men left the district to avoid the severe winter but early in 1911 Jarbidge again boomed and attained a population of 1200. Once more the district declined by fall and mining development was irregular until 1918, when the Elkoro Mining Co. bought the principal claims, set up a mill on which $250,000 was spent to bring electricity 73 miles from a source in Idaho, and began 14 years of large-scale production which continued until the Depression. Some work has continued until the present time. Total production at Jarbidge has exceeded $10 million in gold and silver.

The West's last stagecoach robbery occurred near here on a cold December night in 1916, when the Idaho stage was held up by a lone robber who killed the driver and escaped with important mail and over $3000 in cash. He propped the body up on the driver's seat, smearing his own hands with blood in doing so. Leaving tracks along the way, he scurried to a nearby river where he washed his hands and opened envelopes which he carelessly scattered. Soon he was caught, convicted of murder and sent to the state penitentiary on the basis of palm- and fingerprints on the envelopes. This case was one of the first in the nation in which this type of evidence was admissible in court.

Several cabins, stone ruins and about a dozen permanent residents remain in Nevada's most isolated important mining camp.

GOLD CREEK, via graded road 6 miles northeast of SR 51 at a point 65 miles north of Elko and 19 miles south of Mountain City.

After placer gold discoveries in August 1873 a huge influx of Chinese and some Americans came to sluice 6000 acres of gravel. A hotel, blacksmith shop and Chinese store were among the businesses established in a district and camp which took the name Island Mountain. The district's co-founder, "Manny" Penrod, whose mining experience also included ore discoveries on the Comstock in 1859, built a fine home.

The district was abandoned by 1890 but a wild mining rush began in 1895 when newly discovered open lodes were rumored to be very rich. The Gold Creek Mining Co. staked out a townsite just east of the older settlement, and soon graded streets were lined with an assortment of buildings including a three-story hotel, mercantile company, a dozen saloons, stores, lodging houses, post office and a stage line offering three runs a week to Elko. The camp's first frame structure housed the Gold Creek *News* edited by Charles Sain who already had two published books to his name and ran his third novel serially in the paper. Offices were opened by professional men including doctors, assayers, engineers and architects.

The most optimistic predicted that Gold Creek would be Nevada's largest city by 1896 or 1897. Dynamic as it was, the camp did not last more than a year or two, for rich veins were not found. The district was nearly deserted at century's end; the large hotel was moved to Mountain City about 1907; less than four dozen people were left by 1910; and by 1928 all buildings had been removed. A cemetery, a few cellars and a cement sidewalk slab identify the townsite, and placer tailings remain in surrounding canyons.

Less than a year after the initial rush to Gold Creek, substantial buildings had erupted at the townsite.
(John Zalac Collection)

After completion of the Central Pacific across northern Nevada in 1869, many Chinese took up mining at Gold Creek and other districts. This aged Oriental may have been one of the state's early arrivals.
(Northeastern Nevada Museum)

The placer fields at Gold Creek were washed by the use of hydraulic water pressure. The monitor, six to eight feet in length with a nozzle about four inches in diameter, cuts away the bank to reach the coarse valuable gravel beneath, as seen in the bottom of the bank beyond the men in the foreground. The stone-filled box (counterweight) behind the monitor made manual control easier.
(Mae McCubbin Collection)

ROWLAND, 27 miles north of SR 51 at a point 19 miles south of Mountain City.

Placer gold was mined in this vicinity as early as the 1870s and two mining districts were organized nearby, Alder and Gold Basin. A post office known as Bucasta was located just south of here from 1896 to 1898. The Rowland post office opened in March 1900 and a decade later about thirty people had settled here. The community then consisted of a general store, post office, school and a few log and frame dwellings. A cyanide mill was built in 1911, but it saw only limited use. During the 1920s and 1930s mining occasionally took place and the population of about two dozen was primarily engaged in stock raising. By 1942 all businesses had closed and today mill ruins and abandoned cabins remain.

IVADA, 3½ miles north-northeast of Rowland by road and trail.

After two prospectors found silver ledges in 1907, a few hundred other treasure seekers rushed to Taylor Creek Canyon to look for other prospects. A tent town sprang up and soon it contained a store, saloon and a restaurant run by Mulligan Mike, a habitual camp follower. With no road to camp, supplies packed in by horses were expensive. The camp never grew because the cost of taking ore out of here by pack horse ate up potential profits. Then when the Jarbidge boom hit the county in 1909-10, the few people still here left to participate in the new excitement. Nothing remains.

MOUNTAIN CITY, on SR 51 at a point 84 miles north of Elko.

Some gold mining activity started when Chinese placer miners began sluicing nearby ravines and hillsides in 1868 during and immediately after construction of the Central Pacific through eastern Nevada. Jesse Cope and other prospectors en route to White Pine from Silver City, Idaho, made both placer gold and lode silver discoveries early in 1869, and that spring a camp was founded and initially named Cope. A townsite called Mountain City was laid out, and lots sold for several hundred dollars to speculators. A $10,000 ditch diverted water from the Owyhee River to the placer ground, but when rich quartz ledges assaying several thousand dollars a ton were found late in the summer of 1869, placering was left to the Chinese.

An influx of several hundred miners in 1870 increased the population of the Cope district to over 1000, and by 1871-72 the camp contained over 200 adobe, frame, stone and log buildings as well as a few built of brick. Businesses included twenty saloons, a dozen hotels, six restaurants, two bakeries, two breweries, post office, bank, "hurdy-gurdy house" and a gambling emporium which featured a faro bank. Mountain City was one of the state's most prosperous camps because the miners worked their claims instead of making coyote holes and awaiting capital for development.

The district's first mill began running in the fall of 1869, and two others were soon built. The federal mining commissioner remarked in 1871 that few places in Nevada were a more inviting field for capital or energy and ability than Mountain City. But the closing of the Excelsior mine in 1873 signaled a decline, and a decade later operations virtually ceased after over $1 million had been produced. Thereafter the district wavered between prosperity and decay.

In 1898 the Mountain City *Times* briefly appeared, and early in this century during a significant revival three gold mills were built. The largest and longest revival began in 1932 when copper deposits were discovered at Rio Tinto (which see), and during 1938 the *Mail* was published weekly. Only a few old buildings are still left amid many newer occupied structures.

PATSVILLE on SR 51 at a point 2¼ miles south of Mountain City.

After copper mining began two miles west at Rio Tinto in 1932, the Copper King mine was discovered close to the Owyhee River, and Patsville started up near the new operation. Eventually this camp had a drug store, garage, boarding house, cafe, saloons and a thriving sporting house which served Mountain City and Rio Tinto. Patsville faded in 1947 and now only a cluster of wooden buildings remain.

RIO TINTO, 2 miles west of SR 51 at a point 2¼ miles south of Mountain City.

The moribund Mountain City district in 1932 revived through the persistence of S. Frank Hunt.

Mountain City (above) was a lesser supply point in 1930. As a mining camp it has led a checkered existence, enjoying several revivals with the introduction of new mining methods and the discovery of new ore bodies. Mountain City regained some vigor a few years later when copper was discovered at Rio Tinto (below). Early buildings are shown in this view of the west end of the camp. On the left are the garage, the commissary, the change room, and the shaft where S. F. Hunt made his strike. The main shaft buildings are on the hill to the right. *(Two photos: George Nelson Collection)*

Rio Tinto in 1940 was an orderly company town with neat attractive dwellings. The main shaft at the right leads to the high-grade copper deposit which kept the district booming for a decade and a half. Company buildings and storage areas (below) were located immediately to the left of the main shaft. The neatly stacked timber was used underground. (*Top: Earl A. Frantzen Collection; bottom: George Nelson Collection*)

Working without adequate financial backing, he uncovered a rich copper vein in 1931 climaxing a dozen years of painstaking exploration. The new find was christened Rio Tinto after large copper mines in Spain which predate the Romans. The Mountain City Copper Co., a subsidiary of Anaconda, bought the discovery and as development started the company town of Rio Tinto emerged. Wide tree-lined streets and rows of houses and apartments were built. Other facilities such as electricity, water, sewage system, movie theater, recreation center, grammar and high school and an athletic field attracted miners with families. Within five years after its discovery Rio Tinto was Nevada's second largest copper district and a total recorded output of $23 million was attained before the deposit was exhausted in 1947. Rio Tinto post office was no more after February of the next year. The large shell of the school dominates the site.

COLUMBIA, 1 mile north of SR 11A at a point 17 miles southwest of Mountain City via SR 51 and SR 11A.

Initial silver discoveries in the Bull Run district took place in 1867, and a year later the new finds attracted attention when the first shipment yielded $4000 a ton in silver. The district was organized in 1869, about 200 locations were made, and by 1871 a twenty-stamp mill handled production of the Infidel, Big Four and eight other active mines. Columbia soon became the headquarters for mining in the Centennial Mountains. Another mill was built in 1875 and by 1879 isolated Columbia had a post office. But conditions for operations were most trying, as bulky supplies had to be hauled more than 75 miles over crude wagon roads from Carlin on the Central Pacific. Burdensome transportation costs and faltering lodes disheartened many in 1881 and 1882, and they turned away to other fields. Four buildings remained in 1966.

AURA, on SR 11A at a point 19 miles southwest of Mountain City via SR 51 and SR 11A.

After the Bull Run district revived early in 1906 when gold was discovered, another boom was on and the townsite of Aura was platted in March, a mile and a half below Columbia which did not revive. Early in 1907 the young town had a saloon, general store, post office, the weekly *Concentrator*,

school, and several houses. Aura was the supply point for old and new mines on the east side of the Centennial Range, but as that year wore on operations slowed and then finally stopped because of the difficulty of obtaining capital for additional prospecting and development work. Some work was done in later years, especially during the Depression. Walls of one stone building still stand.

BULLION CITY, or Railroad City, 27 miles southwest of Elko via graded road.

After silver discoveries on the east flank of the Piñon Range in 1869, the Railroad mining district was organized, the name reflecting the miners' elation at being only 14 miles south of the newly completed Central Pacific. Within months the district's principal mines had been located in a crescent around the east side of Bunker Hill, and northeast of the workings rose the camp of Highland. During the early 1870s that camp had a hotel, assay office, store, butcher shop and stables. The more important town of Bullion City was platted two miles east, closer to water sources.

In 1870 a crude smelter was blown in at Bullion City but it operated inefficiently because of mismanagement and shoddy construction. Litigation almost forced the new district into oblivion as early as 1871, but the mines received new impetus in 1872 when the Empire City Mining Co. took over operations and built an efficient blast furnace that summer. A San Francisco firm soon built another smelter, and Bullion City flourished for the next decade. After 14 years of operations more than $3 million in silver, lead, copper and gold were produced, but in 1884 operations tailed off considerably and mining stopped entirely two years later when the price of copper dropped.

Interest revived in 1904 when the mines were reopened after their consolidation, and a new camp known as Bullion started up between the sites of Highland and Bullion City. A 7000-foot tunnel was built to tap the downward extension of known ore bodies on Bunker Hill so that operations could be carried on the year around. The Nevada Bunker Hill Mining Co. and its successors extracted limited amounts of ore during the next sixty years of intermittent operation. Rock walls of one smelter and the slag pile of another, foundations, and graves mark the site of Bullion City; rock ruins are left at Highland; and wooden cabins remain at the newer Bullion.

SHEPHERD'S STATION, 1 mile west of SR 46 at a point 19 miles south of Elko.

In the spring of 1869 George Shepherd (sometimes spelled Shepard) established a station on the South Fork of the Humboldt River, a station which within months became the most important hostel and first overnight stop south of Elko on the White Pine toll road. The proprietor gained a reputation for spreading a fine table and providing comfortable lodgings, especially for teamsters, and the dances that were held here early in the 1870s drew people from surrounding ranches. In March 1870 a post office known as Coral Hill was established here, or possibly a few miles east; it closed for good in 1877, though the station saw regular use well into the 1880s.

JIGGS, earlier Skelton, on SR 46 at a point 33 miles south of Elko.

Since the late 19th century this small community in Mound Valley has been the social center for ranchers in the surrounding valleys. Governor Bradley and others brought cattle here in the 1860s and Mound Station was a stop on Hill Beachey's toll road to White Pine. Post offices established through the years in this area have been named Dry Creek 1874-79, Mound Valley 1879-81, Skelton 1884-1911, Hylton 1911-13 and Jiggs since 1918. Early in this century the hamlet of Skelton had a hotel, community hall, school, saloon, a store with everything from aspirin to saddles, dwellings and about three dozen people. In the 1920s the local trade diminished in favor of Elko and original buildings still stand. Stamps continued to be sold and mail to be handled at Jiggs post office, perhaps named after the comic strip character in "Bringing Up Father."

JACOB'S WELL (White Pine County), approximately 10 miles south of SR 46 at a point 57 miles south of Elko.

Early in the 1860s, both the Pony Express and the Overland Mail built stations at this point in Huntington Valley, and the transcontinental telegraph line was strung through in 1861. A stage station on the Elko-Hamilton road was established here in 1869, but sometime before 1900 the station finally fell into disuse.

JOY (White Pine County), 25 miles east-southeast of SR 46 at a point 57 miles south of Elko.

Silver was discovered in Water Canyon in 1869, and a small camp formed about six years later in a ravine between Bald Mountain and South Bald Mountain, where mining activity centered. Freight was hauled into the camp from Elko and Halleck, each over eighty miles north. For the remainder of the century only one mine produced.

Additional properties opened in 1905 and this camp of fifty miners gained a post office the next year. Mining was never extensive because a few men held the choice mining properties. With good ground tied up, others could not get workable claims, and interest in Joy never developed. Insufficient capital and backing, great distances to mills and high transportation costs prevented earnest exploitation of the mines.

FORT RUBY (White Pine County), via Harrison Pass and Ruby Valley, 32 miles east and south of SR 46 at a point 37 miles south of Elko.
Designated "Hobson" on many road maps.

The first permanent settler in the south end of Ruby Valley was "Uncle Billy" Rogers, an old scout who had been sheriff of El Dorado County, California. He built a trading post and planted a garden here in 1859. This locality was chosen as a station site by the Pony Express in 1860 and the next year by the Overland Mail & Telegraph Co. Though the Pony Express ceased operations in October 1861, the Overland company continued its station through the 1860s. Ruby Valley post office opened here in April 1862.

It was soon evident that travelers and stages using the Overland mail route needed protection, for Indians were particularly hostile in this area, midway between Salt Lake City and Fort Churchill. The army established Fort Ruby in September 1862; a company of California volunteers arrived and at once began cutting timber for the construction of barracks and a storehouse in the six-square-mile reservation. Later that fall most of these men left for Fort Douglas near Salt Lake City, but a detachment remained behind.

Early in this century the store (above) at Jiggs sold dry goods, hardware, and miners' and ranchers' supplies. In this typical country store of that era, the post office was housed. *(John Dewar Collection)*

In the late 1860s the enlisted men's quarters on the west side of the parade grounds at Fort Ruby looked like a movie set. This fort gave Overland trail users full-time protection instead of occasional assistance from patrols sent from distant Fort Churchill in western Nevada. *(Bancroft Library)*

The fertile acres around Ruby Lake were suitable for cultivation of barley, oats and grain. Mormons in the area had many farms, but because their prices were considered exorbitant, the Overland company planted about 1000 acres of grain on a large farm east of the fort in 1865, employing as many as 300 men during peak periods to raise feed for animals. Potatoes, beets and other vegetables were also grown for use at Ruby Station and other Overland stations to the east and west. The local stopping point was one of the most flourishing and popular between Salt Lake City and western Nevada and here the stage-cramped traveler was served baked goods, fresh meat, fish, fowl and vegetables from the Overland farm. A small whiskey shop was a welcome site to the thirsty.

By 1869 the Shoshones had become less troublesome and traffic on the central Overland trail diminished on completion of the transcontinental railroad farther north. Fort Ruby, then named Camp Ruby, was abandoned that September and troops were transferred to Fort Halleck in Elko County. The great Overland farm was subdivided and sold to small operators; the festive coyote gamboled about the abandoned Overland station and jackrabbits burrowed in the flower garden.

In later years a ranch was established and Hobson post office was open nearby between 1902 and 1914. The ranch continues to use for storage a few buildings which date from the 1860s, although barrack structures on the parade ground have been reduced to foundations. Only rock remnants are left of the Overland stage station, and a spring and historical marker indicate the site of the Pony Express station. Several ditches have scarred the landscape where the Overland farm once was. Ask owner's permission to visit.

RUBY CITY, 1½ miles east of the Ruby Valley road at a point 9 miles south of its junction with SR 11 (30 miles east of Elko).

Early in 1915 a corporation of Utah Mormons conceived of the wildcat development of Ruby City in the northern part of Ruby Valley. A generous Homestead Act and continued talk of dry farming in eastern Nevada and Utah encouraged the scheme, and a townsite was platted that May. During the next month a grand opening dance was attended by dozens of people whose ears were filled with descriptions of the town's wonderful layout and a nearly completed canal, five miles long and ten feet wide, which was intended to bring in enough water for dry farming operations. The promoters named the principal streets after the ranchers, hoping that they would build homes in the new town and commute to their ranches.

Advertisements promising good soil and favorable climate enticed several dozen settlers, mostly Mormons, and the new town rapidly rose from the sagebrush. Soon Ruby City had a fine hotel, two school buildings, a Mormon church and Lurline post office. Unfortunately dry farming proved unsuccessful because of alkali in the soil, the short annual growing season — from about June 15 to September 15, and because so little water came through the magnificent ditch. In less than a year the scheme folded; fewer than a dozen buildings were erected in the town which consisted mainly of many tents scattered about. Only a few depressions and the famed ditch mark the site.

FORT HALLECK, 6 miles south of SR 11 at a point 11 miles southeast of its junction with I-80 at Halleck exit.

Established in 1867 at the base of the Ruby mountains to protect Central Pacific construction workers against Indian forays, Fort Halleck saw 19 years of service until 1886, long after the Indians had quieted down. The nine-square-mile military reservation contained a cantonment with two companies housed in several structures arranged around a parade ground. Officers' quarters consisted of frame and adobe buildings, and the enlisted men's barracks were built of adobe and logs. A bakery, kitchens, messhalls, hospital and unofficial post office were housed in other buildings. A contemporary travel guide described the fort as delightfully located, well watered and surrounded by thriving groves of cottonwoods.

The railroad station nearest the fort was appropriately named Halleck. Some troops were usually there, and from that station, government stores were freighted and post business was conducted. In the 1870s Halleck station had a post office, hotel, store, and saloons where "lingering death" and "blue ruin" were doled out to soldiers and travelers. Early in this century Halleck station grew to a village of 150 people, with a few stores

With the beautiful Ruby Mountains as a backdrop (above), the photographer with Wheeler's 1871 survey party captured Fort Halleck on film. From the left are the storehouse, surgeon's quarters, and the hospital. The center picture shows other buildings edging the parade grounds, while below are the officers' quarters. Though built only five years later, these buildings show a marked departure from the architecture at nearby Fort Ruby. *(Three photos: Smithsonian Institution)*

serving ranchers on the North Fork of the Humboldt River and in Ruby and Secret valleys. It is now little more than a siding.

After the fort was abandoned in 1886 the premises were not guarded and consequently no structures are left, but many cottonwood trees remain. A marker indicates the site.

DEETH, 1 mile south of I-80 at a point 33 miles east of Elko and 17 miles west of Wells.

After the Central Pacific began running past this point in 1869 a sidetrack station with telegraph was established. By the fall of 1875 a post office was opened for nearby ranches, and a decade later a tourist guide noted that a few buildings had clustered here. The weekly *Tidings* appeared in 1895, but the editor soon moved on to Elko.

As county-wide ranching and mining activity grew early in this century, shipping from here increased. During its early years Jarbidge received its supplies through Deeth, and a fast stage rushed people there for $10 by way of Charleston. The Western Pacific began running through Deeth in 1910, and early in that decade this community had another newspaper, the *Commonwealth*, mercantile stores, schools, Mormon church, blacksmith, livery stable, saloons, hotels, barber shop, and a population of 250. Many dairies and farms flourished in Starr Valley, and this lively cattle town also served as depot and trading center for ranchers in Ruby Valley, Mary's River, North Fork of the Humboldt River, and the Charleston and O'Neil country far to the north. A fire in 1915 destroyed two-thirds of the town, and as autos made Elko more accessible, Deeth declined. One store and several inhabited houses remain at this community which is noted throughout the county as one of the coldest places around.

METROPOLIS, 14 miles northwest of Wells, via graded road.

The New York-based Pacific Reclamation Co.'s scheme of building a city and surrounding it with farms looked like a good idea late in 1909. When the plan was on the drawing board the next year it looked even better. In the midst of over 40,000 acres of farms was to be a modern city of 7500. An office opened in Salt Lake City in the summer and the great reclamation project soon to rise on the Nevada desert was heavily publicized.

Streets, lots and two parks were staked out in 1911. The semi-monthly *Chronicle* began publication in September, boosting the sale of dry farm land at $10 to $15 an acre, irrigated land at $75, and town lots for from $100 to $300. Metropolis eventually had graded streets, broad cement sidewalks, hydrants and street lights in the four-block commercial district. Later that year the Southern Pacific built an eight-mile spur from its main line at Tulasco and erected an elaborate depot and a small park with trees.

A hundred-foot-high dam was built early in 1912, along with large canals and an expensive water distribution system for the town. A reservoir began to form behind the dam and land sales boomed; by the year's end about 700 eager colonists, over two-thirds Mormon, had settled in the vicinity. The town then had a post office and several businesses including a wagon factory, five saloons and a modern brick hotel costing about $75,000.

That same year farmers in Lovelock Valley initiated a suit enjoining the Pacific Reclamation Co. from using certain creeks in the headwaters of the Humboldt. A court decision allowed only enough water to irrigate about 4000 acres in the Metropolis vicinity. The irrigation ditches were proving unsatisfactory, too, in that they delivered too little water to many farmers and too much to others. Plagued by these and other difficulties, the company went into receivership in the spring of 1913; the promotional paper ceased publication that December.

Though a fine $25,000 brick school was opened in 1914, it was clear that the reclamation scheme was not successful. Farmers were moving away because of the water problems, which were compounded by several drought years, high interest rates charged buyers, litigation over water and land rights and general discontent. The farms that remained had more water available after the exodus and for the rest of the decade were successful in raising turkey-red wheat and potatoes as well as in dairying. In the early 1920s they shipped cream to Reno by railroad. Social life centered in the recreation hall with dances and parties, and at the hot springs where picnics and baseball were enjoyed.

Showplace of Metropolis was the Hotel Metropolis which after its formal opening early in January 1912 became the finest hotel between Reno and Ogden, Utah. It boasted all modern conveniences including steam heat, electric lights, a fine water system, billiard room, and a barber shop. Parties and dances held here were attended by people for miles around. *(Mrs. Myrtle Myles Collection)*

The Pacific Reclamation Co.'s grandiose scheme for cultivating thousands of acres of wheat was responsible for making Metropolis a thriving town. The dry farming activity declined as early as 1913, and by 1940 there was very little farming for most of the land had reverted to sage. Caving basements, empty ditches, and stone walls mark the site of this overpublicized town. *(Bud Triplitt, Wells Progress)*

221

Beginning about 1925 the town and farming activity steadily decreased. The Southern Pacific abandoned its branch that year. Buildings were moved away and land was abandoned. The famed hotel succumbed to fire in 1936; the post office closed in 1942 and the school was shut down five years later. No one lives in the town today, but about seven ranches are left.

CONTACT, ¾ mile west of US 93 at a point 50 miles north of Wells.

Ore discoveries in the early 1870s sparked no boom but did result in periodic shipments of gold and copper. A five-ton smelter built in 1897 ceased functioning after three test runs, but with a renewal of mining in 1905 Contact City was laid out below the older camp in a more favorable location near the Salmon Falls River. Businesses were established including a hotel, several saloons and a store. The weekly Contact *Miner* provided a voice beginning in 1913, and during World War I large amounts of copper were mined.

When the Union Pacific (Oregon Short Line) was built nearby in 1925, mining resumed, and between 1928 and 1930 Contact had 260 people, saloons, hotel and post office. Electric power and water were brought to the camp in anticipation of large mining expansion, but a depressed copper market shelved the camp's dreams of permanence. Thereafter Contact was relocated on US 93 and became a tourist stop.

COBRE, 2 miles west of SR 30 at a point 8 miles northeast of its junction with US 40 (I-80).

Cobre (Spanish for copper) was born when the Nevada Northern Railway decided to build its line to Ely from this point on the Southern Pacific instead of from Wells, as originally planned. Construction actually started in November 1905; by March 1906 Cobre had officially acquired the post office from nearby Toano. It was also anticipated that rails would be laid from a point four miles north of here to Twin Falls, Idaho.

This railroad junction town by 1910 had over sixty people, store, hotel, saloon, mercantile company, railroad station, and several houses in a neatly laid out townsite. For the next several decades Cobre remained alive with store and post office but as traffic on the N. N. dwindled Cobre

outlived its usefulness. In May 1956 the post office finally closed. Left are several cabins and a small population.

TOANO, or Toana, 2 miles northwest of Cobre.

Founded late in 1868 as a Central Pacific Railroad division point and eating station, Toano quickly became an important center for staging and freighting of supplies destined northward to Idaho and to eastern Nevada mining camps as far south as Pioche and Pahranagat. The new town which grew around the varied activity took its Indian name, meaning "black coated," from the mountain tops of the nearby Toana Range, dark in appearance due to a thick growth of cedar. The railroad soon erected repair shops and a 14-stall roundhouse. Large freight yards occupied several acres, and other businesses included saloons, hotel, boarding house, grocery store and post office. Many buildings were built of sandstone blocks quarried nearby, and this town of 250 people was regarded as one of the finest along the line.

Toano prospered until 1902-03 when railroad changes involving shortening of lines resulted in a rearrangement of railroad districts. The railroad dropped Toano as a repair depot and after completion of the Nevada Northern southward to Ely from nearby Cobre in 1906, many buildings were moved from here to the new junction point. Earlier that year the post office was removed. In later years when the Southern Pacific doubled its track, Toano's deserted stone buildings were destroyed but the cemetery remains nearby.

MONTELLO, on SR 30 at a point 24 miles northeast of its junction with US 40 (I-80).

Completion of the Southern Pacific's Lucin Cutoff across western Utah in 1904 bypassed its division point at Terrace, Utah. The new engine terminal was located at Bauvard (or Banvard), about ten miles into Nevada, and a post office opened there in June 1904. Houses were shipped on flatcars from Terrace to help start the new town, and some of the water came from springs to the south at a watering place and campground long used by the Indians and called by them Montello, meaning "rest" in their language.

In 1905 the Southern Pacific created the town of Montello, three miles northeast of Bauvard, as a

Cobre, a busy railroad community in 1910, was the place where Ely passengers from the Nevada Northern Railway made connections with the transcontinental Southern Pacific. This general view of Cobre (above) with the Pequop Mountains in the background shows the town when it was only five years old. Immense loads of baggage await transfer. The office crew at the Cobre depot relax from the day's work of processing baggage and freight. *(Three photos: E. R. Sanderson Collection)*

new division point and soon built shops and a seven-stall rectangular roundhouse. Here freight trains changed crews and helper engines were added for the haul over Pequop summit. The new town acquired stores, saloons, rooming house, hotel, restaurants and the Bauvard post office (which officially retained that name until early in 1912). Besides housing railroad personnel and their families, this town of 800 bustled as a shipping point for big cattle outfits and for the Utah Construction Co. which maintained a headquarters here. The community built a substantial high school.

In the 1920s Montello also served as supply point for the Delano mines, 36 miles north. Since then the population has steadily decreased, though the town continued to thrive until the advent of Diesel engines on the Southern Pacific early in the 1950s. Thereafter helper crews were no longer required, and personnel were transferred to Ogden and Carlin. Roundhouses and shops were removed a few years later, and now Montello is a sleepy town of about 150 to 200 people.

TECOMA, on SR 30 at a point 8 miles northeast of Montello.

A post office was established here as early as December 1871, and by the 1890s the community had a school, saloons, hotel, store and boarding house. Early in this century Tecoma was an important shipping point for the Sparks-Herrell Co. and for other ranches more than 100 miles away in Utah and Idaho; it also thrived as the railroad station for the nearby Jackson and other mines. The hotel burned in 1918; the post office closed three years later, and only shipping corrals remain.

BUEL, approximately 7 miles east of Montello.

Many locations were made after copper and silver discoveries in the Toana Range in June 1869; in the 1870s a tourist guide described the district as "populated." A local smelter treated the silver-lead ores, and bullion was also shipped to San Francisco. This camp, named for Col. David E. Buel of Austin fame, had a post office from 1871 to 1878, but died before 1880. Early in this century the district was known as Lucin, and copper mining encouraged the building of a railroad spur from Tecoma to connect with a cable tramway from the Copper Mountain mine. Over $1.7 million was pro-

duced before operations shut down in 1912, although occasional efforts kept the branch line open until 1940.

SHAFTER, 12 miles south of I-80 (US 40) at a point 36 miles southeast of Wells.

The Nevada Northern Railway established Bews siding here in 1906 and by November 1908, when the transcontinental Western Pacific began service to this point, a small community was beginning to form. Shafter post office had opened in August of that year, and the renamed community soon had a saloon, store of general merchandise, boarding house, restaurant and about thirty people. Shafter still functions as a railroad intersection point, but by 1957 all businesses including the post office had closed. Less than half a dozen people remain.

TOBAR, via graded roads 3¾ miles east of US 93 at a point 15 miles south of Wells.

When the Western Pacific laid its line across Elko County later in 1908, Tobar got its start as a construction camp. As the story goes, an enterprising man living in a tent nailed a tipsy sign reading "to bar" to a post and that name stuck to the settlement. Attempts at farming were soon under way and a post office was established in December 1911. A townsite was platted in May 1913 and a two-story frame hotel was built. The Elko paper proclaimed Tobar as the busiest spot in the county. A real estate broker from Salt Lake City proclaimed Tobar as the "home of the big red apple"; elaborate advertising lured people from as far away as Canada and the east coast to settle and dry farm in the desert. It was anticipated that 50,000 acres would be brought into cultivation and that Tobar would have 3000 people. The broker was believed to be selling public land and was brought to trial on the charge of defrauding through the mail. Eventually he was acquitted.

At its peak around 1916 Tobar had two saloons, a rooming house, hotel, hardware store, lumberyard, blacksmith shop, two mercantile stores, a school, post office and the *Sentinel*, which was replaced in July that year by the weekly *Times*. Tobar had become a trading center for at least a few hundred people and the shipping point for cattle from surrounding ranches in Clover Valley and for mines in the Spruce Mountain and other districts.

This general view of Contact, Elko County's northern outpost, shows the camp before 1930. *(Ida Le Nord Collection)*

In Montello's early years there were no saloons in the original townsite. This bar was opened on an adjacent section. Note the early slot machine which turned up poker hands on the reels. *(Mrs. Marjorie Dowler Collection)*

In 1905 the recently-completed Southern Pacific Clubhouse (Railroad Hotel) was a popular meeting place where travelers mixed with the townspeople of Montello. Dances and other recreations were held here, and a dining room occupied the center. At the left end was the town library and the upstairs rooms were rented by the day or week. *(Mrs. Marjorie Dowler Collection)*

This big red apple never grew at To-bar — nor were many acres transformed from sage to cropland. Flamboyant circulars and notices such as this one helped publicize the Tobar agricultural development. The camp of Sprucement (left) was on the west side of Spruce Mountain. Buildings at the Monarch mine in the Sprucemont district (below) are shown as they were in 1920. The mine was at an altitude of 8500 feet. *(Top: Nevada Historical Society; two others: U. S. Geological Survey)*

After World War I the settlement declined. From 1918 to 1921 both the name of the settlement and the post office were changed to Clover City. In the mid-1920s only a garage, school, post office, store and railroad station were left. The Western Pacific closed its station in the early 1930s and the Tobar post office finally closed in 1942. Only cellars remain amid weed-choked graded streets.

SPRUCEMONT, or Spruce Mount, via unimproved road 7 miles northeast of US 93 at a point 36 miles south of Wells.

In a setting of pine and spruce forest, the Latham mine was discovered in 1869, and because of satisfactory returns, prospectors searched the area for additional ledges. On the west slope of Spruce Mountain a camp was started during the next year, and with the development of five mines and construction of a smelter in 1871 the camp was relocated two miles eastward in a sheltered canyon near the smelter. The camp acquired livery stables, saloons, butcher shop, post office, blacksmith shop and a population of 200.

Operations ceased early in 1872 when the smelter could not handle the district's lead-silver ores satisfactorily, although work resumed at intervals until 1874. Other companies worked the mines with indifferent success, experimenting with new smelters to treat the ore, but by 1880 the camp had only fifty miners and seven businesses. Another attempt at mining early in 1907 was snuffed out by the national financial panic that year.

By the early 1930s the camp had revived, again with post office. Large annual outputs during World War II brought the district's total production to barely less than $3 million. One log building and ruins of a smelter remain at Sprucemont. At the Black Forest mine, almost four miles east via steep road, are the cookhouse, mill and cabins of a lead-silver producer active from the mid-1920s until 1942, when its camp also had a post office.

CURRIE, on US 93 at a point 62 miles south of Wells.

As early as the 1870s a freight station known as Bellinger's Spring and a ranch functioned here on the Toano-Cherry Creek road. A community called Currie developed during construction of the Nevada Northern Railway early in 1906 and the post office which was established that August is still open. By 1910 a depot and section house had been built, along with store, saloon, and hotel. Currie developed into a rail shipping point for sheep and cattle from nearby ranches, and about twenty people have lived here through the years. A school was also established and the state highway department has a maintenance station here.

DOLLY VARDEN, 3½ miles northwest of US 50A at a point 20 miles northeast of its junction with US 93 (68 miles southeast of Wells).

The Dolly Varden shown about 20 miles north of this location on many highway maps is a siding on the Nevada Northern Railway.

Silver-lead discoveries in 1869 led to the organization of a district and founding of a camp which took its name from a bewitching character in Charles Dickens' popular novel of the day, *Barnaby Rudge*. A smelter was erected the same year, but the ores were anything but promising, and only intermittent small efforts were made during the next several decades.

KINGSLEY, approximately 12 miles south of US 50A at a point 18 miles northeast of its junction with US 93 (78 miles southeast of Wells).

Elko County's first ore find was in the Antelope Mountains near here in December 1862. The district was reorganized by 1865 and two years later several claims were worked for copper, but in the early 1870s the camp was abandoned until a revival in this century. A mill built in 1909 was unsuccessful and soon shut down. At Kingsley all work was sporadic and of small extent.

Ely's early growth was stimulated by two booms. Though only a sagebrush village before 1887, it was selected as the seat of White Pine County that year because important county roads converged here. A boom then followed, and within two years, when the above picture was taken, a business district emerged and a courthouse and jail were built at a cost of $8500. In the 1890s and early 1900s Ely thrived as a ranching center and a gold camp, but after a big copper boom got under way in 1906, Ely soon became Nevada's largest copper-producing district. Substantially built business buildings were then erected, as shown below. *(Both: Charles D. Gallagher)*

Ely, Nevada.
Copyright 1908 by
Gallagher & Cutter

WHITE PINE COUNTY

The vicissitudes of mining are more evident here than in any other part of Nevada. Initial settlement came in 1868 with the rush to White Pine which centered at Hamilton, Treasure City, and Shermantown. A furious boom lasted two years, and by 1873 Cherry Creek briefly surpassed Hamilton. After 1876 Ward was the county's largest camp until Cherry Creek revived in 1880. When that camp faltered in 1883, Taylor was the liveliest camp until Ely gained prominence around 1890. Osceola was an important placer camp between 1880-1900.

Lane City rose in 1897, and large-scale copper mining which commenced at Ely beginning in 1905 continues to the present, a longevity not common in the industry. Only Black Horse, Cherry Creek, and Taylor revived early in this century. In the 1960s the Ward and Taylor districts were active, and smaller operators worked other mines.

ELY, at the junction of US 50, 6 and 93, 320 miles east of Reno, 190 miles southeast of Elko and 289 miles north of Las Vegas.

Though gold and silver may have been found here as early as 1864 or 1865, locations were not made until November 1867, when an Indian guided prospectors from Egan Canyon to gold deposits near Murry Creek. By March of the next year the Robinson district was organized, and soon a settlement was started at Mineral City (see Lane City). Until the mid-1870s, mining activity and population centered there, but the prevalent copper ore was looked upon with disfavor because it interfered with gold and silver mining processes then in use.

In the fall of 1878 a few cabins beside the Selby Copper Mining & Smelting Co. furnaces were called Ely City, named for Smith Ely, the company president. Though in November of that year a post office was established, a business district did not develop, and through the mid-1880s Ely was little more than a "jerkwater" stage station with a post office. In the four elections between 1880 and 1886, the district of which Ely is only a part averaged a mere eleven ballots cast, and mining during that period was only desultory.

Not until 1887, after the state legislature designated Ely as the seat of White Pine County, was a town started near the mouth of Robinson Canyon. The county offices required goods and services, and so businesses from throughout the county relocated here. Times were lively; there were no idle carpenters to be found and lots in the townsite were in brisk demand. A mill on Murry Creek treated gold from the Aultman mine. A race track three miles below town soon became a favorite gathering place. By October 1887 Wells, Fargo & Co. had set up shop, and in October 1888 the *White Pine News* moved here from Taylor, the "town which made Ely." The population by the end of that year was about 200.

These developments stimulated a renewal of mining. In 1889 a water-powered stamp mill began treating ore from nearby gold mines, but yields were small. During the 1890s some gold ore was

Aultman Street in Ely had become a smooth boulevard by the 1920s. The barber shop at the left had a bath house attached, and egg shampoos were also available. A pioneer hotel, the Oldfield (just beyond the Riepe building) was noted for its midnight dinners during big dances. After eating, most of the revelers returned to dance again until daylight. On the right was the Golden Rule store, the forerunner of J. C. Penney Co. In this later aerial view (below) Ely is in the foreground and East Ely is in the background. (*Charles D. Gallagher photos*)

freighted to Toano and profitably smelted in Salt Lake City. Local smelters erected to treat copper ore were so crude that it was impossible to handle the red metal on a commercial basis.

In 1900 Ed Gray and Dave Bartley took a lease and option on the Star Pointer and D. C. McDonald's Ruth claim. Mark Requa bought these properties in 1902 and formed the White Pine Copper Co. the following year. Through 1902 the district's total yield has been generously estimated at about $500,000, but beginning early in 1903 things began to happen. That same year the Giroux Consolidated Mining Co. was organized and one of its shafts showed promising ore at the 450-foot level. Smaller operators were also busy. Further experimentation took place in 1904. With talk of a railroad for the district and a large smelter to be built, a boom and a rush from throughout the West started in the spring of 1906.

A new entity the Nevada Consolidated Copper Co. under Requa had acquired properties of the White Pine Copper Co., the Boston & Nevada Copper Co. and other holdings. On the basis of their having over 26 million tons of ore in reserve, Requa began construction of the 140-mile Nevada Northern Railway late in 1905 from Cobre on the Southern Pacific main line.

Attracted by stories of the wealth and great opportunities of Ely, hundreds of people came and went during 1906. Real estate was quoted in the thousands, and Tex Rickard of Goldfield fame paid $15,000 for property in the center of town on which to build the Northern Hotel. For miles around, incoming prospectors eagerly took up claims formerly thought to be worthless. In the summer of 1906 a few thousand miners, prospectors and speculators crowded the streets, and the magic name of Ely was heard in the financial centers of the East.

On September 29, 1906, Mark Requa drove a copper spike, signifying completion of the Nevada Northern Railway. Yards and freight depot were located as they are today at Ely City (now East Ely). By year's end more than fifty mining companies had been organized, many of them with Ely-hyphenated names. The Steptoe Valley Mining & Smelting Co.'s big smelting facilities were under construction at nearby McGill (which see), and by the beginning of spring 1907 there were over 5000 people in the town. In May, Ely became incorporated to handle the growing problems of the burgeoning town.

The national financial panic in the fall of 1907 dampened the boom and most small companies failed. But completion of the smelter at McGill in May 1908 starated a new era for the district. Production jumped from $2,363 in 1907 to over $2 million in 1908 to an early peak of $26.4 million in 1917. Three years previously the Consolidated Coppermines Co. had taken over the Giroux and other small properties and remodeled the concentrating plant. The town meanwhile experienced a rapid growth. In 1914 it had electric lights, two banks, stores of all kinds, a brewery, an ice plant, the *Ely Daily Mining Expositor,* two other weeklies, and schools and churches.

Because of the low price of copper after World War I, the Consolidated Coppermines Co. closed down operations in 1920, and during the next year the Nevada Consolidated followed suit. The latter resumed operations the next year, as did its rival after reorganization as the Consolidated Coppermines *Corporation.* Healthy development then followed, and during 1924-30 production of the two companies totaled over $100 million.

In 1933 a new entity, the Nevada Consolidated Copper *Corporation,* came into being when the Kennecott Copper Corporation, which had stock interests in the former company as early as 1915, acquired full ownership of the Nevada Consolidated Copper Co. Ten years later Kennecott's properties around Ely were given their present name — the Nevada Mines Division of the Kennecott Copper Corporation. In 1958 that company acquired virtual control of all mines in the area when it bought out the property of the Consolidated Coppermines Corporation. The total yield has been over $1 billion, more than twice that of the famous Comstock Lode.

Though mining and processing copper dominates the town's economy, Ely is also sustained by ranching and tourism. In the last forty years population has remained relatively stable at about 4000. Today Ely also serves as the supply and distribution point for many eastern Nevada mines and settlements.

231

LANE CITY, earlier Mineral City and Robinson Canyon, north side of US 50 at a point 3 miles northwest of Ely.

An Indian showed a prospecting party from Egan Canyon the location of silver-bearing rock in November 1867; the Robinson mining district was organized the next March and a camp started up taking the name Mineral City. A furnace and a ten-stamp mill erected in 1869 handled local ores. Completion of the Central Pacific stimulated Robinson and other mining districts, and by 1870 the population reached 400, but later that year miners left because of low-grade ores. By 1872 Mineral City revived with mercantile stores, post office, express office, six saloons, hotels, restaurants, livery stables, four boarding houses, blacksmith shop, and a floating population of nearly 600 people. A tri-weekly stage ran to Hamilton. However, by 1876 illusions of rich mines vanished, the camp declined, and the post office closed.

For the rest of the century production was quite sporadic, and most of the time Mineral City was deserted. In 1896 Charles Lane, an eastern capitalist, bought underdeveloped claims because, he said, spirits told him of great wealth to be found here. He invested over $168,000 in building a water ditch, power plant and a 100-ton cyanide mill which began running in March 1902, and the camp took the name Lane City. Evidently the spirits misled Lane, because after less than five years of sinking shafts no large gold vein was struck and the ore that was mined would not respond to cyanidization.

The wooden and rock buildings on the site belong to this century.

RUTH, via SR 44, 2 miles southwest of its junction with US 50 at a point 5 miles northwest of Ely.

Ore was discovered at the Ruth claim just before 1900, and exploration and development after 1903 led to the founding of a settlement of tents and shacks near the main mine. In 1904 the Nevada Consolidated Copper Co. began explorations in earnest after building an experimental mill at the mouth of the main shaft. During the next year the company acquired Copper Flat and adjacent properties. With the increased development, Ruth by 1905 had a modest commercial district which included a post office that was established in February 1904.

Robinson Canyon has been the scene of mining for over a century. Lane City grew around the Chainman mine and mill early in this century, and by 1907 or 1908, when this picture was taken, a few businesses had opened. Most supplies were obtained in Ely, over the low hills down the canyon in the background to the left. *(Charles D. Gallagher Collection)*

A boarding house, bunkhouses, a hospital and other company buildings were built, and all utilities were provided for by the Nevada Consolidated. Ruth soon became the second largest company town in the district, dwarfed only by McGill, and in 1910 this camp of about 500 was considered a pleasant place to live. The population more than doubled during the next decade.

At first, the major copper deposits of the Nevada Consolidated were mined underground, but in the summer of 1907 steam shovels began stripping the overburden from the area above the Eureka mine. Within three years a large oval pit had taken shape, and in 1916 it was combined with a nearby pit to form the large Liberty pit. The Ruth mine continued to be developed underground.

Until 1958 the Liberty pit was partly owned by the Kennecott Copper Corporation (Nevada Consolidated Copper Corporation before 1943) and the Consolidated Coppermines, but in that year Kennecott acquired full ownership. Inside the pit were fourteen miles of railroad which operated until pit trains were replaced in 1958 by trucks.

The town of Ruth attained its peak population of over 2,200 people just before the Depression. Scattered over the hillsides were attractive houses which in many cases had to be moved when mining operations were extended. Around 1955 all buildings were relocated in the present site called New Ruth to allow for block caving of ore in the new Deep Ruth shaft. In 1970 about 600 people lived at Ruth, while at the old site is the Ruth pit. That huge excavation, which was started in June 1968, will by 1971 become the center of Kennecott mining operations after removal of sixty million tons of overburden.

Scattered in the foreground is the migratory town of Ruth, shown here in the late 1950s when it was moved for the fifth time to allow expansion of the Liberty pit. When abandoned in 1967 that famed operation was more than a mile long, about ⅝ of a mile wide and nearly 1000 feet deep. It was started in 1906 when this low-cost method of mining was found to be more feasible than mining copper underground. Beyond the pit are the towns of Reipetown and Kimberly. *(Kennecott Copper Corporation)*

In these two photos of pit operations at Ruth, over a half century of excavation techniques are spanned. The three-ton steam shovels (above) were used in the Liberty pit in 1910. To loosen the copper ore, great charges of explosives are set off in the pit. Many holes are drilled and filled with explosives. All are connected electrically and set off simultaneously. The huge blasts shatter thousands of tons of ore which is then hauled by trucks to the railroad, which delivers it to the concentrator at McGill. *(Both photos: Kennecott Copper Corporation)*

Kitty's place in Reipetown was established before the days of piped-in water. This combination bar and dance hall was staffed nightly by women who lived in cabins at the back. *(Effie Read Collection)*

REIPETOWN, or Riepetown, via paved SR 44, 3 miles southwest of its junction with US 50 at a point 5 miles northwest of Ely.

Richard Reipe laid out a townsite in December 1907 which quickly had a busy boulevard of saloons, dance halls and gambling clubs patronized by miners from nearby Kimberly and Ruth. By mid-1909 Reipetown had gained the distinction of being the wettest town in the county and one of the state's toughest communities. It thrived on liquor, gambling and prostitution, and knifings, robberies, and fist fights were regular occurrences. Numerous cribs and 16 saloons adequately served the district.

A post office opened in 1909 for three years. A small frame building served as a jail to hold Reipe-town's most exuberant patrons, but its first occupants easily escaped one night by removing the floor and mining for their liberty. A fire wiped out the saloon district in 1917 and Reipetown's days of easy money were thought to be numbered. But because about 200 people had established homes, the town rose from the ashes and again became a seat of pleasure after saloons and restricted districts were reopened. When the county began imposing strict controls for liquor licenses for saloons late in 1917, Reipetown incorporated so that it could liberally issue its own licenses. The town was forced to disincorporate in 1919 by act of the state legislature. Saloons were eliminated early the next year by the 18th Amendment, but bootleg joints maintained Reipetown's reputation as a wide-open town. Old shacks remain amid occupied homes.

KIMBERLY, at terminus of SR 44, 4 miles west of its junction with US 50 at a point 5 miles northwest of Ely.

The Ely district's oldest copper properties are on a hill called Pilot Knob, immediately north of Kimberly, but not until the turn of the century were they developed. The Giroux Consolidated Mining Co. organized in 1903 took over Pilot Knob to begin development, and amid the activity the company town of Kimberly sprang up, taking its name from an old Pilot Knob financier.

By the time the Nevada Northern Railway entered the district in September 1906, Kimberly had a post office, general store, boarding house, and dwellings. During the next year the railroad extended its line past Kimberly, and production increased. By 1910 this little camp had its own newspaper, the Kimberly News.

When the Consolidated Copper Co. acquired Giroux's holdings in 1914, Kimberly, with its neat white-painted barracks and houses, became one of the district's attractive company camps. In the mid-1920s this camp had a school, hospital, Nevada Northern depot, bunkhouses, boarding houses and dwellings for about 500 people. The Depression slowed operations early in the 1930s, and after further declines the Kennecott corporation bought out all mines near Kimberly as well as the townsite around 1958. Only dumps indicate where Kimberly once was.

VETERAN, ¼ mile west of Kimberly.

At the shaft of the Cumberland-Ely Copper Co. this camp sprang up about 1906 and soon had about fifty buildings, among them a three-story office building, boarding house, and bunkhouses. It became the western terminus of the Nevada Northern Railway and after 1908 that line's depot was prominent in the local landscape. Veteran never grew large and when operations ceased at the Veteran shaft in 1914, the camp's buildings were moved to Ruth.

McGILL, on US 93, 12 miles north of Ely.

Among the company-owned towns of the Ely district, McGill on the east side of Steptoe Valley was the most important because here the Steptoe Valley Mining & Smelter Co. erected its smelter during 1906-08 to process copper ores from the mines west of Ely. Initially, the company planned to build a 1500-ton smelter at Ely City (East Ely), but early in 1906 the McGill site was selected because water was available in quantity from nearby Duck Creek. Also, the Cumberland & Ely, which owned a half interest in the smelter, had eight square miles of land here which was ample for the building of a tailings pond.

After plant construction began in the fall of the year, a cluster of drafty tents and company-owned buildings below the mill became known as McGill, named for a local ranch owner. During 1907 the

---

The camp of Veteran, shown here after the modern buildings were built in 1909-10, was pleasantly situated at the west end of the Ely district. At the left is the six-compartment Veteran shaft. Unfortunately, the Veteran mine proved to be a disappointment during early development, and the expensive underground operations here caused work to close down in 1914. At a later date, this was the scene of the famous Veteran pit. (Charles Gallagher photo)

In McGill's Greek tent suburb in 1908, laborers had to sleep ten to a building. The main part of town, then also known as Smelter, is in background left. The Greek area was soon supplanted by modern residences. Mid-20th century McGill and the mill and smelter are shown below. The trees planted in the early 1930s hide most residences. To the right of the town are large tailing ponds in which the residue from the concentrator is deposited. *(Top: Charles D. Gallagher photo; bottom: Kennecott Copper Corporation)*

The concentrator and smelter at McGill is Nevada's largest single industrial unit. In the grinding section (left) the ball mills reduce ore to a thin pulp which is then treated by flotation to remove the valuable minerals. (*Kennecott Copper Corporation*)

Above the concentrator at McGill was the famous 1720-foot-long hiline trestle, shown before a fire destroyed it. To the left of the tiered concentrator is the smelter, where reverberatory furnaces and Bessemer converters make the concentrates into blister copper which is then shipped to refineries elsewhere. (*Mrs. Nelda Cole Collection*)

Steptoe Valley Co. built modern quarters for company officials and comfortable concrete houses for several of its skilled employees. A few stores opened their doors, and a boarding house, bank and saloon were built. The post office, which had been established in 1891 when McGill was a ranch, was then briefly known as Smelter.

Beginning in May 1908, the mill began processing 8000 tons of ore daily, though by World War I capacity was increased to 14,000 tons. Later in 1908 the company built many low-cost wooden houses, and during the next year a modern Nevada Northern Railway depot began serving the town. By 1910 McGill, with a population of nearly 2000, supported many businesses, including the weekly paper *Copper Ore*. Later in the decade McGill had surpassed Ely as the county's largest town, and the census of 1920 showed that there were 2,850 permanent residents.

In July 1922 the huge concentrator covering about nine acres was completely burned at an estimated loss of nearly $2 million. It was soon rebuilt however. By 1930 this trim, well-built town had about 3000 people, over half of whom were employed at the mill and smelter. During the Depression those facilities ran in regular cycles of two weeks of operations and then shut down for four weeks. The Nevada Northern Railway continued regular shipment of immense tonnages of ore from Ruth and Kimberly to the smelter which in the late 1930s was again treating 14,000 tons of ore daily.

World War II stimulated production which was maintained at a high level through the mid-1950s. Since 1930 the town of McGill has steadily lost population, but about 2000 people made their homes here in 1970.

STEPTOE CITY, a half-mile east of US 93 at a point ¾ mile north of McGill.

The Steptoe shown on many maps, about 10 miles northwest of here is a ranch.

After the orderly milling town of McGill was established in 1907, three fringe communities known as Smelterville, Ragdump and Steptoe City emerged nearby, all containing saloons, dance halls, gambling dens and cribs. Smelterville, two miles southwest of McGill, rose on a platted townsite, and Ragdump, two miles north of McGill, initially grew to be the biggest of the three cities of pleasure. Ragdump had four dance halls which offered free round-trip buggy shuttle service from McGill.

Lead was mined in the canyons east of Steptoe City and that city had stores, Miners' Union hall and school in addition to its allotment of saloons, dance halls and women. In the spring of 1909 a grand jury investigated the prostitution, numerous beatings and robberies in the three communities, but not until 1912 was anything else done about the situation. In that year federal agents stunned Ragdump by ending an interstate white slave traffic with the arrest of several persons from that community. Two years later an aroused public citizenry in McGill and Ely made county officials refuse to renew licenses for Ragdump and that sinful burg quickly expired.

Steptoe City lived on and was occasionally populated with McGill workers when housing at the mill town ran short. A few individuals built modest homes from time to time and rented them at low prices. During the early 1920s Steptoe City had businesses, community church and 150 people, but most buildings went up in smoke in 1926 when a fire visited the town. A few people have always lived here amid the old houses and foundations.

BLAINE, 21 miles west and north of US 93 at a point ¾ mile north of McGill.

Prospecting was lively on the eastern slope of the Egan Range in the mid-1870s and the Granite mining district was founded, but the gold ore would not pay and the district was largely abandoned. Additional discoveries were made in 1894 and the ore was worked at a five-stamp mill on the nearby Campbell ranch. The nearest post office was Steptoe on the west side of Steptoe Valley.

Governor Denver Dickerson and his associates sparked a revival in March 1908 by developing the Blaine silver mine. His Ely *Mining Expositor* that month exclaimed, "Come, come to Granite. Come on foot or come on horseback, but come, come; Blaine is the town." A few hundred men rushed here and a camp rose with saloons, assay office, boarding house, blacksmith shop and stage service to Ely. The boom soon subsided though some activity continued until 1918. Mining again took place at the end of the 1930s.

RUBY HILL, or Rubyville, 7 miles east of US 93 at a point 17 miles north of McGill (33 miles north-northeast of Ely).

The Ruby Hill district was organized about 1871 after silver discoveries on the top of the Schell Creek Range, and a small camp with mill was active briefly and in later years. Fallen-down log ruins are left.

SCHELLBOURNE, a half-mile east of SR 2 at a point 3 miles east of its junction with US 93 (43 miles north of Ely).

Schellbourne led three lives — station, fort, mining camp. The Pony Express established Schell Creek Station with corral and station house in the spring of 1860. When the Pony Express ceased running 18 months later, Schell Creek became a minor stock exchange station and inn for Overland stages. This place briefly took the name Fort Schellbourne in 1862 after a detachment of troops camped here to head off troublesome Indians who harassed the stages and the mails. As the decade wore on things quieted down; the Indians were subdued and the troops were transferred elsewhere; and the stage station saw less use after 1869 after completion of the Central Pacific further north.

Gold discoveries in the surrounding hills in 1869 led to the founding of a mining camp two years later. A post office was established in December 1871 and in July of the next year the Schell Creek *Prospect* began weekly publication. Schellbourne got off to a fine start and had over 300 people that year, but its hopes were blasted away by the sensational discoveries at Cherry Creek, ten miles west across Steptoe Valley at the end of 1872. The new boom drained all but a few people even though Schellbourne's promising silver ledges had been scarcely worked. Houses and machinery were hauled overnight to Cherry Creek. Meanwhile, a few hopefuls stood by for capital to revive the district. Later in the 1870s mines resumed production to feed a five-stamp mill and the camp was lively, but by 1880 Schellbourne had declined to fifty inhabitants. Stone and log buildings remain in a tree-studded area — a good campsite with plenty of cool water.

TUNGSTONIA, 22 miles southeast of SR 2 at a point 21 miles east of its junction with US 93 (47 miles northeast of Ely).

After employees of the Overland Mail Co. discovered silver ore sometime in the 1860s, a district was founded in 1868 which eventually took the name of Eagle. It was reorganized twice before the Glencoe mine began operations in the early 1880s, and a camp called Glencoe had a post office from 1891 to 1894. The district's real importance came after discovery of tungsten in 1910. Several properties then began opening up and in 1915 a tungsten mill was built. During the next year two Utah firms also began construction of mills of which one was completed, and the tent and wooden town of Tungstonia had a post office beginning in January 1917. But when World War I was over the price of tungsten dropped and the camp died. Mill ruins are left.

SIEGEL, earlier Centerville, 4 miles west of the Spring Valley road at a point 3 miles south of its junction with SR 2 (38 miles north of Ely).

Silver mining on the east flank of the Schell Creek Range on Siegel Creek early in the 1870s gave rise to the camp of Centerville which lasted intermittently through the 1880s. Early in this century a Utah financier began renewed operations and the camp that was named for him had a post office during most of 1907-08. Stone ruins remain.

AURUM, 3 miles west-southwest of the Spring Valley road at a point 3½ miles south of its junction with SR 2 (40 miles northeast of Ely).

The district was organized in 1871 during an era of much prospecting on the east flank of the Schell Creek Range, and soon the new gold mines in Silver Canyon gave birth to the camp of Aurum which contained two boarding houses, saloons, blacksmith shop, store and a ten-stamp mill. But the mines did not live up to expectations and most of the ore ran low-grade, ending Aurum's lackluster career in the early 1880s, except for sporadic activity in later years.

Mail service had been provided by a special run from nearby Schellbourne before Aurum post office opened in Spring Valley below and south of the mining camp. Aurum post office ended in 1938. Mill ruins, foundations and cemetery remain.

Ranching and occasional mining are still carried on near Schellbourne. Prominent in this winter scene is a former warehouse or store, incorrectly thought to have been a Pony Express station. *(Gerald "Casey" Fisher Collection)*

Siegel in 1918 after its abandonment had log houses with sod roofs. These buildings have long since been removed. *(U. S. Geological Survey)*

MUNCY, 2 miles west of the Spring Valley road at a point 13 miles south of its junction with SR 2 (32 miles northeast of Ely).

During the late 1870s and early 1880s the mines on Muncy Creek gave promise of being a good copper district, and the camp had a post office beginning July 1882 until 1898 and again in 1909-11 when the mines again made a small showing.

PIERMONT, 2½ miles west of the Spring Valley road at a point 21 miles south of its junction with SR 2.

Little work was done after the district's organization in July 1869 until a San Francisco company purchased half-interest in many locations after rich silver discoveries in the spring of 1871. A camp then formed which at its peak in 1872 had a ten-stamp mill and about 400 inhabitants. But by the end of 1873 Piermont had played out, though some work was done during World War I, in the 1920s, and just before World War II. Log cabins and mill foundations remain.

CHERRY CREEK, at western terminus of SR 35, 9 miles west of its junction with US 93 at a point 45 miles north of Ely.

After the White Pine district faltered, Cherry Creek led the county in mineral production from 1873-75 and 1880-83. Initial silver discoveries in October 1872 brought an immediate influx of prospectors, and the next spring Cherry Creek rose on a platted townsite at the mouth of Cherry Creek Canyon. The new camp soon became the county's largest, with a business district which included a Wells Fargo agency and post office after June 1873. The election of 1874 reflected the town's remarkable growth; over 500 ballots were cast that November. During 1875 the camp declined, but the district remained a somewhat steady producer and the 1880 census showed 639 permanent residents.

After rich new veins were uncovered among older workings in the spring of 1880, another boom was under way, and in only a few months' time the population streaked to 1500 or 1800. The Star, Exchequer, Teacup, Grey Eagle and other mines kept at least three local mills busy. Several merchants relocated here in 1881 and the White Pine *News* moved in from Hamilton on New Year's Day. The town's social calendar reflected the great ac-

tivity of the early 1880s; people from as far as modern Wells and Ely attended local banquets and dances. The jockey club sponsored seasonal horse races at the track three miles south, and the town also boasted a coursing and rifle club.

Cherry Creek unsuccessfully challenged Hamilton for the county seat in 1882, and then the district crashed early the next year. Production practically ceased within another decade, but the district revived during 1905-08 and in later years, especially 1935-1940. Estimates of production range up to $20 million. Less than a dozen people remain to tell tales of the town's lively past, and these yarns linger around several old stores including assay office, jail, saloons.

EGAN CANYON, 5 miles southwest of Cherry Creek.

Named for Howard Egan who pioneered a mail service through here in the 1850s, Egan Canyon was the site of a Pony Express station on a meadow at its west end. Here, too, the Overland Mail Co. had a station in the early 1860s. Gold veins were tapped in 1863 by a company of California volunteer soldiers and in the fall of that year the Egan mining district was organized, the first in eastern Nevada. In 1864 the Gilligan mine began operations after building a five-stamp mill at the east entrance of the canyon.

A year later a second company erected a ten-stamp mill and began mining and by 1865 Egan village contained stores, blacksmith, post office, school and several houses. The district's two companies merged in September 1866 to form the Social & Steptoe Mining Co., which operated until late in 1868, producing $80,000. The next year, after completion of the Central Pacific Railroad, the Overland stages stopped running through the canyon. By this time virtually all mining activity also had ceased.

Egan Canyon revived during 1873-76, after discovery of silver at Cherry Creek, and made regular bullion shipments. Again in 1880 the camp began another two-year reincarnation when Cherry Creek had its second boom. By 1883 the district was nearly finished and after the demonetization of silver a decade later operations ceased. Later road building and small mining attempts during this century have obliterated the site.

Around the turn of the century, Cherry Creek was still one of the county's more productive camps. The two-story Masonic hall is prominent in the town.

Bicycling was a fashionable pastime in Cherry Creek in the early 1900s. Cyclists considered riding horses was for the lower classes.

In 1878 the twenty stamps of the Star mill (bottom) began to drop on ores hauled from the hills in the background. A constant flow of bullion continued until 1883, when mining declined. The mill became the property of Wells, Fargo & Co. and ran only occasionally thereafter. *(Three photos: Gerald "Casey" Fisher Collection)*

False-fronted buildings were typical on the business streets of Cherry Creek. Unlike other large White Pine County boom towns, Cherry Creek has managed to stay alive through the years because of periodic revivals when mines were reopened.

During the last century, Cherry Creek was the county's most important social center. In the early morning, happy revelers (below) decide to hunt rabbits after dancing all night in the large two-story dance hall. These men were probably from towns and ranches several hours distant; and when they came to Cherry Creek for the dances, they stayed a day or two before returning home. *(Both photos: Gerald "Casey" Fisher Collection)*

In 1898 Cherry Creek still looked like a firmly established town, although the decline of the camp had started fifteen years earlier. Most of these buildings met their end when they were destroyed by fire in February 1901. (Bud Triplitt, *Wells Progress*)

"Let's have a drink," was the most common expression in a mining camp. At the Elk Saloon in Cherry Creek, it was possible for a hard-working drinking man to think of himself as a wealthy mine owner for the price of a few beers. Why be a pauper when you can be a millionaire for a dollar? (*Gerald "Casey" Fisher Collection*)

Leishmann's mill (above), operating around 1916 and the Stewart mill in Egan Canyon (below) were two of the mining operations near Cherry Creek. *(Two photos: William A. Kornmayer Collection)*

BUTTE STATION, approximately 22 miles west of Cherry Creek via Egan Canyon.

Initially the Pony Express built a station here in the spring of 1860 and during 1861-69 the Overland Mail & Telegraph Co. also had a station. Maintaining a station in the desert was as monotonous and lonesome as it was dangerous. The company agent received $50 a month in gold to manage the station and to give flour, bacon or other food to passing Indians, keeping the peace at any price. A hostler cared for horses and helped harness and change teams after coaches arrived. An Indian greased and cleaned harnesses.

Sir Richard Burton stopped here in the fall of 1860 and described this typical station in his diary, calling it "Robber's Roost." The thirty-foot-long walls were made of logs, sandstone and big limestone slabs compacted with mud, and the roof was of split cedar trunks. Portholes served as windows. Behind the house was a corral of rails and a shed.

A canvas partition cut the inside into unequal parts with one section containing two bunks, standing bedsteads of poles, all heaped with ragged coverings, probably army blankets and buffalo robes. Underneath were saddles, harnesses and straps, clothes and several sacks of grain and food kept off the earthen floor by logs. The uneven unswept floor was a sea of mud in one corner because part of a spring oozed through one wall. A fireplace occupied half of another wall.

Chairs consisted of posts mounted on four legs and stools with reniform seats. Rough dressed planks served as tables. The walls were pegged to hold spurs and pistols, whips, knives and leggings. A niche over the door held a coffee mill, while a nearby shelf contained a tin skillet and dipper. A handful of gravel and evaporation served as soap and towel. Carelessly strewn about the room were rifles, pistols, ax, saw, hammer, large borers and chisel. There was no sign of a Bible, Shakespeare or Milton.

Only foundations now mark the site.

HUNTER, 19 miles north of US 50 at a point 21 miles west of Ely.

Lead and silver discoveries on the west flank of the Egan Range late in 1871 ultimately attracted a small camp which by 1877 contained a post office, half a dozen saloons, blacksmith shop, three restaurants, two general stores and about forty houses. After 1884 the mines lay idle until about 1905 when the district resumed limited activity for another four years. During the 1920s a bootlegger operated a still, but today not a drop of liquor can be bought anywhere within thirty miles. Smelter ruins and building remnants mark the site.

ROUND SPRING, 1¾ miles south of US 50 at a point 36 miles west of Ely.

During the 1870s and early 1880s this wayside inn was also a toll station on the road from the eastern part of the county into Hamilton, and here travelers had to pay tribute in passing and repassing. Only the spring remains.

HAMILTON, 11 miles south of US 50 at a point 36 miles west of Ely.

After discovery of rich silver lodes on Treasure Hill late in 1867, the newly formed White Pine district needed a town with a desirable location. In May 1868 a promoter named Hamilton laid out a townsite near a campground which was dubbed Cave City because of a number of caves where the earliest arrivals first sought shelter. The first business established was a saloon. Beginning that June the sensational stampede to White Pine started, the West's noisest, fastest and most intense mining rush since the gold rush in California.

Electrified by promise of quick wealth, several thousand prospectors flocked here through the rest of 1868, and so great was the furor that by the next spring, despite the poor climate and outbreaks of disease, over 10,000 shivering miners had established themselves in such meager retreats as huts of hay, mud and stone, houses of rough lumber, slabs and posts, in caves and in drafty cotton tents. While the thermometer was at zero, mines and land, wood and water were claimed and reclaimed in a carnival of speculation and disorder. Even snowbanks with all their "dips, spurs and angles" were coveted because of the water they contained. Several towns were platted, lot prices rose into the thousands, toll roads extended in every direction, and before 1869 dawned the Bank of California and Wells Fargo had established branches in Hamilton.

Chinamen, Mexicans and men of dozens of other nationalities were represented in this noisy

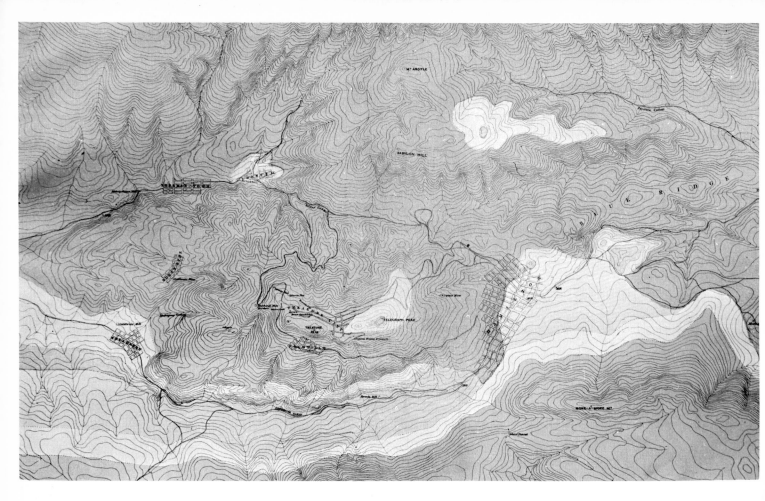

Hamilton and six other towns of the White Pine district are shown in this map prepared in 1868 by the King survey of the fortieth parallel. (*E. W. Darrah Collection*)

Among the buildings being constructed on the main street of Hamilton in 1869 was the two-story Withington Hotel. Each of the 17 rooms on the top floor had a fireplace. The hand-hewn stone of the facade came from a quarry three miles east, in the direction of Eberhardt. Several tents are in the background, at the foot of Treasure Hill. (Las Vegas *Review-Journal*)

The $60,000 Smoky mill built in 1869 at the east edge of Hamilton is receiving ore teamed from the mines at Treasure Hill, nearly four miles distant. (*Nevada Historical Society*)

The school and Masonic lodge are shown as they looked around 1910. The lodge was organized in 1870 and in 1901 it forfeited its charter. (*Both photos: Charles McShane Collection*)

Mourner's Point, a mile north of Hamilton, was the main cemetery of the White Pine district, the "poor man's paradise." (*Gary Allen photo*)

assemblage of miners, merchants, brokers, speculators, drifters, thieves and desperadoes, but several at Hamilton thought beyond the day when its inhabitants would have only chloride on the brain. Before a child lived in the camp, a school district was organized with an elected board of trustees and a school site. A debating club and reading room were established, and the town "fathers" provided free land for religious purposes.

When White Pine County was organized in March 1869, Hamilton was selected as the first county seat, and an imposing brick courthouse with jail was built months later at a cost of $55,000. Hamilton had also developed into the business center for a district with almost 20,000 people. Solid fronts of offices and stores occupied several blocks in the two-square-mile townsite. There were 101 establishments selling liquor — most with billiard tables and cigar counters, 59 stores of general merchandise, a few dozen lawyers, doctors, fire companies, churches, fraternal orders, Miners' Union, banks, jewelers, theaters, skating rinks, dance halls, auction houses, a soda factory, breweries, pawnbrokers, gunsmiths, express facilities, and every morning the *Daily Inland Empire*. Anticipating that the population might shortly reach 50,000, a San Francisco firm organized a water company and steam pumping works.

In all, 195 White Pine mining companies were incorporated; their stocks had a total list value of over $70 million, with shares enthusiastically traded throughout the nation. Daily stagecoaches laden with bullion ran to Elko, the nearest railroad point, and for awhile stages were being robbed at the rate of about two per week.

Any mining excitement eventually subsides, and revulsion followed the White Pine excesses in the winter of 1869-70. Uncertainty over mining development led to depression. Speculators unable to realize $20,000 from the sale of a hole in the ground withdrew; miners took up their blankets and walked away; and merchants in Hamilton closed shop. Census figures of 1870 reflected the immediate decline, with the count showing about 6800 in the district, though hundreds of transients were undoubtedly missed.

Later fires also hastened the town's demise. In June 1873 a cigar store owner set fire to his establishment to collect insurance, but the flames spread through town and destroyed $600,000 in property. The arsonist was brought to trial and sent to the state prison. Another major fire in 1885 destroyed the courthouse and two years later the crippled town lost the county seat to Ely. Since then the White Pine district has been occasionally active, especially early in this century at the Belmont mill, and lead-silver ore was shipped to Eureka. As late as 1925 a few hundred people were in the district, but the camp is entirely abandoned today.

TREASURE CITY, via graded road 3 miles south of Hamilton.

Treasure Hill! The very name suggests a rich strike in romantic surroundings. Near the top of that eminence, on its western slope, the first cabins were built in November 1867, and early the next year Treasure City townsite was laid out with the White Pine district's first business center. The Hidden Treasure and Eberhardt mines, both multimillion-dollar silver producers, began large-scale development and a swarm of adventurers arrived that summer. Within a year, after additional rushes, this "city above the clouds" contained about 6000 souls, second only to Hamilton in the district. White Pine was considered much faster than the Comstock; more men made and lost fortunes in its first year than in the early days of Virginia City. Every White Piner was on the sell and the district was filled with self-proclaimed millionaires. In less than two years' time, over 13,000 claims were located on Treasure Hill; most of them were never worked. "Feet" changed hands at enormous prices, and buying and selling of real estate took place at a furious pace. Claim-jumping was such a common occurrence that on a certain night sixty lots were jumped in Treasure City. Personal occupation and a well-oiled revolver often constituted clear title.

The town grew on a sloping surface amid several hundred claims, and shallow shafts and pits crowded streets and alleys. Many two-story structures and fireproof buildings extended along Main Street for over half a mile; stores and saloons occupied the lower side while the upper side had lawyers' offices and stores.

Treasure City was said to have altitude, silver, population and whiskey — everything except an agreeable climate. Situated on the exposed side of

These lithographs of Treasure Hill's west side in 1869 show Treasure City near the summit at an altitude of nearly 9000 feet above the sea. The main street ran parallel with the crest, about 300 feet below. The Hidden Treasure, the richest mine in White Pine, is on the east side of the ridge north of town. The important mining areas known as Bromide Flat, Chloride Flat and Pogonip Flat are below and to the right of town; that area was perforated with thousands of claims and yielded rich ore. The first rock mined there averaged several hundred dollars a ton at the mill. Hamilton, shown at the left in the bottom picture, was connected to the mountaintop town by a winding three-mile toll road. *(Top: Getchell Library, University of Nevada; bottom: Bancroft Library)*

a mountain, the town took the brunt of bleak, fitful blasts of icy winds that howled through the district most months of the year. Its citizens were often plagued by the horrid pogonip — a merciless lung-stinging fog which hung over the city in the wintertime. Deep snowdrifts not only destroyed buildings but also blocked roads and hampered mining development. But the people on Treasure Hill were caught up in an incessant whirl of excitement and endured the grim discomforts because of the rich ore.

At its height in the spring of 1869, Treasure City had the daily White Pine *News*, post office, stock exchange with seats worth $300 each, theater, Masonic and Odd Fellows lodges and other amenities of an incorporated city. The business district had at least 42 stores, a bank, Wells Fargo office and several saloons. Prices were outrageously high for most goods.

In August 1869 a bitter labor dispute hit the mines, marked by parades and beatings of non-union workers. Order was finally restored when several union officials were arrested for inciting riots. The union had to disband as a result of the strike.

Later in the year shallow veins and excessive litigation brought the district into decline. By the end of 1870 most of the population had left for greener fields. In the spring of 1874 Treasure City's business district succumbed to flames and little if any of it was rebuilt. The 1880 census showed only 14 voters left in the town where 11 years earlier the mines were allegedly so rich that they threatened to glut the world money market. Probably as much as $20 million in silver had been recovered by 1880. Remnants of buildings, tunnels, and caved-in shafts extend for over a mile. The only digging on Treasure Hill is now done by squirrels and foxes.

PICOTILLO, 1 mile southeast of Treasure City.

After this townsite was platted in the White Pine district in 1868, its lots were extensively advertised, but purchasers found their property on the steep east side of Treasure Hill "which a kangaroo might climb, but not a human being." A town actually developed on Picotillo Flat in 1869 but succumbed when White Pine lost its magic early in 1870. Rock foundations remain.

BABYLON, approximately 3 mi. west of Hamilton.

This primitive camp was started in the summer of 1868 on Babylon Ridge, high in the White Pine Range "where the wind blew and the snow fell as in few places west of the Rocky Mountains." Even in the summer miners built fires to keep warm.

Babylon was only one of nearly a dozen satellite "cities" platted in the White Pine district which were little more than names on maps and promotional literature glibly issued by speculators. On one occasion a newcomer to White Pine desiring to learn particulars about one of these cities questioned a miner who, on the strength of a month's residence in the area, laid claim to the title of one of the oldest inhabitants and received the reply that the city "was about as large as New York, but was not built up yet." Babylon and other outlying camps such as Greenville, White Pine City, Sunnyside and Menken consisted of mere dugouts, crude shanties, primitive tents, and had no businesses except perhaps a saloon and an assay office. Babylon was abandoned in 1869 after less than a year of activity and the Hamilton paper quipped, in biblical style, "Babylon has fallen!"

SWANSEA, 3¼ miles southwest of Hamilton via graded road.

In the spring of 1869 the Hamilton press described Swansea as the new magic town situated in a lovely valley north of Shermantown, and said that it "bids fair to become an important place." At the height of the White Pine boom that summer, Swanseans anticipated that larger mills would be built and that the main street might soon stretch to larger Shermantown nearly a mile south. But Swansea's swan song was sung when Shermantown annexed this industrial settlement late in 1869 and thus it was not destined to have a separate development. Rock ruins remain.

SHERMANTOWN, 4 miles southwest of Hamilton.

With abundant water and wood supplies, Shermantown Canyon, southwest of Treasure Hill, was a natural spot for construction of stamp mills to pound out ore from silver mines at Treasure City. The camp of Silver Springs rose amid the milling activity, but was renamed Shermantown early in 1869 when a townsite was platted. Eight mills with

A wall of the Wells Fargo building in Treasure City is framed by the arch of the town's other remaining stone structure, probably another bank. The stone shell (below) of this stamp mill at Shermantown, built in 1869 to crush ore for the Eberhardt mine, makes its last stand against invasion by heavy sage growth. *(Frank Mitrani photos)*

69 stamps were eventually constructed, as well as four furnaces and two sawmills.

With this activity Shermantown grew to about 3000 residents in 1869. The town incorporated in April and on the business street were impressive structures built of light sandstone quarried nearby. A towering three-story building housed the Masons and the Odd Fellows; at different times two daily evening newspapers carried the Shermantown dateline; and near the peak of the boom in mid-1869 lots sold for from $800 to $2000 each.

Of all the towns in White Pine, Shermantown was the most desirable as a place of residence, for it was sheltered by mountains from cold winds which swept the district most of the year. But with the town's economy inextricably tied to the mines on Treasure Hill, Shermantown diminished with their decline in 1870. A decade later the town housed a solitary family. Adobe mill ruins and roofless stone walls remain.

EBERHARDT, 5 miles southeast of Hamilton. .

This camp sprang up in 1869 at a point in Applegarth Canyon near the thirty-stamp Stanford & Eberhardt and California mills and mines in Eberhardt Canyon immediately to the west. The Federal Mining Commissioner described the largest mine, the Eberhardt, as having walls and ceilings of sparkling silver; dust from a walk in the tunnel covered the visitor's boots and clothing with a gray coating of fine silver. One small cut, about 70′x 40′x 28′ yielded over $1000 per ton and a certain four-ton boulder of silver chloride was so fine that the silver could be hammered into sheets without milling.

Although the boom and extravagant hopes of the rest of the White Pine district collapsed in 1870, Eberhardt expanded when the British-owned Eberhardt & Aurora Mining Co. Ltd., capitalized at $12 million, began extensive operations. In June 1871 the camp had a post office, saloons, carpenter shop, wagon shop, blacksmith, stores and an active temperance organization. Activity slowed after 1873 but picked up again in 1876 and in 1880 the permanent population was 170. Five years later after irregular operations, the British company shut down and Eberhardt quietly slipped into history. Rock ruins of mills and foundations remain.

MONTE CRISTO, via graded roads 15 miles south-southeast of US 50 at a point 51 miles west of Ely.

Monte Cristo was the pioneer camp of the White Pine district after its organization in the fall of 1865. During the next year a five-stamp mill, transplanted from La Plata in Churchill County, began to treat local ores. Wagons also hauled high-grade worth up to $100 per ton to mills in Austin.

In July 1867 the Monte Cristo company began prospecting the west slopes of Mount Hamilton but found no veins of value. The discovery of the rich silver veins on Treasure Hill actually began later that fall when an Indian showed A. J. Leathers a rich chunk of ore. He then piloted Leathers and others five miles east to a rich chloride ledge that became the Hidden Treasure mine. The initial shipment sent to Austin yielded several hundred dollars a ton. The richness of that find ignited the famous stampede to White Pine and the subsequent boom at Hamilton and Treasure City (which see). Monte Cristo was forgotten during the height of the White Pine excitement in 1868-69, but early in the next decade a new company rebuilt the mill and added a furnace to treat ore from mines 15 miles west. That activity lasted only a few years. Rock walls and mill stack remain.

SELIGMAN, 4 miles northeast of Monte Cristo (3½ miles west of Hamilton).

Initially a mill camp known as Leadville in the early 1880s, this camp which grew around lead mines at the west side of Mount Hamilton by 1887 had a blacksmith shop, Wells Fargo office, boarding house, assay office, store of general merchandise, mill and post office. Gambling dens were conspicuously absent in this peaceful camp which succumbed probably sometime around 1895 when the post office was removed. Rock ruins remain.

BUCK STATION, 21 miles north of US 50 at a point 51 miles west of Ely.

After the Central Pacific Railroad began running to Elko in January 1869, that station became the jumping-off point for the White Pine silver mines 110 miles south. Buck Station was only one of several stations which were established between Elko and the land of fortune, others taking such colorful names as Black Hawk, Salty Williams,

On the southeast side of Treasure Hill (above) was the portal of the famed Eberhardt mine. From there down to the town of Eberhardt (below), a three-mile aerial tramway costing $137,000 was built to carry ore to the sixty-stamp $257,000 Eberhardt (or International) mill, built late in 1870. Some of the wooden towers of the nation's largest cable tramway in the 1870s are shown leading from the mill toward Treasure Hill. In the foreground left is the superintendent's home, while the main part of the camp was located around the base of the hill where the smaller Stanford mill is situated. All buildings have been removed. (Both photos: Bancroft Library)

Pancake, and Do-Drop-In. Many types of rigs continually passed through here, including freight wagons loaded to the hilt drawn by long lines of mule teams and dusty four- and six-horse stages crowded with humanity, supplies and machine parts.

Stage travelers awaited such welcome stops as Buck Station to stretch their limbs and eat at a waiting table if the station was reached at the dinner hour. Limited lodging facilities were probably available, though passengers regularly slept on the jolting stages. Besides conveyances, a throng of men on horseback and footpackers carrying blankets and gear also passed through here, often begging and stealing along the way. But when Hamilton declined after 1870 the station saw less frequent use. Later a small ranch thrived here and buildings of it remain. Miles-long segments of the old Elko-Hamilton stage road scar the barren landscape at many points both north and south of this site.

POGUE'S STATION, on SR 20 at a point 16 miles south of its junction with US 50 at a point 67 miles west of Ely.

Because of a welcome water supply, a stage station was built here in the early 1870s to accommodate traffic on the Palisade-Pioche road. Later a barn, adobe building, corral and other structures providing simple lodging were erected. The miserly stationmaster who operated the place around the turn of the century was said to have buried treasure nearby which after his death in 1915, was the object of an unsuccessful search. Stone walls mark the site.

PINTO, or Silverado, via unimproved road, 2 miles north of US 50 at a point 65 miles west of Ely.

After silver discoveries in 1865 and organization of the Silverado district four years later, a camp called Pinto emerged with blacksmith shops, boarding houses, post office in 1870-71, stores, dwellings and 75 people. In 1872 an English company erected a £30,000 mill before opening up mines, but subsequent explorations revealed that company-owned ground had no valuable deposits, and the mill treated only a few thousand dollars worth of ore before shutting down in January 1874.

Thereafter the mines led an irregular life, and by 1880 Pinto had declined to four businesses and 25 people. District activity ceased by 1884 although Pinto briefly revived about 1902-03. Stone walls remain at Pinto, while smelter ruins are east of US 50 just south of Pinto Summit, Eureka County, where there was another district camp called Pinto, with post office from 1875 to 1884.

PINTO CREEK STATION, 2½ miles northwest of the Newark Valley road at a point 5 miles north of its junction with US 50.

This station situated on the east flank of the Diamond Range served travelers on the Austin-Hamilton stage road in 1868. When Eureka boomed early in the 1870s the stage road to Hamilton was rerouted south of here and this station saw less use.

NEWARK, ¼ mile west of the Newark Valley road at a point 11 miles north of its junction with US 50.

Austin prospectors discovered silver on the east flank of the Diamond Mountains in October 1866, and mining development gave rise to a camp the following year. In 1867 the Centenary Silver Co. purchased the most important workings in this little-known district and spent $180,000 to build a twenty-stamp amalgamation mill with eight furnaces imported from the Reese River area. The Methodist Church provided capital with the stipulation that initial returns would be used to build a church in Austin. The agreement was made good late in 1867, Methodism's centenary year. During 1868-69 rich ore from the White Pine district accounted for most of the milling activity, and the mill also treated ores from Pinto and the local company mine.

Newark had 200 men working in 1874, but the mines closed a few years later after only producing $100,000 in silver from shallow workings. Newark reawoke about 1905 when production from old mines allowed limited shipments for a few years. Mill foundations identify the site.

WARD, 2 miles west of the Cave Valley-Charcoal Ovens State Monument road at a point 7 miles south of its junction with US 6, 50 and 93 (12 miles south of Ely).

256

"Like a tin can, a mining camp often lies where it is thrown," wrote an early editor about mining camps. The town of Ward sprang up in an unfortunate position on the shelf of a hill; the north side of the main street was ten feet higher than the south side. Steptoe Valley is beyond the town to the right. (*White Pine Museum*)

The primitive aerial tramway of the Martin White Co. at Ward used gravity to bring the loaded buckets from the shaft house (right) to the loading bins. The empty buckets were returned on the cable at left. (*White Pine Museum*)

The extensive Martin White Co.'s smelting and milling facilities are shown in these two early lithographs. (Las Vegas *Review-Journal*)

Charcoal for the furnace in the smelters was manufactured in these ovens three miles south of Ward. The taller three are thirty feet high and the diameter at the base is about 27 feet.

Teamsters on the Toano-Pioche freight run, while hunting for bulls turned loose to graze and rest, stumbled onto a rich silver outcrop in Ward Gulch in March 1872. The discovery later became the Paymaster, the district's best producer. In the spring of 1876 a rush developed and mining began. By fall a school district was organized and the Ward *Miner* began weekly publication. In January 1877 a post office was opened.

By the summer of 1877, Ward, with a population of 1500, was the county's largest camp. Two smelters which had been built in 1875 were joined by a twenty-stamp mill with three furnaces, costing $85,000, connected with the mines by a tramway. Two breweries kept the town in good spirits; fraternal orders were established; a hook-and-ladder company was founded and a city hall was built. Another paper, the *Reflex*, began publication in April. Within another year's time Ward's 680 registered voters controlled county elections.

In sharp contrast with most young mining camps which experienced frequent shootings and robberies, Ward's vigilance committee dispensed with lawbreakers immediately. After a camp follower, without provocation, gunned down a local merchant on the main street, morning found the drifter hanging from a tree. Later when a stage was held up while approaching the camp, one bandit was shot during his attempt at robbery and his partner escaped, only to be captured and sent to prison.

When the lead content of the ore decreased significantly in 1878, the larger of the two smelters was converted into a mill, and mining continued into the early 1880s. Revival of Cherry Creek in 1880 beckoned the mining camp crowd and Ward declined further when a major fire in the summer of 1883 destroyed one-third of the town. The *Reflex* then moved across Steptoe Valley to the growing town of Taylor and the post office was discontinued by 1887. Short-lived revivals of mining took place in 1906, in the late 1930s and in the 1960s. Cemetery, smelter and mill foundations are left at Ward, and six coke ovens built about 1876 remain at the Ward Charcoal Ovens Historic State Monument three miles south.

TAYLOR, via graded roads 4 miles east of US 6, 50 and 93 at a point 14 miles south of Ely.

Though initial discovery of silver had been made on the west slope of the Schell Creek Range as early as 1873 and rich chloride ores were found in 1880, mining excitements elsewhere stole the headlines. A camp emerged in 1880 and became a boom camp three years later after Cherry Creek and Ward had folded. Buildings were moved from nearby camps and a business district soon embraced saloons, butcher shops, restaurants, boarding houses, stores, drugstore, a Wells Fargo office, brewery, post office, opera house and school. That same year the Monitor Co. mill built two years earlier was joined by a new facility on Willow

The Monitor mill on Steptoe Creek, seven miles northwest of Taylor, handled much of that district's ore. In front of the blacksmith shop at the right, a man is sharpening tools at a grinding wheel. The mill was built in 1881 when machinery for ten stamps was brought in from Seligman, west of Hamilton. (*Gerald "Casey" Fisher Collection*)

In the mid-1880s when the Taylor mines on the west slope of the Schell Creek Range were in full swing, Taylor was the county's largest camp. Its south end shown in these two views had a compact business street. At the head of the street (above) was the opera house. (*Nevada State Museum*)

A view of the same street from the opposite direction (below) shows the district's two leading mines. The dumps of the Argus mine are high on the ridge to the right while the hoisting works and the dump of the Monitor mine appear at the head of the street.

Creek owned by the Argus Mining Co. For the rest of the decade Taylor was the center of county mining activity.

During the mid-1880s Taylor, with a population of several hundred people during peak operating periods, was a quiet orderly town and experienced only occasional violence. Indians often brought wild ducks into the camp and peddled them at two bits apiece. A brass band, programs in the town's opera house, and an occasional traveling circus provided entertainment. In August 1885 the influential White Pine *News* moved here and merged with the already established *Reflex*.

Through a mining report published in 1886 said that the mines were producing well and had excellent prospects, the district began to decline, spurred by the fall of metal prices. By the end of 1889 Taylor was through and most of its businesses had moved to the new town of Ely. The Argus and Monitor mines continued significant production after 1890, bringing the district's estimated total to $3 million.

Today Taylor is a pathetic ruin, desolate. Mill remnants north of the camp are those of the 100-ton Argus cyanide mill built in 1919.

OSCEOLA, 3¾ miles east of US 6 and 50 at a point 8 miles east of their junction with US 93 (29 miles southeast of Ely).

The Osceola district was organized in October 1872 after placer gold was discovered the previous summer. Lack of water to wash the gravel initially hindered development — and a placer district without water is like a Virginia City saloon without whiskey! At peak times between 1873 and 1877 as many as 400 miners worked claims employing pans, rockers and arrastras to recover the ore. By 1878 a small five-stamp mill was pressed into service, the same year that the district got its post office.

Beginning in 1880 the Osceola Placer Mining Co. began two decades of operations, with the best years coming after canals were completed in 1884. That company was the first in Nevada to use hydraulic hoses, a process imported from California. The canals lost efficiency about 1900 and major work ended, but the company had recovered an estimated $2 million in gold. Various individuals continued working claims and enough miners remained to support a store, saloons and the post office which finally closed in 1920. Thereafter, some activity was evident most of the time at least through the 1960s.

In the early days Osceola had the reputation of being a good steady district. While other placer camps wavered between lean and fat years, this one had consistently produced gold and the "dry wash boys" always had plenty of coin. The camp

In this view of Osceola around 1890, several canvas-topped freight wagons are delivering supplies to the camp. For cooking and heating purposes, each house had its own woodpile, a necessity in this cold climate. The rock walls of the general store (the building with a sign on the right) still stand. In back of the camera, a well-kept cemetery contains headstones showing names of several nationalities. *(Mrs. Wayne Cole Collection)*

Three hydraulic giants attack the gravel found at Osceola. The resulting mud and rubble flows through the sluice boxes where riffles charged with mercury collect the gold. *(Gerald "Casey" Fisher Collection)*

This tent saloon at Black Horse was set up by building a box with a wooden floor and three-foot walls and then adding lumber to frame the top. Thick canvas was then stretched over the boards and fastened to hooks on the outside walls. The frame door is not shown. Such a building was typical; it was very cozy and warm when heated. The wooden box type of construction kept out snakes and vermin. *(Theron Fox Collection)*

262

has gained at least three distinctions: its pioneering use of hydraulic hoses in the 1880s, a $6000 nugget — probably Nevada's largest — that was found in 1886 and, most important of all, it has survived longer than any other placer camp in Nevada. Small but mighty was Osceola!

BLACK HORSE, 2 miles north of US 6 and 50 at a point 23 miles east of their junction with US 93 (34 miles southeast of Ely).

The discovery of gold here in 1905 was accidental, as at Tonopah. A lone prospector caught in heavy winds and rain found shelter under an overhanging ledge, and while waiting out the storm made a few taps on the rock. What he chipped off looked interesting, and after an assay revealed a high gold content a rush developed in which most miners in nearby Osceola joined. Within six months a camp had formed with 400 people housed in tents and wooden shacks. A crude mill began operating in 1909 and was replaced by a slightly larger one the following year. By the end of 1911 the ore veins had thinned and Black Horse came to a halt in 1913. Only cellars and a few graves now mark the site.

MINERVA, 17 miles southeast of US 93 at a point 4 miles south of its junction with US 50 and 6 (39 miles southeast of Ely).

Three mining districts were organized on the west flank of the Snake Range during an era of intense silver prospecting after 1869, but each was abandoned by the mid-1870s. After 1900 tungsten claims were developed on a small scale and the Tungsten district was organized in the area of the Hub mine, 9½ miles north-northeast of Minerva. The U. S. Tungsten Corporation built a fifty-ton concentrator in the Hub Basin which operated briefly in 1911 and during World War I, producing a recorded $670,000. Below the mill a camp developed with about fifty people and a store was started. A post office known as Tungsten Mines existed from October 1916 to June 1917.

Also during the war the Minerva Tungsten Corporation was active and equipped with a 150-ton concentrating mill built about four miles south of Minerva below the Chief mine. There the first camp of Minerva was started. Mining activity subsided after 1918 and practically ceased after 1920. A decade later mining resumed; in 1937 the Tungsten Metals Corporation built a mill of about 200-ton capacity at Minerva and the camp had several cabins and about sixty people. A post office and school known as Shoshone were located about 1½ miles north of Minerva. Production through 1944 was an estimated $3.4 million and after World War II the mill was dismantled. A smaller mill built about 1949 treated tungsten ore until about 1957. The camp of Minerva is now abandoned; part of a mill and several cabins remain.

The main street of Black Horse, shown here in 1906, eventually had three saloons, a barber shop, a blacksmith shop and two boarding houses. A school district was organized. Now only cellars and a few fenced graves mark the site. (*Theron Fox Collection*)

The portal of the Potosi mine is on the west face of an almost perpendicular cliff 150 feet high, near the summit of Potosi Mountain. (*U. S. Geological Survey*)

A half-mile north of the mine and 700 feet below it is the camp of the Potosi mine. Completion of the transcontinental railroad through the county in 1905 and a boom at nearby Goodsprings made possible a revival at Potosi. (*Elizabeth Harrington Collection*)

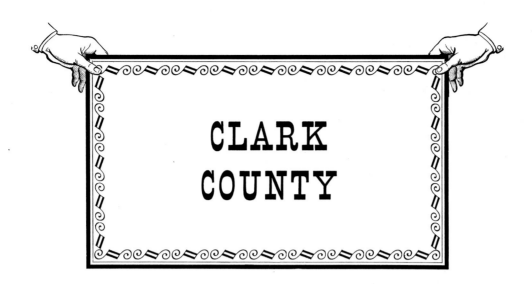

CLARK COUNTY

The state's earliest lode mining activity took place at the Potosi mine, initially worked in 1856. Systematic mining began at Eldorado about five years later and in the 1860s settlements such as Callville, Junction City and St. Thomas were important points on travel routes to the West Coast. Though not heavily populated this area prospered until the Mormon exodus of the winter of 1870-71, which crippled developments for six years. By 1881 many had returned from Utah to populate farms and settlements, and in the 1890s mining saw better days with continued development at Eldorado and the discoveries at Searchlight.

Completion of the transcontinental San Pedro, Los Angeles & Salt Lake Railroad in 1905 stimulated county mining and led to the founding of Las Vegas as the freight and passenger depot for southern Nevada. The Potosi and mines near Goodsprings made large outputs during World War I, and though activity slowed in the 1920s Nelson (Eldorado) resumed large-scale mining in 1935. That district and Goodsprings shut down because of World War II, and since 1952 only small operators have mined precious metals.

POTOSI, 4½ miles southwest of the Spring Mountain road at a point 20 miles west of its junction with I-15 at Arden exit (25 miles southwest of Las Vegas).

Many legends have been associated with the Potosi, Nevada's oldest lode mine. It is said that a Mormon batallion returning from California in 1847 initially discovered ore and that the mine was named for an Indian guide. Another story has it that Indians carried on mining and cast silver bullets before the advent of the white man, but where guns and powder were obtained is not made clear. One myth which has gained wide acceptance insists that lead ore was hauled on ox wagons to the Las Vegas mission for smelting in a furnace built in an adobe fireplace.

Mormons at the Las Vegas mission initially found lead deposits here in April 1856 through the help of a Paiute guide. Early the next month Nathaniel Jones came from Salt Lake City to examine the newly found "mountain of lead" and eventually named the mine Potosi after his boyhood home in Wisconsin. Jones did not begin mining until August after returning to Utah for blasting powder and other essentials. In September the first wagonload of ore was taken to Utah for trading purposes.

By December three wagons loaded with supplies, including bellows, furnace, hearths and other apparatus arrived at the camp below the Potosi mine so that larger development could begin. Beginning Christmas day a crudely built adobe furnace began smelting ore packed by mules down the 700-foot descent from the mine more than a half mile away. But this effort was abandoned before the end of January 1857, as the lead proved too flaky and brittle for use, probably because of the complexity of the ore and its high zinc content.

In the spring of 1861 the Colorado Mining Co. set up a larger smelter at Potosi Spring, and silver mining operations attracted attention all over the far West. The town of Potosi was laid out below the "Las Vegas Silver Mines" as they were then also called and the camp soon had 100 miners and two manuscript newspapers. Though the district was made more accessible with completion through it of a wagon road to the San Bernardino Valley, operations ceased in 1863. Seven years later the Silver State Mining Co. reopened the Potosi, then known as the Comet mine, and a cluster of stone buildings at the springs made up the camp of Crystal City.

Work was only desultory between 1873 and 1906, when the Salt Lake railroad was built, and then development of the mine resumed in earnest, continuing for 14 years. Late in 1913 the Empire Zinc Co. acquired it and for the next four years the Potosi was Nevada's largest zinc producer. An aerial tramway and baby gauge track connected the mine with a vertical kiln at the camp.

Activity declined after 1920, but from 1925 to 1928 the mine again produced well. During later years, activity by leasers helped push Potosi production to an estimated $4.5 million in lead, silver and zinc over more than a century of development. Stone ruins remain, as well as remnants of the tramway, railroad and mine entrance. Good water is available at Potosi Spring.

GOODSPRINGS, on SR 53 at a point 7 miles northwest of I-15 at Jean (34 miles southwest of Las Vegas).

A group of prospectors found silver-lead ore here in 1868 and formed the New England district which was soon renamed the Yellow Pine, but the early effort was eventually abandoned because the lead did not contain enough silver values. A prospector and cattleman named Joe Good remained here after the others had left and the local springs were named for him. Several Utah prospectors searched for lead in 1886 and considerable development then followed resulting in the permanent settlement of Goodsprings.

The Keystone gold mine was discovered in 1892 during a year of much prospecting which was encouraged by completion of the Nevada Southern Railway from Goffs on the Santa Fe to Manvel, 45 miles south of here. By the beginning of 1893 there were about 200 people in the Goodsprings area. Keystone ores were milled at Sandy (which see), and for the next five years interest centered on that

mine and other gold deposits. Continued prospecting turned up additional ore deposits, and the Keystone mine remained active until 1906 producing about $600,000, principally in gold.

The Yellow Pine Mining Co. combined many properties in 1901. Long wagon hauls to Manvel prevented shipment of any ore except high-grade until the San Pedro, Los Angeles & Salt Lake Railroad was completed to Jean in the spring of 1905, and district production quadrupled in less than a year. The value of mineral reserves increased vastly that same year when a New Mexico mining engineer named T. C. Brown recognized that the heavy gray-white ore thrown on the dumps after lead ores were milled was actually high-grade zinc. Several lode deposits of zinc were then discovered, and the Yellow Pine Mining Co. was reorganized in 1906 to begin large-scale operations.

Beginning in 1906 the district made steady progress and attracted wide attention. Subsequent experimentation with the local lead-zinc ores led to economical methods of separating the two metals, and the mill on the hillside at the south end of town was enlarged to a 75-ton concentrator. The completion of a narrow gauge railroad from Jean in June 1911 lowered transportation costs greatly, and the $1.2 million production for 1912 was four times that of 1911.

Mining activity peaked during 1915-18 when wartime demand for lead and zinc and the high price of metals encouraged large outputs, and during that time over 85 million pounds of zinc were produced, and a third as much lead. The Yellow Pine Mining Co. paid handsome dividends and at least fifty smaller mines were active. The town had about 800 people and several stores, saloons, post office, school, first-class hotel, hospital and the weekly *Gazette* from 1916 until 1921.

The district lay dormant during 1921-22, but a revival in the mid-1920s lasted until the 1930s. During the mid-1930s gold became the chief metal produced, at an average rate of $300,000 a year until the beginning of World War II. During that time about 150 people lived at Goodsprings. After the war through 1952 the district again produced well, but now the mines are relatively idle. With a total recorded production exceeding $31 million, this district is Clark County's outstanding producer, accounting for about 40 percent of the total.

An eight-horse team hauls lumber into Goodsprings from Jean, a station on the main-line Salt Lake railroad, before the Yellow Pine Mining Co. built its own railroad into the district in 1911. The pile of juniper and fir for the boilers at the concentrator was teamed in from the Spring Mountains. Later firing was done with oil. The bottom picture shows a section gang ballasting the newly laid track of the Yellow Pine Mining Co.'s railroad. *(Both photos: Leonard Fayle Collection)*

In Goodsprings around 1917 was the two-story Fayle Hotel at the left, the Yellow Pine mill and an engine of the Yellow Pine Mining Co. railroad on the hill at the right. The twenty-room Fayle Hotel (left) opened in 1916 with a banquet and an all night party with a live dance band imported from Las Vegas. For years the Fayle was considered one of southern Nevada's finest. It burned down in 1966. At the cookhouse of the Yellow Pine mine (lower) are some of the belles of Goodsprings who lived here around 1910. (*Top: Jack Hardy Collection; middle and bottom: John Yount Collection*)

268

This train, loaded with ore from the Yellow Pine mine, is at the mill in Goodsprings. The ore will be dumped one car at a time into the bins opposite the scales on the platform in foreground. The engine is one of the Shays owned by the company. The Yellow Pine mine crew (right) takes a break from a busy work day. From a point east of Goodsprings (below), the small business district and the Fayle Hotel are shown on the right and the Spring Mountains, where the Yellow Pine mine and other mines are located, are in the background. *(Top and middle: John Yount Collection; below: James Hardy Collection)*

Both single jack and double jack drilling contests were held on Independence Day in Goodsprings. Cars and buildings were decorated, and excitement was also provided by mucking contests and foot races. Speeches and band music filled the air. A popular saloon is in the left background while over the hill to the right was the restricted district. A favorite pastime was poker or solo in a Goodsprings bar. A holiday minstrel show in Sam Yount's store was another diversion.

Around 1910, oval tracks marked off by stakes on the dry lakes below Goodsprings were the scene of auto racing two or three times a year. The event drew quite a crowd, and drivers from Las Vegas entered cars. Spectators usually watched the races from their own cars. The noisy mufflerless cars (below) are all tuned up to race distances of a mile or two. (*Lower right, opposite page: William Ellis Collection; all others: John Yount Collection*)

Several homes, mill foundations and a small population remain. Abandoned mines abound in the district.

SANDY, 11 miles west of Goodsprings via Columbia Pass (36 miles southwest of Las Vegas).

This small milling settlement had its beginning when the ten-stamp Keystone mill was built in September 1893 at Taylor's Well to treat ore from the Keystone gold mine, five miles east in the Spring Mountains. A store and saloon were established in 1894; a post office was established in January 1896; and at times until 1910 a hotel, feed corral, and school were open at this peaceable, though at times drunken, town. The sturdy shade trees and springs here were a welcome sight to travelers on the stage road from Manvel and Ivanpah on the Nevada Southern northward to Manse and Bullfrog.

The Nevada Keystone Co. terminated operations at its mine in 1905 and the mill shut down permanently in 1906. The post office was moved in 1910 and Sandy was abandoned. Mill tailings were cyanided in 1910 and again in 1916-18. Buildings, mill ruins and cemetery remain. Another point of interest on the road to Sandy and two miles south is the thirty-ton Shenandoah mill, built in 1935 to treat ore from the Keystone-Barefoot mine.

Near the edge of a chalky flat in the south end of Sandy (or Mesquite) Valley, hundreds of cones four to eight feet high seem like a village of brown tents. Whirlwinds (dust-devils) blow dirt and sand against a bush or small mesquite tree, and when moisture is present the sun bakes new layers into place. *(John Yount Collection)*

The town of Sandy in 1902 functioned as a milling settlement for the Keystone mine. The top view shows 18 tons of ore being delivered to the Nevada Keystone Co.'s mill by a team which entered from the far side of the mill to discharge its cargo. Indians cut wood and yucca growing nearby to fire the boilers. In the bottom picture the company office and laboratory are in the building just to the left of center. The cyanide plant is in the foreground while the mill is at the extreme right. To the right of the tents were the store and the post office. The road skipping off into the distance goes to the mine, five miles distant, in the Spring Mountains. *(Both photos: James Hardy Collection)*

PLATINA, ¼ mile southeast of Sandy.

Active mines, agricultural possibilities and hopes for a railroad all made the Sandy Valley (or Mesquite) area between 1904 and 1915 a promising place for promoters who could count on public readiness to invest in get-rich-quick schemes. The first of these impossible towns was started about 1904. With the Salt Lake railroad under construction nearby, a promoter from Los Angeles started the townsite of Lincoln City about three miles south of Sandy, advertising it as a place with superb agricultural and mining resources. Many lots were sold and a store was established, but the town developed no further and investors soon decided that they were left with worthless sagebrush. Four years later homesteaders began to arrive in Sandy Valley, a promoter started the townsite of Mandolin in August 1908 between Sandy and the state line. Many people who had never seen the valley bought lots and one tent was erected, but that was all.

In March 1914 a Goodsprings assayer found platinum in ore from the Boss mine, three miles east of Sandy. This created considerable excitement and much publicity for platinum is seldom found in lode form. When high assays of selected ore gave the impression that the mine contained extensive deposits, promoters were quick to take advantage of the news. On a mesa a half-mile west of the Boss mine the townsite of Boss was staked out, and a rival townsite was started near the Ripley post office. Californians and others eagerly bought about 100 lots, but a small tent constituted all the building. Another townsite called Ripley was also platted. Adjacent to it on the north was Platina, born on paper in January 1915, the only one of the promotions to achieve town status.

Active mining of the platinum lode at the Boss mine began in October 1915. A post office opened the following January and within the year Platina had its Broadway Department Store, a hotel and other businesses for 200 people. People bought lots on speculation as well as mining stock. Some individuals actually came to live, but in 1917 when the big talk and hopes were over, capital for future development was no more and the boom collapsed. The Los Angeles Realty Board publicly denounced the promotion and by early 1918 Platina was a thing of the past. Now only depressions remain where buildings once stood and no trace is left of the other townsites, although wooden pegs which marked the streets at the Boss townsite may sometimes be found.

KINGSTON (California), 2½ miles southwest of Sandy.

A small influx of homesteaders came to Sandy Valley about 1908 and settled especially on the California side, but most moved away in about two years. In the early 1920s a second wave of homesteaders came, mostly from California, and the community of Kingston was started on one of the homesteads. A school was opened and Kingston post office was established in May 1924. Many World War I veterans came and attempted to start dry farms, but the growing season was too short and most raised only a few vegetables. Vineyards were planted and bootleggers were active during the prohibition era.

During the Depression of the early 1930s unemployed people tried to eke out an existence here, and perhaps as many as fifty or more were at Kingston and on adjacent farms at peak times. The community consisted of a post office, grocery store, community hall and branch of the San Bernardino County library. As the depression waned the era of homesteading near Kingston ended, and the post office closed in 1938. A cellar remains where the community hall once stood.

IVANPAH (California), via graded roads 10 miles west of Yates Well exit on I-15 (49 miles southwest of Las Vegas).
Not to be confused with another Ivanpah southeast of I-15 on the Union Pacific Railroad.

Silver-bearing lodes were discovered in the spring of 1869 on the east slope of Clark Mountain. Mining was soon under way and large teams began hauling ore to San Pedro, from where steamers carried it to San Francisco smelters for reduction. Early in the 1870s a mill was built at the east end of Clark Mountain and a camp formed. Salt for milling came from a crude salt works at the extreme south end of Sandy Valley. During 1875-80 the district contained 500 people and two mills, and before the principal mines closed in 1881 at least $4 million had been extracted with the help of Indian labor. The few prospectors who remained

This pack train of burros (above) is carrying empty kerosene cans and supplies back to the Boss mine. From time to time as needed, packers made short run hauls to carry ore from mines to loading bins where wagons completed the delivery to the railroad.

These wagons (right) pulled by a Holt tractor, the forerunner of the caterpillar, are being loaded at a bin which received ore by aerial tramway from the hills at the left. The ore was then taken to Jean, where it was loaded into railroad cars for shipment to smelters near Salt Lake City. Trucks also hauled ore to the railroad. *(Three photos: John Yount Collection)*

as late as 1890 were lured away by the boom at Vanderbilt, 25 miles southeast.

Just before 1900 the Copper World mine opened in the district near Pachalka Spring and a smelter was built at Valley Wells, twenty miles west. Both mine and smelter closed by 1910. Several rock and adobe buildings remain at Ivanpah.

LAS VEGAS MISSION, on Las Vegas Boulevard North in Las Vegas.

The welcome springs at Las Vegas were a popular campground on the old Spanish Trail since the time when that route was broken through Las Vegas Valley about 1830. For the next two decades the good water and abundant grass for stock were known the full length of the trail by the annual caravans packing supplies from Santa Fe to California and returning to New Mexico with horses and mules. John C. Fremont also stopped here in the spring of 1844 on his second expedition in the West.

The strategic location of Las Vegas between northern Utah and San Bernardino led to the establishment of a way station in 1851 on the mail route between the two points. During that decade the wagon road through here was well worn, and in the spring of 1855 Mormon authorities expanded their interest in Las Vegas Valley by starting a mission. A party came here under William Bringhurst and planted crops, dug irrigation ditches, built corrals and buildings and constructed an adobe fort for protection against the Indians. A post office which took the name of their leader was established in August 1855 in this part of New Mexico territory.

After three years of arduous missionary efforts and reclamation of desert land the Mormons abandoned the mission, though this primitive beginning paved the way for later Mormon settlement of southern Nevada in the 1860s. It has often been written that two men conducted lead smelting operations of Potosi ore at the mission and that their operation was the first parcel of silver-lead ever smelted in the West, but evidence indicates that one of these men was smelting lead in southwestern Utah during the mid-1850s.

After 1861 it was anticipated that army troops would be garrisoned at the fort, which became known as Fort Baker, but there is no record of any military movement here. By the mid-1860s the springs and fort buildings were acquired by Octavius D. Gass, who maintained the Las Vegas Ranch until he sold out to Archibald Stewart in 1882. Stewart was killed in a shooting the next year, but his widow carried on and in 1903 sold 1800 acres to the San Pedro, Los Angeles & Salt Lake Railroad Co. which developed the Las Vegas townsite and sold lots in May 1905. Until that time area travelers obtained food at the ranch as a limited amount of supplies were also sold.

A fenced-in adobe building and monument mark the site.

ALUNITE, ¼ mile west of US 93-95 at a point 17 miles south of Las Vegas.

During several months in 1908 a New York syndicate conducted explorations for the mineral alunite, and in September the Las Vegas *Age* reported that the Alunite district was making a great showing in values. Since alunite is a mineral associated with gold, the *Age* hopefully proclaimed the rise of a new Goldfield on the eastern edge of Las Vegas Valley. A rush developed and a month later bunkhouses, stables, blacksmith shop, an office building and rows of tents made up the embryonic town. The Alunite Mining Co. began sinking shafts and building roads, and it appeared that Alunite was here to stay, but the initial excitement wore off early in 1909, as nothing of importance was found. The Quo Vadis mine produced briefly in 1915, and since then smaller operators have unsuccessfully tried to make a go·of the mines. Dumps remain.

CALLVILLE, now under Lake Mead, 25 miles east of Las Vegas by air.

Founded by Anson Call in December 1864, Callville in Arizona Territory soon became a small river port consisting of a landing, post office, corral, warehouse and other buildings. This settlement occupied an important position on the Colorado River as a small freighting center and river landing from where the small stern-wheel steamers *Esmeralda* and *Nina Tilden* made occasional runs to Yuma in southern Arizona. When that territory created Pah-Ute County in 1865 Callville was made its seat, but never functioned as such and the distinction was lost to St. Thomas in May 1867.

Members of the Las Vegas Mission in 1855 built this house and stone wall and planted the cottonwood trees. The Mormon missionaries returned to Utah in 1857 and 1858, and for the next nine years the ranch often stood abandoned. Thereafter this main ranch house was occupied by the Gass and Stewart families, and lonely prospectors regarded these grounds as a sort of resort. Here the "sons of toil" and travelers on the Los Angeles-Salt Lake City trail received fresh milk, beef and vegetables. *(Fenton Gass Collection)*

In the early 1930s, the rising waters of Lake Mead buried these stone walls of Callville, a cargo receiving point and gateway to Mormon settlements in southern Nevada. Steamboat travel to this point from Yuma in southern Arizona was profitable but risky; navigation was possible only a few months of the year. *(Both photos: Elbert Edwards Collection)*

In this Techatticup mine stope, the man in the center is singlejacking, drilling holes in the rock with a hand-held drill. Candles provided light before carbide lamps were introduced about 1920.

The wagon below hauled ore from the Techatticup mine five miles east to the mill on the Colorado River. The wagon is of unusual construction in that the brake is on the left side.

278

The Southwestern Mining Co. dominated mining at Eldorado in the last century. Organized as the El Dorado Mining Co. in 1862, the company purchased the Techatticup mine from its original locators and erected a ten-stamp steam-powered mill in 1867 which in the early 1880s had been enlarged to this 15-stamp facility. A little over a decade later major operations had closed and leasers worked the area.

In the early 1880s the *Mohave* was one of several steamers that plied between Eldorado and Needles, California, bringing supplies up the river and hauling out bullion for rail shipment. The Southwestern Co. mill at the left and the other mill farther upstream were abandoned early in this century. In the mid-1950s Lake Mohave formed behind Davis Dam, flooding the old camp of Eldorado. *(Four photos: Nevada State Museum)*

The Mormons planned to use Callville as a transfer point for European converts who were to be transported by boat up the Colorado, would disembark here and begin the 500-mile trek to northern Utah, but this project was never put in operation. By 1869 Callville was abandoned after travel and trade in the area fell off on completion of the transcontinental railroad in northern Nevada.

ELDORADO, later Nelson, on SR 60 at a point 16 miles southeast of its junction with US 95 (39 miles southeast of Las Vegas).

According to local legend, the Eldorado district had been mined for over 150 years by Indians, Spanish explorers and occasional Mormon emigrants before 1857. In that year soldiers from Fort Mohave, forty miles downstream, discovered placer gold and commenced mining. Four years later important silver locations were made, and by 1863 the Eldorado mines had created considerable excitement on the Pacific Coast, even though this remote district was in the middle of an unexplored desert over 1000 miles across. It took six months for supplies to come from San Francisco; flatbottom steamers carried the cargo the last leg of the journey from Yuma, Arizona, and often more than a month passed between steamer visits.

In this wilderness, part of Arizona Territory until 1867, a ten-stamp mill started running near the mouth of Eldorado Canyon in 1864 which reduced the amount of overland ore shipments by way of Los Angeles to San Francisco smelters. This was Arizona's first stamp mill. Because it was constructed of old machinery, the mill lost values in the tailings, and so another of similar size was built in the spring of the next year. Later in 1865 a post office was established. The El Dorado Mining Co. added another mill in 1867 which ran successfully into the 1890s.

During its early years Eldorado was a rough and tough lawless camp, and the sheriff at the Lincoln County seat at Hiko (1867-1871) or at Pioche (after 1871) was nearly 300 miles distant, by dubious roads through treacherous terrain where Indians and robbers lurked. Not even a killing was sufficient reason for authorities to come; the locals formed their own posse and vigilante groups to capture and punish wrongdoers.

It is said that about 1882 a Mexican expedition came to Eldorado seeking a certain mine which was clearly marked on their tattered yellow map supposedly found in an old church in Mexico City. The map noted the site of the Techatticup mine, but seeing that the Americans had beaten them to the discovery, the disappointed Mexicans paddled home.

After 1905 the district revived and the townsite of Nelson was platted seven miles west at the head of Eldorado Canyon, and old Eldorado was abandoned in favor of the new site. A fifty-ton smelter was constructed a half-mile below Nelson but produced only limited amounts of lead before blowing up in 1909. Production lagged for the next two decades, but Nelson fought its way back in the mid-1930s, when operations resumed. A paved highway was extended to the town and trucks transported their loads to rail shipping points.

By 1941 the population had reached a stable 600 and three cyanide mills treated 220 tons of ore daily. Two of the mills shipped bullion directly to the San Francisco mint, but increased labor costs prohibited continuance of operations and the mines closed. Production is estimated to be as high as almost $10 million, with the Techatticup, discovered in 1861, accounting for well over half that amount.

The site of old Eldorado is submerged under Lake Mohave; ruins of the Techatticup, several other mines, many old buildings and a population of about fifty are left at Nelson.

SEARCHLIGHT, at intersection of SR 68 and US 95 at a point 55 miles south of Las Vegas.

Veteran prospector G. F. Colton discovered an exposed gold vein in May 1897 near ground which had been initially located in the early 1890s. Several hundred yards east of the discovery Colton found more gold and made a shipment to a Colorado smelter which assayed the ore as high as $2900 a ton. Reports of this encouraged additional prospecting and in July 1898 a district was organized; by October a camp with a post office was established three-quarters of a mile west of the present townsite.

The district became populated after a rush in the following winter. The next year Boston inter-

During the boom days, Searchlight's main street ran east and west. The well-stocked store (below) sold boots and shoes, fine whiskey and cigars, mining supplies, fresh food, and up-to-date ladies' cosmetics including Florida Water and face powder. Also sold were hay, grain and candy. Record of payment was kept in the store's ledger and in small paper books carried by the customers who paid their bills monthly. (*Top: James Cashman Sr. Collection; bottom: E. C. Braswell Collection*)

The Quartette mill (below) was Searchlight's principal producer; from its mine came $2.2 million between 1898 and 1911 — almost half of the district's total production. This mill, built in 1903, was one of the first in Nevada to use the cyanide process extensively. *(James Cashman Sr. Collection)*

Quartette Mill.
Searchlight, Nev.

By 1910 Searchlight was a mature mining town that had outgrown the crude conditions of only six years previous. In 1904 there were mostly tents and cloth-lined houses, only a few of which had running water. A business street soon formed, which included 13 saloons. The town that developed was conveniently situated in the midst of a golden triangle of mines. The local paper called booming wild Searchlight the "camp without a failure." Many prominent Las Vegans made their start here. The camp took its name from the Searchlight claim, probably named for a popular brand of sulphur matches of the day. *(Gordon Colton Collection)*

In Searchlight the smaller Duplex Mining Co. owned this twenty-stamp mill. That company mined more than a million dollars worth of ore. *(Gordon Colton Collection)*

ests acquired important properties with "picture rock" and incorporated the Quartette Mining Co. Other mining companies also formed and the Duplex mine was organized around the Searchlight claim.

Ore was shipped by wagon to Manvel, California, for rail delivery to a smelter at Needles. Costs were reduced when the Quartette company built a twenty-stamp mill on the Colorado River in 1900, and further savings in transporting ore were realized when a 15-mile narrow gauge railway began shuttling between mines and mill in May 1902. The next month the weekly *Searchlight* began beaconing the news of the burgeoning camp and several tent saloons were in evidence. Some of the whiskey's influence "splashed" on nearby mines which bore such names as Cyrus Noble, Little Brown Jug and Old Bottle.

A three-month strike in 1903 suspended work of the Quartette company until a new crew of non-union miners and millers resumed operations. Later that year the Quartette mine discovered enough water near at hand to build a second twenty-stamp mill in Searchlight; its capacity was doubled in 1906 when the river mill was dismantled and its machinery was moved to the new facility.

The Searchlight boom peaked in 1907 when the camp supported the competing *Bulletin* and *News,* well-furnished stores, over a dozen saloons, telephone exchange, 44 working mines, several mills, an active chamber of commerce and a fluctuating population of up to 5000 according to local boosters. Several mining companies were organized as stock-selling ventures.

In the spring of 1907 a whooping crowd led by a fifty-piece cowboy band greeted the arrival of the first train of the Barnwell & Searchlight Railroad. A barbecue, contests and tours of the mines celebrated the opening of the new connection by which cars from Searchlight could be taken to Barnwell, formerly Manvel, and there coupled onto trains of the Santa Fe.

The panic of 1907 hit the district severely because rich ore bodies had been worked out and low-grade ores required additional capital for continued development. Production tailed off drastically after 1910 and leasers replaced the large mining operations of the Quartette and the Duplex. Many families moved away, especially to Las Vegas. Tailings were cyanided in later years with little success. A new flotation mill was built in 1934 and a thirty-ton custom mill ran briefly after 1935, finally shutting down for lack of ore. Total district production is estimated at about $7 million. Old buildings remain amid many modern structures.

CRESCENT, south side of SR 68 at a point 17 miles west of Searchlight, via paved road.

The district's earliest inhabitants were Mexicans, said to have extracted over $500,000 in gold from 1863 to 1878. Burros transported ore to Goodsprings where crude arrastras recovered gold which was melted into bullion bars. This effort abruptly ended in July 1878 when a band of renegade Mormons raided the camp's burro wagon and in a shooting foray killed most of the miners. The search for minerals resumed after 1894, and about two years later an Indian known as "Prospector Johnnie" discovered turquoise deposits worked by Indians in the distant past. In 1897 the Toltec Gem Co. began three years of operations, and various individuals mined turquoise until 1906.

After a party of eastern mining men relocated a silver mine in the spring of 1904, a mild boom ensued with 300 claims recorded in six months. Crescent townsite was staked out in 1905 and tents and wooden buildings quickly appeared. That summer a post office opened, and the young camp soon had six saloons, restaurants, the weekly *Times,* lodging houses, bakery, union hall, school district, and another house "off by itself which little boys were warned to stay away from." At least ten incorporated mining companies were active from 1905 to 1907.

Miners worked seven days a week, but occasional dances in the union hall furnished diversion. In 1906 Crescent began to wane, and after 1907 production was intermittent for a decade. A revival failed in 1908. The reactivated Big Tiger mine produced for awhile in 1916 and increased metal prices two decades later encouraged a mild revival. A lone fireplace marked the site until 1960, but even that is gone now.

Townsite promoters arrived early at the scene of a strike, platted a townsite, and with the help of journalists' superlative-filled reporting and advertising, lured hard-earned money from excited investors throughout the nation. (Las Vegas *Review-Journal*)

SUNSET, by road and trail 8 miles north and east of Nipton at a point 19 miles west of Searchlight.

Though some ore was uncovered in the 1890s, the district's only significant producer, the Lucy Grey mine, was not found until December 1905, when a lone prospector searched the district's ledges for gold. Sunset townsite was laid out near the Nevada-California border two miles from Lyons (now Desert) siding, California, where water was available. A cyanide mill was installed near the mine in 1912 and for several years it produced some bullion. For three more decades leasers added to the district production which reached about $50,000 by mid-century. Buildings remain at the mine.

VANDERBILT (California), via graded roads, 5 miles southeast of Ivanpah on the Union Pacific Railroad.

Though the first gold discoveries were made in the 1870s, no large boom got under way until rich gold veins were found in 1891. Numerous claims were then located in all directions, and by 1893 Vanderbilt had stores, post office, the weekly *Shaft,* and six saloons in full swing for 500 people. The camp folded by 1897 but some mining continued, and though the California Eastern Railway began running through here in 1902 the camp did not revive. Wooden buildings mark the site.

MANVEL, or Barnwell (California), 7 miles southeast of Ivanpah on the Union Pacific Railroad via graded road (21 mi. west-southwest of Searchlight).

The town of Manvel was born early in 1893 in anticipation of being the northern terminus of the Nevada Southern Railway, then being built from Goffs on the Santa Fe main line. A post office was established in March, and about six months later the new line began running to here. For the next eight years this town of 75 to 80 people served as the supply and transshipping center for Eldorado, Goodsprings, the Ivanpah district, Searchlight after 1898 and adjacent Vanderbilt. Stages and large freight wagons plied between those and other camps and mines, and this community had two stores, butcher shop, blacksmith, doctor, a small school, and two saloons including one named the Last Chance. Though a transient town, Manvel was not considered wild.

When the Nevada Southern, by then renamed the California Eastern, pushed construction north into Ivanpah Valley in 1902, Manvel lost some trade but assumed even more importance between 1902 and 1908 because of the increase in freight traffic to Searchlight. Manvel served as the railroad station for that boom until early in 1908 when the Barnwell & Searchlight Railroad was completed. Loss of the Searchlight trade and a fire in September 1908 led to the town's decline. The California

These businesses thrived at Vanderbilt during the 1890s, when the district was producing over $2 million, chiefly in gold.

After 1893 the frontier railroad community of Manvel served as the jumping off point and railhead for eastern California and southern Nevada. The middle view shows a stage about to depart for Searchlight. Wood-frame buildings and tents comprised most of the settlement. *(Three photos: Huntington Library)*

Eastern ceased operations several years later and the post office closed in 1915. Wooden ruins remain.

HART (California), 9 miles east of Manvel via desert roads.

Gold-bearing ledges were discovered late in December 1907 with ore so rich that assayers supposedly went "crazy with the figures." A rush ensued and a town was founded; by the end of January 300 people had settled here. The weekly Hart *Enterprise* appeared that same month and wagons began hauling ore to Searchlight for treatment. The town soon had a first-class hotel; a post office opened in April and most of the other mining town businesses were on hand except that Hart had no booze. Liquor licenses were hard to obtain and private bottles had to be augmented by water which sold for as much as eight dollars a barrel. A businessmen's league was organized to encourage legitimate mining, and with the presence of a "law and order" committee Hart was a conservative camp. Months later the boom was over but the post office lasted until 1915.

FORT PIUTE (California), 17 miles west-south-west, via desert roads, from US 95 at a point 13 miles south of Searchlight.

Never an official army facility, this outpost of Fort Mohave on the east side of the Piute Range was first used about 1860 to protect springs used by travelers on the government road between northern Arizona and San Bernardino. During the Civil War Fort Piute may have been occupied, and afterwards it was probably used on occasion as a base for protection of travelers. Buildings were made of native rock and the thick walls of the largest structure had several rifle ports. Fort Piute probably fell into disuse about 1870 when troubles with Indians had subsided in the area. Thick rock walls and a stone corral are left.

WEST POINT, 1 mile south of SR 7 at a point 3 miles north of I-15 at Glendale exit (50 miles northeast of Las Vegas).

Mormons founded this small settlement in the upper Muddy River Valley in 1867 and within two years about twenty families were there. After marauding Indians, hunger, disease, insects, flash floods and poor harvest had taken their toll during 1869-70, the church granted permission for settlers to vacate the community in September 1870. Less than a month later the entire population of 119 moved to fairer parts of the valley and re-established farms. The breaking up of West Point was the signal for a visit by church president Brigham Young to Muddy River Valley and eventual abandonment of southern Nevada by the Mormons by February 1871.

ST. JOSEPH, 1½ miles north-northeast of Overton on SR 12 at a point 6 miles south of I-15.

First established in May 1865 as a Mormon fort atop a high bluff on the east side of the Muddy River, St. Joseph rose a month later as a settlement scattered over an area of a few miles on a level sandy beach northwest of the fort. Several adobe buildings were built with willow roofs and floors of clay and straw, and at a place called Mill Point or Simonsville a large wooden structure was finished in December. It housed a gristmill which ground wheat, corn and salt.

In August 1867 a post office was opened. A year later some small boys playing near one of the houses built a fire to roast potatoes, and runaway flames quickly spread throughout the settlement, destroying several buildings. Attempts to rebuild the old site and dig a six-mile canal later met with failure, and by 1869 most of the people had moved to the new site of St. Joseph, 3½ miles northwest, leaving the old site abandoned.

The new St. Joseph by late 1869 had grown almost as large as the older Mormon community of St. Thomas (which see), a dozen miles to the southeast, with several hundred residents. To bring an orderly administration to the valley of the Muddy River at that time, Utah Territory created Rio Virgen County with St. Joseph as county seat, but a survey showed Muddy Valley to be in Nevada, and St. Joseph was abandoned when most Mormons returned to Utah early in 1871. About a decade later the new St. Joseph site was resettled as Logan's Ranch or Logandale, and continues as a small community of about 150. Only the ditch remains to mark the site of old St. Joseph.

KAOLIN, 3 miles south-southeast of Overton.

This community was started about 1910 when a few dozen destitute Armenian Mormon converts coming down from Utah chose this spot to begin farming because it reminded them of their native land. The name Kaolin was derived from the type of mineral being mined just west of the settlement. Dissatisfied with this location, the Armenians moved on about two years later. Kaolin was resettled shortly thereafter, a post office opened in 1914, and as many as 100 people were in the vicinity by 1930. A few years later farms were abandoned in anticipation of submersion by Lake Mead.

ST. THOMAS, now under Lake Mead, 8 miles southeast of Overton.

After Brigham Young ordered wholesale colonization of Muddy (now Moapa) Valley in October 1864, St. Thomas was founded when the first arrivals circled their wagons here the following January. Five-acre farm lots and vineyards were surveyed, as well as a townsite near the confluence of the Virgen and Muddy Rivers. By April 600 acres had been assigned for crops and Mormons began to seek other sites for settlement. Over the next four years St. Joseph, Overton and West Point were founded.

St. Thomas was settled quickly and within three years had 600 inhabitants in town and on nearby farms, and streets and irrigation ditches were shaded by thousands of cottonwoods. Meanwhile it gained its post office in July 1866, at which time it was thought to be in Utah Territory. Early the next year Arizona Territory named St. Thomas as the seat of its Pah-Ute County, but the Mormons made no attempt to organize a government; their ties were with Utah, not with Nevada or Arizona.

A boundary survey in 1870 showed that the disputed Muddy Valley was in Nevada, and the state ordered the Mormons to pay back taxes for the previous two years. If this demand had not been placed upon the Mormons, the stability of Southern Nevada undoubtedly would have been maintained. Instead, the Mormons refused to pay either the back or the current taxes and abandoned Muddy Valley for Utah during the winter of 1870-

Two men of the Stanton survey of 1890 are sitting on the bank of the Colorado River near its junction with the Virgen River. These surveyors were determining the feasibility of running a railroad from Grand Junction, Colorado, to San Diego. Daniel Bonelli's ferryboat is also shown. *(National Archives)*

71. On February 20 the last train of settlers left St. Thomas. The sheriff from Hiko plastered tax suit notices on a few hundred empty houses. Only a few remained, including Daniel Bonelli, to operate the post office and lodging facilities for travelers.

The Mormons returned to Muddy Valley after 1880 and the area's population gradually increased to several hundred inhabitants. St. Thomas finally came to an end in the mid-1930s when the waters of Lake Mead filled the lowlands behind Hoover Dam. The town was evacuated and its residents settled at Overton and elsewhere. The townsite emerges when the lake's water level drops low enough to expose cement foundations and a lone chimney.

JUNCTION CITY, later Rioville, now under Lake Mead, 26 miles south of Overton.

When Major John Wesley Powell traveled down the Colorado River in his famous expedition of 1869, he noted late in August that Junction City was being laid out at the confluence of the Rio Virgen and the river which he had been exploring for over 14 weeks. The community, which had actually started in February 1869, was to be a crossing point for Mormon settlement of Northwestern Arizona Territory. Indian harassment had kept Junction City from growing and in the general Mormon exodus of 1871 the place was abandoned.

About 1875 Daniel Bonelli came to install a ferry service across the Colorado to accommodate north-south travelers going between eastern Nevada and the Arizona goldfields at Cerbat and Mineral Park. Bonelli built an inn and farm and employed Indians to run the ferry. He also owned salt mines just below St. Thomas and sold that product to mills at Eldorado. Activity increased in 1880 when the Mormons returned to Muddy Valley, and this place was renamed Rioville with the opening of the post office the next year, though little was done to establish a town. Destruction of the ferry boat, Bonelli's death in 1904 and the building of the railroad through southern Nevada a year later all led to the end of Rioville. The post office closed in June 1906.

KEY WEST, 5 miles east of the Gold Butte road at a point 19 miles south of that road's junction with I-15 at Riverside exit.

Copper deposits were first located in the late 1890s after an Indian had made the initial discovery. The Copper King district was organized and mining continued on a small scale. After 1900 the Key West mine was worked for nickel and platinum, but production was small and since 1913 the district has been generally inactive.

GOLD BUTTE, on the Gold Butte road at a point 56 miles south of I-15 at the Riverside exit (33 miles southeast of Glendale).

Daniel Bonelli found mica here in 1873, but the first precious metal to be discovered was gold, in 1905. Enough people had come by 1906 to warrant the opening of a post office, and another mild rush developed in 1908 when the Gold Butte Mercantile, Townsite & Mining Co. capitalized with 500,000 shares at $1 each and laid out a townsite. The camp contained a hotel, livery stable, post office, store and residences. A sanitarium was also proposed, as its planners believed that in time Gold Butte would be a popular stopping place for travelers. A number of small companies were organized in the district and the camp of Copper City was started two miles west around the short-lived Lincoln copper mine, but no sustaining developments were begun and by the end of 1910 most mining had ceased in the district. Little of interest remains.

GRAND GULCH (Arizona), approximately 16 miles southeast of the Gold Butte road at a point 23 miles south of I-15 at Riverside exit (44 miles southeast of Glendale).

Americans discovered copper in Grand Gulch about 1853, though Indians knew of the existence of metal in the area before that time. A Mormon from St. George, Utah, bought the prospect from the Indians for a horse and a few bags of flour, and for several years hauled ore to St. George for treatment. A crude adobe smelter was built in 1870, but it saw only limited use. Other small attempts to mine and smelt the ores met little success until 1906, when the Grand Gulch Copper Co. began shipping out regular loads of rich copper. By 1913 a smelter in Salt Lake City was receiving an average of 120 tons of copper ore per month. District production is estimated at $500,000. Wooden buildings and mine ruins remain.

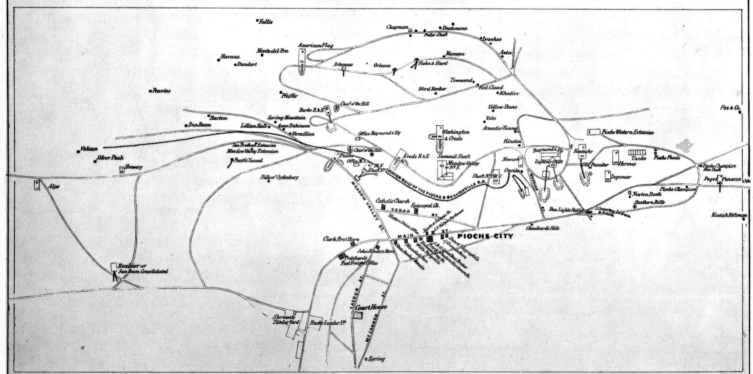

ELY DISTRICT, NEV.

COMPILED & DRAWN BY F.E. DURAND C.E.

A. NOËL, AGENT.

ROOM N? 20 HAYWARDS BUILDING, S.F.

LITH. BRITTON & REY. S.F.

0. Pioche City
1. Kentucky.
2. Lightner Shaft. Ray'd & Ely.
3. Old Panaca.
4. Hermes.
5. Pioche West Extension.
6. Pioche Phenix.
7. Pioche Champion.
8. Newton Booth.
9. Ingomar.
10. Meadow Valley Shaft N°3.
11. Meadow V. Summit Shaft.
12. Washington Creole.
13. Burke (Ray'd & Ely.)

14. Pioche.
15. American Flag.
16. Chapman.
17. Arkansas.
18. Huhn & Hunt.
19. Ivanhoe.
20. Chief of the Hill.
21. 4 Mile H°. (road to Hamilton.)
22. Meadow Valley Street.
23. Main Str.
24. Lacour St.
25. Page & Panacca.
26. Tanks of Meadow Valley,
    Ray'd & Ely. Kentucky, Newark.

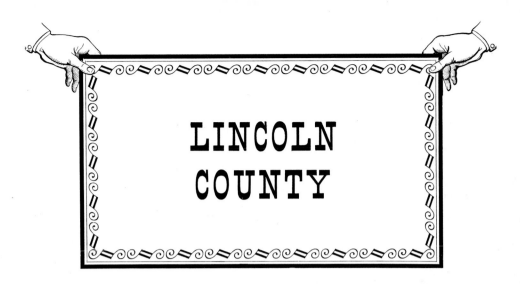

LINCOLN COUNTY

When the Pahranagat district boomed in southeastern Nevada during the mid-1860s, this new county was carved out of Nye County to meet the need for local government. Pahranagat soon declined but mining activity at Pioche, which had begun in 1868, increased dramatically in 1871 until Lincoln became an influential county, second only to the Comstock in the entire far West in terms of mineral production. A decline in the mid-1870s brought the county into the doldrums; the only significant mining activity was at Bristol and some revivals at Pioche, especially in 1890. After 1892 Delamar began its boom which continued until 1909 when the county lost its southern half in the creation of Clark County.

Small districts early in this century were Fay and Atlanta. For several years after 1912 intermittent mining activity took place in the Pioche-Ely Range region, and during the 1920s at Jackrabbit. Pioche revived significantly in 1937, and Tempiute joined Pioche as a major tungsten producer after World War II, but both districts folded by 1958. In the mid-1960s Pioche's mines awoke from seven years of dormancy.

PIOCHE, on US 93, 107 miles south of Ely, 193 miles north and east of Las Vegas.

Southeastern Nevada's richest and most important mining camp was also notorious as the state's most lawless community. Pioche began with a silver discovery in the winter of 1863-64 when Paiutes showed a Mormon missionary ore which they called "panacre," and disclosed its source in exchange for food and clothing. Though a district was organized the next year, serious development did not begin until 1868 when San Francisco financier F. L. A. Pioche bought several claims and erected a smelter on the hillside behind the now-abandoned courthouse. A camp formed around the activity later in the year. Though 1869 passed uneventfully, during the next year two large rivals, the Meadow Valley Mining Co. and the larger Raymond & Ely Mining Co., furiously developed mines at Pioche and each built a stamp mill at Bullionville, ten miles away. In September the Pioche *Record* published its first issue and began boosting the district.

Production in 1870 amounted to more than $600,000. During that and the following two years most of the output came from high-grade silver ores hauled to mills by wagon. No railroad existed in southern Nevada in 1870; the nearest station was Palisade on the Central Pacific, 275 miles north. From there large freight wagons hauled supplies and mining machinery to this isolated camp. The boom continued through the winter of 1870-71, and that spring the county seat was moved from Hiko.

The fame of Pioche's rich mines was matched by the disrepute of its crime. Law enforcement was ineffective at this remote place, over 400 miles from more populous western Nevada, and most offenses generally went unpunished. The frequency of homicide alone made Pioche notorious for frequent gunplay. Nearly sixty percent of Nevada's killings reported in 1871 and 1872 occurred in the Pioche area.

The surgery in the Pioche hospital would have put many of its big city counterparts to shame in 1910. *(Dorothy Ronnow Lee Collection)*

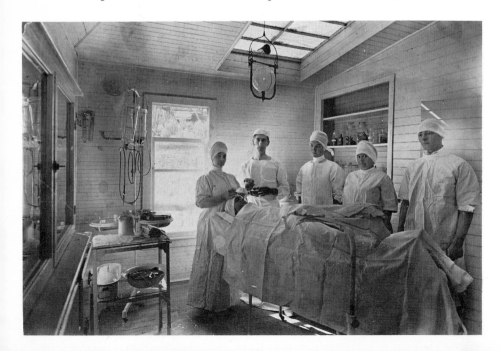

Early in 1872, Pioche (above) was southern Nevada's leading city. In the west end of town, streets ran without regard for symmetry or direction, following the ravines to secure the best grades for teams and wagons. On Treasure Hill in the background were the district's most important mines. There were all types of business establishments. The present Main Street enters from the middle left, behind and above John Ely's residence (with picket fence) and then turns toward the camera at a point just above the Pioche Hotel, labeled "baths." The new Lincoln County Museum is housed in the stone building just below the hardware store on the left side of the street. *(Fred Steen Collection)*

292

After Pioche became the seat of Lincoln County in 1871, this courthouse was built on Lacour Street in less than a year's time. Its scandalous financial history began with mismanagement and extravagant purchases during construction. The completed building, worth about $30,000, actually cost nearly $75,000. Compound interest on discounted bonds and subsequent dubious refinancing skyrocketed costs attributable to the building to about $800,000 by 1938, when the debt was finally returned. The so-called "million dollar courthouse" was abandoned during World War II in favor of new offices built in 1938 in the lower part of town. (*Top: Fred Steen Collection; bottom: Frank Mitrani photo*)

293

A new gasoline hoist is being hauled up the hill to the mines. (*Dorothy Ronnow Lee Collection*)

The output of Pioche's two-year-old Combined Metals mine and mill was 4000 tons a month during 1926, when this picture was taken. In 1940 a mill was built on the other side of this range at Caselton. The Combined Metals mine was connected at the 1200-foot level with a shaft driven at Caselton, and ore was hauled underground to the mill. Production from these operations during 1937-1957 totaled about $73 million, an output that exceeded the famous production in the 1870s. (*U. S. Geological Survey*)

In the early 1880s (above, right), the inhabitants of Pioche were thinking of more than silver and whiskey. The streets were wide and well cared for, and trees would soon line this street. The Raymond & Ely Mining Co. main shaft house is plainly visible on Treasure Hill. In the foreground left is the town gallows where due process was administered quickly and completely. (Las Vegas *Review-Journal*)

The west end of Pioche (below, right) has withstood nearly a century of fires and flash floods. Compare with the earlier view on the previous page. (*Frank Mitrani photo*)

Business and population grew with the increasing shipments of bullion, and much of the camp's floating population consisted of unemployed drifters on the lookout for a "big thing" but not willing to endure hard work. Seven dozen saloons thrived, as well as a flourishing red light district, in this town of over 7000 restless souls. During 1871 real estate values rose handsomely; lots formerly worth $100 or less sold in the thousands.

Shortly after midnight September 16 while Mexicans celebrated their homeland's independence, 300 kegs of powder exploded in a mercantile store, touching off a $500,000 fire. The furious flames quickly moved through the town licking with crackling tongues at the camp's dry wood-frame buildings, and before it was all over, about 2000 people were homeless. Substantial frame buildings soon rose from the ashes and the district continued its growth.

During the early years of the camp until adherence to laws, records and titles improved in 1872, the excessive amount of claim-jumping, fraud and killings made guns the only law, and "reliable legend" insists that violent deaths accounted for over six dozen graves in Boot Hill before a citizen of Pioche succumbed to natural causes. The dead were often buried with their boots on, and some men dug their own graves before being shot. Murderers often gunned down or without provocation stabbed innocent men and openly boasted of their crimes. If one of them were arrested, he was released on "straw bail" or on a technicality. Professional gunmen stalked the streets, and the wealthy hired their own protection. Hired guns of the two large mining companies often turned the Treasure Hill mining area into a virtual battleground.

Lawlessness decreased as churches and benevolent institutions were established. Production peaked in 1872, but no charter governed the wild town even at that date. Construction was begun on the narrow gauge Pioche & Bullionville Railroad which after June 1873 eliminated onerous transportation costs of hauling ore via wagon and encouraged increased production at the mines. But the district began to decline and litigation tied up many important mines. Flash floods during 1873 and 1874, and another ravaging fire in 1876 which gutted the commercial district, were additional

damaging blows. Later in 1876 both the large mining companies ceased major operations and through 1889 activity was minimal.

The district was invigorated in 1890 by talk of the Union Pacific extending its line from Milford, Utah, to Pioche, but silver prices went down and the metal was demonetized in 1893. The panic which ensued and abandonment of plans for railroad extension all nipped the budding revival. Not until early in this century, after completion of the Salt Lake railroad through the county lowered costs of shipping ore to mills, did the district re-awaken. The railroad extended a branch from Caliente in 1907 and five years later the mines began producing regularly. Pioche became an attractive camp with several substantial business houses, water system, school, bank and the Pioche *Record.*

The depression in the early 1930s closed the mines, but beginning in 1937 Pioche was an outstanding lead-zinc producer for two decades. Most mining ceased about 1958 but serious and promising exploratory work resumed in the mid-1960s. Much of interest remains today including abandoned mines, museum, Masonic temple, Boot Hill cemetery, and the "million dollar" courthouse.

BULLIONVILLE, via graded road ¼ mile east of US 93 at a point 1 mile north of its junction with SR 25 (10 miles south of Pioche).

After the relocation of the five-stamp Raymond & Ely mill here in February 1870, a camp named Ely City, soon renamed Bullionville, formed later that year. During the next two years most of Pioche's mills were built here because of a plentiful supply of water which was lacking at the mines. In 1872 construction began on the 21-mile-long narrow gauge Pioche & Bullionville Railroad which the next year began transporting ore between mines and mills. This was Nevada's second internal railroad, following by less than a year the completion of the Virginia & Truckee to Reno.

Bullionville grew rapidly around the milling and between 1872 and 1875 reached its peak population of 500 which supported stores, hotels, saloons, hay yards, blacksmith shop and daily stage service to Pioche. Five mills with 110 stamps crushed Pioche ore and several substantial dwellings were built. In 1875 a waterworks was completed at Pioche, at last supplying that city with

After a busy morning loading tailings at Bullionville early in this century, workers take time out to eat lunch. In the middle view, horse-driven slip scrapers recover the tailings and dump them onto a conveyor. They were then sent by rail to processing plants in northern Utah. *(Both photos: Nevada Historical Society)*

Foundations of early Bullionville mills abound, including these ruins of a 20th century mill. *(Frank Mitrani photo)*

enough water for milling; Bullionville then declined and its mills were removed during the next two years. The railroad ceased most operations by the end of the decade, the last remaining mill stopped running by the spring of 1880 and the town was soon virtually abandoned. The erection of a new smelting and concentrating plant later that year to work tailings of the former mills sparked a brief revival and at various times up to World War I smaller operators have shipped out tailings. Bullionville is entirely abandoned today.

CLOVER VALLEY, 23 miles east and south of US 93 at a point 11 miles south of its junction with SR 25 (31 miles south of Pioche).

Mormons farmed and raised stock in a settlement here in the late 1860s, with perhaps as many as fifty people and a post office between 1871 and 1877. In April 1899 Barclay post office was established, and the siding of the Salt Lake railroad, built through here in 1904, took the same name. Later another settlement named Joseco had a post office here for most of the time from 1916 to 1943.

DELAMAR, 12 miles south of US 93 at a point 16 miles west of Caliente (37 miles southwest of Pioche).

Gold discoveries by farmers from Pahranagat Valley in 1890 and 1891 led to the organization of the Ferguson district the next year, although Indians may have found gold over a dozen years earlier. The first rush developed out of Pioche after reports reached there of assays of $75 to $1000 a ton and people flocked to Ferguson using all types of conveyances. Ferguson, or Golden City, was located west of the Monkey Wrench mine. At the Magnolia mine the tent town of Helene sprang up with a newspaper — the Ferguson *Lode*, and a post office from June 1892 until December 1894.

The district's fortunes rose when Captain John De Lamar of Montana purchased the principal claims in 1893 for $150,000, and stepped-up development led to the founding of the camp of Delamar. The new town eclipsed the others after the Delamar mine began development early in 1894. The Delamar *Lode* commenced publication in June and two months later a post office opened. By the end of 1895 the camp contained many business structures and dwellings built of native stone. A

fifty-ton mill, that began running that May, was within a year handling up to 260 tons of ore daily.

For five years beginning in 1895 Delamar was the premier ore producer in generally inactive Nevada, accounting for over half of the state's output during that period. A second cyanide plant of 400-ton capacity was built in 1897 to keep up with the demand for milling. Unsuccessful attempts at obtaining water by drilling wells locally (one hole went down 900 feet) ended with the building from Meadow Valley Wash 12 miles east and 1500 feet lower, of two 3½-inch pipelines with three booster stations which delivered an inadequate forty gallons a minute to the town.

Because of improper ventilation in the dry process mills, silica dust continually drifted through the mills as well as in the mine tunnels, striking down miners and millers with the fatal silicosis — "Delamar dust"—so frequently that this camp acquired the sobriquet of "The Maker of Widows," a stinging indictment of early mining and milling methods. A sure symptom of this dreaded disease was severe coughing spells. Yet, with the lure of $3-a-day wages, jobs at Delamar did not go begging.

In 1897 Delamar's 3000 dusty citizens supported numerous saloons, stores, theaters, and professional offices. From 35 to 120 mule-driven freight outfits brought in supplies from the railhead at Milford, Utah, 150 miles northeast. Convoyed stagecoaches transported bullion from here until 1897 when an eight-mule-team wagon began hauling away the valuable stuff in a five-ton steel safe equipped with a time lock.

After fire destroyed half of the town in the spring of 1900 it was partially rebuilt. Two years later Captain De Lamar sold his mines which had produced $8.5 million in gold. The new owners headed by Simon Bamberger installed a new 400-ton mill in 1903, and Delamar still ranked third behind Goldfield and Tonopah in statewide mineral production as late as 1906, outproducing such high publicity booms as Bullfrog, Rawhide and Manhattan. After the Bamberger-Delamar mine closed down in 1909, major mining ceased. An estimated $13.5 million was made including $600,000 during a revival from 1929 to 1934 which saw both post office and school re-established. Rock buildings, mill ruins, and a cemetery remain.

298

These rare views of Delamar show most features of the camp. In foreground (left above) is the Delamar mill and tailings dump. High on the mountainside is the Hog Pen, the glory hole of the Delamar mine. To its right is the bold outcrop of the April Fool vein. The tree-lined main street (below) had several wooden stores which were transported from Pioche on wagons. With the decline of Delamar in 1909, many of the buildings were moved back to their original home. Above the main street are weather-proof stone houses owned by the Delamar Co. Note the laundry drying near the buildings in the foreground. *(Both photos: Ashley Cook Collection)*

The *Delamar Lode* was printed on an old proof press. Inking was done with a hand roller. Note the type cases in the background at the right. The flag contains pictures of Teddy Roosevelt and his running mate. Behind the young helper, known as a printer's devil, are several specimens of *Delamar Lode* job prints. *(Fred Steen Collection)*

Death rode through Delamar with such alarming frequency that the dry, dusty Griffin mills originally used were finally replaced by a wet process mill, shown here. The slowness of the owners to convert to the wet process suggests that men were cheaper than machinery. Wood was the principal fuel. To the right of the mill is the mess hall, and the town is in the rear. (Las Vegas *Review-Journal*)

This pumping plant lifted water over the Meadow Valley Range into Delamar. (Las Vegas *Review-Journal*)

CRYSTAL SPRING, on the south side of junction of SR 25 and SR 38 (52 miles southwest of Pioche).

Before Crystal Spring was settled in 1865, the springs supplied water for an Indian village for several generations. After the mid-19th century, westbound travelers stopped here to partake of cool water before striking out over deserts to the southwest. As a result of the nearby Pahranagat silver discoveries in 1865, the state legislature created Lincoln County and Crystal Spring sampled brief glory in 1866 by being designated the provisional county seat.

The attempt to organize the new county almost cost the life of Nevada's first elected governor, Henry G. Blasdel. To reach Pahranagat he and his party journeyed by way of Death Valley, far from the usual routes, and after passing Ash Meadows, south of modern Beatty, they found themselves running out of supplies. Without enough food to complete the trip to Crystal Spring, the six-foot-five-inch Governor and State Geologist White rushed ahead to Logan City (which see), 12 miles west of their destination, to obtain food and supplies. With wagon loaded and a fresh team, they returned to the rest of the party stranded on the desert. Exhausted under the hardship, a man had died and the others subsisted on lizards and other desert creatures. When the Governor and his party finally reached Crystal Springs they learned that the county lacked the number of voters required for organization which had to be postponed until the next year, at Hiko.

During its short five- or six-year existence, Crystal Spring was probably little more than a stage station, although with abundant water it was an inviting site for a town or mill. No evidence of the community remains; springs and a pasture cover the site.

HIKO, on SR 38 at a point 2 miles north of its junction with SR 25.

Indians who knew of silver in the Pahranagat district revealed its location to whites in March 1865, and by October a camp was effected at Hiko, an Indian expression for "white man's town." The new district caught the attention of Austin and central Nevada during the winter of 1865-66 and after a rush early in 1866 Hiko and vicinity had a few hundred residents. That spring William Ray-mond purchased many "squatters' claims," laid out a townsite and, after obtaining necessary capital in the East, had mill machinery shipped up the Colorado River to Callville and hauled by oxen the 140-mile distance to set up a five-stamp mill. The new facility started up in November 1866 but soon failed. In all, Raymond spent $900,000 building roads, erecting dwellings, setting up the mill, prospecting and mining; but with the absence of skilled workers very little return, actually only about $150,000, was realized. Everything proved costly because Austin, the nearest supply town, was more than 165 miles away and freight charges ran twenty cents a pound!

Hiko won the seat of Lincoln County early in 1867, but Raymond gave up on Pahranagat in 1869 when he and his partner uprooted the mill for the fairer grounds of Pioche. Hiko lost the county seat to Pioche in 1871 and then died. Its only hope for better days came in 1880-81 when the Eureka & Colorado Railroad was projected through here; that line never became a reality and Hiko never did revive. Stone ruins and a graveyard remain.

LOGAN CITY, via unimproved dirt road, 12 miles northwest of Crystal Spring.

Lingering rumors of a mountain of silver near the Colorado River tempted a few inquisitive prospectors to venture southward from Austin early in 1865 to look for it, and while returning north from the futile search an old Indian led the party to the east slope of Mount Irish and a rich silver-bearing ledge. That March locations were made and then everyone left for Panaca to obtain supplies. But less than a month after the group returned in June to begin exploratory work, Indians attacked the camp and chased everyone away.

By the fall of the year a permanent camp was established near springs in a wide pass south of the mines and within a few months it had over 100 people, among them William Raymond later of Pioche fame. More than 1000 claims were soon recorded in the Pahranagat district and a mill was built at nearby Hiko. During 1866 the district population climbed to 300 including the nearby camps of Silver Canyon, four miles north, and Crescent, two miles west, where another mill was installed. By July 1867 Logan City received its own post office.

Two mills have been built on this hill overlooking the town of Hiko, in the valley below. The $100,000 mill of the Hiko Silver Mining Co. ran on ore from the Pahranagat mines from 1866 until later in the decade when the rich surface veins disappeared. Later, around 1893, another mill built here worked some of the first gold-bearing ore from Delamar. *(Frank Mitrani photo)*

Logan City (below) with its fine stone buildings was situated near the mines in the Pahranagat district. One way to identify the site is to look for this cliff with its dramatic formation of water-deposited volcanic ash. *(Huntington Library)*

The Pahranagat district declined the next year and died by 1869 when the ore veins lacked depth and the magic name of Pioche was on everyone's lips. Some work was done by small operators early in this century and just before World War II. Rock ruins remain at Logan City and Silver Canyon; remnants of a smelter are left at Crescent.

FREYBERG [also Frieburg, Freiburg], 38 miles northwest of SR 38 at a point 9 miles north of its junction with US 93 (63 miles west of Pioche).

Indians led two prospectors to ore-bearing rock on the eastern flank of the Worthington Mountains in the fall of 1865, and after additional discoveries of lead and silver in 1869 the Freyberg district was organized in May 1869. A large number of locations were made, but no serious mining effort got under way until after 1919. Some ore was then shipped, but operations probably did not continue beyond the mid-1920s.

GROOM, by graded road 26 miles southwest of SR 25 at a point 15 miles west of its junction with US 93.

The Groom lead and silver mine was discovered in 1864 but no district was organized until the fall of 1869. An English company spent $80,000 on roads and development and then abandoned the mine because it was too isolated. In this century leasers have made small shipments.

TEMPIUTE, by graded road 8 miles east of SR 25 at a point 38 miles west of its junction with US 93 (66 miles west of Pioche).

Silver was first found in the winter of 1865, and a band of prospectors discovered additional lodes in December 1868. Specimens sent to Hamilton for assay that winter promised values from $72 to $300 per ton. A district was organized the next month, but mining was difficult because of the scarcity of water which had to be packed to the camp by Indians from springs 12 miles away. About fifty miners were here in 1870, but when the ten-stamp mill at nearby Crescent was dismantled the next year, most mining ceased. During 1874-77 some ore was hauled to Tybo for treatment.

Tungsten ore was found in 1916, but not until additional deposits were uncovered two decades later and a small mill was built did large-scale mining begin. The Lincoln Mines Co. commenced operations in 1940 after building a mill. Tempiute prospered during World War II, then slumped for five years; but after the price of tungsten rose in 1950 the camp revived. For the next six years it had 700 residents and a school, a post office was open during 1953-57, and the Lincoln mine was one of the nation's major producers of tungsten. When the price of that metal slumped in 1957 the mill shut down. It was soon dismantled leaving bare foundations and remnants of houses.

FAY, 24 miles east of Pioche via Eagle Valley road.

After gold discoveries in the Eagle Valley district, a camp with post office called Deerlodge was started during the next year. When richer veins were uncovered a mile northeast in 1899, Deerlodge was abandoned for prospects at the new camp at Fay, named after the daughter of a major investor in the district. The biggest productions were recorded in 1900-01 when the camp had about four saloons, barbershop, stores, post office, and stage service. Orators and imported singers occasionally performed in the town hall. Fay frolicked until about 1915 when the mines failed and by 1924 the post office was removed. Wooden buildings and a dilapidated mill remain at Fay; Deerlodge contains even fewer ruins.

EAGLE VALLEY, 16 miles east then north of Pioche via Eagle Valley road.

This one-street community at the head of a canyon of the same name was settled as a farming and stock-raising area in the mid-1860s. A recreation hall and houses were here and since 1895 Ursine post office has served the population which for most decades has remained a steady forty to fifty persons.

SPRING VALLEY, by graded road 5 miles north of Eagle Valley.

This community of ranches began when Pioche and other camps needed produce during the 1870s, and in 1896 Newland post office was established, named for the Nevada senator who was then promoting bills in Congress to allow for reclamation of arid lands. Around 1900 about fifty people lived here, but in 1912 the post office was removed, and only one family remained in the 1960s.

This 1902 view of the town of Fay shows one of the two principal streets. On the hill in the background at the left is the Horseshoe mine and its 90-ton mill. That mill was enlarged to 120-ton capacity six years later (below). The middle view shows another mill in the Fay district. *(Three photos:* Las Vegas *Review-Journal)*

HIGHLAND, 4½ miles west and south of US 93, via Caselton Road and desert road, at a point 3½ miles north of Pioche.

Silver discoveries on the eastern side of the Highland Range in 1868 led the next year to the founding of a camp with a boardinghouse, brewery, saloon and dwellings. Wagons transported ore to the smelter at Bristol, twenty miles north, where smelting cost seven dollars a ton. A thirty-stamp mill was planned early in the 1870s, but was never built. About 25 tons of ore were taken out daily for weeks at a time until the camp died later in the 1870s. Broken brick and twisted steel mark the site.

JACKRABBIT, earlier Royal City, 1 mile via graded road west of US 93 at a point 14 miles north of Pioche.

Discoveries of silver ore on the east slope of the Bristol Range in 1876 brought Royal City into being. Within months the camp had a store, saloon, boardinghouse, blacksmith shop and restaurant, and it was the last whiskey stop before the southbound stage arrived in Pioche. Its own post office was open in 1878-79. Ores from the Day, or Jackrabbit, mine were milled at nearby Bristol and Pioche. Production dipped during the 1880s, but when the 15-mile narrow gauge "Jackrabbit road" opened in 1891 between a new smelter at Pioche and the Jackrabbit mine, operations increased for two years. The railroad station took the name Jackrabbit and the Royal City moniker was not used. After about 1893 the mines fell silent until 1906-07 and 1912-1914, when Jackrabbit became the terminal of the Bristol mine tramway (see Bristol). The 19th century camp has long since disappeared, but some mining operations have been conducted in most years since 1920.

BRISTOL WELL, 7 miles via graded roads west of US 93 at a point 14 miles north of Pioche.

As early as 1872 a furnace was erected to treat silver-lead ores hauled from the Bristol mine, four miles east at National City. A five-stamp mill with smelter was built in 1880 after the Hillside mine began development, and ovens of shale and sandstone converted pine logs to charcoal for the smelter. About 1890, when a new smelter began treating copper ores, Bristol Well had a post office and a population of about 400.

After its second burst of mining activity ended about 1893, Bristol Well was inactive until a small leaching plant was installed about 1900 to recover copper from the Bristol mine's ores. That mill operated only two years. Any likelihood that local milling might be resumed was permanently killed about 1905 when the Salt Lake railroad was built through Lincoln County. Foundations and three beehive coke ovens remain.

SILVERHORN, 7 miles north of Bristol Well.

A silver strike was made in 1906, but no work started until the fall of 1920 when the district was rediscovered. Outsiders then took note and a boom was on in the spring of 1921. By June the camp had a barber shop, department store and saloons, but the excitement was over by fall.

BRISTOL, earlier National City, 10 miles west of US 93, via graded roads, at a point 14 miles northwest of Pioche.

Mormons discovered silver in 1870 and the new finds on the western flank of the Bristol Range gave rise to a camp called National City in April 1871. Sixty locations were made that year and a smelter was built which operated for a short time, then did not fire up again until 1878 when discovery of the Hillside mine revived the district. That year a 12-stamp mill was installed, and after the older smelter was repaired the flow of bullion commenced. About that time the camp was renamed Bristol.

By 1882 the town had five stores, eight saloons, two hotels with restaurants attached, three stables, a lodging house, express office, printing office which published the weekly *Times*, two barbershops, butcher, laundry, shoemaker, blacksmith shop, post office, plenty of whiskey and "more prospective millionaires than any camp of comparable size!" Bristol became the trading point for about 700 mines, and the camp was said to be assuming the airs of a metropolis because the Star brewery had hired a female who served the fluids with all the graces of a modern Hebe.

Itinerant ministers occasionally held services until population had dwindled away by 1884, though the camp revived in the early 1890s. In 1911 operations at Bristol and at Jackrabbit, two

The main shaft of the Bristol mine was constantly in use early in this century. *(Charles Labbe Collection)*

Jackrabbit for many years was consistent in its ore production, but today the only buildings remaining are these shacks and the ruins of the tramway terminal. *(Theron Fox photo)*

These kilns at Bristol Well manufactured charcoal for a nearby lead smelter in the Bristol district. *(Frank Mitrani photo)*

miles northeast, were combined, and after 1913 an aerial tramway linked the two points. Bristol's ores were then sent on the tram and loaded on railroad cars for delivery to Salt Lake City smelters via Pioche. The Bristol mine still produces ore, but the town has been a ghost for many decades.

ATLANTA, 21 miles via graded road northeast of US 93 at a point 29 miles north of Pioche.

After the discovery of "exceedingly rich ledges of silver ore" early in 1869, a district was organized and the small camp of Silver Park was started. But picks and shovels were soon cast aside here because of the glamor of White Pine. Two mills began working the ore after 1872, and annual outputs were made until 1878 when one mill was shut down and the other moved to Utah.

The area lay quiet for over three decades until a few men began working in the summer of 1909. A mild boom ensued and soon additional locations surrounded the old workings. A celebration with dance and free food greeted the establishment of a townsite, and its promoters sold many lots. News circulated that a projected railroad from Ely to Pioche would pass near Atlanta, and development of this district was watched closely. About 100 people were attracted here, but by 1910 Atlanta "fell" as it was a low-grade camp.

The Atlanta Consolidated Mining Co. began extensive development of claims in 1911 and for the rest of the decade made a limited production. During the 1930s the mines were worked off and on, and a new mill was built in 1965 in preparation for large mining operations, but a lawsuit forced cessation of work in 1966. Wooden cabins remain of old Atlanta while newer installations are guarded by a watchman.

MONTEZUMA, via graded road, approximately five miles west of US 93 at a point 54 miles north of Pioche.

An Indian revealed silver ore bodies to whites in January 1869, the Patterson district was organized the next month, and during the spring over 400 persons came here. A camp formed on a slope of a hill near the mines and soon had a blacksmith shop and stores. Lots sold for $100 to $300 and the district's several promising mines began production as a result of enthusiastic prospecting. Another town known as Patterson, or Springville, was laid out a mile and a half east in a small valley where there was enough water for a substantial town, but the rich ore bodies gave out and the district was abandoned probably about 1873. A post office was opened in 1872-73. Early in this century limited mining revived the district.

Atlanta was located amid junipers and sagebrush-covered hills on the north flank of the Wilson Creek Range. (U. S. Geological Survey)

In the early months of Beatty's existence the Northern Saloon was opened as an obvious imitation of Tex Rickard's successful saloons in Alaska and Goldfield. It seemed that a new mining camp early in this century was incomplete without a Northern. *(National Park Service)*

At holiday time the main street in Beatty shows a horse-drawn stage arriving at the Montgomery Hotel, a renowned hostelry. Each of its 23 rooms had a telephone, a Brussels carpet, and red curtains. Most rooms had private baths. Farther down the dusty street were many saloons. Late in 1906, the first railroad was built into the town, supplanting most of the stagecoach traffic. In 1907 Beatty was a great transportation center with three standard gauge railroads. *(Los Angeles County Museum)*

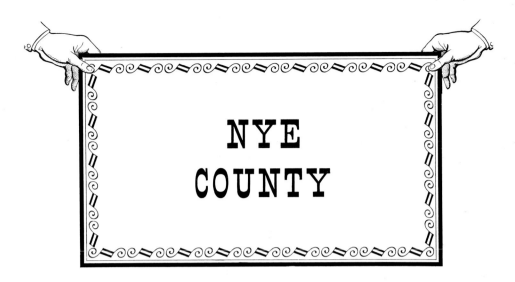

NYE COUNTY

This huge mineral-studded county was first settled in the summer of 1863 during a rush southward from Austin which resulted in the founding of such camps as Ione, Washington, Grantsville, Ellsworth and Ophir Canyon. By the mid-1860s settlement had extended eastward across the county to Belmont, Hot Creek, Northumberland, Danville and Reveille. But the White Pine excitement at the end of the decade emptied most of these towns and forced the mines to shut down.

The 1870s were highlighted by outstanding production at revived Belmont, Jefferson, Tybo, Downeyville and Grantsville. Many smaller mines were also active in northern Nye County; because water and timber were inadequate for mining and milling, the south experienced no development. After 1881 mining was depressed county-wide for the rest of the century.

The discovery of silver at Tonopah in 1900 triggered a series of mining rushes which went far beyond the county's borders. As the Tonopah mines became known throughout North America, the whole area was prospected at a furious pace and at least nine dozen camps rose. Rhyolite in the Bullfrog district also gained nationwide attention after discoveries in 1904. Johnnie and Bonnie Claire were also important southern Nye camps; Troy, Reveille and Silverbow boomed in the east; and Round Mountain, Manhattan and smaller camps along the huge ridge of the Toiyabe Range were producers of ore.

The greatest single decade of mineral output was 1910-1920 when Tonopah made its largest pro-duction and Round Mountain enjoyed a sustained boom. Wahmonie briefly flared up in 1928 and Tybo, Manhattan and Round Mountain revived in the 1930s. Lodi, Northumberland and smaller districts thrived around 1940, and after World War II large operations resumed at Manhattan and Round Mountain. Smaller mines in many districts have also been active in the 1950s and 1960s.

BEATTY, junction of SR 58 and US 95 at a point 114 miles northwest of Las Vegas.

Beatty is the sole surviving town of the Bullfrog mining district, a 20th century boom area which embraces the mineral-bearing Bullfrog Hills. Before discoveries in the summer of 1904, this area was relatively quiet. Oasis Valley, directly to the north, attracted several ranchers who had taken Indian wives and established small homesteads along the running stream known as the Amargosa River. Itinerant prospectors often spent the night at one of these ranches before again braving heat and the dry shadeless plains north and south of the valley.

All this quietness changed after the fall of 1904 when mining excitement from Tonopah and Goldfield extended southward to this area. Mining activity brought the camps of Rhyolite and Bullfrog into being near the newly discovered mines, while Beatty rose at the eastern edge of the Bullfrog district on the Amargosa. Within a year's time Beatty blossomed into a thriving freighting center serving the entire district, and an array of businesses were established including a hotel built by the town's founder, Bob Montgomery.

In the summer of 1905, Beatty was an impressive tent city, though no important mining activity took place near the town. The Bullfrog district's major mines were at Rhyolite, just beyond the hills in the background. During 1906 the Porter brothers' store (below) began serving the locals. It advertised itself as having the lowest prices —"you know that!"— and here prospectors completely outfitted themselves with mining supplies, dry goods, clothes and other necessities. *(Top: National Park Service; bottom: Mrs. H. H. Heisler Collection)*

310

Stores in Beatty soon moved from tents into wooden buildings. Additional saloons, clubs and cafes had been opened, and the telephone company opened an office just beyond the Porter brothers' store. From this adobe office (right), the Bullfrog district's pioneer newspaper was issued weekly, beginning in April 1905. The plush $25,000 Montgomery Hotel (bottom) was the center of social activity in Beatty and the gathering place for important mining men. It is shown here after its completion in the fall of 1905. In 1908 the building was moved to the camp of Pioneer where during the next year it was destroyed by fire. (*Top: Ray McMurry Collection; right: Getchell Library, University of Nevada; bottom: National Park Service*)

311

The speed in which Beatty emerged is illustrated by the Beatty *Bullfrog Miner* in contrasting the 1905 Thanksgiving dinner at the Montgomery Hotel with the one supposedly enjoyed the previous year by Montgomery and friends:

THANKSGIVING DAY, 1904
MENU
Bean Soup
BOILED
Beans and Bacon
BAKED
Bacon and Beans
ENTREES
Mulligan, a la Scraps
DESSERT
Flap Jacks   Coffee
Dog Leg Tobacco   Clay Pipes
CORDIAL
Dr. Jesse Moore

THANKSGIVING, NOVEMBER 30th, 1905
THE MONTGOMERY CAFE
Casey & Arden, Props.

✓   ✓   ✓

Blue Point Oysters
SOUP
Chicken Soup, a la Montgomery
FISH
Amargosa Trout, a la Tammy
SALADS
Lobster Salad, a la Mitchell
Potato Salad
BOILED
Boiled Chicken, a la Parky
ENTREES
Calf's Brains, Porter Sauce
ROASTS
Roast Young Turkey, a la Malcolm Macdonald
Suckling Pig
RELISHES
Olives   Pickles
VEGETABLES
Green Corn   Stewed Tomatoes
DESSERT
C. & A. Hot Mince Pie
Pumpkin Pie, a la Hoveck
English Plum Pudding, Hard & Brandy Sauce
Nuts   Cheese
Manhattan Cocktail
WINES
St. Julien   White Seal   Numm's
CIGARS
Egyptian Cigarettes   Cafe Noir

With a population of over 1000 in 1906-07, Beatty boomed with three railroads and a bank. After the Bullfrog district boom subsided in 1909, Beatty continued as a supply base for small adjacent mining operations, as southern terminus of the Bullfrog Goldfield Railroad until 1928 and as northern terminus of the Tonopah & Tidewater Railroad until 1940. This town of several hundred continues to thrive as the northeast entrance town into Death Valley National Monument.

RHYOLITE, 2 miles northwest of SR 58 at a point 2 miles west of Beatty.

Two penniless prospectors named Eddie Cross and Frank "Shorty" Harris spent the summer of 1904 with their pack train of five burros prospecting in the hills but found nothing until early in August when they came to the Bullfrog Hills. Harris struck his pick into croppings of quartz and finding gold in the green stained rock he named his claim the Bullfrog. News of this rich discovery quickly circulated and the Bullfrog district was organized.

That fall the new district rapidly came to the front, and many people rushed here despite the approaching winter season. Assays of $3000 per ton were reported in the mining press, and hundreds of people tempted by this latest Nevada mining siren were lured into the district. Beginning early in 1905 the trail was especially hot from the north, and the rush from Tonopah and Goldfield raised "a string of dust a hundred miles long." Daily four- and six-horse Concord stages came from Goldfield and Las Vegas with passengers, express and mail.

In February 1905 Rhyolite townsite was platted in a draw close to the district's most important mines, offering free lots to merchants, and a town virtually sprang up in a day. During the first few months the crude new community consisted of rag dwellings, canvas lodging houses, tent saloons and stores. Fuel was scarce; sagebrush and greasewood were used to feed the few stoves in the camp. All food had to be teamed into the camp, and water was hauled from Beatty at from two to five dollars a barrel. Lumber was in such demand that three suppliers could not bring it in quickly enough. But amid the primitive surroundings the restless crowd was developing mines and a city was emerging.

In May 1905 the three-month-old town of Rhyolite was a sea of tent houses. The camp grew rapidly and substantially, and by January 1908 (below) the town's expansion was just about completed. The tracks of the Las Vegas & Tonopah Railroad enter from mid-foreground and lead to the depot, where a smoking engine has stopped. The tracks then lead past the freight yards before disappearing into the hills in the mid-background. From the depot Golden Street extends through the heart of town past the John S. Cook Bank building at its intersection with Broadway Street. On the far side of town is the depot of the Bullfrog Goldfield Railroad. *(Top: Marion Schendel Collection; bottom: Mrs. H. H. Heisler Collection)*

RHYOLITE, NEV.   JAN. 1908

FROM BONANZA MT.   A.E. HOLT

When millionaire Charles Schwab inspected his mines at Rhyolite (top), he probably stayed at the Southern Hotel. It opened about July 1905 with 36 furnished rooms, a private banquet hall, and a first-class grill and bar. (*Mrs. H. H. Heisler Collection*)

William Stewart, Nevada Senator for five terms, retired from politics in 1905 to open a law office in Rhyolite. Though his fine building lasted past the boom era, only low walls now mark its site, just southwest of Ladd Mountain. (*Mrs. H. H. Heisler Collection*)

Though Death Valley Scotty condemned empty bottles as worthless (he was only interested in full ones), beer and champagne discards were often used as building materials. The West's most famous bottle house was this one at Rhyolite, built of several thousand empties in the early years of the camp. In the 1920s it was reconstructed for use in the Zane Grey movie "Wanderers in the Wasteland." People still live in it. (*Mrs. H. H. Heisler Collection*)

314

The Bullfrog district's richest mine was the Montgomery-Shoshone, which produced nearly $1.4 million. Its 200-ton cyanide plant ran for three years.

On Independence Day 1908 (middle), volunteer firemen pull hose carts down Rhyolite's Golden Street. Posters on the left advertise the coming of the Barnum & Bailey circus, which on the morning of its arrival (below) paraded through the town. The band played such spirited songs as "There Will Be a Hot Time in the Old Town Tonight" to arouse interest for performances later that day. *(Three photos: Mrs. H. H. Heisler Collection)*

Golden Street in 1968 is nearly deserted. These grand ruins are the John S. Cook bank building and in the background are the remains of the Overbury block. From the left (below) are the skeletal walls of the Cook building, Dr. Quimby's office, the Las Vegas & Tonopah Railroad depot (still used as a residence), and the Porter brothers' store. *(Top: David Muench photo; bottom: Gary Allen Photo)*

In May 1905 the Rhyolite *Herald* began publication, and a post office was established the next month, replacing a subscription mail service which paid a stage company to bring letters to the camp. During the rest of 1905 and 1906 thousands of people came and went. Property values soared into thousands of dollars per lot. The mining stock boom which captivated the nation at that time put the Bullfrog district in the limelight of speculation and investment; individuals with the "fever" who were unable to make a killing at Goldfield poured millions into local mining developments and into townsite lots. Wildcat companies flourished but a dozen of the better Bullfrog stocks went above par value. The Las Vegas & Tonopah Railroad reached nearby Gold Center in May and service was extended to Rhyolite before the year ended.

By 1907 this thriving town of only two years had 6000 hustling inhabitants and possessed a modern telephone exchange, three water companies, three ice plants, electric street lights, board of trade, hotels with private baths, three railroads, four banks, dozens of saloons, opera house, symphony orchestra, four competing newspapers and two locally printed magazines. Block after block of substantial wood and stone structures had been built, and wide smooth streets were lined with comfortable and ·commodious homes. A modern city developed before any of its highly touted mines had begun to operate in the black.

Among the mines within the radius of a few miles many had received nationwide publicity including the Montgomery-Shoshone, Denver, Original Bullfrog, National Bank, Gibraltar, Tramp, Polaris and Eclipse. When financial panic struck the nation late in 1907 these mines folded as did others in the mining West. By the end of the decade major mining in the district had ceased; the lower grade veins under the rich surface deposits were unprofitable to work. People who only a few years earlier had arrived in stages or on foot rode the trains out of town to settle in Las Vegas and Los Angeles.

Rhyolite had only 700 people in 1910; a decade later the town had completely expired; and during the 1920s and 1930s dozens of abandoned buildings with furniture and office records and stock remained exposed to the Amargosa wind. Vandals, the weather, and the need for building materials

in Beatty and Las Vegas have taxed the town so that ruins of less than a dozen buildings are left. The expensive depot still stands inhabited, as well as the famous bottle house.

BULLFROG, one mile southwest of Rhyolite.

Townsites galore were platted in the Bullfrog district during the first seven months after the original gold discovery in August 1904. The tent village of Orion, soon renamed Amargosa City, sprang up below the Original Bullfrog mine as the district's pioneer camp, and the first mining recorder and telephones were established there. A Bullfrog townsite was laid out nearby. Amid important strikes three miles east of Amargosa City, the rag town of Bonanza sprang up near the foot of Ladd Mountain. Other towns were Beatty and Gold Center. Claims blanketed the area for miles around these camps.

After still another townsite, Rhyolite, was platted early in 1905 and important mining centered there, Amargosa City was moved entirely to the flat below Rhyolite to start the present town of Bullfrog. Bonanza also moved en masse to the Rhyolite townsite that spring, and thereafter the two towns briefly engaged in a wild race for com-

Frank "Shorty" Harris, co-discoverer of Bullfrog, was a veteran of mining stampedes from Tombstone to British Columbia. *(Mrs. Stella Brown Collection)*

317

In May 1905 the main street of Bullfrog was clearly defined. The tents in the draw to the right are the south end of Rhyolite. Against the base of the hills in the middle distance is the Original Bullfrog mine. *(Marion Schendel Collection)*

Shorty Harris, a "single-blanket jackass prospector" did not become rich because of the Bullfrog discovery; too much "Oh Be Joyful" allowed the fruits of his labor to get away. He died penniless in 1934. *(Mrs. Stella Brown Collection)*

Before arrival of the railroad to Bullfrog, immense freight teams hauled in supplies to the district. *(National Park Service)*

mercial supremacy. Within a year's time this camp of over 1000 people had its own water line, bank, post office, hotels, chamber of commerce, and the business district converged with Rhyolite's. Telephones and fast auto stages gave Bullfrog rapid communication with the outside world.

Later in 1906 Rhyolite had extinguished Bullfrog's commercial light, and many of the business buildings were moved on wagons up the draw to the larger camp. Bullfrog still retained many fine residences, and its post office did not close until the district collapsed in 1909. Stone and adobe walls mark the site.

LEADFIELD (California), by one-way road westbound, 14 miles west of SR 58 at a point 6 miles west of Beatty.

Two decades after major mining of borax and precious metals in Death Valley had practically ceased, the Western Lead Co. acquired low-grade lead ore bodies in picturesque Titus Canyon for the purpose of promotion. Oil magnate C. C. Julian controlled that company, and during 1926 he skillfully advertised Leadfield as a large mineral-studded district, inducing thousands of investors to pour their savings into this speculative operation. The Leadfield boom was kicked off on March 26, 1926 when a special train was chartered to bring some 3000 eager investors from Los Angeles to Leadfield, although probably less than half that number actually made the trip. Almost 100 autos converged on Titus Canyon that day and at the townsite a banquet was served, complete with live entertainment. The flamboyant Leadfield *Chronicle* spread the news of the district's supposed riches, and other autos came loaded with mining implements and supplies. Frame buildings soon rose among the tents, and a telephone line connected the new camp with Beatty.

Bunkhouses were built, as well as a mess hall, blacksmith shop, hotel, an inn, and a half-dozen other types of stores. Townsite lots brought $260 each and thousands of claims were staked in the canyon. By August enough people lived here to warrant a post office, and 200 persons picked up letters on its opening. But the boom was spurred by smooth salesmanship instead of sustaining strikes, and when the post office closed in January 1927, only one person called for mail. Cement foundations and walls mark the site.

Leadfield in March 1926 promised to be a rich mining district but it never got beyond this unimposing collection of tents and shacks. *(Mrs. Henrietta Revert)*

At Gold Center, misguided business judgment erected this brewery to supply fluids for the Last Chance and other saloons in the camp. The brewery also furnished distilled water and ice. (*Dickenson Library, University of Nevada*)

When Gold Center consisted of these few buildings a townsite promoter tried to induce the Bullfrog district's new arrivals to settle at the place south of Beatty and the mines. But promotion here was not as successful as at nearby Rhyolite, and by 1908 the camp had become "Dead Center." (*History Division, Los Angeles County Museum*)

GOLD CENTER, ½ mile west of US 95 at a point 3 miles south of Beatty.

The placid Amargosa River, not as bitter as its name and usually only about a foot wide in its huge bed here, was an important water source for mining camps in the Bullfrog district in 1904, when a townsite was platted at this point. It was called Gold Center, although no gold was found here and the place was the center of nothing but sand and mountains.

Gold Center grew in stature after becoming the terminus of the Las Vegas & Tonopah Railroad in May 1906, and it served briefly as railhead for Rhyolite until that booming camp first saw the smoke of locomotives in December 1906. The L. V. & T. maintained a yard and freight depot at Gold Center until the extensive Rhyolite yards were completed.

At its height early in 1907 Gold Center had a post office, bank and trust company, the *News*, hotel, stores, feed corral and several saloons. These served draft beer brewed locally by the Gold Center Ice & Brewing Co. This firm was housed in a large stone structure complete with steam whistle. A visitor remarked that a brewery in this hot desert country was as far removed from malt and hops as it was possible to be this side of Hades.

The community finally got into the mining act when the Gold Center Water & Mills Co. sank shafts and extended tunnels, but found no valuable rock. A thirty-ton mill erected here briefly served

the district. Indeed, Gold Center developed into quite a town, but as Rhyolite and Bullfrog faded it too became a thing of the past. Foundations of the mill and brewery mark the site.

CHLORIDE CITY (California), 13 miles southwest of US 95 at a point 7 miles south of Beatty.

Silver discoveries near Chloride Cliff in 1873 led to limited mining, but the district died after 1880. Rhyolite men purchased the mines in 1908 and erected a cyanide mill in 1916. A camp formed, consisting of superintendent's house, blacksmith shop, assay office, bunkhouse and cookhouse, but operation was brief and Chloride City folded, probably by 1918.

CARRARA, on east side of US 95 at a point 9 miles south of Beatty.

First attempts at quarrying marble in the Carrara hills began in 1904, but operators soon found the marble too fractured to provide large desirable pieces. Additional deposits were uncovered about seven years later and the American Carrara Marble Co. laid out a town to develop quarries in Carrara Canyon, high above the desert. The Las Vegas & Tonopah Railroad was already at hand, and water was piped in from Gold Center, 5½ miles north.

The townsite was officially dedicated early in May 1913, and the celebration that day included a dance with music by a band from Goldfield, a

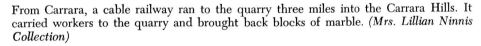

From Carrara, a cable railway ran to the quarry three miles into the Carrara Hills. It carried workers to the quarry and brought back blocks of marble. (*Mrs. Lillian Ninnis Collection*)

baseball game and swimming in the town pool. Carrara had its weekly *Obelisk,* and later in the month a post office opened, and a hotel, restaurant and store to serve about 100 people. A company railroad was completed in the spring of 1914 to move large marble blocks from the quarry to the Tonopah & Tidewater station at Carrara, whence they were shipped to Los Angeles for finishing.

Operations had slipped by 1917 when the paper suspended publication, and Carrara declined further in the early 1920s. The post office closed in 1924. Only foundations and the road to the quarry remain at Carrara. Concrete structures 1¼ miles to the north were never part of the marble company town; they are remnants of a cement company of Philippine ownership which abandoned its buildings early in 1936 before production began.

ROSE'S WELL, 1¼ miles southwest of US 95 at a point 17 miles south of Beatty.

This was a minor station on an old stage road between the Bullfrog district and points south where meals and forage were available. A well was sunk 210 feet deep and yielded 110 barrels of water a day.

Three miles south of the station is the Big Dune, a 300-foot hill of sand, replenished periodically by Death Valley winds. Sandstorms have been so severe that following the stage road was sometimes exceedingly difficult. One day in 1910 a teamster was caught in a sandstorm near the Big Dune and had to cut loose his whiskey-laden wagon so that he could take his team to Rose's Well to wait out the storm. After the heavy winds subsided, he returned to the dune but could not find his hooch wagon. It is said that many witnesses testify to the validity of this apocryphal story and several bottles of well-aged whisky may yet be under the Big Dune. Only the well remains at the station site.

LEELAND, 10 miles south of US 95 at a point 17 miles south of Beatty.

When the Tonopah & Tidewater Railroad built northward in 1906, Leeland was established with facilities for minor service, including water tank and station. The camp of Lee boomed five miles to the west that year, and Leeland served as the railhead for developments there. In 1911 a small post office was established which lasted for three years. Leeland had long outlived its usefulness when the T. & T. pulled up its track in the early 1940s.

LEE (California), 5 miles west of Leeland.

Gold was found in 1906 on the east flank of the Funeral Range and a tent camp formed near the mines. In the spring of the next year a platted townsite straddled the state line. At its height many buildings were built, mostly on the California side. The Lee *Herald* began publication and a telephone line was extended to the camp, but when the veins pinched out Lee quickly folded.

WAHMONIE, 34 airline miles east-southeast of Beatty. The site is within the Las Vegas Bombing and Gunnery Range and is not accessible for exploration.

Mining began on the east edge of Jackass Flat before 1905, but the area remained quiet until the discovery of high-grade silver-gold ore in February 1928. Over 200 miners and builders hastened to the district within three weeks' time. Others arrived hauling small houses on trucks or in cars loaded to the hilt with grub and lumber, tents and stoves, and some came pushing wheelbarrows tied down with goods. Many people thought that Wahmonie might become another Cripple Creek, and newspapers invoked the adventurous to seek a fortune. "Former knowledge and experience is of little value. Any tenderfoot who has the ambition to get out at 5 a.m. in the cold, and hustle into the mountains and has luck enough to get a claim is liable to have his made right now."

The Wahmonie townsite soon blossomed with tents. Boarding houses opened, tent stores sold dry goods, and cafes offered ham and eggs and coffee for a dollar. Within a few weeks over 1000 claims were staked and with autos continuing to speed across the sagebrush to Wahmonie in the cold wintery weather, the population streaked to 500 by March. George Wingfield organized the Wahmonie Mines Co. which developed the Horn Silver mine. A post office opened in April, and two months later the town reached its peak: 1451 mining locations had been filed and about 1000 busy people were in camp. The Horn Silver mine sank a 500-foot shaft, but only minor shipments were

Nevada's last flamboyant mining rush took place in 1928 at Wahmonie. The mild climate encouraged hundreds of fortune seekers, many of whom had been at Weepah the previous year. They brought their tents and supplies here, believing that Wahmonie was to be a place of promise. *(Mrs. Harry Mighels Collections)*

Some people came to speculate in real estate (center). Frequently more money was made in the sale of townsite lots than at the mines. The useful tent with a wood floor and low wood sides was easily assembled and transported. Little ropes fastened over hooks or nails on the wooden frame held the canvas top in place. *(Nevada Historical Society)*

This pioneer Wahmonie merchant mentally inventories merchandise in his open air store. Coca Cola, Pep cereal, Snowdrift, and canned cream are shown. The haphazard display emphasizes the fast pace of the district.

made, and the pervading optimism subsided. By the end of that hectic year the town was bust; Wahmonie had produced more excitement than minerals. But since 1950 the ghosts of Wahmonie have been disturbed by atomic testing.

AMARGOSA, on north side of US 95 at a point one mile west of its junction with SR 16 (40 miles southeast of Beatty).

Named for the bitter water encountered after wells were drilled forty feet, Amargosa began as a temporary construction camp when rails of the Las Vegas & Tonopah Railroad were being laid northwestward through the Amargosa desert in the spring of 1906. When trains began running here from Las Vegas, this community became the railroad station for many nearby mines, especially for the camp of Johnnie, and Amargosa was briefly known as Johnnie Station.

The community eventually had a blacksmith shop, store, hotel, restaurant, and an agent of "Alkali Bill" Brong's Amargosa-Greenwater auto stage run, better known as the "Death Valley Chug Wagon," which whizzed passengers to that new copper boom 45 miles to the west in less than three hours. Great quantities of supplies were unloaded here and freighted to Greenwater in mule- and horse-drawn wagons. Traffic was brisk on the toll road to Greenwater through most of 1906 and continued so even after the Tonopah & Tidewater Railroad was built closer to Greenwater early in 1907. After mining declined at Johnnie about 1912 Amargosa was finished as a depot for mining camps. Only a concrete slab foundation remains.

STIRLING, 9 miles south of US 95 at a point 14 miles east of its junction with SR 16.

Silver discoveries around the northwest end of the Spring Mountain Range in 1869 led to the organization of the Timber Mountain district but no mining followed. A small mill treated gold ores from the Sterling mine, and water was piped in from Big Timber Spring, two miles south. Early in this century the Ore City Mining Co. took out some gold and copper, and a speculative townsite was laid out on a nearby hill in April 1907. A post office was applied for two months later but the boomlet was soon over and mines were abandoned. No buildings remain.

JOHNNIE, on SR 16 at a point 13 miles south of its junction with US 95 (51 miles southeast of Beatty).

Though the Johnnie area was visited by prospectors as early as 1869, no sustained developments were started until after the winter of 1890-91 when a five-man prospecting party left the ranch at Indian Springs to search for the lost Breyfogle mine. After bold outcrops of gold were found on the northwest edge of the Spring Mountains, a rush developed early in 1891 from throughout Nevada and California to the newly formed Montgomery district. By May over 100 men and women were in the camp which soon acquired stores and dwellings. Hay, groceries and machinery had to be freighted in from Daggett on the Santa Fe railroad 150 miles distant over rough wagon ruts, and water was packed in canvas bags and hauled by donkeys from springs four miles away. Montgomery post office opened in August in this remote camp, but by 1893 shallow veins had chased away capitalists and prospectors.

The camp revived about 1898 when Utah capitalists acquired the Johnnie and Congress (Chispa) mines, the district's two largest. Situated over 180 miles from the county seat at Belmont, Johnnie was a rough camp. When a dispute raged concerning title of certain mining properties, an occupant who refused to give up one mine barracaded the entrance. After a gun battle of several hours' duration the stubborn occupant lay dead and three other men were wounded in the foray. Another dispute between leasers and mine owners ended after two men were killed, cookhouse and ten-stamp mill burned and the mine house dynamited. The safe came to rest minus its door 200 feet away.

Situated on the center of the "Searchlight belt" a broker-invented term for the mineralized region extending from the Comstock in the north to Searchlight farther south, Johnnie was caught up in the mining hysteria which advanced south from Goldfield and Bullfrog after 1904. A post office was opened in May 1905 and six months later a townsite was laid out in a flat central to the mines. An advertisement in a Rhyolite paper admonished the readers to hurry or they would not get a lot in Johnnie because they were selling like pink lemonade at a circus. In 1907 the town had 300 citizens who supported several saloons, stores, restaurants,

Named for the bitter water encountered after wells were drilled fifty feet down, Amargosa (above) served as a busy regional shipping point early in this century. (Las Vegas *Review-Journal*)

The recreation hall, dwellings and mine buildings of the Johnnie mine are shown in the 1930s. This district was active for nearly a half century, one of southern Nevada's longest-lived mining developments. (*Mrs. Charles Labbe Collection*)

hotels and daily stage to Amargosa, the nearest railroad station. The fare was three dollars. This attractive mining camp had cold and tasty water, watering troughs, fire hydrants and tree-lined streets that furnished grateful shade in this hot, arid region.

The Johnnie mine and 16-stamp mill continued production until 1914, but after changing hands the next year operated only intermittently. Placer gold was found in the gulches surrounding Johnnie in 1920, and it was worked occasionally for three decades. The Johnnie townsite had only about a half-dozen people in the late 1930s when another camp had started at the Johnnie mine five miles east, with Johnnie Mine post office, a store, pool hall and other businesses. World War II forced a shutdown and the post office closed in 1942. Production is said to have exceeded $1 million at the Johnnie mine alone. A few houses remain at both the townsite and the mine.

MANSE RANCH, south side of SR 16 at a point 6 miles southeast of the town of Pahrump.

In 1876 Joseph Yount came to Pahrump Valley and established what eventually became a famous 160-acre ranch and fruit orchard. A bountiful spring helped the ranch to prosper. Miners and prospectors passing through here were heartily welcomed and treated as members of the family. From 1891 to 1914 a post office named Manse was at this place, and four or five buildings here consisted of a big ranch house, storerooms, corrals and stables. Until the Johnnie boom of the 1890s, Yount's nearest Nevada neighbor was the Gass or Stewart family at Las Vegas, 50 miles east.

Early in this century Yount's Ranch raised much alfalfa and beef cattle that were sold to the Tecopa mines or freighted to Goldfield and Bullfrog before railroads were laid to those towns. Yount's sawmill in Clark Canyon, ten miles east on the west slope of the Charleston Mountains, supplied the Bullfrog district with lumber hauled there by Yount's teams. Freighters and stages on the run from the Ivanpah area to Bullfrog regularly stopped here where eating and lodging as well as some supplies were available. The ranch later became part of a dairy farm and now its activity has diminished.

FAIRBANKS RANCH, 7 miles southeast of SR 29 at a point 6½ miles south of Lathrop Wells.

Early in this century this well-known ranch was a travelers' stop on various roads. Initial traffic north to the Bullfrog district from Manvel and Ivanpah passed here, as did freighters to Bullfrog out of Las Vegas after rails reached there in the spring of 1905. After 1907 another road led from Amargosa on the Las Vegas & Tonopah Railroad through here to Greenwater.

TRANSVAAL, 11 miles east of US 95 at a point 4 miles north of Beatty.

This district was appropriately named. In South Africa Transvaal means "across the river," and here it means the same — across the Amargosa River from Beatty and Rhyolite. In March 1906, after discovery of gold in Beatty Wash, the trend was toward Transvaal and the district became the new firing line of the gold-seeking invasion.

A tent camp soon formed, and as usual the refreshment people arrived in advance of the dry goods and grocery merchants. During April the camp acquired about 75 rag habitations and tent businesses which included assay office, saloons, lumberyard, eating stands and lodging houses, and the floating population reached 800 at times. Every morning daily stages left Beatty for the new camp at a fare of five dollars. One man even boasted, "I carried away from Transvaal enough gold *on my boots* to buy a dinner in Beatty!" Competing Transvaal papers, published in Beatty and Rhyolite, were distributed during April and May, but no permanent veins were found and the boom was over by the beginning of summer. Transvaal would not have been worse off if it had been named "Flybynight."

SPRINGDALE, on east side of US 95 at a point 10 miles north of Beatty.

During the 19th century the meadowed area around Springdale contained an Indian campground and many small ranches. When the Bullfrog Goldfield Railroad was being laid north from Beatty in the winter of 1906-07 a section house was built to take advantage of the bountiful water supply.

After Pioneer rose three miles west early in 1907 Springdale thrived as a "blowoff" town, fea-

Sam Yount of Goodsprings, son of the founder of the Manse Ranch, engages in a game of pool with another well-known desert character, Chief Tecopa, who is attired in his habitual dress — shoeless, but with a top hat and vest. He begged his way through life and it is said that he bathed only annually.

Up to ten acres were devoted to raising grapes at the ranch. Stage travelers and teamsters who stopped here described the wine cellar as "tempting in the extreme." Visitors were treated to everything that was typical of a desert ranch — fresh fruits and vegetables from the orchard and garden, and fresh eggs, butter, milk and meat. *(Della Fisk photos; John Yount Collection)*

At the Yount sawmill in Clark Canyon (above) lumber was cut and then hauled by one of Yount's teams (below) to the Bullfrog district. The peak of activity at the mill was in 1905-06, before the completion of railroads to Bullfrog made cheap lumber available. Travelers were put up at the ranch house (top and middle right). Miners also came for a little rest instead of "going inside" as it was said when a trip was made over Cajon Pass and into Los Angeles. Hunting dove and quail, an occasional game of pool and swimming in the big spring were the principal recreations. (*Della Fisk photos, John Yount Collection*)

The camp of Pioneer in July 1910 (above) had been partially rebuilt after the crippling fire in 1909. Only a few buildings now remain. (*Nevada Highways and Parks* magazine)

A distinctive feature in the desert mining camp was the water wagon. Everyone depended on the precious liquid which they stored in a water barrel or can behind their tents. (*Nevada Highways and Parks* magazine)

The Pioneer mine's ten-stamp mill used amalgamation followed by cyanidization to process ore from its nearby mine. (*Los Angeles County Museum*)

turing four saloons and a flourishing red light district employing about a dozen girls, as well as a hotel, post office, restaurants, rooming house and livery stable. Springdale also served as the railroad shipping point and depot for Pioneer. Independence Day that year not only had the usual mining camp celebrations but also included a Wild West show imported from Goldfield and attended by over 1200 persons from nearby mining camps.

With the temporary decline of Pioneer about 1911, Springdale's palmy days ended. The post office closed in 1912, and trains rumbled through the lifeless station until 1928. In those days bootleggers were active in town. A couple of service stations operated until about 1958 when US 95 bypassed Springdale on the west side. Several buildings still stand on a ranch.

PIONEER, 2½ miles southwest of US 95 at Springdale.

The discovery of the Pioneer gold mine in 1907 was an outgrowth of mining developments in the Bullfrog district, and by the end of 1908 a camp formed between the Pioneer and Mayflower mines. With rich surface findings optimism flourished, and owners of the Pioneer mine hoped soon to hear their property mentioned in the same breath with the famous Mohawk in Goldfield.

The neatly-laid-out townsite soon embraced several small businesses, many of which were branches of Rhyolite and Beatty firms, and Pioneer had competing newspapers, as well as a post office beginning in March 1909. That year the Las Vegas *Age* called Pioneer the liveliest place in the state and remarked that autos were continually traveling to all neighboring towns.

The Tonopah & Tidewater Railroad advertised through passenger service to Pioneer via Rhyolite where automobiles met the incoming train. "Ask your railroad agent for a through ticket to Pioneer" was the beckoning call to the camp which already had a population approaching 1000. Both the T. & T. and the Las Vegas & Tonopah railroads projected branches, but before construction was begun by either line, fire visited Pioneer in May 1909, and with the help of prevailing high winds quickly destroyed the camp's wooden buildings. The camp partially rebuilt and mining continued. In 1913 the Pioneer mine installed a ten-stamp mill which operated for three years and then shut down. The Mayflower mine reopened after 1910 and its mill made fair productions. Pioneer last produced in about 1940.

BONNIE CLAIRE (or Clare, or Clair), earlier Thorp, southeast side of SR 72 at a point 7 miles west of its junction with US 95 (30 miles northwest of Beatty).

Gold mining began in the early 1880s and a five-stamp mill at Thorp's Well, four miles south, handled ore from three active mines. The mill operated satisfactorily for over two decades before the Bonnie Claire Bullfrog Mining Co. acquired the mill early in this century to pound out ores from its mines in the Gold Mountain district. About 1904 the Bonnie Claire mill was built near the stage station of Thorp, where travelers going to and from Goldfield and Bullfrog found accommodations for man and beast. After June 1905 Thorp post office was open as well. The settlement was also briefly known as Montana Station.

Three months after the rails of the Bullfrog-Goldfield Railroad reached this point in October 1906, Bonnie *Clare* townsite was platted at Thorp and a tent town grew around the shipping activity. In the spring of 1907 the Las Vegas & Tonopah Railroad began running through here and a handsome two-story wooden depot was built, the most prominent structure in the community which by then had saloons, mercantile companies and a population of 100 at the height of activity that year.

Bonnie Claire diminished in importance after mining declined nearby and at Rhyolite in 1909, with a consequent drop in railroad traffic. During a revival in 1913 a new mill was built; activity slowed a few years later until 1928 when Death Valley Scotty shipped building materials here, for his famous castle 23 miles west in Grapevine Canyon. When that traffic ended the Bullfrog Goldfield Railroad was abandoned and Bonnie *Clare* post office was removed in 1931. Nearby mines have occasionally been worked since then, and in the 1950s another mill began running. Only walls of the railroad depot and remnants of cabins are left.

GOLD CRATER, 23 airline miles southeast of Goldfield. The site is within the Las Vegas Bombing and Gunnery Range and is not available for exploration.

In the spring and summer of 1904 a rash of gold discoveries took place at Gold Crater, Wellington (O'Brien's), Wilson, and Trappman's Camp in the large Pahute Mesa area of central Nye County. The most important of these finds was Gold Crater, and in the fall of 1904 several hundred people flocked here. Official townsite lots were placed on sale, and 200 lots were purchased in three days, with the sale of corner lots averaging about $50 and inside lots for half that price. Many astonished investors had seen lots advance in price from $50 to $6,000 and even more in Goldfield and other towns, and speculators placed their money and hopes here. A pipeline was planned from Stonewall Mountain to provide water for the burgeoning camp, but within a couple of months the boom subsided and only a few waited out the winter of 1904-05 for spring to come. After 1905 only leasers sank shafts and performed development work. In the same area other camps in later years were Jamestown, a camp with post office which developed after gold discoveries in 1908; Antelope Spring, a silver camp of about 150 people in 1911; and Mellan, a short-lived gold camp which followed discoveries in 1930.

KAWICH or Gold Reed, 53 airline miles east-southeast of Goldfield. The site is within the Las Vegas Bombing and Gunnery Range and is not available for exploration.

"Kawich is a h - ll of a place! No mines, no water, no feed, no women," said a disgruntled early visitor to this remote camp in 1905. Stunted sagebrush had been the only sign of life until gold discoveries late in 1904 led to founding of the camp in December. During the following spring several hundred men rushed to this tent camp which had a few saloons, stores, feed yard, and post office beginning in April. As the year passed, Kawich became the main camp in the region around the north end of the Kawich Range where many smaller camps formed about locations that were being worked. In 1905 and 1907 the number of inhabitants fluctuated from 50 to 400, and during the most active months a stage ran irregularly to Tonopah, 70 miles to the northwest — fare $10. The Gold Reed Co. worked the most significant properties, but by the end of 1907 the town and mines were dead.

Auto stages loaded with passengers and baggage are ready to depart from Tonopah on a cross-mountain journey to Kawich. Around 1910 the auto stage was rapidly replacing the horse-drawn stagecoach. (Tonopah *Times-Bonanza*)

TONOPAH, junction of US 6 with US 95 at a point 93 miles north of Beatty and 207 miles northwest of Las Vegas.

The discovery of silver at Tonopah by Jim Butler on May 19, 1900 triggered the beginning of the fast-paced twentieth century mining era in Nevada; as the size and richness of this bonanza became known to the North American mining community, mining was stimulated throughout the West for over a decade, and Nevada awoke from hard times and declining population.

Butler's discovery came about innocently enough. While traveling with a camping outfit packed on a burro from his ranch north of Belmont to visit friends at Klondike, he made camp at a small spring known by the Indians as Tonopah, a Shoshone word for "little spring." In the morning his burros were gone, and after a brief search he found them near an outcropping which immediately attracted his attention. He broke off a chunk, studied it, and decided to take it with him to Klondike. The camp's assayer gave Butler's samples one look, declared they were no good, and eventually threw the rocks away.

On Butler's return journey to Belmont several days later, he gathered additional samples and in Belmont tossed them onto the porch of Wilse Brougher's store, where they remained unnoticed for several days. Butler's friend Tasker L. Oddie, later Nevada Senator and Governor, offered to ask his friend Gayhart, a schoolteacher in Austin, to run an assay on the samples.

The results showed values of $50 to $600 per ton — a real strike! Gayhart contacted Oddie, who immediately dispatched an Indian with the good news to the Butler ranch. Butler was away at that time and thus did not act promptly to locate claims, but after the camp of Klondike heard the news, prospectors there including the camp assayer searched the area in vain for Butler's find.

Finally on August 25 Butler and his wife located eight claims and christened the first three the Desert Queen, Burro and Mizpah. The latter ultimately proved to be a producer for over forty years. Butler began working these claims in October with his partners Oddie and Brougher, and the first ton of sorted ore netted $600.

Butler issued the number one lease in December. Additional leases were granted early in 1901, all stipulating a 25% royalty on the ore extracted, and that spring over a hundred more were given. All were oral leases backed by Oddie's integrity. By mid-spring the camp, then known as Butler City, had elevated itself from the status of an unproven camp to a recognized producer. W. W. Booth began publishing the Tonopah *Bonanza* on June 15; one of its first issues announced that the camp had 650 hardy souls. Veteran prospectors, gamblers, con men, and ladies of the night mingled with writers from the national dailies looking for the big story in this land of adventure.

By the end of 1901 leasers using hand windlasses, buckets, and wheelbarrows had extracted $4 million in ore from Mount Oddie east of the camp. When the leases expired on midnight January 1, 1902 the lucky miners hurried off to impress home folks with newly acquired wealth.

Early in 1902, the Tonopah Mining Co. which had earlier bought six claims from Butler and associates for $336,000, began extensive development work. Tonopah's isolation made obtaining supplies an acute problem. Most freight came by way of the nearest railhead at Sodaville (which see). Prices were high, sanitation was crude, and many men died under the primitive living conditions. Bed space was so scarce that rooms were crammed with single cots which were rented for eight-hour shifts.

By the fall of 1902 the tent and wooden town of Tonopah had over 3000 inhabitants supporting 32 saloons, six faro games, two dancehalls, two weekly newspapers, school, two churches and two daily stages. The camp was peaceful and orderly; it experienced only one stage robbery through 1902. Many rich ore bodies had been struck, fortunes were made and lost, and the fame of Tonopah had spread to all parts of the world.

In the winter of 1902-03 additional fine ore bodies were discovered. Capital was attracted to central Nevada after April 1903, when Tonopah stocks were listed on the San Francisco exchange. The Tonopah Mining Co. began building a narrow gauge railroad from a mile below Rhodes on the Carson & Colorado Railroad that year, and for three days beginning July 25, 1904, the town celebrated the railroad's completion with speeches, sporting events, horseracing on the main street, and dances. The railroad was standard gauged

After the spring of 1901, regular shipments of sacked ore left Tonopah by mule team. During that year leasers (below) dug into Mt. Oddie, cut it, and crosscut it, feverishly mining ore until midnight on January 1, 1902, when all leases expired. By that day over a million dollars' worth of ore had been piled near leasers' shafts awaiting shipment. The Main Street in 1902 is clearly defined, and Tonopah, already one of the West's busiest places, had the makings of a permanent camp. *(Top: California State Library; bottom: Mrs. Willard Hanson Collection)*

At this lease in the Tonopah district, a horse-powered whim brings ore from the stopes below. Some ore is sacked for shipment by wagon to Sodaville, where the railroad finished delivery to the smelters. (Tonopah *Times-Bonanza*)

The entire population (below), which included three ladies, is grouped for this picture early in 1901 when the camp was only six or eight months old. *(Mrs. Della Dodson Collection)*

During its third year, Tonopah (above) rapidly filled the sandy waste that had bridged the area between Mt. Oddie (in the background) and Mt. Brougher (behind the camera). *(Mrs. Willard Hanson Collection)*

When the saloon district emerged in the winter of 1901, the first whims and windlasses had been installed and prospecting cuts had defaced the foot of Mt. Oddie. *(Charles Hendel Collection)*

At Tonopah's railroad depot, a steam tractor hauls away empty ore wagons. Here immense shipments of supplies and machinery for the intensely active camp were received. *(Thomas W. Miller Collection)*

336

Tonopah's first funeral in May 1901 was conducted under most trying circumstances. Despite the lack of an undertaker, prayer books, and minister, the service, consisting of eulogies and prayers and hymns sung from memory, was held with extreme reverence. This Concord stage (below) from Sodaville arrived in front of the camp's first business establishment early in 1901. Long jerkline teams hauled supplies and ore to and from the camp. (Above: Nevada Historical Society; middle: E. W. Darrah Collection; below: Thomas W. Miller Collection)

The Tonopah Stock Exchange kept in constant communication with the major national exchanges. Because stocks moved up and down with lightning rapidity, men were rich one day, poor the next, then rich again. *(Nevada State Museum)*

Tonopah assumed a convivial air during the passing of a parade. Uniformed bandsmen were followed by floats and men and women in festive attire. Spectators lined the broad streets to watch the event. *(Huntington Library)*

On the east side of Mt. Oddie the Tonopah-Belmont Development Co. built this 500-ton mill in 1913. It was the nation's finest silver cyanide mill in its day, but was closed in 1923, and now only concrete foundations remain. *(Getchell Library, University of Nevada)*

The Main Street of Tonopah in 1906 was dominated by the five-story State Bank Building. Brokerage houses, mining engineers, and saloons occupied other business buildings. At the Big Casino dance hall, fine musicians played for the men and taxi dancers who had such nicknames as "Slivers," "Slats," Dirty Dory," "Spider Lip," "Frenchy," "Blondie," "Stringbean Annie," and "Mona Lisa". The red light district was in back of that club, but other girls lived on Corona Avenue in the mid-foreground. *(Huntington Library)*

months later and renamed the Tonopah & Goldfield Railroad when the line was extended to the latter camp in the fall of 1905. With the beginning of railroad service, the district's population soared and so did the town's problems. An epidemic during the winter of 1904-05 took 56 lives, and conditions were so bad that in April committees of sanitation were organized to improve the town. The problem of the county government being so far removed from this population center was no more after May when the county seat was moved here from Belmont.

By 1907 Tonopah had evolved into a modern mining town and possessed five banks, modern hotels (with private baths, steam heat, elevators and eventually telephones), cafes, opera house, schools, lavish gambling palaces, electric and water companies, and an array of other businesses housed in fine stone edifaces, a few reaching four and five stories. Besides three weeklies, the Tonopah *Sun* and the Tonopah *Bonanza* spread the greatness of the camp. The slopes of the hills off the main streets contained some of the finest homes in the state. Feverish activity in a maze of underground tunneling showed itself on the surface by massive ore dumps, mine buildings, and gallows frames. Most of the ore was treated at nearby Millers.

From its infancy Tonopah was the outfitting point for hundreds of prospectors who scoured Nevada's wild mountain ranges in search of mineral-bearing ledges. As a result, Goldfield, Bullfrog, Rawhide and scores of other districts were discovered during 1902-1907. With its central location Tonopah served as distribution and supply point for the new camps.

The peak of production was attained during 1910-1914 when the mines' annual yield averaged $8.5 million. New mills built at Tonopah along with the facilities at Millers had a combined daily capacity of 1830 tons and were in operation day and night working the ores. Tonopah had become the most prosperous mining camp on the Pacific slope and some of its pioneers such as Jim Butler, Ben Edwards, Wilse Brougher, Frank Golden, Zeb Kendall, George Bartlett, Key Pittman and Tasker Oddie were now millionaires and statesmen.

After World War I Tonopah still had many good years until the Depression, and the district's four principal companies, the Tonopah Mining Co., the Tonopah-Belmont, the Tonopah Extension and the West End Consolidated all were active until World War II. A notable event in 1947 was the abandonment of the Tonopah & Goldfield Railroad. The district's total production ranges upward from the recorded figure of nearly $150 million, chiefly in silver. Tonopah as a historic spot has been immortalized — and justly so. Virginia City had put Nevada on the map; Tonopah kept it there.

HANNAPAH, 2 miles west of US 6 at a point 18 miles east of Tonopah.

The Hannapah silver mine was discovered in 1902 and for the next few years limited mining took place. Serious steps were taken toward founding a town early in 1906 after a townsite was platted and lots were placed on sale. A well-advertised barbecue in February lured many investors to buy a piece of the desert, but other than 1908-09 and 1914 little mining activity ever took place. Wooden buildings remain.

ELLENDALE, 3 miles south of US 6 at a point 27 miles east of Tonopah.

After the discovery of float gold by Ed and Ellen Clifford near Salisbury Wash in April 1909, rumors quickly circulated and soon a rush was under way. Nevada mining papers described it as a repetition in miniature of the stampedes that followed discoveries at Manhattan and Goldfield. Reports of ore assaying up to $80,000 a ton brought four or five hundred people almost overnight. Ellendale townsite was laid out, many lots were sold, and saloons, boardinghouses, stores and dwellings were built. A gang of surveyors projected a rail line from Tonopah, and a telegraph line connected the two towns. Two weekly papers, the *Lode* and the *Star* were printed in Tonopah for distribution here during the summer of 1909.

Late that summer the Rhyolite and Tonopah newspapers blasted Ellendale's hopes of permanence by implying that this camp was another swindle. Only one ore shipment went to Millers for treatment that year. Leasers stayed on that fall but none of the developments sustained the camp and Ellendale died. By 1912 everyone had left. One structure, waste dumps and mine ruins remain.

After the Ellendale townsite was laid out in the spring of 1909, the usual establishments opened, including one inevitably known as The Northern. Rich gold pockets in this district promised to startle the mining world and some thought that here was Brey-fogle's phantom ledge; but when the veins proved to be shallow, the miners folded their tents and left. *(Top: Huntington Library; bottom: Dr. James Herz Collection)*

Near the site of the original Ellendale strike, the locators (top) discuss the possibilities of the district while well-dressed representatives of moneyed men look over the ground for possible purchase. The voice in the wilderness at Ellendale (right) was a promoter selling sagebrush lots. The auctioning of a townsite drew investors from near and far. The few ladies in the camp were on hand when a photographer came to Ellendale. *(Above and right: Dr. James Herz Collection; below: Mrs. Ida Le Nord Collection)*

Golden Arrow Development Company

E.M.KIERON.
PRESIDENT.

T.J.DOYLE.
VICE PRESIDENT.

F.M.KIERON.
SEC.-TREAS.

DIRECTORS.
E.M.KIERON.
F.M.KIERON.
HANNAH KIERON.

MINES AT
GOLDEN ARROW.
NYE COUNTY, NEV.

GEO.L.BAILEY.
SUPERINTENDENT.

Tonopah, Nev.

Golden Arrow's largest company had a fancy letterhead. After a strike was made at Silverbow (center), locations were made for miles around, as the claim map shows. Ownership of mineral rights extended into the platted townsite itself. Though town lots were often expensive, nearby land could be had for the squatting. *(Center: U. S. Geological Survey; top and bottom: William Metscher Collection)*

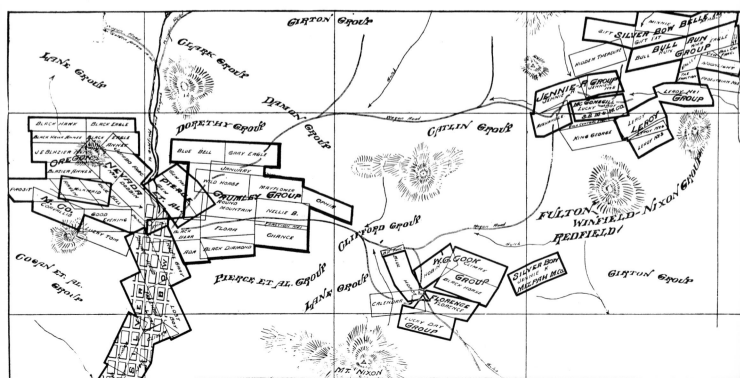

DANVILLE, 3½ miles west of the Little Fish Lake Valley road at a point 46 miles north of its junction with US 6 at a point 34 miles east of Tonopah.

In July 1866 a party of prospectors returning to Austin from a trip farther east, headed along the east flank of the Monitor Range. Running short of provisions, the party traveled through Danville Canyon in the belief that they were making a beeline for the nearest settlements. On the way they discovered silver.

Nothing came of this find until 1870 when the reorganization of the district resulted in a camp. Several wagonloads of ore were shipped to Austin for treatment, but after about 1872 the mines were abandoned. A revival in the 1880s was large enough to support a camp with post office. Thereafter Danville had many ups and downs, with heavy stress on the downs. Revivals also took place between 1909 and 1914 and as late as 1940-1942. Wooden cabins remain.

GOLDEN ARROW, 12 miles south of US 6 at Five Mile Spring, 34¼ miles east of Tonopah.

The postmistress at Tybo found a small ledge of rich gold ore in October 1904, the Page brothers made additional discoveries in September 1905, and late in 1906 the Golden Arrow Mining Co. laid out a townsite. Wagons loaded with ore began making hauls to shipping points and bringing back supplies. A surveying party routed a railroad from Tonopah to Ely through Golden Arrow in October 1906, but the new line was never built. In 1907 the camp had a wood-frame hotel, store and saloons, but the boom was brief, and ten years of erratic mining efforts brought little production to show for the time and money spent in development. Remnants of wooden buildings and headframes of shafts mark the site.

SILVERBOW, 27 miles south and east of US 6 at Five Mile Spring, 34¼ miles east of Tonopah.

After silver discoveries some claims were filed in November 1904. By the following summer George Wingfield and George Nixon platted a townsite and Silverbow became supply center for several hundred men living here and in nearby camps. Silver ore mined nearby was compared to the deposits at Goldfield; and with timber and water in abundance, Silverbow soon was the larg-

est mining camp in eastern Nye County. By September 1905 the business district embraced a post office, stores, saloons, meat company and the *Standard,* which published one edition with the ink on the front page mixed with gold dust that supposedly assayed at $80,000 a ton! A weekly stage ran to Tonopah — fare seven dollars.

Claim jumping was such a problem that deputy sheriffs from Tonopah frequently had to be summoned to help settle disputes and round up claim jumpers to populate the county jail. In one instance a fight over a noted claim between two friends culminated in gunplay on the camp's main street. The survivor was later acquitted on his plea of self-defense.

The first shipment was made early in 1906, but Silverbow lasted only until mid-year before joining the multitude of dead towns in the county. Small stamp mills were built following strikes in 1913 and 1920, but neither revival was long enough to sustain a camp. Wood cabins mark the site.

CLIFFORD, later Helena, 2 miles south of US 6 at a point 8 miles west of Warm Springs and 42 miles east of Tonopah.

Ed and James Clifford discovered silver in this barren desolate region in December 1905. News of this find and the sale of their claim for $250,000 created a stampede in a night. In less than two weeks the camp had forty tents and a saloon, and with many additional strikes made in the immediate vicinity, Clifford promised to become one of the best towns in southern Nevada.

During 1906 Hale and Schwab of Pittsburgh, McCarthy of Tonopah, and "Diamondfield" Jack Davis of Goldfield had heavy holdings of property. Population peaked in 1908 when Clifford had about 100 houses and tents including saloons, dance hall, stores, a post office known as Helena, a stage line to Tonopah, and boardinghouses. The camp soon died and thereafter leasers were active at times, especially in the late 1930s. A couple of buildings and evidence of mining remain.

BELLEHELEN, via unimproved road, 18 miles south then west of SR 25 at a point 1 mile east of its junction with US 6 at Warm Springs.

After discoveries in 1904, Bellehelen emerged a year later as an outgrowth of the Silverbow discovery with silver and gold mines in the west flank of the Kawich Range. Mining eyes briefly focused on the district in 1907 when George Wingfield's engineers came to the camp to inspect properties, but nothing came of their visit. The camp's best years were 1909-10, when about 500 tent dwellers congregated in the district. Bellehelen post office opened in October 1909 and closed two years later. After 1910 one operator was said to have extracted $500,000 from the mines, but the district was generally silent until 1917 when the Pacific States Mining Co. began large operations. That company produced about $117,000 before it merged with the Tonopah-Kawich Co. in 1922 to build a new cyanide mill the next year. This new facility ran unsuccessfully and irregularly before shutting down for good in 1927. Mill ruins and tailings pond indicate the site.

REVEILLE, 8 miles south and west of SR 25 at a point 20 miles southeast of Warm Springs.

When brave prospectors made explorations of the inhospitable southern Nevada deserts in mid-1866, silver was discovered on the east side of the Reveille Range, and initial assays revealed values of $300 to $800 a ton. A camp of wood, stone and brick formed, taking its name as a salute to Austin's widely read daily, the *Reese River Reveille*. Within a year the district on the east side of the Reveille Range had fifty mines under development with veins of "immense proportions" and the remote camp gained a post office. Supplies came via Austin, and freighters took six days to make the trip over vast desert valleys and mountain ranges. In 1867 a five-stamp mill was built nearby, followed by another of double that size in 1869 in Reveille Valley, twelve miles to the west. Each shut down after running briefly.

By 1875 the Gila Silver Mining Co. acquired the principal properties, repaired the ten-stamp mill, and began four years of operation which grossed over $1.5 million. By the spring of 1880 Taps had sounded for the Reveille district and since then production has been irregular.

In 1904 lead mines opened at New Reveille, six miles southwest on the western side of the Reveille Range. Small operations kept the Gila mill operating until as late as 1945, and more than

$4 million has been taken from the district. The shell of the Gila mill stands alone in Reveille Valley; stone and adobe ruins mark the site of New Reveille, while the desolation of old Reveille consists of rock walls and a few weathered graves on a nearby hill.

ARROWHEAD, via unimproved roads, 3½ miles north of Reveille.

A small but active silver camp in the sandy gulches of the barren wasteland around the north end of the Reveille Range, Arrowhead after World War I consisted of a few stores, garage, several dwellings and a post office operated by "Whispering Joe" who had lost his voice after being buried in a Montana snowslide years earlier. The Arrowhead Mining Co., incorporated with 1.5 million shares valued at 10 cents each, began developing the properties in 1919. Only small productions were made, and most activity ceased about 1923. Cement foundations and one wooden building remain.

TROY, 4 miles east of the Currant-Nyala graded road at a point 32 miles east of its junction with SR 25 (90 miles east of Tonopah).

Alexander Beatty, the first white settler in Railroad Valley, and who later homesteaded Butterfield springs, discovered silver in the Grant Range in May 1867. Further prospecting by others that summer led to the founding of a camp which took the classical name of Troy. Later in 1867 the Old English Gold Corporation bought up several claims and proceeded to work them. By 1871 Troy had two general stores, boardinghouse, blacksmith shops, school, unofficial post office, and the population numbered 70 miners and their families. The English company expended $500,000 in mining development and in building a modern 20-stamp mill with furnaces, completed in 1871. But like its ancient namesake, Troy fell, and the company closed shop when the district's low-grade ores proved unprofitable to reduce. After the big mill's machinery was moved to Ward in White Pine County in 1872, all mining ceased and the district became quiescent. Small revivals were made later in the decade, in the 1900s, and during 1936-1946. Mill ruins and a few buildings remain.

This 50-ton cyanide plant at Bellehelen was born a failure. (California State Library)

A bath at New Reveille often consisted of about two inches of cold water, a piece of dirty brown soap, and a wrinkled towel. (Mrs. E. R. Bongberg Collection)

Since Reveille was far from the railroad, everything had to be shipped in by large wagons (center). In the bottom view, old and new types of transportation are contrasted. (Both photos: Mrs. E. R. Bongberg Collection)

GRANT CITY, 6 miles east of the Currant-Nyala road at a point 40 miles east of its junction with SR 25.

After organization of the district in October 1868 Grant City was surveyed, streets were laid out, and several stone houses were built. In the spring of the next year this camp of fifty miners had several businesses, and the newspaper at Hamilton anticipated a great future for the camp. The population increased rapidly in the summer of 1869 and local enthusiasts boasted that in the fall of the year silver bricks would be regularly leaving the district. But the low-grade ores could not sustain the camp and it was soon abandoned. A few stone ruins mark the site.

After the silver discoveries in the Troy and Grant districts in 1867-68 the area in between was organized as the Seymour district, and early in the 1870s the small camp of Central City emerged. It lasted less than two years.

BLUE EAGLE SPRING, on the Currant-Nyala road at a point 50 miles east of its junction with SR 25.

In the late 1860s the traveler was said to be all right at this place — a good station house, good fare, and a splendid big spring full of little fish were here. A store was maintained for over four decades until about 1910. Two structures are left on a private ranch.

TYBO, 8 miles northwest of US 6 at a point 10 miles northeast of Warm Springs.

The word "tybo" is a corruption of the Shoshone word "tybbabo" which means "white man's district." The first locations were made in the summer of 1870 after an Indian revealed the location of ore to white men, and initially small seams of rich silver were worked. The main lode — the Two G — was found later that year, but a boom did not get under way until the spring of 1874. Mining development then began in earnest, a townsite was platted and two smelters were built.

Tybo in its infancy was such a peaceful camp that one chagrined individual wrote to the Belmont paper, believing that not enough shootings and fights were taking place to speak very well for a bright future. He concluded by saying, " It is not expected that a new camp will amount to much

unless there have been three or four men for breakfast." As the camp grew, it did have its share of violence. But Tybo's greatest problem was the continual strife between the Irish, Cornish and Central Europeans. In May 1875 racial difficulties were compounded when local wood contractors imported several Chinese to cut piñon timber to provide charcoal for use in the smelters. The white factions united against the Orientals and chased them from the camp with bullets and whips, because they cut wood at less than the prevailing wage.

The tri-sectioned municipality of Tybo was the sensation of the county during 1875-1877. The population approached 1000 and the business streets boasted several wood and stone edifices. Numerous whiskey shops, a brick school, literary society, good Templars' lodge, and post office had been built, and the valley below the camp contained many cattle ranches. The Tybo *Sun* commenced publication in May 1877 giving the district literary enlightenment.

During 1877 at least 16 mule freight outfits were employed to bring on the average of 187.5 tons of freight and merchandise from the railhead at Eureka, resulting in a monthly bill to the Tybo merchants of $11,250. The same wagons carried up to 262.5 tons of lead-silver bullion monthly for rail shipment to the Pacific coast. Tybo had become the county's most important producer of metal and for awhile was second only to Eureka as the leading lead-producing district in the nation.

In 1879 the Tybo Consolidated Mining Company failed because of difficulties in ore reduction, despite substituting a crushing and roasting process to reduce the ore, and by the spring of 1880 Tybo was nearly dead. Intermittent production continued by different operators until 1891 when all work ceased.

For the next 40 years Tybo hovered between two worlds, one dead, the other powerless to be born. Attempts at revival in 1901, 1906, and 1917-1920 resulted in only limited outputs. In May 1929 the Treadwell-Yukon Co. finished construction of new smelters and concentrators and began milling up to 300 tons of lead-zinc ore per day. During the next eight years, except for 2¼ years in 1932-1934, the mill operated steadily, processing almost

In 1875 Upper Tybo had saloons, a bootery, and other stores along the bottom of the canyon. On the flank of the mountain to the left of center is the 2-G fissure. *(John Zalac Collection)*

Trowbridge's store on lower Main Street sold general merchandise for cash or approved credit. This building served as a miners' recreation hall during the revival in the 1930s and still stood in 1970. *(Philip R. Bradley Collection)*

After large-scale mining began at Tybo, this twenty-stamp mill and smelter (top left) was fired up for the first time in August 1874. That facility was soon joined by a larger smelter (bottom left) on the opposite side of Tybo Canyon. These operations of the Tybo Consolidated Mining Co. failed before 1880 and two years later all equipment was sold in a sheriff's sale. In the foreground is the heart of the business district which included Trowbridge's store.

The shaft house and boiler room (top) of the 2-G mine was located above the smelters. Around World War I, the Louisiana Consolidated Mining Co. acquired the principal mining properties and erected a flotation concentrator and lead smelter (below) on the site of an earlier smelter. The venture was unsuccessful and the plant closed in 1920. *(All photos: Philip R. Bradley Collection)*

The revival of 1929-1937 enabled the Tybo district to climb into second place in Nye County mineral production. The major buildings in this 1935 view show (from top left, descending) the hoist house, head frame over the 1500-foot shaft, crushers, flotation mill (long low building) and conveyors for lead and zinc concentrates. Three modern residences are in the foreground, while the company general offices are immediately in back. Still farther beyond are the superintendent's home, commissary, store and men's dormitory. (*Nevada State Museum*)

On this winter night at Tybo, about 100 men are snug in the three-story dormitory. To its left was the boarding house; assay office and mill are to the right. (*George Barnett Collection*)

500,000 tons of lead and zinc ore until September 1937 when operations ceased and the plant was dismantled. Recorded production to 1944 after over seven decades of mining showed $9.8 million, but the value of the output is considerably higher than that figure suggests because of low metal prices during the years of greatest activity. Cemetery, brick and wood buildings, and stone remnants remain in a deep canyon with fine mountain scenery.

HOT CREEK, 17 miles north of US 6 at a point 10 miles northeast of Warm Springs (58 miles northeast of Tonopah).

Before the white man came to Hot Creek, the area was an Indian paradise where an abundance of game and plant life supported a small population. Prospectors first ventured here in the spring of 1866 and silver deposits were revealed to them by the Indians. The whites rewarded the natives with silver coins which the red men considered worthless and threw over a cliff into a canyon. As the year progressed people from districts near and far swarmed into the region. A two-sectioned town emerged in 1867 and within a year embraced saloons, post office, hotel, restaurant, blacksmith shop, assay office and a district population of 300. Ox teams dragged two stamp mills into the district; the ten-stamp Old Dominion was installed in Upper Town which was also known as Carrolton in 1867 while a five-stamper was erected in Lower Town. After beginning operations the former mill was partly burned, then rebuilt and operated for awhile, stopped again, and then was finally dismantled and moved to White Pine.

Mining activity peaked early in 1868 before the lure of White Pine drew away all but a handful. The district then remained silent until the Tybo Consolidated Mining Co. built 15 kilns five miles to the north to supply charcoal for their furnaces at Tybo. Over 600,000 bricks were used in building the oval-shaped kilns. When mining revived in earnest just before 1880 another ten-stamp mill was set up, but it also saw only limited use, and the district turned in the following year after producing about $1 million. Early in this century the mines were reactivated and the camp again had a post office. The stone and adobe structures which remain are now used for storage purposes by the Hot Creek Ranch.

MOREY, 17 miles north of US 6 at a point 21 miles northeast of Warm Springs.

Among the Austin prospectors who fanned southeastern Nevada in 1865 were some who discovered silver here and organized the Morey district. The new find and the district's natural resources were favorably mentioned in Austin's *Reese River Reveille* but development did not begin until the following summer. Chinese laborers worked some of the mines.

By 1869 a camp had started. In the spring of 1873 a twenty-stamp mill was constructed of old parts and pressed into service, but it often broke down and was silent most of the time. Morey that year had its own post office, stores, saloons, blacksmith shop, livery stable, boardinghouse, daily stage service to Belmont and Eureka and a population approaching 100. During 1874 the Morey Mining Co. of New York built a ten-stamp mill, but it did not run continuously and ore was freighted to Belmont and Eureka for treatment. Production continued until 1891. Remnants of rock cabins remain in this minor camp in Nye County's galaxy of ghost towns.

MOORE'S STATION, 18 miles north of US 6 at a point 21 miles northeast of Warm Springs.

Stages on the Tybo-Eureka run stopped here after two brothers in the mid-1870s planted an orchard, dug a reservoir, built log stables with sod roofs and erected a fine stone building that still stands.

RAY, 10 miles north of Tonopah via desert roads.

Judge L. O. Ray discovered silver ore on Christmas Day 1901 and immediately staked out several claims. Ore assaying about $240 a ton in February 1902 sparked a small rush by the end of that month, and nearly 200 men started working claims. While the camp awaited the building of a suitable wagon road to haul out ore, the excitement died. A few wagonloads were shipped in February 1903 but Tonopah's northern neighbor did not develop except for one mine later in the decade. The site is marked by depressions where buildings once stood.

It is amazing to come upon this well-constructed stone house at Moore's Station miles from anywhere.

Judge Ray's mining camp (below) near Lone Mountain was briefly a place of promise in 1902. Serious mining did not get under way and the camp died in its infancy. *(Nevada Historical Society)*

SPANISH SPRING, 3¼ miles north of SR 82 at a point 25 miles north of Tonopah via SR 8A and SR 82.

This stage station was the main stop on the Tonopah-Manhattan road from about 1905 until after the boom. Wooden ruins identify the site.

MONARCH, 4 miles southeast of SR 82 at a point 25 miles north of its junction with SR 8A.

Early in this century, when screaming head-lines announced news of rich ore discoveries every week, thousands of people clamored for a chance to share in profits and become millionaires. Stocks of dubious value as well as mining claims and townsite lots were sold by ambitious promoters who were obliging enough to relieve the unwary of their hard-earned savings. Such a man was the Reverend Benjamin Blanchard, who conceived Monarch in the summer of 1906 and platted a wildcat townsite with adjacent ranch estates and mining claims. These were offered for sale in Tono-pah and in other cities, and by September Mon-arch contained four stores, boardinghouse, the pro-motional *Tribune,* and about 130 residents. Fast stages and express operated to and from Manhat-tan, and that same month the telephone and tele-graph company began preparations to extend serv-ice to the new town.

Blanchard peddled property as far away as Missouri and eventually sold about 2400 lots and salted away about $45,000 in investors' funds. Trouble came to a head when supply bills and mechanical claims fell due, and Blanchard told creditors that no money was available to pay bills because eastern backers failed to deliver promised funds. Blanchard then announced that he was heading East to obtain money and when he failed to return at the time agreed upon by creditors, buildings and other improvements were attached for mechanics' liens and other claims which amounted to $73,000. Most settlers left during Oc-tober and were replaced by watchmen and Mon-arch died a-borning. Three outhouses mark the site — you can get inside any of them without a dime!

BELMONT, on SR 82, 28 miles northeast of its junction with SR 8A (43 miles north-northeast of Tonopah).

Initial locations were made in October 1865 after an Indian discovered silver earlier in the year, and soon a camp rose on a slope of the Toquima Range amid the nut-pine- and cedar-studded hills. A rush early in 1866 lured many from Ione, Austin and other camps in western Nevada to look for high-grade surface ores yielding from $200 to $3000 a ton. The district took the name Silver Bend or Philadelphia. A ten-stamp mill was built near the camp in 1866 at a cost of $30,000 and during the next two years five local sawmills supplied the district with cut lumber.

With an ample supply of wood, water, rock and clay, the townspeople constructed many substan-tial stone and fireproof brick buildings as well as numerous frame structures. By the time Belmont became the county seat in February 1867 it had become an important mining and milling area and trading center for settlements in a radius of a hun-dred miles. The handsomely laid out town had a bank, a school, the competing *Silver Bend Reporter* and the *Mountain Champion,* telegraph service, post office, and several stores and shops including Hatch's Meat Market which featured choice Chi-cago hams and Iowa butter.

Prices of goods were not high considering the remoteness of the camp. Delivery from Austin cost 4½ cents a pound on fast freight and 2½ to 3 cents on slow. A thousand feet of lumber ran $140, a ton of hay was $75, and eggs were $1.25 a dozen. Tea cost $1 to $1.50 a pound. Belmont's population reached almost 2000 early in 1868 and it was the most flour-ishing town in eastern Nevada, but a decline in the tenor of local ores and the exciting White Pine boom made heavy raids on the population later in 1868 and 1869.

Dull times then prevailed for over four years until rich discoveries at the Belmont and other mines in 1873 started another healthy boom. The large mills built in the late 1860s ground anew with ore from the Arizona, Belmont, Highbridge, Monitor-Belmont and Quintero mines situated in the mineral belt one mile east of town. The Bel-mont *Courier* commenced publication in February 1874 and dwellings and business establishments faced streets shaded by maples, locusts and balm of Gilead trees.

This town of 2000 people gave an 1874 visitor a nostalgic feeling with its beautiful ladies, troops of

Belmont, in the midst of an important mining region, had already started to decline
when this picture was taken around 1890. The courthouse sits on the knoll to the right,
while the business street leads toward the Monitor-Belmont mill beyond the town.
(Theron Fox Collection)

Built in 1876 of brick manufactured at nearby kilns, the $25,000 Nye County court-
house at Belmont replaced a string of county offices scattered throughout the town. The
formidable-looking prisoner, handcuffed and wearing leg irons, has just been removed
from the jail in the rear and is being led away to an undetermined place. *(Mrs. Della
Dodson Collection)*

The twenty-stamp Monitor-Belmont mill, located a mile south of Belmont, looks impressive even after its machinery had fallen silent. It was originally built in 1867 by the Belmont Silver Mining Co. *(Griffen Collection, Nevada Historical Society)*

During Belmont's balmy days, this lodging house was the popular Cosmopolitan Saloon which also contained a first-class dance hall. Traveling theatrical companies performed on a small stage at the rear; there the famous 19th century actress Lotta Crabtree played the part of Little Eva in "Uncle Tom's Cabin." Respectable dances were held here at holiday times. *(Theron Fox Collection)*

Belmont view from the east summit around 1904 was a charming little country town surrounded by rugged mineral-stained hills. The Catholic church in foreground was at that time, "a house left desolate," in the language of Scripture. It had been built in 1874 at a cost of $3,000 and the last service was held in 1901. Seven years later the building was moved to Manhattan, where it still stands. On the extreme right is the Episcopal church. *(Western History Research Center, University of Wyoming)*

Impressive buildings which have outlived the mines still remain at Belmont. Below is the Highbridge mill, showing 19th century architecture. The magnificent photographic studies on the opposite page show the ruins of Belmont's substantially built commercial district. These buildings as well as an abandoned courthouse are protected by a few permanent residents. *(Below and opposite page: Frank Mitrani photos)*

"San Antone" irregularly functioned as an important stage station for over a third of a century until railroads were built into southern Nevada, displacing much of the area's stage traffic. At times in the last century the station was completely deserted. Its builder is unknown, but it may have been originally owned by the Liberty Mining Co. which mined gold and silver in the San Antonio Range to the south.

The town of Baxter Springs was platted amid gold claims on the edge of Ralston Valley. The primitive beginning of the camp in January 1906 is shown here. *(Mrs. Nevada Browne Collection)*

healthy children, and its handsome church with organ and a rector who "not only pointed the road to heaven but led the way!" Diversions included dances, coasting on bobsleds down the main street, and croquet on grounds located at the lower end of that thoroughfare. A race course known as Monitor Park was laid out southeast of the suburb of East Belmont and such nags as "Nigger Baby" and "Belmont Brown" raced there.

Production continued until 1887 when most mines were shut down after recovering over $15 million. By 1900 only a few businesses and a score of people were left, and in May 1905 the county seat was moved to Tonopah. The extensive Belmont dumps were reworked in 1907-08, and production during the World War I years fed the new Highbridge mill. Belmont now contains a small population and ruins of mills, stores and residences.

BARCELONA, 10 miles west of Belmont via unimproved road.

Mexicans discovered silver in the Spanish Belt district as early as 1867 but the mines saw little development until 1874 when five large mines opened and a camp formed. During that year the Austin-Belmont stage was rerouted to serve the new town of 150 which contained a blacksmith shop, store, assay office and three boardinghouses. Cessation of mining the next year saw the camp deserted by the end of 1877. Some mining was performed in 1879 and at other times, and in 1921 a ten-stamp mill was installed only to shut down a year later. Rock ruins remain.

SMITH'S STATION, 1½ miles west of SR 82 at a point 8 miles north of Belmont.

A stage station of the 1860s on the Belmont-Austin road was established here and housed in a large two-story stone building. That landmark is now situated on a private ranch.

PINE CREEK, approximately 3 miles west of SR 82 at a point 18 miles north of Belmont.

This station on the Belmont-Austin stage run also had a post office between 1873 and 1875 and again in 1879-1881. It was probably discontinued before the end of the century.

NORTHUMBERLAND, 11 miles northwest of SR 82 at a point 25 miles north of Belmont.

Silver discoveries in the west part of Northumberland Canyon on the Austin-Belmont stage run in June 1866 attracted only limited attention, but months later a camp started after several well-defined ledges were located on the east slope of the Toquima Range. Ore was shipped to Austin for reduction until early in 1868 when a ten-stamp mill was moved from Indian Springs near San Antonio and installed by the Quintero company. That summer another camp known as Learnville formed near the mill, but soon after starting operations the mill closed down because of financial embarrassment. Work then suspended and by 1870 the mines were abandoned.

Development of the Monitor and Blue Bell mines brought about a revival late in the 1870s, and another ten-stamp mill operated for three months. The town which started was also known as Bartlett and it briefly contained a store, boardinghouse and saloons, but in 1881 the district was totally abandoned. A revival in 1885-86 was large enough to support a camp with post office, and mining again resumed occasionally from 1908 until 1917 when silver veins were found and a new mill was built. The Northumberland Mining Co. took over the properties in 1939, and its modern cyanide plant capacity was increased to 280 tons after moving mill machinery from Weepah. Company operations ceased at the end of 1942 after over $1.1 million was extracted. Several buildings and mill ruins are left at the site.

BAXTER SPRING, 5 miles northeast then north of SR 8A at a point 27 miles north of Tonopah via US 6 and SR 8A.

Early in the 1870s Baxter Spring, then also known as Cedar Spring, began as a stage station on the Belmont-San Antonio stage road. After gold discoveries early in 1906 in a gulch west of the station, a tent town formed which had four saloons, a lodging house and two grocery stores which did a rushing business. A couple of small mercantile stores also opened, one of which had to pile its wares on bare ground, lacking a shelter large enough for supplies. By the end of February about 400 people had come, but the camp lasted less than three months before shallowness of the veins sent the gold seekers elsewhere. A few buildings remain as well as the spring, with good water available.

SAN ANTONIO, 10 miles west then southwest of SR 8A at a point 42 miles north of Tonopah via US 6 and SR 8A.

Nevada's most famous stage station, a twenty-room two-story structure of adobe and brick, rose from the sage about 1865 to accommodate north-south travelers to Silver Peak, Gold Mountain, Death Valley, and east-west travelers to Belmont.

In October 1863 Mexicans had discovered gold in the west flank of the San Antonio mountains 15 miles to the south. Within a year 200 miners were working the Liberty and other mines and a camp called Potomac rose near San Lorenzo Spring. Arrastras treated local ore, but high grade was hauled to the mill at Washington, almost 100 miles north. Returns of $600 a ton prompted the building in 1865-66 of the ten-stamp Pioneer mill at Indian Springs, five miles north of San Antonio. A settlement also started there.

Though the Liberty Mine and the mill shut down by 1868, "San Antone" remained open, and early in this century it was a noted landmark and station for individuals headed for the Tonopah and Goldfield bonanzas. With the arrival of the railroad at Tonopah, this stage station had outlived its usefulness and probably became a mere dwelling. Crumbling walls surrounded by thick sagebrush and two gaunt poplars are left at San Antonio; rubble remains at Indian Spring; and extensive old mine workings can be found in the San Antonio mountains.

MANHATTAN, eastern terminus of SR 69, 7 miles east of its junction with SR 8A at a point 42 miles north of Tonopah.

Silver ledges were initially tapped in 1866 and a mill at Belmont treated a few ore shipments. In 1869 the district was abandoned until April 1, 1905, when John Humphrey and two friends discovered rich float while riding after cattle and appropriately named the claim the April Fool. Richer discoveries that summer brought an influx of prospectors who located claims for several miles around. Though no sustaining veins had been found by August, indications were favorable and

eight townsites were staked. A ledge said to have assayed $10,000 a ton attracted additional gold seekers in September, and at the end of 1905 Manhattan had several hundred inhabitants.

After the district's rich ledges came to the attention of speculators and promoters in January 1906 the boom turned red hot and Manhattan became a pulsating camp of 4000 in only two weeks' time! Autos, stages, freight wagons and many other types of rigs carrying supplies and fortune seekers crowded the road from Tonopah all hours of the day and night. Saloons sold floor space for sleeping room, and a bath in a round wooden tub cost up to three dollars. Several wood frame business buildings rose on the canyon floor; lots on the main street sold for $1300 to $1900 each and dozens of tents and wooden houses filled the canyon and hillsides. By the beginning of spring Manhattan had three banks, the competing *Mail* and *News*, numerous thirst parlors, assay offices, schools, telegraph and telephone service, electric lights and water, and stage lines running north and south served the camp.

Then when the camp was "humming loudest" Manhattan was financially jolted by the famous San Francisco earthquake of April 1906. Heavy investors from the Bay Area withdrew funds from mining stocks and developments to finance the rebuilding of their city, and in less than a month the district's mines practically ceased production. The population fell to only a few hundred but the camp refused to give up. Rich strikes in the summer and fall of 1906 and in June 1907 revived the district, although the financial panic later that fall killed many budding mining companies.

In 1909 Manhattan once again rebounded when placer operations began below town, and three years later a rich lode strike at the White Cap mine encouraged the building of a 75-ton mill. Thereafter Manhattan was one of the best camps in Nevada, a mature town of 800 to 1000 people with many gold, silver and copper mines, mills, a business district and the well-received weekly *Post* which was run by Frank Garside, later editor of Tonopah and Las Vegas newspapers. Hospitals were built and the town was served by a large electric plant and water system.

Operations subsided in the mid-1920s, but Manhattan was a strong camp during the depres-

This Manhattan merchant offers tools and services for sale before erecting his building. The proprietor mended furniture and had the necessary equipment for most types of repair work: a grindstone, an anvil, saws, paint brushes, and sawhorses. Two customers have axes to grind. *(Mrs. Lillian Ninnis Collection)*

In 1906 Manhattan sprawled over several adjacent slopes on the west flank of the Toiyabe Mountains. Located in a setting of pinions and juniper-covered hills, Manhattan in the cool atmosphere of a high altitude was quite a contrast to other southern Nevada mining camps situated in bleak deserts. (Las Vegas *Review-Journal*)

Even a Pierce-Arrow sporting car found its way into Manhattan in 1906. *(Mrs. Rose Walter Collection)*

The main street quickly acquired numerous false-fronted buildings and an array of stores. During the boom, there was activity on the streets day and night — men discussing ore samples, buggies bringing visitors to town and low wagons hauling supplies. (Las Vegas *Review-Journal*)

Manhattan around 1914 had reached stability. There were stores to fill every need, and the mines were regular producers. Even private residences had electric power. (*Mrs. Lillian Ninnis Collection*)

The Horse Shoe Club at Manhattan, built in the early months of the camp, was a favorite miners' gathering place for gambling, drinking and entertainment. This was no place for a lady. Note the unshaded electric lights hanging from the ceiling. (*Mrs. Myrtle Myles Collection*)

365

The financial panic of 1907 did not frighten the Manhattanites and in 1912 when lode mining was begun in earnest the Associated Milling Co. built this mill.

Just before World War II started, this huge gold dredge operated in Manhattan gulch just below town. Nevada's first successful bucket line dredge operated in an artificial pond, and below the water's surface huge buckets dug into the bank to scoop up placer gravel. A ladder line carried the gravel onto the boat, where the gravel was washed and separated into fines and coarse gravel. In eight years of operation the dredge recovered $4.6 million in gold. *(John James Collection)*

sion, producing several hundred thousand dollars of ore annually. The Manhattan gold dredge, better known as the "big boat" operated from 1939 until the fall of 1947. Since World War II the mines have been quiet. The district's total recorded production was a bountiful $10.3 million, a good showing despite periods of depression and bad luck in the camp's infancy.

CENTRAL CITY, 2¼ miles west of Manhattan.

After rediscovery of the Manhattan district in 1905, several promotional townsites were laid out around the main camp: Palo Alto by springs west of Manhattan and near the site of original gold discoveries in the district, Central City between there and Manhattan, North Manhattan and East Manhattan, where 75 people were served by two stores, two saloons and a restaurant briefly in the spring of 1906.

Central City was the most important of the peripheral camps, and gold discoveries in 1906 seemed to assure a great future. It soon acquired two stores, two hotels, buildings for mining and brokerage companies, post office, steam laundry, bakery, lumber company, assay office, cold storage building and five saloons. Before an electric light plant could be built, additional strikes at Manhattan raided the population here and Central City's boom collapsed like a pricked balloon. Only dumps mark the site.

JETT, approximately 5 miles west of SR 8A at a point 11 miles north of its junction with SR 69 and 1¼ miles south of its junction with SR 92.

Silver discoveries in 1876 gave rise to a camp with sawmill, butcher shop, cabins, and then in 1880-81 a post office, at the townsite three miles up Jett Canyon. During the 1920s a camp started at the mouth of the canyon and cabins and a boardinghouse were built.

ROUND MOUNTAIN, eastern terminus of SR 92, 2¾ miles east of its junction with SR 8A at a point 54 miles north of Tonopah.

Gold was discovered in 1905, but outsiders took no notice until February 1906 when Morgan and Scott found high-grade ore on the south slope of a hill called Round Mountain. So sensational was the new strike that several men from Goldfield hastened across the desert to seek golden wealth. With marvelous rapidity a camp emerged, with rooming houses, saloons, stores and restaurants, and a few months later Gordon post office opened. Mining companies by the dozens were organized overnight, and money began to pour in for development work.

The townsites of Brooklyn and Shoshone were laid out in March, but were replaced a few months later by Round Mountain, platted on a gradual slope north of the mine workings. Early in June the camp had 400 people and several wood-frame buildings. A few gallows frames also appeared as well as numerous hand-operated windlasses, and the exhausts of gasoline hoists were heard for miles around. Bullion shipments, each worth thousands of dollars, left the district and incoming freighters from Tonopah brought in much-needed supplies.

Before the year ended, Thomas "Dry Wash" Wilson of Manhattan discovered extensive placer gold below the lodes, and from two small hand dry-wash machines worked by two men evolved the Round Mountain Hydraulic Mining Co. early in 1907. It installed a five-mile-long pipeline and hydraulic equipment to work the placers on a large scale.

The district's lode mines kept two mills running that spring crushing $80,000 monthly, and the most active producers were the Antelope, Sphinx, Fairview and Sunnyside, the latter being the largest. Daily stages ran to Manhattan and other camps. Round Mountain had the usual complement of mercantile stores, brokerage offices and other businesses, the weekly *Nugget*, school, and library. Nearby ranches raised considerable stock. Over $1 million had been taken from the mines through 1909, and the Sunnyside mill alone treated 100 tons of ore daily. That mill had started running in 1906 and was in continuous operation until 1921.

During the 1920s all claims were consolidated into the Nevada Porphyry Gold Mines, which still owns most of the district. Underground mining ceased by 1935, while the Dodge Construction Co. continued surface operations using dirt moving equipment for another five years. Placer mining resumed in 1950 when a dry land washing plant was built which could process 15,000 tons of gravel

The town of Round Mountain (top left) derived its name from the humpbacked oval hill which rises nearly a thousand feet behind the town. In its infancy, Round Mountain (lower left) was laid out with broad streets at right angles. The camp is shown as it was in 1914 with Mt. Jefferson and the Toquima Range in the background.

Gold panners (top right) are looking for rich placer gravel at Round Mountain late in 1906. In this humble plant (center), every Friday the Round Mountain *Nugget* printed the latest mining camp news. Touring cars have arrived in Round Mountain, bringing forth some response from the locals. *(Top left: Frank Mitrani photo; top right: Albert Silver Collection; all others: George Barnett Collection)*

The Round Mountain Mining Co., the district's largest early producer, had its own private bus. Perhaps the passenger was bound for the beer drinking contest. *(George Barnett Collection)*

Beer drinking contest
July 4th 1911
Round Mountain
Nevada

Since the early years of the camp, the mining of placer gravel has sustained the Round Mountain district. Hydraulic mining (above) employed streams of water from nozzles about five inches in diameter to cut away the overburden to reach the gold-bearing gravel. The bottom view faintly shows the pipeline extending across Big Smoky Valley toward Jett Canyon in the snow-capped Toiyabe Mountains, the source of water for the hydraulic operations. The bottom view on the opposite page shows the Sunnyside mine about 1915. The boulders in the foreground were left by the hydraulic mining. (*Both photos, this page: Albert Silver Collection; middle photo, opposite page: U. S. Geological Survey*)

daily, but operations were not successful and it shut down about 1957. District production is estimated to be over $8 million. Round Mountain is now a sleepy camp of about 75 people, and only a few leasers are now active.

JEFFERSON, 7 miles east of Round Mountain.

Though silver had been discovered in 1866 and production began in 1871, not until the summer of 1874 did Jefferson attract much interest, and parties from other camps made frequent visits to spy on the business outlook. By October a two-sectioned town with post office thrived; the lower camp was near the district's two mills and mines and the upper town was three-quarters of a mile to the east in a wider spot, higher in the canyon. Jefferson contained two stores of general merchandise, three blacksmith shops, three boardinghouses, a Wells Fargo express office, drugstore, barbershop, restaurants, hotels, lumberyard, sawmills, brewery, bakeries, school and livery stable. A toll road was built over Jefferson summit to Belmont. Almost every day a 16-mule team arrived from Wadsworth bringing supplies.

At its height in 1876 Jefferson had 800 citizens and in the election that year polled about 600 votes. A forty-pound specimen of Jefferson ore worth $400 was exhibited at the Centennial Exposition in Philadelphia. By 1878 both mills had been closed and the town was virtually abandoned. The post office was discontinued in 1879, and by the following year all but about a dozen people had left. Several later revivals were attempted, including a big one in 1908 when New York interests purchased the mines for $350,000 and built a new mill. Charles Stoneham of the New York Baseball Giants bought the properties in 1917 and renewed mining and milling operations, but soon gave up what had become an unprofitable venture. Stone ruins and houses dot the canyon.

DARROUGH HOT SPRINGS, ¼ mile east of SR 8A at a point 8 miles north of its junction with SR 92.

Darroughs is the oldest stage station in Big Smoky Valley. John C. Fremont stopped here in 1845 on his way south and wrote in his diary that Indians had used these waters for many centuries.

Swimming in a mineralized pool fed by water from the springs may be enjoyed for a modest fee.

OPHIR CANYON, earlier Toiyabe City 3½ miles west of SR 8A at a point 16 miles north of its junction with SR 92.

Silver was discovered early in 1863 by a Frenchman named Boulrand who remained secluded and alone for over a year, packing in provisions from Austin by night to prevent others from finding his lode. News of the discovery finally leaked out after Boulrand confided in a countryman on a trip into Austin. R. B. Canfield purchased the principal ledge, the Murphy, in 1864, and the Twin River Mining Co. was organized to raise funds for development. A wagon road costing $8000 was constructed 2½ miles from Big Smoky Valley into Ophir Canyon during 1865. Stretches of the road attained 10° grades and nine wooden bridges were built over creeks.

When exploitation of the Murphy and adjacent mines began the new Toiyabe City became a prosperous village of 400 with tri-weekly stage to Austin. In September 1866 construction was completed on a twenty-stamp mill encased in a building of native shale, granite bricks, and rock. The Murphy mine and mill produced more than $750,000 in silver during the next two years but paid no dividends to stockholders because of the rock's extraordinary denseness. The mine logged over 2500 man hours in sinking one ten-foot shaft, and 18,000 drill steels were sharpened monthly for the forty-man crew. In a few instances round-the-clock operations resulted in deepening shafts less than ten feet in a month's time.

Lack of millable ore halted production, and mismanagement forced the company into bankruptcy by 1869 as discouraged stockholders refused to pour additional funds into the operation. During the mid-1880s the Murphy resumed day-and-night operations, out-producing the fine effort of the 1860s, and the revival which lasted until about 1890 boosted production to over $3 million.

During this century small operators were occasionally active but the camp never revived. Remaining today are the roofless walls of the company building, foundations of the mill, and cabin walls all in a steep picturesque canyon setting. A graveyard remains at the canyon entrance.

A small party is crossing Jefferson summit with a prospecting outfit in 1902. *(Mrs. Rose Walter Collection)*

The mining camp of Jefferson contains stone walls of old cabins amid the wooden ruins of newer operations. *(Frank Mitrani photo)*

The dean of settlements in Big Smoky Valley is Darrough Hot Springs (below), shown here in 1895. This building was built in 1863 as a way station for mail routes. A large wooden annex containing a ten-room hotel and bar was added in 1908. This noted landmark was still in use in 1970. *(Mrs. Myrtle T. Myles Collection)*

At the settlement of Ophir Canyon, these saloons, hotels and stores all reopened in the revival of the mid-1880s. The miners had built substantial rock cabins. The crew of the Murphy mine at that time is shown in the middle picture. The Murphy shaft house and mill (below) were at the upper end of the canyon above the mining camp. The revival of mining here was one of Nevada's most significant operations during that decade. Now only roofless walls and foundations remain of the Murphy operation. *(Three photos: Mrs. Myrtle Myles Collection)*

This store (page opposite) which opened at Millett in 1906 served the central part of Big Smoky Valley. *(George Frawley Collection)*

MILLETT, ¼ mile east of SR 8A at a point 22 miles north of its junction with SR 92 (66 miles north of Tonopah).

Before the Millett gold boom early in this century several ranches and stage stations had been established in the area. Minnium's Station, or Baumanns, east of SR 8A at a point eleven miles north, was a stopover point for travelers in Smoky Valley as early as 1862. Charles Scheel started a ranch in 1873 which Mike Millett bought in 1896. Tate's Station, built two miles south in 1886, gained importance as the halfway stop on the Austin-Belmont stage run and junction of a line running to Ophir Canyon. The post office for the area was at Junction (1873-1906) on the Lognoz Ranch, five miles north of Millett. Other than in Ophir Canyon, the east base of the Toiyabes was only superficially worked during the 19th century.

Discoveries at Manhattan and Round Mountain in 1905 sent prospectors into all nearby canyons of the westerly Toiyabes in search of rich leads. After the finding of $200 a ton ore in the hills west of Millett Ranch early in 1906, a townsite was platted at the ranch, and many people bought lots when mining development began. A three-foot ledge of $5000-a-ton ore was found near a long-undiscovered skeleton in March, and Pueblo townsite was laid out three miles southwest of Millett between two running streams and close to the mines. Sixty tents and a dozen frame buildings were built there in a few weeks' time, but that camp lasted only several months.

At the beginning of summer the Millett district had 300 or 400 people frantically searching for lodes. Telephone service had been extended from north and south, and Millett had a post office, store, wagon repair shop, and the two-story Lakeview Hotel. In June 1906 the first gold shipment was hauled to Austin for delivery by railroad to Salt Lake City. The principal operator, Manual Mining Co., also maintained a small stamp mill. Though Millett town died out a year or two later, some mining continued until 1916. Dugouts remain at Millett, as well as Scheel's original ranch house; picturesque rock ruins are left at Minniums; a house and sod cellar remain at Tates; while at Pueblo there is nothing of interest.

375

These three pictures show the early days of Broken Hills, a camp that took its name from a rich mining district in Australia. At the camp's first lease (bottom), ore sacks are being loaded for shipment to the railroad at Fallon. Later trucks made the haul at a cost of $4 per ton. *(Three photos: Western History Research Center, University of Wyoming)*

PARK CANYON, 3 miles west of Millett.

The North Twin River district was organized in 1863, and two years later silver ore began to be shipped to mills in Austin. Early in 1867 the La Plata Mining Co. uprooted a ten-stamp mill from Yankee Blade and installed it in a substantial building built of brick and stone found in nearby canyons. Initial runs were made in July, and the mill saw regular use briefly until it closed down before 1869.

The district revived several times, enough so in the mid-1880s to support a camp with post office. Another revival in 1905 lasted a decade. A legend lingers at Park Canyon that a deposed Hawaiian monarch lived here awhile after 1867 and owned several mining properties. This may be true, as Hawaiians settled elsewhere in the Great Basin, especially at Iosepa, Utah.

DOWNEYVILLE, 2¼ miles north and east of SR 23 at a point 2 miles north of Gabbs.

After silver-lead discoveries in May 1877, several locations were made and development work started. Most of nearby Ellsworth flocked to this new boom, and a camp sprang up which had great expectations — so great that the newcomer, unless he had friends or acquaintances, had to sleep in the sagebrush, "house room being too valuable to be wasted in furnishing lodgings." By 1878 Downeyville contained 200 men, stores, saloons, stables, and office for stage lines and Wells Fargo express. Stages from the northwest brought in supplies and occasional visitors.

A post office opened in March 1879 and after 1881 ore was freighted to the newly-completed Carson & Colorado railroad and sent away for treatment until a lead smelter was constructed at Downeyville a few years later. The extent of the stone ruins suggests that the camp grew quite large before passing out of the picture about 1901, when Tonopah and other discoveries beckoned. The post office was officially discontinued in October 1901. Stone ruins and dumps remain.

LODI, later Marble, 2 miles west of Lodi Valley road at a point 8 miles from its junction with SR 23 (9 miles north of Gabbs).

Gold was discovered at the Illinois mine in 1874 and the Lodi district was organized early the next year. A ten-ton smelter was built and by 1878 the camp boasted a general store, blacksmith shop, saloon, boardinghouse, stone dwellings and a population of a hundred. After producing about $400,-000 the Illinois mine ceased operations about 1880 and the camp died.

That mine resumed operations in 1905 and the revived camp was also known as Marble after the post office was established in March 1906. In the spring of 1908 a Lodi townsite was platted at Lodi Tanks, where a good water supply was available. Buildings went up including the usual quota of thirst parlors, corrals and mercantile companies. At the Illinois mine another townsite known as Bob was laid out. There a new 100-ton smelter was blown in during June 1909, the second built to treat ore from the Illinois mine. Development of the mine was halted by water from 1914 to 1919 when further attempts were made. Some ore was again produced about 1940. Smelter ruins and buildings of recent origin remain at Lodi near the Illinois mine; brick foundations indicate the site of Lodi Tanks.

BROKEN HILLS (Mineral County), 1½ miles east of SR 23 at a point 15 miles north of Gabbs.

James Stratford and Joseph Arthur discovered silver-lead ore in 1913 and within six months a boom developed, only to be cut short because the original discoverers had already claimed the most promising locations. For the rest of the decade these two men extracted $70,000 and in 1920 sold out for $75,000 to the Broken Hills Silver Corporation backed by George Graham Rice. The new company started development but ran into difficulties and ceased operations after making only one $7000 shipment to a nearby mill. Other short-lived companies fared no better.

Broken Hills reawoke early in 1926 when nearby Quartz Mountain in Nye County boomed a few miles east, and a post office and businesses reopened. After 1928 activity declined and smaller operations continued work, producing about $180,-000 from 1935 to 1940, the district's most productive era. But the camp was most populous during the World War I years when it had a few hundred residents, hotel, saloon, stores and a school. Several wooden buildings poke up out of the flat landscape to mark the site.

Around the turn of the century Ione was a peaceful hamlet where a few people had brought some land into cultivation. Ione Valley is in the background. (*Theron Fox Collection*)

A prospector and his outfit are at Berlin. The Berlin mill and mine office are in the background. (*Western History Research Center, University of Wyoming*)

Grantsville in the mid-1880s had a main street with 42 business establishments. Adjacent canyons contained many houses. (*Mrs. Myrtle Myles Collection*)

QUARTZ MOUNTAIN, 2 miles southeast of Broken Hills (13 miles north of Gabbs).

The first discoveries were made in 1920 and ore was shipped the following year; but then the district lay dormant until 1925, when three men leased certain mines. In the course of development work a rich lead-silver ore shoot was hit, and the news of this strike early in 1925 coupled with the rumor that Nevada's millionaire banker George Wingfield was interested in the district started a stampede in the spring of 1926. Fortune seekers from the Idaho panhandle to the Mexican border transformed this part of the desert into a hive of activity. Claims were staked out for miles, development work began and a camp quickly formed.

As each new day broke, prospectors cooked breakfast over a hundred campfires, and afterwards the purr of autos was heard as one by one the men drove to their claims for the day's work. By spring several hundred had come, and big trucks shuttled back and forth to Fallon, hauling out ore and bringing in water, supplies and mail for the burgeoning district. Incoming letters and parcels were left at a saloon at nearby Broken Hills, which revived because of this boom. During May and June several buildings were moved in from Rawhide and Goldfield, and businesses had opened up: four cafes, grocery stores, barbershops and stores of general merchandise. The townsite of Quartz Mountain was staked out in June, the same month that the *Miner* began weekly publication. "Keep your eyes on Quartz Mountain," advised the first issue, declaring that the district would become a second Coeur d'Alene. Work continued through 1926, when the camp folded. Several wooden structures, weathered appreciably by the wind, stand scattered among a few low hills.

PHONOLITE, 2½ miles east of the Lodi Valley road at a point 12 miles northeast of its junction with SR 23.

Initial work started on the west side of the Paradise Range in the Bruner district in July 1906 when the Black Mule mine opened up after assays promised $2500 per ton in gold and silver. Phonolite soon came into the limelight and gained a post office in January 1907. Promotion was handled in typical 1907 style; the Phonolite Townsite & Water Co., incorporated at $1 million, laid out an official

townsite and devised elaborate plans for an electric light plant and a water system. By spring another townsite christened Duluth was platted one mile east; that camp had its promotional *Tribune* and a post office. The boom was brief and both camps folded after the summer of 1908.

Another corporation known as the Kansas City-Nevada Consolidated with a capital stock of 6 million shares at one dollar par value, tried to make a go of the district's mines in 1915 and built a fifty-ton cyanide mill in 1919, which they enlarged two years later. It ran with only limited success. The district's only profitable producer was the Penelas mine, which gave forth nearly $900,000 during 1935-40. Concrete mill foundations are left at Phonolite; a few buildings remain at Duluth and the Penelas mine is abandoned.

IONE, at eastern terminus of SR 91, 24 miles east of Gabbs (64 miles north-northwest of Tonopah).

After silver discoveries in the northern part of the Union district in November 1863, the camp of Ione rose and at once nearby mines acquired a reputation on the Pacific slope for rich minerals. The camp grew to about four dozen buildings in a beautiful canyon, but was found to be too distant from the principal belt containing the mines. Early in 1864 the present Ione townsite was founded in a lower part of the canyon broad enough for a commodious commercial street. In February 1864 the state legislature designated Ione the seat of newly-created Nye County, believing that here was the center of another rich mineral region. Later that spring after another rush the camp boasted about 100 houses and over 500 inhabitants. In June the *Nye County News* began publication and the business district served outlying camps.

Milling began in the spring of 1865 when stamps began to fall in the Pioneer mill, but the unprepared miners were unable to supply enough ore, and after litigation the sheriff closed down the plant. That same summer eastern capitalists erected the $130,000 twenty-stamp Knickerbocker mill three miles south of town. Beginning in 1866 this facility intermittently treated ore from nearby districts for about a decade. Mining conditions were depressed later that year, the county seat was moved to Belmont early in 1867 and a budding revival in 1868 was quickly extinguished by the

White Pine boom. Finally, after 1870 the mines near Ione registered several respectable annual productions, especially in 1872-73, and by 1880 this camp had weathered many vicissitudes, at times prosperous and then all but deserted.

Although no big revivals have taken place at the mines since 1880, the camp has never been totally deserted. Quicksilver operations in the 1920s and 1930s have elevated the total production to over $500,000. Several buildings still stand, including a wooden structure supposed to have been the courthouse.

ELLSWORTH, 10 miles west of Ione via graded roads.

Late in 1863 an Indian revealed a silver ledge to whites who organized the Mammoth district a few months later. Two rival camps developed near the mines, Ellsworth and Upper Weston or Summit City, and each had small business streets. Mining development was slow and discouraging until a ten-stamp steam-powered mill with furnace was completed in the summer of 1871. Activity increased and owners returned to work their claims. That year Ellsworth had 200 citizens, businesses, and a post office and dwellings built of rock. Stage and freight service brought in supplies from Wadsworth, 108 miles northwest, at a cost of 2½ cents a pound.

The mill ran for the next two years, the foreman employing several Indians to tend the pans, settlers and concentrators. In 1872 it encountered difficulties in ore reduction and in 1874 when the mill was sadly out of repair most people drifted away. Only twenty people and two saloons remained in 1880 but later operators, particularly in this century, worked the mines and attained some production. Only rock walls and a cemetery remain in Ellsworth Canyon, half a mile below newer wooden buildings.

BERLIN, 2 miles south of SR 91 at a point 19 miles east of Gabbs.

State Senator Bell originally located the Berlin mine, which was first worked for silver about 1895, and sold out to John G. Stokes of New York. The aggressive Nevada Company bought the properties in 1898, acquired the Pioneer and Knickerbocker mills near Ione, moved all machinery to help build a new thirty-stamp mill, and began systematic development.

At the height of operations Berlin had a population of 250 which supported a store, post office, auto shop and a stage line to nearby camps. But the yields were small and the mill fell silent in 1909, although in the previous year the Goldfield paper reported that enough ore was in sight to run the mill for at least three years. A fifty-ton cyanide plant worked the Berlin tailings between 1911 and 1914 but recovered only about $2.50 in each ton. The larger mill was stripped of its equipment during World War II, but a large shell remains, surrounded by an assay office, boardinghouse and wooden cabins.

UNION, 1¼ miles south and east of Berlin.

After nearby Ione and Grantsville were founded in 1863 Union emerged as the smallest of three camps in the Union mining district. The camp faded by the mid-1860s but revived in the 1890s when the nearby Berlin gold mine was worked. Several miners built stone buildings, ruins of which remain.

GRANTSVILLE, 5 miles east-southeast of SR 91 at a point 18 miles east of Gabbs.

After silver discoveries in the Union district in the summer of 1863, a camp formed in the upper part of Grantsville Canyon where a nest of ledges was being worked. Development was slow and the camp was forsaken for White Pine in 1868-69. In 1877 the Alexander Company began working the silver mines and built a twenty-stamp mill; the camp then reawoke after nearly a decade of dormancy, reaching a population of about 800 in 1879.

That year the business street boasted ten stores of general merchandise, drugstores, a hardware store and tin shop, furniture store, bakeries, many saloons, three barbershops, blacksmith shops, assay offices, jewelry store, brewery, a modern post office and the print shop of the weekly Sun. The mill doubled its capacity in 1880 and the Bonanza began weekly publication, filling the void left by the eclipse of the Sun. Stages ran to Austin via Ione and Eureka via Belmont. Townsite lots sold for $500 and some optimists considered building a railroad line to connect with the Nevada Central at Ledlie, near Austin. For diversion the Grantsville people had balls and dances, banquets and various sports including an occasional baseball game for a keg of lager.

The town's lively days were over by 1885, but numerous revivals have augmented the district's earlier production. The largest modern development was just before World War II, when several new structures rose at the lower end of the canyon. Fallen adobe walls, stone buildings, foundations and a cemetery remain in a mountain setting which commands a fine view of Ione Valley to the west.

ATWOOD, 7 miles southeast of SR 23 at a point 4½ miles south of Gabbs.

Gold was discovered in 1901, the Fairplay district was organized in the summer of 1903, and a camp was formed by 200 people, most of whom came from Goldfield. A Tonopah realty firm promoted Atwood townsite late in 1905, and the first business establishment, a hotel, threw open its doors on New Year's Day of 1906. A month later the camp had a post office. In a mild rush early in the year a smaller camp emerged a mile southeast, Goldyke, which soon had its own post office, the *Daily Sun* and five-stamp mill. In Atwood, the *Fairplay Prospector* was published briefly in 1907. Both camps folded that fall when the mines played out. A few wooden and adobe buildings are left at Atwood; mill ruins and one building remained at Goldyke in 1960.

PACTOLUS, 14 miles southeast of SR 23 at a point 2½ miles south of Gabbs.

Gold and silver prospects were worked at various times during 1903-07, but unlike the banks of the Pactolus in ancient Lydia, its sands did not turn to gold. A few dozen men worked here in the 1920s and several buildings were built. Only a well and one structure mark the site.

CLOVERDALE, 6 miles north and east of SR 89 at a point 30 miles southeast of its junction with SR 23 (36 miles northwest of Tonopah).

This stage station and ranch has been a landmark for travelers in western Nye County since about 1872. A post office was established briefly in the late 1880s. The ranch still remains.

GOLDEN, approximately 6 miles north of Cloverdale.

The south end of the Shoshone Mountains attracted some attention early in 1906 but mining stampedes to Manhattan and Round Mountain eclipsed these prospects. The mining press gave favorable notice to gold discoveries in the spring of 1907 but bank failures later that year brought a slump in activity. A small mill was built in 1909 and placer operations took place at times since the year of the district's discovery. After favorable testing for placers in 1931 a Los Angeles group delivered dragline equipment to the district but for unknown reasons production did not begin.

The Divide boom of 1919 was another case of big promotion and little ore. Vast sums were spent in exploratory work, and nearly 100 prospects were being developed in the summer of 1919. The above picture shows a closeup of an operation and a camp on the slope of the mountain. Numerous stock companies issued handsomely engraved certificates, but only the Tonopah Divide Mining Co. produced enough ore to suggest dividends. *(Top: Pete Moser Collection; bottom: William Metscher Collection)*

ESMERALDA COUNTY

In the early years of the state Esmeralda County extended halfway across southwestern Nevada — from the verdant East Walker River area to the Death Valley country. After Mineral County was carved out of northern Esmeralda in 1911, the remainder consisted of isolated basins and rugged mountains, with no railroads or important trails. In this remote and uninviting setting, silver was discovered at Silverpeak as early as 1864. The borax town of Columbus boomed during the 1870s and other 19th century camps were Montezuma, Palmetto, Lida, Gold Mountain and Tule Canyon.

Esmeralda County rapidly assumed importance in the mid-1900s, after the discovery and development of Goldfield, one of the West's greatest single gold districts. Because of that camp, mining throughout the county was stimulated. Old areas such as Montezuma, Lida and Palmetto were re-worked and Blair, Diamondfield, Hornsilver (later Gold Point) became important camps. After World War I Divide City became a promoters' paradise and Gilbert and Weepah followed. During the next decade Silverpeak, Goldfield, Gold Point, Weepah and Lida were active, but most mining ceased at the beginning of World War II. Since then the Columbus and Silverpeak districts have been significant producers.

DIVIDE, earlier Gold Mountain, 1 mile south of US 95 at a point 4½ miles south of Tonopah.

Two Tonopah prospectors discovered gold veins at the Tonopah-Divide mine in 1901, and within a year the Tonopah Gold Mountain Mining Co. began development. In the spring of 1903, the Tonopah paper proudly described Gold Mountain as an Esmeralda County suburb, with boarding-house, general store, and three saloons going full blast. But brighter prospects in Goldfield and Bull-frog soon drew everyone away and the camp did not last long.

Leasers worked the district occasionally until late in 1917, when high-grade silver was accidentally found in a worked-out gold vein. The value of this find, its nearness to Tonopah, and the soaring price of silver all created a psychological setting which resulted in an intense rush in the spring of 1919. Hundreds of tenderfoot and experienced prospectors wildly filed claims, and most of the forty surrounding square miles were quickly spoken for. Many of the new arrivals came by Pullman berth on the Tonopah & Goldfield Rail-road, with steamer trunk, safety razor, and an antidote for snake bite — essential because the nation would soon become "dry." About 350 companies were speedily organized, nearly all with "Divide" as part of their designations.

Divide was the daily destination of commuters whose bedroom was Tonopah. Each morning men crowded outbound autos for the mines at Divide and at night inbound ones back to the city.

Divide had a post office known as Sigold and a newspaper, the *Times*, which first appeared in March 1919. Later in the year the expiration of the Pittman Silver Act, coupled with unimpressive results of exploratory work, ended the boom and except for a few companies, most of the ground

Gold Reef was only one of scores of small mining camps that rose near newly found allegedly rich ore bodies. A multi-purpose store such as the one above was quickly and easily built, and a lot sale or a banquet kicked off a small real estate rush. Some came by autos but others relied on the established burro train (below). Most of these boom-lets lasted but a few months, and their ruins stand as monuments to folly and wasted effort. (*Both photos: Mrs. Nevada Browne Collection*)

was abandoned. The outstanding mine was the Tonopah Divide which in its first four years produced a recorded $1.4 million. A hoist-house remains as well as many prospect holes.

GOLD REEF, approximately 6 miles south-southeast of Tonopah.

A gold strike was made probably in the summer of 1909 and by October a camp started up which included a store, cafe and saloon. In the same month a banquet with champagne and other delicacies brought out from Tonopah by a caterer was enjoyed by miners and owners together. Some publicity followed, but the tonnage was not there and the camp did not even last out the year.

KLONDIKE or Southern Klondike, 2½ miles southeast of US 95 at a point 10 miles south of Tonopah.

Gold and silver were discovered in March 1899 and for about six years various leasers took out ore. Klondike was a small ordinary camp and would have passed into oblivion except for one event. When Jim Butler discovered silver-bearing veins at what soon became Tonopah in May 1900, he was en route to this camp. Butler brought samples into Klondike, gave them to an assayer named Frank Hicks, and offered to give a quarter interest for an assay. Believing that the rocks were worthless, Hicks threw the sample out the window to the waste pile. The rest of the story is well known: Butler gathered additional samples and an assay revealed that the ledge was rich in silver (see Tonopah). After learning of the strike, Hicks retrieved the original samples, assayed them and reported results, claiming a quarter interest in the find. Butler generously gave him a one-thirty-second interest, although he had no moral or legal obligation to do so.

Klondike never grew large but it had a post office from 1901 to 1903. Tonopah was the supply and shipping point, and water was obtained from Klondike Well, four miles west. Some small shipments of ore have been made through the years. Wooden ruins mark the site.

ALKALI SPRING, on Silverpeak-Goldfield road at a point 7 miles northwest of its junction with US 95 at a point 4½ miles north of Goldfield.

For over a dozen years this spa was the scene of picnics, dances and parties for the people of Goldfield, and there was also swimming in a large concrete pool. A restaurant served fine dinners. With the decline of Goldfield after 1918 the resort lived out its usefulness. Foundations remain.

PHILLIPSBURG, approximately 5 miles west of Alkali Spring.

Veteran Tonopah prospector G. H. Phillips spent six weeks with his pair of mules, wagon and camp outfit, prospecting the Lone Mountains before striking silver early in May 1906. News of the find created a furor at Goldfield and in a few days a saloon, restaurant and assay office opened up among a collection of tents. The town of Phillipsburg was surveyed and 150 lots were sold at once, but the rush was cut short when the gold and silver veins proved smaller than publicized, and the camp was probably abandoned by midsummer.

MONTEZUMA, 7 miles south of the Silverpeak-Goldfield road at a point 11 miles west of its junction with US 95.

Mexicans who mined silver with Indians in the mid-19th century performed the earliest work in the area on the northwestern side of Montezuma Peak. Three prospectors who found ore in August 1867 organized a district, and within a year several dozen claims were staked and a camp formed. By 1870 the mining activity demanded a mill, and machinery of an abandoned ten-stamp mill at Yankee Blade was relocated here. With the help of 14 laborers and two brick masons, machinery was moved 140 miles over rough wagon roads and put in running order in only three months, a speedy job considering the remoteness of this region.

The mill served local mines intermittently through the 1870s and into the next decade. Mining continued until about 1887 and the camp was large enough to support a post office during most of 1880-88. After prospectors ventured westward from Goldfield in 1905, mining revived here and some shipments were made before operations ceased in 1907. Montezuma has yielded over $500,-000 — a good showing for such a remote area. With no extensive help from outside capital the district took care of itself. Ruins of a stone oven and remnants of other buildings are left on the site.

GOLDFIELD, on US 95, 25 miles south of Tonopah and 182 miles northwest of Las Vegas.

Splendid, magnificent, Queen of the Camps,
Mistress of countless Aladdin's lamps
Deity worshipped by kings and tramps,
The lure she is of the West.

— J. W. Scott

Worthy was Goldfield to receive such praise in 1907. Its magical name was a byword on the lips of mining men throughout the world, and in 1906 and 1907 alone over $15 million had been produced by the camp's mines, the chief of them already numbered among the world's greatest.

In the fall of 1902 an experienced Indian prospector, Tom Fisherman, brought gold samples to Tonopah and two young prospectors there, Billy Marsh and Harry Stimler, decided to go to Rabbit Springs where Fisherman hung out. In a heavy storm of howling winds and alkali dust they discovered float gold on Columbia Mountain and named their first claim the Sandstorm. Anticipating an extensive deposit they christened the camp Grandpa in the optimistic belief that it might be the granddaddy of all camps.

After news of assays running $12 to $97 per ton of ore had circulated early in 1903 a mild spring rush developed. In May the district was renamed Goldfield. Claims were developed under lease; if this system had not been adopted Goldfield would not have been exploited with such energy in so short a time. In June 1903 George Nixon and George Wingfield became the district's first important backers, and a mining excitement developed which soon simmered down when these men failed to take up their mine option. In October a Tonopah syndicate opened up rich ore bodies on the five-month-old Combination claim, and two months later shipments were begun.

A full-blown mining stampede early in 1904 transformed the desert into a burgeoning camp of several thousand within a year. From every direction adventurers swarmed across the sagebrush using any possible means of travel — wagons, horses, a few autos, and even their own feet — each hell-bent to grab himself a claim. The colorful Goldfield *News* began publication that April proclaiming Goldfield as the greatest camp ever known, and before midsummer the Jumbo, Florence and January leases began shipping ore. By August daily output from the leases was estimated at $10,000 a day!

During 1905 handsome adobe brick and stone buildings were erected, as well as many frame houses, keeping carpenters busy 24 hours a day. Electricity and water connections to residences made Goldfield a modern place. Real estate values rose to $150 and $210 a front foot on the main thoroughfares. Completion of the Tonopah & Goldfield Railroad into the camp in September improved the district's transportation facilities, although freight charges remained high.

The boom grew red hot in 1906, aided greatly by the rich ore discovered on the Hayes-Monette lease of the Mohawk. Townsite lots sold in the five figures, one lot bringing $45,000, and expensive buildings were erected. The Gans-Nelson world lightweight championship fight in September brought Goldfield a real publicity bonanza. The mines became targets of greedy high-graders who used specially made overalls, false soles and heels in shoes and hollow pick handles to carry away each week hundreds of dollars worth of rich ore which was later discounted at assayers' offices.

Emerging behind the restless crowds, experienced promoters and operators developed the mines and planned ways of bringing efficiency to district mining. Two of these were George Wingfield and George Nixon, who organized the Goldfield Consolidated Mining Co. late in 1906 to begin systematic development. Early in 1907 Goldfield boosters succeeded in winning the county seat from Hawthorne, and a year later a substantial stone courthouse was built.

From 1906 until the spring of 1908, fierce labor disputes rocked the town when the Industrial Workers of the World and the Western Federation of Miners vied to control labor in the district. Strike after strike in the mines followed disagreement over wages, change rooms (an attempt to eliminate high-grading), and the use of script. Threats of violence in December 1907 moved Governor Sparks to call in federal troops though local authority had not collapsed.

Nevertheless the boom attained its height in 1907-08, when this modern city of 20,000 was served by five banks, two daily and three weekly newspapers, two mining stock exchanges, three

386

Some of Goldfield's earliest visitors were moneyed men's representatives who stayed in comfortable hotels in Tonopah while looking over the mines. These cars traveled the thirty-mile distance between the towns in two hours flat. A few frame structures (middle) amid drafty tents had been built in Goldfield in 1903. Two years later St. Pierre's up-to-date store contained the usual line of shoes and a repair shop. The variety here nearly equalled that found in Reno or San Francisco. *(Top: Orlo Parker Collection; two other photos: Huntington Library)*

Goldfield by October 1904 had begun to look like a city. Columbia Street, the main thoroughfare, has taken shape in the townsite which was laid out on a comparatively level area midway between Rabbit Springs and Columbia Mountain to avoid the possibility of huge mine dumps blocking the streets as at Tonopah. A good water supply also determined the site. At the base of the mountain in the background was the town of Columbia. Only a few prospects are evident there, but in the three years to follow that same area was to be heavily developed.

Development of early leases in the Goldfield district are shown in the two pictures on this page and at bottom opposite. High-grade ore is sacked and shipped to smelters, while ore of lower grade was piled separately to be worked when milling facilities would be built in the district. At lower left a group of fortunate leasers line up to observe their work. (*Top: Orlo Parker Collection; bottom left: Mrs. Myrtle Myles Collection*)

Columbia Street, shown in the top two photos, was in 1905 continually crowded with all types of conveyances and people moving about from stores to saloons, brokerage offices to banks. Ahead of the delivery wagon (top left), a stylish surrey moves past freight wagons loaded with lumber, furniture and whiskey. New construction is everywhere. The Malpais mesa is in the background.

With Columbia Mountain as a backdrop (top), the east end of Main Street shows evidence of bustle. Goods are stacked in front of stores, and delivery wagons and a large freighter piled high with lumber trek through the dust.

Goldfield was the receiving point for ore from nearby districts. A wagon from Hornsilver (bottom left) passes a clothing store on its way to the freight depot. Autos soon began crowding animal-drawn conveyances off the streets. These stages (below) prepare to take passengers to Diamondfield, Lida, Tonopah, Bullfrog, and other points, attesting to Goldfield's importance as a hub of mining camps. (Two top photos: Western History Research Center, University of Wyoming; bottom left: Orlo Parker Collection; bottom right: Mrs. Harry Mighels Collection)

Goldfield's tenderloin district, in the northwest section of town on lower Main Street, had row after row of cribs. At the height of the boom about a hundred girls were employed at three large establishments. *(Center: Las Vegas Review-Journal)*

Gambling establishments numbered 25 to a block, according to one observer early in 1907. The click of the ivory balls in the roulette wheels, the rattle of dice and the flip-flap of cards were heard day and night. *(Pete Moser Collection)*

During 1906-07 chaotic crowds were everywhere, especially at holiday parades (above) and at drilling matches (below), both common features of all mining camps. These contests tested the skill of the miners. The driller able to put a hole into a solid granite block or boulder deeper than his opponent within a specified time, with single jack and drill, was declared the winner. Spectators often placed bets on the participants, and women at times sang patriotic songs during the match. Tex Rickard's famed Northern saloon at the right was on the corner of Main and Crook streets, Goldfield's main intersection, where the Hermitage, Palace and Mohawk saloons also stood. (*Both photos: Douglas Robinson Jr. Collection*)

The John S. Cook & Co. Bank (above) also had branches in Tonopah and Rhyolite. This institution along with the Nye & Ormsby County Bank were Goldfield's two largest. (*Mrs. Harry Mighels Collection*)

At the bank, sacks of high-grade ore from the Mohawk, Jumbo, Florence and other mines were stored under the watchful eyes of stern guards. (*Huntington Library*)

394

The inquiry, "How are stocks today?" was asked by everyone; the rise and fall of the value of various mining companies started a conversation anytime. The "big board" (below) shows the bid and asking prices of mining stocks in Goldfield, Manhattan, Round Mountain, Virginia City and Tonopah. Promising development of ore bodies resulted in big variations in stock prices and sudden changes in fortunes. *(Top: Mr. W. B. Mercer Collection; bottom: Fred Steen Collection)*

The huge 100-stamp mill of the Goldfield Consolidated Mining Co. (above) was situated northeast of town on the north side of Columbia Mountain. George Wingfield and George Nixon organized that company in November 1906 after acquiring the Mohawk, Jumbo, Red Top, and Laguna mines and capitalizing them at $50 million in five million shares at $10 par value. Subsequently the Combination and January mines were bought. The mill began running in 1908 and continued until 1918, when the company ceased operations. The interior view (below) shows the stamps in batteries of ten. (*Bottom: Orlo Parker Collection*)

Goldfield, Nevada's largest city late in 1907, had many solid business blocks — substantial testimonials of progress. The largest building shown is the Goldfield Hotel, on the right side of Columbia Street, in center of picture. That street is flanked on the left by Main Street and on the right by Fifth Avenue. At middle left are the high school and the Esmeralda County courthouse under construction. At the base of Columbia Mountain is the suburb of Columbia; faintly visible under a cloud of steam in the same area is a Tonopah & Tidewater train. The town's expansion is nearly completed. Comparison of this picture with the 1904 view on a previous page dramatically shows the growth of this mining metropolis. *(Getchell Library, University of Nevada)*

When troops were sent to quell the labor disturbances in 1908, they camped near the Combination mine. *(Orlo Parker Collection)*

During 1908, auto stages regularly left the Goldfield Hotel for the new boom at Rawhide. The most famous ex-Goldfielder to exchange allegiances that year was Tex Rickard. (Las Vegas *Review-Journal*)

Plenty of beer, whiskey and wine bottles are in evidence at this stag banquet with all the trimmings at Goldfield. (*Dickenson Library, University of Nevada*)

When construction was finished on the modern four-story $450,000 Goldfield Hotel in June 1908, three days and nights of dancing took place to the stacatto popping of corks from $5 bottles of champagne. The town's aristocracy and visiting nabobs shared its luxuries. Vestibuled Pullmans carried San Franciscans here without a change of train, and at the depot a dozen taxis whisked guests to the hotel. Its 150 rooms had brass beds and deep carpets; about half of the rooms had private baths. The spacious lobby (right) was finished in solid mahogany and had overstuffed black leather chairs. In the dining room (lower), special chefs served a distinguished cuisine which included oysters on the half shell, lobster, quail, squid, Roquefort and other imported delicacies. After the guests feasted, an orchestra entertained dancers far into the evening. The hotel closed in 1936 but it reopened in 1942. Again the doors were locked in 1945. *(Three photos: Mrs. W. B. Mercer Collection)*

399

This Goldfield bar interior was typical of the era. A few tables occupied the front (not shown), near the swinging doors. Opposite the bar, and stretching along in similar fashion was a short-order chop house. Lucky purchasers of beef at this meat market (below) might have chunks of liver thrown in free of charge. *(Two photos: Orlo Parker Collection)*

400

The fashionable Palace Club on the corner of Main and Crook Streets had a fine bar and many gaming tables. The Montezuma Club and the Elks regularly gathered here. From his corner stand the news vendor did a brisk business selling papers from all over Nevada, San Francisco, and the East, as well as the latest mining journals. (*Mrs. W. B. Mercer Collection*)

At the brewery on the west side of town, low-grade steam beer was manufactured for local consumption. With a wagonload of kegs, the team is ready to make deliveries. (*Orlo Parker Collection*)

The home of Tex Rickard, built during the boom era on the corner of Crook and Franklin streets, still stands, but today takes in guests. Rickard brought the Gans-Nelson fight to Goldfield in September 1906 and thereafter rose to national fame as a promoter in the fistic world.

Goldfield's progressive citizens saw that the children had fine schools. The high school (below) was condemned in the late 1940s but the building still stands. (*Orlo Parker Collection*)

Goldfield has been visited by the twin curses of flood and fire. In September 1913 a violent flash flood quickly descended upon the declining camp, further dampening its spirit. The terrible effect of the flood is shown. A decade later a fire leveled 53 square blocks of the city. The destructive blaze is viewed from the balcony of the Goldfield Hotel. *(Two photos: Mrs. W. B. Mercer Collection)*

railroads and four fine schools. Saloons numbered 25 to a block and brokers' offices abounded. Imposing block buildings, some four and five stories high, housed commercial activity, and many fine residences graced the side streets. The productive mines tantalized mineral-conscious investors, and brokers at major east and west coast exchanges traded Goldfield mining shares at a furious pace.

The leasing era of the camp ended in 1908 when the Goldfield Consolidated Mining Co. confined its work to developing the Mohawk and Combination mines and building its new 100-stamp mill northeast of town. The fever over Goldfield receded as mining was put on a businesslike basis. The nearly $9 million production in 1909 more than doubled that of the previous year, and mining output peaked in 1910 when $10.7 million was recorded. Eight years later major mining ceased when the Goldfield Consolidated mine nearly exhausted its ores and closed its mill. The camp's production to that date was a recorded $80 million, though some say about $125 million is a reasonable estimate considering high-grading and unrecorded outputs.

Goldfield also declined for reasons other than the labor wars and diminished mineral outputs. A cloudburst that flooded the town in 1913 damaged many homes beyond repair, and the great fire of 1923 leveled 53 square blocks of the city including many commercial structures. Enough remains at Goldfield to rate it among the best historic spots in Nevada.

COLUMBIA, 1 mile north of Goldfield.

After gold was discovered in the Goldfield district in 1902, the first settlement, called Stimler, was near the mines at the base of Columbia Mountain, for which the camp was soon renamed. To avoid the crowding about the mine works that so inconvenienced Tonopah, the town of Goldfield was laid out on a more spacious and level site farther to the west, but Columbia continued to flourish and many businesses, including a bank, opened in 1904. A newsy weekly, the Goldfield *Review*, appeared in October 1904; the next month a post office and a large hotel opened. Businessmen organized a chamber of commerce, capitalized at $10,000, to raise money for a two-story edifice on the main street; in this building were also a lodge hall and office suites.

It was not uncommon in early Columbia for builders to "squat" on lots and extend structures over alleys. When the situation got out of hand, incensed owners went about kicking the squatters off their properties. One man actually sawed off the rear of a wooden building which encroached on an alley.

Columbia grew to 1500 by 1907 and had many two-story brick and wood-frame buildings, including the depot of the Tonopah & Goldfield Railroad, but when the initial excitement over Goldfield wore off in 1908 Columbia became a mere suburb. It finally died after the district's big mines closed in 1918. Acres of foundations, cellars and brick walls remain.

Adjacent to the mines in the Goldfield district (off the picture to the left) was the suburb of Columbia. On the Main Street, the camp's first two-story building, a hotel, is shown. The ten-stamp Combination mill (below) is shown to the left of the town of Columbia. Soon after construction was finished, its capacity was doubled. Only a few shafts had been sunk when this picture was taken, late in 1903 or early in 1904, but in another three years' time the foreground was filled with headframes, hoist houses, and waste dumps. (*Top: John Zalac Collection; bottom: Marion Schendel Collection*)

DIAMONDFIELD, 5 miles north-northeast of Goldfield.

The camp never acquired the color of its founder, "Diamondfield Jack" Davis, who came from Idaho to Tonopah in January 1903 fresh from an eleventh-hour pardon after he was convicted of murder. When news of richer gold strikes in Goldfield broke out in the spring of 1903, Davis headed there and uncovered promising ledges on McMahon Ridge northeast of Goldfield. Later that year, several excited prospectors swarmed the discovery site within a few weeks' time. Davis laid out a townsite and built a toll road to Goldfield.

By August 1904, when the town probably attained its height, it embraced a post office, restaurants, three saloons, two stores of general merchandise, school, church, miners' union hall, butcher shop, livery stable, assay office, blacksmith shop, drugstore, two lodging houses and many dwellings near the main street. Doctor, deputy sheriff, a lawyer and a notary public had also set up shop. There was constant communication with Goldfield via auto, wagon and telegraph.

It was said that if enough capital were directed here Diamondfield might become a formidable rival to Goldfield, but this suburb never had more than two or three hundred residents, and was through by 1906-07 when mining development was most spectacular at Goldfield. The town Davis founded has two large stone dwellings amid ruins of many rock walls and foundations.

CUPRITE, one mile east of US 95 at a point 2 miles north of its junction with SR 3 at Lida Junction (13 miles south of Goldfield).

This comunity's short but varied career began about 1902-03 when copper ore was found in nearby hills to the north. After the Bullfrog district opened up in 1904, a saloon-and-inn was maintained for north-south travelers. By 1905 a camp developed when a cooperative company began mining nearby copper and silver deposits. When the Bullfrog Goldfield Railroad established a station here after laying track through this point in September 1906, Cuprite became the shipping point and depot for several camps including Hornsilver, Lida, Palmetto, and the Stonewall and Tule Canyon districts. A post office was established in April 1907 and a business district had formed.

Freighting traffic fell off with the decline of nearby mining districts and by 1910 Cuprite was reduced to one saloon, roadhouse and garage. Only a few foundations remain.

STONEWALL (Nye County), 6 miles east of US 95 at a point 2 miles north of Lida Junction.

After a silver strike on the north side of Stonewall Mountain in August 1904, a mild rush from Tonopah developed. Nothing came of the early discoveries but the district was worked sporadically thereafter for over two decades. Mine ruins remain.

GOLD POINT, earlier Hornsilver, on SR 71 at a point 15 miles southwest of Lida Junction via SR 3 and SR 71.

This camp has had three different names, depending on what was being mined at the time. Initially it was called Lime Point because of lime deposits found in 1868. Silver mining began after 1880 and ore was hauled to Lida for milling, but huge costs at that inefficient mill and remoteness of railroads led to virtual abandonment of operations in 1882 until the growth of Tonopah provided better facilities for development. The rush to Goldfield in 1903-04 virtually emptied the district but interest revived when the Great Western mine began operations in 1905.

After discovery of high-grade hornsilver in the spring of 1908, a feverish stampede developed and the camp of Hornsilver was founded. In May the Hornsilver *Herald* began publication, followed a week later by the establishment of a post office. The *Herald* optimistically declared that Hornsilver would soon shine as the brightest star in Nevada's crown, and the Goldfield *Review* in May reported that new stores were opening up every week. "Hornsilver is the latest wonder in Nevada mining districts . . . a comer . . . Main Street is extending almost as you watch it." A chamber of commerce was organized and a railroad was projected to haul ore. Auto stages ran to Goldfield ($7.50), Lida, and also to Cuprite ($5), where rail connections were available. Hornsilver's broad streets were flanked by several stores and shops, and 13 saloons amply supplied the camp with liquid refreshments. Over 225 wood-frame buildings, tents and shacks covered the slope of the town.

Diamondfield (above) had become quite a town late in 1904. Its main street had businesses supplying the miners' every need. *(Top: Nevada Historical Society; middle: Orlo Parker Collection)*

In the sprawl of tents (below) that was Hornsilver in 1908, the nucleus of false-fronted wooden buildings of the business district is shown to the left of center. *(Theron Fox Collection)*

These views of the isolated camp of Gold Mountain show the hoist building of the State-line mine (above) and the interior of the Stateline mill. *(Douglas Robinson Jr. Collection)*

Deep ore bodies were extensively developed until litigation early in 1909 brought many mining properties into the courts, and inefficient milling practices also made mining unprofitable. About 1915 large operations resumed, and at a receiver's sale in 1922 baseball interests headed by Charles Stoneham of the New York Giants purchased the Great Western mine, the camp's greatest producer with a recorded $500,000 production. After 1930, when more gold was being mined than silver, the camp assumed the name Gold Point. All major mining efforts ceased in October 1942, when essential war industries drew away the workers. All business establishments have closed, and about four dozen windowless wooden buildings face the deserted streets.

GOLD MOUNTAIN, later Stateline, 2 miles northwest of SR 71 at a point 6 miles southwest of Gold Point.

Thomas Shaw originally discovered gold outcroppings on Slate Ridge in 1864 but after repeated trials abandoned his claims. In the winter of 1866-67 four roving prospectors relocated the ridge and leased the location to others who began mining. However, earnest prospecting and exploitation of the district's many fine ledges did not take place during the 1870s because of lack of water, poor transportation facilities and Indian harassment. Despite these disadvantages, the Stateline mine was regarded as one of the best in the state in 1880.

In the summer of 1881 a surveyed townsite had five saloons, two stores, chop house, livery stable, bakery, butcher, boardinghouse, post office, a hurdy-gurdy, and wooden, stone, canvas and dugout dwellings. The Stateline Mining Co. erected a ten-stamp mill costing $40,000 and the laying of a pipeline from Tule Canyon eliminated hauling water at $3.50 a barrel from Oriental. The arrival of the Carson & Colorado Railroad to Candelaria in 1882 replaced the expensive freight charges of mule runs from Wadsworth over 190 miles away, and Gold Mountain produced well for the rest of the decade. Removal of the post office in 1891 followed a decline in mining, and the statewide boom after 1905 brought about an ever-so-brief revival. In later years the Stateline mine built a new mill,

machine shop and bunkhouse, and ruins of these buildings remain amid older rock structures.

TOKOP, by unimproved road 7 miles south and east of SR 71 at a point 2 miles south of Gold Point.

Mining began in the 1890s and early in this century a stage station offered accommodations for travelers. Surface discoveries of gold in December 1904 carried over $100 a ton and extensive prospecting turned up large bodies of low-grade millable ore, but no mines developed which would suggest building a town.

ORIENTAL, later Old Camp, via desert roads 10 miles south of Gold Point.

Thomas Shaw found gold on the north slope of a mountain in 1864 and, elated over his find, he named the peak Gold Mountain. A six-foot arrastra crushed ore for a time, but it was inadequate and all work soon ceased. After rich gold veins were uncovered in the Oriental mine in 1871, several stone buildings and cabins were thrown up, forming a camp that was first known as Gold Mountain and was renamed Oriental later in the decade. Wagons and pack mules shipped ore and concentrates to mills in Austin and Belmont. Many people thought that this discovery might have been the place where in 1864 Jacob Breyfogle obtained rich specimens which he claimed to have found in Death Valley, and in search of which many disappointed people spent much time.

The Oriental yielded some of the richest gold found in Nevada during the last century, and specimens were displayed at the Centennial Exposition at Philadelphia in 1876. But the camp never grew very large because of its remoteness and lack of enough water for milling. Increased operations in 1881 at the Stateline mine, six miles west led to Oriental's abandonment for a few years, but it revived and a post office functioned from 1887 until 1900. Since then there has been no new activity. Rock ruins remain.

TULE CANYON, 10 miles west of Gold Point by dirt roads.

Placer mining operations have been carried on in 15-mile-long Tule Canyon for over a century with the first digging performed by roving Mexicans about 1848, long before Americans first came in 1867. Mexicans extensively combed the canyon during the 1870s and at other times Indians and Chinese worked the placers. A post office known as Senner was open for over three years in the early 1890s, and a little later the camp of Roosevelt Well, at the south end of Tule Canyon was described by the contemporary press as being "at the top of Death Valley." Though the gold was never rich enough to sustain large or lengthy development, it is estimated that almost $1 million has been taken from the district. Stone ruins, mine shafts and placer dumps remain.

LIDA, on SR 3 at a point 19 miles west of Lida Junction (22 miles southwest of Goldfield).

Indians and Mexicans first found gold in the surrounding hills, probably sometime in the early 1860s, and with primitive means extracted all they could and departed. American prospectors invaded Lida Valley in the spring of 1867 and organized a district. The town of Lida Valley was laid out in March 1872 and soon gained several stores and shops, livery and feed stables, and a post office which was initially established as in Inyo County, California. A fine road was pushed through the mountains to Silverpeak and freight from Wadsworth, the nearest railroad station in western Nevada, was $100 a ton. Steam-powered mills of five and eight stamps were constructed at nearby springs, though high grade which at times ran up to $500 and $1000 a ton continued to be hauled to Austin and Belmont for treatment. Later in the 1870s mining declined here and by 1880 this remote camp had only ten operating businesses. For the balance of the century operations were desultory.

When Goldfield started to boom in 1905, Lida caught its second wind and soon had a chamber of commerce, the weekly Lida *Enterprise,* and stage service to Goldfield. Nearby springs helped supply Goldfield with water, and a big pipeline was laid between the two towns. Lida thrived for three years but by 1907 the most important properties were tied up in litigation and the camp declined. Serious mining efforts were resumed a few years later, and during the years before World War I Lida had a hotel, schools, stores, and a post office for three or four dozen small mining companies in the area as well as for a few ranches. In later years leasers were active. In all, the district has produced almost $1 million in precious metals. The site is now located on a private ranch.

The residents of Lida in the winter of 1906 saw prospecting parties like this one at left headed for the nearby boom at Palmetto. The urgency of getting in on the ground floor was so great that cold weather was disregarded. *(Douglas Robinson Jr. Collection)*

The tent and wooden town of Lida in 1905, under a great bank of clouds, seemed a place of promise. A camp was proud of its first frame buildings; many never got past the tent stage. Graded streets were soon extended over three hundred acres in this valley in anticipation of further growth, but this never materialized.

One of Lida's hotels (below) also had a restaurant and a bakery, run by a "half-crazy old man who had a liking for signs." *(Both photos: Douglas Robinson Jr. Collection)*

PIGEON SPRING, ¼ mile south of SR 3 at a point 29 miles west of Lida Junction.

During the 1890s this spring was the site of the Pigeon stamp mill and the accompanying settlement contained a saloon, store and a roadhouse for travelers. A post office was applied for in 1899 but it did not open because mining in the area came to a standstill. Mill foundations are left.

SYLVANIA, 5 miles south of SR 3 at a point 30 miles west of Lida Junction.

Three years after lead-silver discoveries in 1869, mining began and a camp formed. Stone and eventually log buildings were erected, including a general store that may have been operated by Chris Zabriskie, who later gained fame as a Death Valley borax miner. Desultory operations were conducted until 1875, when the mines produced well enough that a thirty-ton smelter was built. It ran for three or four years before shutting down, and after 1880 only small operators worked the mines. Stone and log buildings remain.

PALMETTO, ½ mile west of SR 3 at a point 32 miles west of Lida Junction.

After three prospectors found silver deposits in the mountains north of here in the spring of 1866, a district was quickly organized and the miners named the camp Palmetto, thinking that the local joshuas were related to the palm tree. Though a 12-stamp mill was erected that year and ran successfully, not enough millable ore was mined to keep it running. Palmetto was then virtually abandoned until discoveries late in 1860 sent miners back to the district for a brief period.

When a third revival got under way in this century, old and new mines opened up and early in 1906 over 200 tents were pitched on a platted townsite a half-mile west of old Palmetto. A mile-long commercial street contained many stores, meat markets, feed yards, bakeries, restaurants, delicatessen, assay offices, lumber company, bank, doctor's office, post office, and an undetermined number of saloons and clubs. Beginning in February the weekly Palmetto *Herald* gave a voice for the district's developments, but the mines were not able to hold up for long — only until the fall of 1906 when the locals drifted to other camps, particularly Blair in the Silverpeak district. As late as 1920 another mill was built and leasers have since been occasionally active. Mill foundations and roofless walls are left at old Palmetto; the newer townsite has only foundations and piles of tin cans.

412

The mill at Pigeon Spring (opposite page) was running around 1895.

Early in 1906 numerous tent businesses served the revived Palmetto district. After clearing the ground of sagebrush and cactus, a merchant with a few boards and canvas was in business within a day's time. After the boom subsided, these buildings could be removed with a minimum of effort. No buildings remain at Palmetto.

The Silver Champion mill (below) was the second of three mills built on this site. Since the very beginning of the Palmetto district, stamp mills have functioned here. *(Three photos: Douglas Robinson Jr. Collection)*

MILLERS, ½ mile south of US 95 at a point 14 miles west of Tonopah.

As early as 1865 or 1866 Desert Wells station was open here as a watering and resting place on the road between San Antonio and Silverpeak. After Tonopah began to boom in 1901, Desert Wells served as the third water station eastward on the busy Sodaville-Tonopah stage and freight runs, the last stop before Tonopah. When the Tonopah Railroad was built in 1904 its repair shops were put here and the place was named Millers after the vice-president of the Tonopah Mining Co. The community gained added significance in 1906 when the Desert Power & Milling Co. constructed a 100-stamp silver mill to treat the ore of the parent Tonopah Mining Co. A camp with post office formed, and the next year another mill was built, a fifty-stamper to process ore for the Tonopah-Belmont Development Co.

During the height of the southern Nevada mining excitement in 1907, Millers had plans of becoming the world's largest shipper of bullion. A railroad line was projected north to Manhattan and Austin, and southward to Montezuma and other camps. None of these lines materialized, but Millers prospered from 1907 until 1911, while the Tonopah & Goldfield regularly brought in huge carloads of ore from Tonopah to the mills. With 250 citizens, this camp even boasted a modest business district and a large park with baseball diamond and grandstand. After 1910 the construction of the sixty-stamp mill of the Tonopah-Belmont Co. in Tonopah was followed by a decline in use of the local mills. In later years leasers profitably worked the immense piles of tailings.

Before these mills and other buildings were built at Millers after 1906, this area contained huge feed yards and corrals for stages and freighters of the Tonopah-Sodaville run. With construction of an ore sampler and stamp mills, and with talk of projected railroad lines, Millers promised to become one of the state's most important towns. (*Mrs. Harry Mighels Collection*)

The huge 100-stamp mill of the Desert Power & Milling Co., or "Desert Mill," could crush 400 tons of ore daily from the Tonopah Mining Co.'s various properties. At first a large coal-fired steam plant with electric generators furnished power to run the mill, but after 1907 a transmission line from Bishop, California, brought in power. The interior view (below) shows the huge stamp batteries and concentrating tables. (*Two photos:* Tonopah *Times-Bonanza*)

ROYSTON (Nye County), 14 miles north then west of Millers via graded roads.

Before the coming of white men, Indians mined turquoise in the Royston Hills. Tiffany & Co. of New York reportedly obtained this gem here during the years 1905-1912. Later some silver was mined and shipped to Tonopah for milling and the camp made headlines in 1921 when a leaser found a deposit of high-grade silver. News of about $20,-000 worth of ore being extracted from a 24-foot shaft in six weeks' time attracted about 300 individuals and a camp was started. The excitement subsided weeks later and Royston was suddenly abandoned.

GILBERT, via graded roads, 15 miles northwest of US 95 at a point 1¼ miles west of Millers.

In a rugged desert setting on the north slope of the Monte Cristo Range the Gilbert brothers had been prospecting for many years without success. They decided to make one final effort, named their property the Last Hope and in November 1924 discovered high-grade gold ore. Others also found gold nearby and in two months the surrounding hills were blackened with energetic prospectors. The discovery of a $50,000 outcropping in February 1925 started a rush and the rise of Gilbert.

Big trucks loaded with houses, lumber, supplies and machinery soon began motoring into the camp. New buildings rose as fast as the material could be hauled in and tools could put them together; autos came and went as leasers in the nearby hills feverishly dug in. The Gilbert *Record* began furnishing high-grade publicity with its first number on February 21. Snow delayed operations in March, but Los Angeles investors arrived in April to begin large-scale development.

As the spring progressed the boom grew hotter, and late in April Gilbert had electric lights and a population of 400. The business district had four restaurants doing a rushing business, an ample representation of speakeasies, bakery, barber — almost forty businesses in all. The curious from Tonopah occasionally drove out to watch the progress of the camp.

Through 1926 Gilbert basked in prosperity, but the district soon declined by the next fall. By 1929 the population was down to a mere sixty hopefuls, and two or three years later Gilbert was gone. In later years a turquoise mine shipped stones by the barrelful to Tiffany & Co. of New York. Wooden shacks and headframes mark the site.

This all-purpose store at Gilbert (above) was located in the heart of the camp. The panorama of Gilbert was taken late in May 1925; nearby mines to the right had familiar names. In the background left a car kicks up dust as it enters the camp. Poor roads were not given a second thought in those days. *(Top: Italo Gavazzi Collection; bottom: Mrs. Nevada Browne Collection)*

CROW SPRING, via graded road 11 miles northwest of US 95 at a point 1¼ miles west of Millers.

Before the Tonopah Railroad was completed in 1904, Crow Spring served as an overnight stopping place for teamsters and as the main stage stop between Sodaville and Tonopah beginning in 1902. Teamsters slept under their wagons using their own blankets. Huge corrals and a feed yard were maintained. After discoveries in 1909 Crow Spring was the scene of turquoise mining, but little evidence remains to indicate the early activity.

WEEPAH, via dirt road 9 miles north of Silverpeak-Goldfield Road at a point 7 miles east of its junction with SR 47 at a point 18 miles south of US 95.

Weepah means "rain water" in Shoshone. After Indians discovered shallow gold pockets early in 1902, about 200 people rushed to Weepah, but the early effort died out in a few weeks' time. The district lay abandoned for 25 years until two young men from Tonopah, Leonard Traynor and Frank Horton, Jr., rediscovered gold early in March 1927. It assayed at about $70,000 a ton and news of this fabulous strike did not remain a secret for long. The magic word "gold" went forth from the desert in a whisper and grew louder and louder until its echo reverberated throughout the mining West and across the nation.

Subsequent publicity extolling the riches of this remote Nevada desert area brought about the wild Weepah boom and an assemblage of autos, tents and people. This motorized rush ultimately developed into the wildest Nevada mining stampede in over a decade and a half — since the days of Rochester and Rawhide. A week after the news broke out, over a thousand adventurers had come, made discoveries and jumped claims left and right.

These "mail order prospectors" fully equipped with squeaky boots, bundled-up bedrolls and new 1927 model cars settled in a hastily-laid-out townsite which saw wood-frame structures rising daily amid the sea of tent houses.

The boom grew hotter as March wore on. By the end of the month the three motor roads to Weepah were jammed with cars; western Nevada railroads had to put on extra coaches to handle the throng of gold-seekers, and the new town soon had a population fluctuating from 1500 to 2000. Reporters sent daily special dispatches to their papers, and Pathé and International movie newsreels featured on-the-site scenes of the wild developments. If Weepah was not the richest gold strike, it certainly was more thoroughly covered by the news media than any other Nevada mining excitement of any era.

By April the town shifted into second gear when it had about sixty frame buildings housing the usual line of businesses including a post office and over a dozen mining companies. Barrels of water hauled daily from Tonopah augmented the liquid refreshments served in the bootleg joints where hopefuls congregated after a day at their claims. By the first of July most of the excitement had died and most of the incompetent rainbow chasers quit the camp, leaving capable miners to work the most promising claims. Even most of these were gone by the end of 1927 when the shrewd Tonopah mining promoter, George Wingfield, lost interest after attempting to buy most claims including the initial discovery site for development.

About 1934 an open-pit silver mine and a 350-ton mill were built, and a smaller camp housed fifty miners employed there. That operation lasted until about 1938. Wooden ruins mark the site.

By the time of the Weepah boom, the auto had come into its own as reliable transportation even in remote deserts. Conspicuously absent were mule teams and burros. The tents of the earliest arrivals (opposite page) were soon joined by hundreds of others which clustered in a townsite. Tents were raised beside autos (bottom) where newcomers put themselves down after traveling hundreds and even thousands of miles in autos packed tightly with household necessities and mining tools. The easy life, comforts and hearth of home did not drive them back, when gold and silver beckoned them to come on! *(Top: Charles Hendel Collection; bottom: Leonard Traynor Collection; opposite page: Mrs. Nevada Browne Collection)*

The three-month Weepah rush in the spring of '27 made the Roaring Twenties roar even louder. This "rich" badger hole (left) contained the ledge where the original strike was made. There visitors got down on all fours and peered into the hole to see the free gold.

Weepah's magic name drew not only representatives of moneyed men but also the mining tycoons themselves. Standing on the right at the bottom is George Wingfield of Goldfield fame.

All types of businesses were opened to accommodate the crowds. Open air restaurants, dry goods stores, sandwich and hot dog stands, saloons, and gas stations all flourished on the main street which resembled a carnival midway. The gold seekers in the bottom picture seem like tenderfeet rather than prospectors of the old guard such as "Seldom Seen Slim." *(Top: Charles Hendel Collection; bottom: Leonard Traynor Collection: three photos, opposite page: Dr. James Herz Collection)*

420

BLAIR, ¾ mile northwest of SR 47 at a point 18 miles south of US 95.

When the Pittsburgh Silver Peak Gold Mining Co. bought the district's significant mines in 1906, rapacious speculators had grabbed all available property at Silverpeak and imposed outrageous prices for mill sites. In September 1906 the new company secretly surveyed a new townsite in the district, about three miles north of Silverpeak near the company's gold mines, and named it Blair. Within a year the company placed into operation a 100-stamp mill, which also had cyanide tanks, and constructed the 17½-mile Silverpeak Railroad from Blair Junction on the Tonopah & Goldfield main line.

In November 1906 the weekly *Press* began publication and a post office was established in a business district that already had saloons, a two-story hotel, and stores sufficiently varied to serve a population of 700. By 1910 the company absorbed the Silverpeak-Valcada and other mines and enlarged its mill.

Mining continued until October 1915, when low-grade ores could no longer be worked profitably. Mill machinery was dismantled and moved to California; the railroad was eventually torn up; the post office was moved to Silverpeak and the orderly company town of Blair was virtually abandoned by 1916. Mill foundations and part of one building remain.

In June 1909 Blair was an impressive town less than three years old. In the foreground is the Silver Peak Railroad whose depot and yards extend toward the right. Dominating the business district is Patty Flannery's saloon and hotel which contained a brewery in the basement. Beyond the lumberyard at the extreme right is the company office of the Pittsburgh Silver Peak Gold Mining Co., where semi-monthly paychecks awaited employees. Between there and Flannery's was the Elite Hotel where miners ate three meals a day for $42 a month. *(Fred Steen Collection)*

Thoroughly modern Blair had on its steep main street several handsome buildings including this mercantile company. Many other nearby businesses used Blair as part of their name. *(Mrs. Nevada Browne Collection)*

In 1907 the Pittsburgh Silver Peak Gold Mining Co. built its mill above and west of Blair. After twenty stamps were added to the original hundred, this mill became the largest of its kind in the state. It operated continuously, filling the air with a steady monotonous roar. In ten years of operation, this company produced more than $7 million. *(Nevada Historical Society)*

SILVER PEAK, or Silverpeak, on SR 47, 21 miles south of its junction with US 95 (31 miles southwest of Tonopah).

Smoky Valley prospectors passing through the region in the spring of 1864 to procure salt for Austin's mills discovered $180-a-ton ore. This find attracted considerable attention and resulted in general recognition of the mineral potential of southern Nevada. In the fall of that year additional gold-bearing ledges were found on Mineral Ridge, seven miles northwest, and there the Silverpeak & Red Mountain Co. began operations. A ten-stamp mill was moved from Jacobsville in the fall of 1865 and a town with the appearance of an adobe Mexican village formed on the western edge of Clayton Valley. The inefficient mill ran only a few months and then shut down because values were lost in the tailings.

During 1866-67 eastern interests headed by John Blair took over the Silverpeak & Red Mountain Co. operations, purchased other mines, and at a cost of $100,000 erected a twenty-stamp mill that was said to be one of the finest on the Pacific slope. Later its capacity was doubled. With this modern mill operated by experienced personnel and a long gravity tramway from Mineral Ridge which delivered ore to the mill at a cost of only two dollars a ton, a bright future seemed assured. For reasons that were never announced, all operations abruptly terminated in November 1870 and mines and mill shut down.

For the next three decades a few companies made unsuccessful attempts to reopen the mines, but at the turn of the century the properties still remained in the hands of John Blair. In 1906 eastern investors organized the Pittsburgh Silver Peak Gold Mining Co. to exploit the mines and operations three miles north at Blair (which see). Silver Peak waned and lost its post office in 1913, but regained it when Blair was abandoned three years later. This time its name was spelled Silverpeak. The rise of metal prices brought several revivals until World War II. A fire destroyed several buildings in 1948, but the camp lives on as a result of lithium and salt mining in the 1960s. You can't keep a good town down.

NIVLOC, at terminus of SR 47, 7 miles southwest of Silver Peak.

An Indian discovered gold in 1907 and a one-saloon camp rose near the short-lived Nivloc mine. That name was taken from the backwards spelling of an early owner of the mine. The Nivloc was later reopened in the 1930s and during the height of gold mining from 1940 to 1943 the camp had a post office. The mine resumed operations after World War II and has been occasionally active. Remains of these operations can be seen.

424

The post office at Silver Peak (below, left) is being visited by a prospector whose burros carry supplies on pack saddles.

At the Mary mine in the Silver Peak district, there was a small settlement with its own post office from 1907 to 1914. From the right are bunkhouses, two-story boarding house, residences, and a mill. The huge playa in the background contained salt water when this picture was taken, about World War I. It is now dry in rainless seasons.

The bottom view shows the Nivloc mine and camp below it. *(Three photos: Tonopah Times-Bonanza)*

COALDALE, west side of US 95 at a point ¾ mile north of its junction with US 6 at modern Coaldale.

Long before the turn of the century a Coaldale stage station served travelers to and from Fish Lake Valley, Bishop, Hawthorne and Belmont. The first woman in Goldfield, Dr. Frances Williams, founded the camp of Coaldale in November 1903. An elaborate forty-acre townsite with a large central park was platted, and in 1904 the Tonopah Railroad made Coaldale a station. This camp was considered promising for two reasons: the coal deposits in the mountains to the south were extensive, and water was available in abundance from the nearby White Mountains. The founder believed that all should have a voice in mining the deposits and that every man should own his own ground. Unfortunately she could not raise enough capital for development, and the town acquired only a few structures.

Early in 1905 employees of the Tonopah Railroad discovered gold stringers worth $350 a ton, and many from Tonopah hunted for the non-existent main ledge. In 1911 two mines began operating and some production continued for five years. Coaldale still had a service station as late as 1959; only depressions now mark the site of the old camp.

COLUMBUS, 5 miles southwest of US 95 at a point 9 miles north of modern Coaldale.

About two years after a company of Spaniards discovered silver, the town of Columbus was founded in 1865 by Americans who began gold and silver mining operations in the newly formed district. At the same time, a rich supply of salt was identified on the forty-square-mile white alkali flat immediately south of the camp. A stamp mill was moved in from Aurora and by 1866 Columbus had a population of 200. Further growth took place five years later after borax was discovered on the flat, and by 1873 four companies began shipping borax to commercial markets. The largest firm, the Pacific Borax Co., which had started operations in September 1872, erected its works about five miles south of town.

By 1875 the borax plants were running continuously night and day for eight months of the year, and three mills with a total of 28 stamps were pounding out ore from nearby silver mines. This town of several hundred had many stores supplying all wants, an adobe school, post office, iron foundry, and a weekly newspaper — the *Borax Miner*. Most structures were of wood and adobe. Competing stage express companies offered service to Fish Lake Valley, Lida, Candelaria after 1876, and to the nearest railroad depot at Wadsworth, 125 miles north. In the summer of 1875 as many as 28 freight teams with 16 horses each hauled silver and crude borax to Wadsworth.

Columbus faded after 1875 when the Pacific Borax Co. built a larger plant at Fish Lake, 30 miles south. After 1877 the west side of the flat below town saw a different kind of activity — horse racing — sponsored by the Columbus Jockey Club which outlined a track and built a grandstand. The population had fallen to only about 100 and a dozen businesses in 1880, but during the next year a soap factory was active. Sometime in the mid-1880s the varied activity here ceased and Columbus became a dead camp.

Mining of borax continued on a small scale at times, and during the next decade operations centered at Calmville, seven miles south, which had its own post office from 1893 to 1895. More recently a flotation mill was unsuccessful during the early 1950s, and after 1955 a cyanide plant ran for the rest of the decade. Foundations and tanks of these later operations, known as Argentum, remain two miles east of the Columbus townsite. Columbus itself has been reduced to walls, foundations and a few graves. The race track oval and two straight tracks may still be traced from the air.

FISH LAKE, or Borax City, 12 miles south and then east of SR 3A and US 6 at a point 6 miles west of modern Coaldale (43 miles west-southwest of Tonopah).

The Fish Lake shown on many highway maps is not the one described here.

After the Pacific Borax Co. started operations here in August 1875, a village with 200 people and forty buildings formed and was named for the nearby Fish Lake, which by the late 1870s was waggishly described as a fashionable watering place for the elite at Candelaria, Belleville and Columbus. The borax mill lived out its usefulness shortly after 1880 when operations in southern California assumed control of the market. Some foundations remain.

426

Though silver initially drew people to Columbus, borax created the boom in the early 1870s. Francis M. "Borax" Smith first learned of that mineral here in 1872. Besides a borax plant, he and his brother established this store (above) which for a year in the mid-1880s was managed by Chris Zabriskie, who afterwards became superintendent of Smith's borax operations.

In the very midst of downtown Columbus in the late 1870s was a borax mill. The White Mountains are in the distance. *(Top: Mrs. Estelle Funke Collection; bottom: Mrs. Dorothy Jennings Collection)*

Though "Borax" Smith's milling operations were transferred elsewhere in 1875, smaller operators carried on. Violent sandstorms sometimes beset the crude operation. In the above area, borax was harvested by a dragline scraper suspended from twin towers, one of which is shown on the left. Since the muddy surface could not support vehicles or animals, this was the only way in which the crude material could be removed.

Chris Zebriskie is at the helm of this steam tractor which was probably used to transport borax to Carson & Colorado Railroad stations.

The top view shows sacked borax ready for wagon shipment. The horse-powered pump in the foreground was used to raise the brine to the evaporating vats. In the refining stage (below) thin wire rods were suspended into the covered tanks and then, as the solutions were allowed to cool, the borates accumulated as crystals on the rods which were then removed. A tap of a hammer jarred the crystals loose, and the product was then ready for sacking. *(Four photos: Mrs. Estelle Funke Collection)*

GOLD HITT, 9 miles south then west of the junction of US 6 and SR 10 at Basalt.

The Buena Vista or Oneota district at the north end of the White Mountains was prospected and organized as early as 1862, but nothing came of the district until its reorganization in 1870 after an Indian discovered rich gold float at the Indian Queen mine. Ox teams hauled limited quantities of its ore to railroads for shipment to Sacramento until 1875, when a four-stamp mill with furnace was built at the mouth of Queen Canyon for the Indian Queen. For about the next five years that mine paid dividends.

The Indian Queen resumed production during the statewide boom early in this century, and the camp of Gold Hitt emerged. A town was laid out in October 1905, lot sales commenced, and during the next month 200 people were in the district. The miners organized a union, and a daily stage connected the camp with Basalt station, six miles away on the Nevada & California Railway. In 1906 the new camp contained saloons, a livery stable, meat market, store and restaurant; the district post office was Oneota, open from June 1906 until February of the next year. But the mines were not of the quality to sustain the camp and Gold Hitt was knocked out of the list of active camps when the Indian Queen ceased production later in the year. A revival in 1915 reopened mines and two mills were built, but about 1919 that activity ceased. Little has been heard of the district since then.

BENTON (California), on SR 120, 4 miles west of US 6 at Benton Station.

Silver discoveries on Blind Springs Hill in March 1865 led to the development of several mines and, on a watered grassy flat two miles to the northwest, the camp of Benton. In less than a year the community had its post office and was a supply center for the surrounding area. Later in the decade a local mill treated ore from as far away as southern Esmeralda County. But the price of silver fell in 1873 and the mines soon closed.

Early in the 1880s the Bodie & Benton Railroad was projected to this point, but grading stopped about 15 miles to the west. During that decade Benton was described as being situated in a rich farming and fruit-growing region where vineyards also thrived. About 200 people lived there.

A small population remained early in this century and a hotel and store did considerable business with adjacent ranches and small mines. Wells Fargo office, jail, school, store-museum and other buildings are left at Benton Hot Springs, as the community is now known.

MONTGOMERY CITY (California), 2¾ miles east of US 6 at Benton Station.

After rich silver discoveries in October 1863, a district was organized four months later to begin mining. A camp formed which briefly had a newspaper, the *Pioneer*, but no continuous veins were found and the camp folded at an early age.

Pleasantly situated in a rolling valley at the foot of White Mountain, Benton has been a small but active town since the post-Civil War years. Before 1900 the town was noted for its brewery (middle) and mill (below) and for its hot springs (not shown), which unlimbered old joints. The Benton Trading Post (opposite page) is still an area landmark. *(All photos: Mrs. Lorena E. Meadows Collection)*

The first Carson & Colorado train is shown arriving at Hawthorne in April 1881 (above). By the mid-1890s young trees lined the streets, and Hawthorne had become the county's largest town. In the foreground the stage has just left the railroad station for Bodie. The general view of Hawthorne at bottom shows the railroad yards and at the left above the trees the courthouse. In the distance is Walker Lake. *(Top: Chester Barton Collection; below: Mineral County Independent-News; bottom; Mrs. W. M. Mercer Collelction)*

MINERAL COUNTY

The area of modern Mineral County initially attracted attention in the 1860s because of development of Aurora. That camp came into immediate prominence and grew as a center of mining for the rest of the decade. During the 1870s mining activity shifted to the southern edge of the present county where Candelaria, Belleville, Rhodes and Marietta thrived with silver, borax and salt mining. Activity was further boosted in 1881-82 when H. M. Yerington built the Carson & Colorado Railroad across the county. This aided mining developments especially at Candelaria.

While the 1890s were years of recession, mining early in this century was carried on at Luning, Dutch Creek, Aurora, Candelaria, Lucky Boy, Rawhide and many small districts. Nevada's largest new boom town in 1908 was Rawhide, but a disastrous fire in September snapped that town's promotional string. During World War I mining took place at Aurora, in the Candelaria country, as well as at Rawhide and Lucky Boy. Most mining ceased before World War II. The county still lives up to its name — mining continues in small mines at various places.

HAWTHORNE, on US 95, 106 miles northwest of Tonopah, 312 miles north of Las Vegas and 135 miles southeast of Reno.

When the Carson & Colorado Railroad began laying narrow-gauge rails southward from Mound House 160 miles to Candelaria in May 1880, the need for a division headquarters between the two points soon became apparent. During the summer H. M. Yerington, the president and superintendent of the C.&C. chose the south end of Walker Lake as the site for shop facilities and a depot from which freight teams would run west to Aurora and Bodie. In advance of the graders, a few tents sprang up here, along the intersection of old freight roads from Bodie and from Candelaria and points north. Local legend has it that mules drawing the freighters would at night wander to a spot two miles south of the lake and huddle in a group, because that point was less vulnerable to the chilly winds from the nearby mountains. Thus it is said that the wisdom of mules aided in determining the site of Hawthorne.

Prior to railroad construction, a trading post known as Knapp's Landing was established about 1875 below the present Munitions Depot. Freight for points south was brought by mule team from the Central Pacific station at Wadsworth, hauled to the north end of Walker Lake, and then ferried by small steamer across the water to Knapp's, where local Piutes helped reload the freight onto wagons.

Early in the fall of 1880 a couple of tents made up the fledgling town of Milbrae, soon renamed for W. A. *Hawthorn,* the contractor of a new wagon road from this point to Bodie. Early in April 1881 the tracks of the C.&C. reached the new townsite which was auctioned off on April 14. On that sunny day Governor Kinkead and about 800 others took advantage of the railroad's offer of free transportation to the new town to speculate in townsite lots.

This Concord stage which has pulled up in front of a building housing both the post office and a bar often carried with other express bars of gold from the mills at Bodie. It is not known whether postal service was impaired or improved by this proximity of letters and liquor. The office of the town's voice (below), the Walker Lake *Bulletin* is shown around 1885. *(Top: Mrs. Lorena Meadows Collection; below: Mrs. Jack Burns Collection)*

The engineer kept the throttle open all the way from Mound House, and the four cherry red passenger cars and twelve flat cars arrived at Hawthorne just in time for lunch. A half dozen tent saloons sold drinks for a bit, though some barkeepers added water to their half-empty beer barrels and continued selling "nice cool lager." A restaurant was open, but enterprising Piutes made more money selling fish. Bidding was spirited, with lot sales averaging about $112, though one buyer under the influence of the lake breeze paid $195 for one lot.

Thereafter Hawthorne was in business. A month later a post office was established; at the end of May there were water connections on every street; and by the first day of summer over thirty houses had been built. Railroad construction southward to Candelaria kept things lively, and in August a handsome depot was finished on F Street.

By then there was talk of removing the county seat from Aurora, but the town was too small to even support a newspaper. The weekly *Oasis* was started in September, but after six numbers the editor suspended it, saying, "It may be possible to publish a newspaper on one square meal a week, but to undertake to do so on one square a month . . . is a little more than human nature can stand."

Nevertheless Hawthorne prospered as the end of a division on the C. & C. and the railroad erected many buildings to accommodate its growing business. Freight wagons and modern Concord stages were arriving and leaving all the time, and the town's public spirit was shown by a costly water works and public park.

A well-received weekly, the *Walker Lake Bulletin* began publication in March 1883, and four months later the town celebrated becoming the county seat with gun salutes and fireworks. No further growth took place for the rest of the century; Hawthorne in the midst of a small mining region kept alive as an outfitting point for scattered mines and ranches.

Because of the Tonopah and Goldfield booms, railroad traffic through here after 1902 was lively, but it ended abruptly in 1905 when the Southern Pacific realigned and standard-gauged the old Carson & Colorado. Thereafter Hawthorne was seven miles from the railroad, and the economic decline led to loss of the county seat two years later. But new mining booms at Lucky Boy, Rawhide and other places around Hawthorne between 1908 and 1910 helped bring about the creation of Mineral County with Hawthorne as the seat.

An increase in county-wide mining made Hawthorne prosper before and during World War I, but after 1920 the town again went into decline.

A visitor to the Naval Ammunition Depot in 1930 entered the main gate at the left and passed the industrial buildings to reach the officers and civilian residential "U" in the mid-background. When the first shipment of explosives came to this desert arsenal in October 1930, there were less than a hundred buildings; in 1970 there were about 2100 magazines and almost 900 other buildings devoted to production and storage. (*Mineral County Independent-News*)

In 1906 the raw desert community of Luning was caught up in the mining craze that swept the state. New businesses were opened, and the increased traffic through here made the town lively.

In 1916 during the height of activity at Luning, this 18-room hotel with second story dance hall was built. A restaurant and first-class bar were downstairs. Rooms rented for $1 to $1.50 a night and each had running hot water. Note the wood protectors around the small cottonwood trees which prevented burros from chewing the bark. *(Top: photo courtesy of Art Haig; bottom: Avoni Frediani Collection)*

With only a two-teacher school and less than 150 citizens, Hawthorne early in July 1926 was further demoralized by a destructive fire that wiped out almost all of the business district and many residences. The courthouse was saved by dynamiting nearby buildings. With the town in ashes, it was fast approaching ghost town status.

An unrelated East Coast disaster that occurred less than a week later ultimately affected the fortunes of Hawthorne. On July 10, 1926 the extensive ammunition arsenal at Lake Denmark, New Jersey, was rocked by a multi-million dollar explosion that also cost about thirty lives in many small nearby towns. Two years later, after much political logrolling, it was decided to relocate the ammunition here because sparsely-populated Hawthorne also offered room for unlimited expansion.

Ground breaking for the new facility took place in July 1928 and it was formally commissioned in September 1930. During the construction period the town boomed mightily. New businesses of every kind were started, including the Hawthorne *News*. But for the rest of the 1930s no further expansion occurred; the depot peacefully carried out its function of receiving, renovating and storing ammunition.

After World War II started, another boom and increase in population followed, intensifying after Pearl Harbor was struck in December 1941. Buildings for assorted industrial activities were built, and here rockets, mines, depth charges and torpedoes were assembled for the armed forces.

In 1944 there were over 4300 military personnel and 2860 civilians working on the base, and the U. S. Department of Commerce that year estimated the population at in excess of 13,000. Tent and trailer suburbs sprang up, and every available shack was utilized for housing. Adjacent Babbitt developed from a village of fifty buildings into a town with over 1100 housing units in 1943. Rail freight charges out of nearby Thorne for munitions was a whopping $91 million in 1944, though many shells were also shipped out by truck.

A gradual decline of activity and population followed after World War II ended, but personnel at the depot was again increased during the Korean and Viet Nam wars. The Naval ammunition depot is still the largest of its kind, but tourism also sustains the town. From here the hunting, fishing and skiing areas of the eastern Sierra are easily reached, and bass and cutthroat fishing are enjoyed the year around at nearby Walker Lake. The town's businesses serve a population of about 6500 within a radius of sixty miles.

ACME, ¼ mile north of US 95 at a point 18 miles east of Hawthorne.

This town sprang to life in the spring of 1907 as the station on the Nevada & California Railway for the many copper mines in the Fitting district, seven miles north. In April a townsite was platted and the *Nevada Copper News* carried the Acme dateline, but later that year the camp apparently folded. No buildings remain.

LUNING, on US 95 at a point 25 miles east of Hawthorne.

Before the Carson & Colorado reached this point in 1881, a stage station known as Deep Wells was here, and stages ran to Downeyville, Grantsville and Belmont. The name was changed to honor a heavy bondholder of the railroad, and during 1881-82 Luning enjoyed a boom when saloons and stores were built. A post office was also established, and the local depot served the Santa Fe silver mines, five miles east of town. Mining activity virtually stopped in 1894, but exploration for copper in 1900 led to active development and the revival of Luning as a copper camp six years later. Several companies were active in 1907-09 and Luning's dozen businesses supplied mines in the area. When the smelter was blown in at Thompson, Lyon County, operations increased in 1912 with the highest output during World War I years. Over $2 million in silver, lead and gold was recovered by 1920. Sporadic mining activity and travelers on US 95 have kept Luning alive during the last five decades, and even today about three dozen people still make their homes here.

MINA, on US 95 at a point 33 miles east of Hawthorne.

In the summer of 1905 Mina was founded as a railroad division point on the Southern Pacific-owned Nevada & California Railway, when expansion of terminal facilities at Sodaville was thwarted by a grasping land speculator. New Boston, three miles north, was briefly considered as a terminus, for there the railroad had a water tank and an

Front Street in Mina (above) shown around World War I is now U. S. Highway 95. The Hotel Mina was the finest watering place between Hawthorne and Tonopah.

Mina's Chinatown was off to one side of the community. Minority groups usually clustered in suburbs.

Built in 1906, the handsome engine house (below) was built to service the standard and narrow gauge locomotives used in the area. In the foreground can be seen the three-rail tracks which could accommodate both gauges. *(Top: photo courtesy of Art Haig; middle and bottom: Mrs. Lorena Meadows Collection)*

excellent pipeline from a spring about five miles west, but here too an opportunist grabbed up available land. The Mina site was then selected and named for Wilhelmina, the daughter of a railroad executive. Two wells provided poor water.

During July and August extensive facilities were built, including a ten-stall roundhouse, tanks, turntable and machine shops. Most of the tracks had three rails to accommodate the traffic interchange between the N. & C.'s newly laid standard gauge to the north and its "Slim Princess" to the south. Here too the Tonopah & Goldfield Railroad met the N. & C.

The townsite of Mina was surveyed in August on a sloping sagebrush plain west of the tracks, and soon several buildings appeared. A post office opened in September and the next June, 1906, a well-received weekly made its debut, the *Western Nevada Miner*, edited by J. Holman Buck, an influential Nevada journalist of the time. Within a year Mina had enough stores and saloons to serve several hundred people, and was an important railroad point. Every day two trains arrived from San Francisco, and two departed for that city.

Mining activity and railroad use began to decrease in 1910, but for the next two decades Mina remained a steady town of 400 with hotels, stores, locally based mining companies and, in time, service stations. The community's showplace was the sixty-room, $100,000, wooden Hotel Mina with its first-class bar.

After the 1920s mining declined further in the area served by the railroad and Mina steadily lost population. The newspaper ceased publication in December 1930, and railroad traffic from the south ended in 1938 with abandonment of a large section of the narrow gauge into California. In 1947 the T. & G. ceased operations, but Mina still functions as the southern end of the S. P. branch from Hazen and as a minor tourist town with motels, restaurants and a few stores. Many of the homes date back to the early boom days, and on the main street the depot and old false-fronted buildings remain in use.

SIMON, 21 miles east then north of Mina via desert roads.

Though the Simon silver-lead mine was discovered as early as 1879 and small quantities of lead were shipped, the district's real importance began after Syrian-born P. A. "Pop" Simon acquired several properties on the west side of Little Pilot Peak and organized the Simon Silver-Lead Mines Co. in 1919. A post office was established that year, and in 1921 a 100-ton flotation mill began treating ore. Adjacent properties were purchased the next year, and after the company's reorganization in 1923 the mill was enlarged to handle 250 tons daily. Beginning that same year company stock was traded on several national exchanges. After producing over $740,000 during four different periods of operation, the mill shut down in January 1927, though work continued in the 1930s and in later years. Buildings remain.

OMCO, 4 miles north of Simon (20 miles northeast of Mina).

After gold discoveries at the north end of the Cedar Range in 1915, the Olympic Mines Co. of San Francisco began development work the next year. The company built a seventy-ton cyanide mill, and during 1917 a post office opened, named with the acronym Omco. Fire destroyed the mill in 1919 but the company rebuilt it within a year and increased its capacity to eighty tons. The large ore deposits were exhausted in 1921 and mine and mill shut down after producing $700,000, mostly in gold. Leasers worked the properties sporadically until 1929. Four years later a severe earthquake caved in the mine workings, but in 1936 mining resumed for a few more years.

DOUGLASS, or Silver Star, 2½ miles southwest of the Mina-Garfield Flat road at a point 4½ miles west of Mina.

Veins carrying gold and silver were discovered on the north flank of the Excelsior mountains in 1893, and during the following decade leasers recovered $500,000 in silver. During the 1893 panic this camp was known as the "dinner pail" because of the opportunity it afforded leasers to make a good living. A five-stamp mill was installed in 1894, and during 1898-1905 a small post office and businesses served the district. The discovery of Tonopah drew most of the camp away and production declined after 1901. A comeback attempt in 1910 was unsuccessful, although many leasers were active in later years.

GARFIELD, south of the Mina-Garfield Flat road at a point 11 miles west of Mina.

Silver was first discovered in 1882 and for the next five years the Garfield mine produced well. The camp was large enough to support a post office from November 1883 to November 1884. About 1890 an English company acquired the mine and erected a ten-stamp mill at Garfield spring, nine miles south, but only a few thousand tons were treated. In the 1920s one mine consistently produced high-grade silver ore, and during the next decade small leasing operations were carried on.

PAMLICO, 25 miles west of Mina via the Mina-Garfield Flat road.

The Pamlico mine was said to have produced several hundred thousand dollars worth of gold ore in the 1870s and 1880s, and leasers worked the lodes later while placer miners operated here during World War I. A twenty-stamp mill was active in the 1920s but by the middle of the next decade was dismantled. The Pamlico mine and its contemporary the La Panta mine, 3 miles northeast, may have produced as much as $1 million, principally in gold. Mine ruins remain.

The placer gravel at Pamlico (above) was obtained by drift mining. This shaft was sunk 170 feet before bedrock was encountered. After gravel was discharged into the bin, it was separated into coarse material and gold-bearing fines which were recovered in the riffles in the long sluice box.

Governor Colcord's twenty-stamp mill (below) was active early in this century. (Two photos: William A. Kornmayer Collection)

SODAVILLE, ¼ mile east of US 95 at a point 3¼ miles south of Mina.

Initially known in the 1870s as Soda Springs because of its twin mineralized springs, this community became a station on the Carson & Colorado Railroad late in 1881. Sodaville came of age in the winter of 1900-01 as a busy terminal for the C. & C. and as shipping point for booming Tonopah and eventually Goldfield and other camps. For three years until 1904 immense twenty-mule freight outfits hauled heavy loads of supplies and machinery daily between Sodaville and the new bonanza. Thousands of early travelers reached Tonopah in a day's travel — from dawn to midnight — by four- and six-horse stagecoaches, each passenger carrying just one bag, six-gun, pocket comb, and the makin's. Stages averaged eight- to twelve-man capacity, and full coaches carried two riders shotgun.

Returning wagons and stages hauled high-grade ore packed in white canvas bags for rail shipment to refineries in Salt Lake City and San Francisco. With the demand for faster passenger service, Stanley Roadsters, auto stages with 32-horsepower engines and 16-passenger capacity, initiated regular service in 1904, promising to make the dusty 60-mile trip in a speedy six to eight hours.

Sodaville's days as a busy railhead for Tonopah and Goldfield abruptly ended when the Tonopah Railroad commenced regular service in the summer of 1904, and suffered further loss the next year when the Carson & Colorado removed its roundhouse and terminal to Mina. Buildings of later origin remain, as well as foundations of the Silver Dyke tungsten mill, active in the mid-1930s. Picturesque walls of the Mount Diablo mill which ran on Candelaria ore around 1880 stand a few hundred yards east of the townsite.

In the mountains just west of Sodaville, tungsten ore was discovered in 1915. The Nevada-Massachusetts Co. stepped up operations in 1929, using caterpillars to haul the ore to the mill. (*Nevada State Museum*)

441

In the early 1880s Soda Springs (above) thrived as a resort and a minor station on the Carson & Colorado Railroad. With the rise of Tonopah at the turn of the century, Sodaville (Soda Springs), shown in 1904 in the middle picture, became a center for teamsters who hauled their loads to the new silver camp. Generally remote and far from the Hawthorne sheriff's watchful eye, Sodaville became one of southern Nevada's wildest and toughest towns. The Mt. Diablo mill (bottom) is shown in the early 1880s. *(Top and bottom: Mrs. Lorena Meadows Collection; middle: William A. Kornmayer Colllection)*

RHODES, ¼ mile east of US 95 at a point 7 miles south of Mina.

Salt pools were discovered in 1862 on the Virginia salt marsh, now Rhodes salt marsh, and imported camels transported salt to mills near Virginia City. Apparently the camel trains became quite numerous, for a Virginia City ordinance prohibited the humped beasts from entering the city during certain hours of the day to prevent stampeding of horses. Before the Rhodes source was known, the Comstock imported all of its salt from San Francisco, and despite high cost, $120 to $180 per ton, many thousands of tons were consumed by Comstock mills before 1862. The new and nearer source at Rhodes considerably lowered the cost of salt for the Comstock, but after only one year Rhodes lost this big customer because of new discoveries at Sand Springs in Churchill County. The marsh still supplied salt for mills at Aurora, and eventually Belmont and Belleville.

A contemporary report said that the immense Rhodes marsh contained enough salt to preserve the world! By 1881 Rhodes marsh had been worked quite extensively for salt, and a significant quantity of borax had also been mined and shipped to Alameda, California, for refining. Borax mining increased and in 1882 Rhodes became a station on the Carson & Colorado Railroad when that line was extended past Rhodes. For the rest of the decade Rhodes continued to ship salt to various users, and a post office established in 1893 lasted until 1911. The Rhodes Salt & Borax Co. was briefly active here early in this century.

One structure and a salt-loading tower mark the site.

At Rhodes, crude borax was semi-processed and then shipped by the Carson & Colorado Railroad for refining. At this plant borax first went into the white cement brine tanks where gangue and slime were washed out with water from the wooden tanks above. The product was then removed from the tanks, dried in sunlight, and sacked for shipment. (*Richard C. Datin Collection*)

443

CANDELARIA, 6½ miles west of US 95 at a point 16 miles south and east of Mina.

First discovered by a band of roving Spanish prospectors in 1863, Candelaria's silver veins were not exploited on a large scale until the spring of 1873 when the Northern Belle, the camp's oldest and richest mine began production. The successful development of that mine attracted several people, and within two years the Columbus district became southwestern Nevada's most productive. In 1873 and 1876 the Northern Belle erected twenty-stamp mills at Belleville, eight miles northwest. Other companies owned mills at nearby Columbus and Soda Springs (Sodaville). Columbus served as the district's town until August 1876, when Candelaria was platted below the Northern Belle.

In September a boom populated Candelaria and within a month it had a post office, two hotels, restaurants, 11 saloons, livery stables and other businesses. Freight had to be teamed in from Wadsworth, 120 miles away, so prices were high for manufactured goods. Poor quality wood from sources 12 to 20 miles away cost $20 a cord; alkali-laden water cost 4½ cents a gallon from Columbus and a bath cost two dollars.

The Northern Belle began paying dividends in 1876 and production averaged over $1 million each year for the next decade. The 1880 census confirmed Candelaria's position as the largest town in the county, a distinction gained four years earlier. During 1881-83 when the mines reached their peak of production, the town's 1500 residents also supported a bank, telegraph office, school, lumber companies, dry goods and furniture stores, two brewer-ies, three doctors, lawyers, a newspaper — the *True Fissure,* and over two dozen saloons. The town's several hotels were noted both for the excellence of the tables they set and the quality of their wines and liquors.

Even in prosperity Candelaria was uncomfortable and uninviting. A relentless sun beat down on flimsy wooden shacks and humble tents, and the continual hot dry wind was pervaded by powdery dust given off by local mills. Rough, crude and isolated from centers of law enforcement, this became one of Nevada's toughest camps. The local paper once boasted, "No one killed or half-murdered during the past week."

In February 1882 the first Carson & Colorado train chuffed into Candelaria and departed with a large shipment of ore from the Northern Belle. Prosperity seemed assured with this new railroad service, an expensive waterworks and plenty of ore in sight, but a fire in 1883 destroyed part of the town. Legal strife between the Northern Belle and the Holmes mines led to their consolidation in 1884 and the next year a summer-long strike resulted in another off year for the mines, with production taking a drastic 50% drop. Candelaria declined after 1885 and the *True Fissure* folded.

The camp revived enough in 1890 to support another weekly paper, the *Chloride Belt,* but in 1892, after over $20 million had been removed, Candelaria fell into decay, with only small revivals early in this century. In 1919 the Candelaria Mines Co. consolidated the most important mines, which produced for about four years thereafter. Extensive rock ruins, wooden cabins and a cemetery remain.

In this barren valley surrounded by black lava mountains, Candelaria was founded in 1876. Though in decline by the late 1880s, the camp had an interesting main street flanked by many wooden buildings (below). At the height of activity in the early 1880s the Candelaria Water Works & Milling Co.'s thirty-stamp "Princess" mill was built at the head of the street. The camp then boasted 27 saloons, but it was without a church despite the town name meaning "candle mass." On the opposite page, Candelaria is viewed from a point east of town. (*Three photos: Mrs. Estelle Funke Collection*)

Metallic Lake, at the top of Pickhandle Gulch high above Candelaria, was a reservoir owned by the Candelaria Water Works & Milling Co. Its office was in the large building below the mill (center), whose interior (below) was adorned by a large map of the mining district.

446

The shaft house of one of the mines is shown above, and the neat saloon interior (below) shows the bartender ready for action. (*Bottom left: Mrs. Dorothy Jennings Collection; all others: Mrs. Estelle Funke Collection*)

Looking as though it was parked in the side yard, this engine of the Carson & Colorado Railroad is probably awaiting orders from the line's agent, who lives in the house in the foreground.

The local "doc," in the distant days of house calls, looks as if he is ready to make his rounds, knowing that patients will be in his office awaiting his return.

Located at the entrance to Pickhandle Gulch was the Holmes hoisting works (above right). The 300-ton mill of the Candelaria Mines Co. ran at intervals from 1922 until 1925, and is shown at right below in a picture from the Art Nelson Collection. *(All other photos: Mrs. Estelle Funke Collection)*

448

METALLIC CITY, ½ mile southeast of Candelaria.

This camp formed in upper Pickhandle Gulch on the Candelaria-Columbus road after 1876 and was originally named Pickhandle Gulch. By 1879 its citizens wanted the camp to be called Metallic City, after the manner of the Slippery Gulchers on the Comstock, who insisted on the more dignified name of Gold Hill for their town. Metallic in 1880 had a population of 300 including two dozen ladies, store, barbershop, five rattling saloons, drugstore, and a post office. But by the next year the population fell by two-thirds, and as Candelaria declined a few years later Metallic became uninhabited. Several rock cabins remain.

Metallic City was a small but active camp in the mining area above Candelaria. The steep canyons in Pickhandle Gulch were pockmarked with prospect holes in the effort to find silver veins.

The modest business district at Metallic City included the inevitable Pioneer Saloon.

Huge ore dumps have altered the sides of the canyon in Pickhandle Gulch, bearing witness to an era of active mining. *(Both photos: Mrs. Estelle Funke Collection)*

BELLEVILLE, ¼ mile east of SR 10 at a point 14 miles south of Mina via US 95 and SR 10.

The cosmopolitan town of Belleville came into being in 1873 after the building of a twenty-stamp silver mill by the Northern Belle mine of Candelaria, and less than a year later a camp with post office had started. Another twenty-stamp mill high above town opened in 1876. The town's 400 inhabitants supported hotels, saloons, restaurants, stables, blacksmith shops, a newsstand where East and West Coast papers were sold, a jockey club which sponsored horse racing, and an amateur magicians' club. Several Chinese lived here as well as about 74 Indians. By the next year the town had grown to 500 or 600 and acquired the *Times*

and other short-lived papers including the *Self-Cocker* and the *Tarantula*. Belleville's sporting district, brewery and numerous gambling dives served Candelaria, and the scene was enlivened by frequent shooting forays and an occasional fandango — a picturesque mélange of Indians, Chinese and others dancing to the accompaniment of grunts and exclamations.

Belleville declined after 1882 when the Northern Belle built a 27-mile pipeline from the White Mountains so that milling could be accomplished close to the mine. Night life was not enough to sustain the camp and Belleville was completely deserted a generation later. Massive mill foundations, dozens of cellars and a few graves remain.

Before 1880, the principal means of freight transport to Belleville was the ox team. Oxen were preferred to horses or mules on long freight runs because of their strength and simplicity of care, even though they made only about a mile an hour. In any team three pair of oxen had special names. The two animals hitched to the wagon, the wheel-

ers, were the hardiest pair. Just ahead of them were the pointers, attached to the tongue of the head wagon; they pulled the wagons around turns in the road. At the teamster's command of "Chain!" the first pair, called leaders, swung around the turn and the rest of the team followed.

In 1882, when the Carson & Colorado railroad tracks reached Belleville, it meant the retirement of the hard-working ox teams. Beyond the station, shown below, is one of Belleville's two mills.

At the height of milling operations at Belleville from 1878-1883, these two twenty-stamp mills handled up to 120 tons of ore daily. Each steam-powered mill required up to 1000 cords of pine per month. In the background the town is shown generally confined to one long street and a shorter back street. As the main street was extended, the town gained additional prestige. *(Top and opposite page: Getchell Library, University of Nevada; bottom: Douglas Robinson Jr. Collection)*

MARIETTA, 10 miles west of SR 10 at Belleville (17 miles southwest of Mina).

Salt mining activity began on Teel's Marsh early in 1867 and the product was sent to mills near Virginia City by long camel trains, and to Aurora by pack mules. While scouting for wood on a nearby mountain in 1872 Francis M. Smith looked with curiosity on the marsh, a dry lake which differed in appearance from other alkali deposits. He and his brother investigated its crusted surface more closely, and after obtaining favorable assays on borate samples, he staked out a large section of the marsh. Word of the discovery brought an influx of California prospectors to stake claims, and soon several small borax plants started operations on the southeastern end of the marsh. Wagon teams also hauled the crude borax to Wadsworth, 115 miles north, for rail shipment to refineries near San Francisco Bay.

These small operations were important in the national development of the borax industry. Here Smith founded the Teel's Marsh Borax Co., forerunner of the Pacific Borax Salt & Soda Co., which also refined borax at nearby Columbus. When Smith made his discovery less than 500 tons of borax were consumed each year nationally; the amount soon increased to 20,000 tons. With the success of these operations, "Borax" Smith eventually extended his activities to deposits at Borate, Ryan and other Southern California localities and controlled the world borax market for about twenty years.

Teel's Marsh at times experienced violent windstorms which would rage for a few days, kicking up dust and borax particles. The *Borax Miner* in Columbus reported that one traveler who crossed the marsh came into that town covered with alkali, gravel, and cobblestones so as to be past recognition. "After the heaviest of the boulders had been blasted out of his ears, the cobblestones and paydirt pried out of his nose and eyes, and a few tons of borax marsh shoveled off his eyebrows, he was subjected to a broom and hose, and then soaked for a few hours before receiving a bath, after which he was sufficiently renovated to be recognized by friends."

Marietta became a town in 1877 and within a year contained 150 people, post office, and several businesses including a store owned by "Borax"

Smith. A five-stamp mill, originally set up by the state of Nevada at Philadelphia's Centennial Exhibition, was moved here in 1877 and put into successful operation. A large red building with a black smokestack housed the mill, and the town consisted of a sunbaked cluster of wooden and adobe structures and rock huts. Among the rows of buildings, 13 saloons had been built by 1880, and road agent activity was then at its peak. The daily six-horse stage was robbed thirty times that year and in one particular week no less than four times.

The borax plants on the marsh maintained a small but steady production until their abandonment in the 1890s because of rich colmanite (borax) discoveries near Death Valley. Foundations and stone walls of several structures, including Smith's store, remain.

THORNE, 8 miles northeast of Hawthorne on SR 31.

When the Southern Pacific standard gauged the northern half of its Nevada & California Railway subsidiary in 1905, it also realigned the track near the south end of Walker Lake, bypassing Hawthorne. The railroad station serving Hawthorne on the new line was designated Thorne and about June of 1905 a two-saloon settlement was started. Freight was hauled to towns as far away as Lundy, California, and stages ran to Hawthorne, Aurora and Bodie. A post office was open from 1912 to 1921. At the height of activity at the Hawthorne Naval Ammunition Depot during World War II Thorne had about 100 people and was among the busiest stations on the S. P. system. A sleepy station and a few houses remain.

BOVARD, 1 mile west of Rawhide-Luning road at a point 4 miles south of its junction with SR 31 at a point 31 miles northeast of Hawthorne.

Prospectors from Rawhide discovered silver on the northeastern end of the Gabbs Valley Range in April 1908, and within a week a noisy throng on horseback, burros, wagons and other forms of conveyance came to the new lodes. In all, several hundred men and a few women arrived carrying a minimum of provisions, several individuals without even so much as a tent shelter. Bovard consisted chiefly of cloth and never acquired a post office, but that spring dozens of canvas habitations covered the slope for about a mile, with businesses in some of the tents. Several saloons appeared and the Bovard *Booster* was distributed for a month.

While Rawhide men founded Bovard, mining men from Luning and Hawthorne — not to be outdone — set up the rival townsite of Lorena in the district, platted streets and opened up a tent saloon. These promoters induced many from Bovard to relocate in the new camp, and the continued defections offended the town daddies of Bovard. In an effort to get even with the upstart camp, the Bovard promoters one day bribed the water haulers not to make the usual daily delivery to Lorena. With very little water left, the Lorenans became concerned, and most returned to Bovard that very day. Those who remained that night pooled their food, and the next morning gathered at the saloon for a last breakfast. After eating stacks of beer pancakes, they packed their tents and supplies and moved back to the "older" camp.

Bovard itself collapsed a few months later, but limited mining continued for another decade. The Gold Pen Mines Co. erected a twenty-ton mill in 1920 but ceased operations months later because of financial difficulties. The site of Bovard has been relegated to the original wilderness; the location of Lorena has been forgotten.

DEADHORSE WELL, 34 miles northeast of Hawthorne on SR 31.

During the early 1860s a station opened at this point to serve traffic on the east-west road between the Walker and Reese rivers. After north-south freighting developed between Columbus and the railhead at Wadsworth in 1869, Deadhorse Well assumed more importance, and it was busiest during the mid-1870s when traffic from Mason Valley to Belleville was also routed through here and the mines at Candelaria and Columbus required continuous freight service with Wadsworth. During the early months of the Rawhide boom in 1908 a small stamp mill here pounded out gold ores and a barrel of local water was worth $2.50 delivered in Rawhide. Fallen buildings, cellars and rubble mark the site.

Well-known Nevada mining camp figures were attracted to Bovard, and among them was Tex Rickard, shown at the extreme right. *(Nevada Historical Society)*

RAWHIDE, 5 miles northwest of SR 31 at a point 37 miles northeast of Hawthorne.

After discoveries in the latter part of 1906, a camp formed in February 1907, a district was organized and serious prospecting began. A cowboy disgusted with his experiences at Buckskin named the camp Rawhide. The first gold values turned up March 1 and high grade was found that summer; the district then came to the attention of mineral-conscious men, generally unemployed and needing a new camp. A rush early in the fall populated a newly-platted townsite with about sixty tents; in one of these a post office opened in October, replacing the tobacco can nailed to a pole where the earliest arrivals had obtained their mail. Within a month W. W. Booth started publication of the Rawhide *Rustler*.

The nationwide financial panic late in 1907 temporarily delayed development work at Rawhide, but all that winter a stream of believers rushed here, braving icy winds, deep snow and sub-zero temperatures. Early in 1908 powerful automobiles — "greyhounds of the desert" — motored their loads from railroad stations at Luning, Schurz and Fallon, and this traffic was augmented by horse-drawn stages and private rigs. In Rawhide men met who had last clasped hands in Alaska's frozen fields, in the Rand of South Africa or in the rugged mountains of Mexico, all drawn here by the lure of the yellow stuff.

When the camp was only a year old it began to take on metropolitan airs. The *Rustler* proclaimed Rawhide the greatest gold camp in the world, and high-pressure promotional techniques so well learned in Goldfield, Rhyolite and Greenwater were practiced here by promoters Tex Rickard, Nat Goodwin, George Graham Rice and others. The resulting publicity and build-up created an atmosphere of hysteria and excitement that attracted thousands of individuals who saw Rawhide as their one last chance to get in on the ground floor of something big.

By March the daily *Press-Times* joined the five-month-old *Rustler,* and other papers briefly appeared. In April construction of a railroad from near Schurz was begun, and a half-dozen stage lines with over four dozen large-capacity autos plied the rough, dusty desert roads. Scores of leasers and leasing companies began shipping ore.

By June 1908 Rawhide was a city of 8000 beings, always on the go; it was said to resemble a beehive as seen from Balloon Hill, where many of the principal mines were located. By actual count there were over 40 saloons (Tex Rickard's Northern being the most famous), 28 restaurants, 30 hotels, 3 jewelers, 13 doctors, 10 barbershops, 9 bakeries, 9 lumberyards, 4 hospitals, 3 banks which were open until midnight, and about 125 brokerage offices. A school had opened and the volunteer fire department had three engines. Lodging houses with corrals provided resting places for six bits a night, or a dollar for Sybaritic ease behind print curtains. Only two churches were built to offset Stingaree Gulch, the camp's quarter-mile-long red light district.

Thus within six months' time a modern city had been built and equipped with all latest conveniences including telephones, refrigeration plant and a $150,000 water system — things which took other camps three or more years to acquire. Then tragedy struck. Early in September a nearly-million-dollar fire wiped out a third of a mile of businesses and leveled several dozen residences. The camp partially rebuilt with bigger buildings, but the smart money noted that less than $1.5 million had been taken from the overpublicized mines, and the boom cooled.

Three custom mills were built in 1909 but operated only a short time before shutting down. Various individuals took out ore in the district during subsequent decades, and only recently has Rawhide been entirely abandoned. Through the years production totaled less than $2 million. Wooden buildings and a stone jail, dating back to the raucous mining era, are left.

EAGLEVILLE, 2½ miles east of SR 31 at a point 10 miles north and east of Deadhorse Well.

This gold camp dating to the early 1880s was worked intermittently for about thirty years. A post office opened in 1889 but the camp never grew large and was described as always running short of ore. Placer miners made a small showing in 1905-08, but after the Rawhide boom subsided the camp died, losing its post office in 1913. Rock ruins remain.

Mouth of Tunnels
Grutt Bros. Leece
Rawhide Nev.

In 1907 Rawhide began a spectacular two-year career. The above view shows the camp's founding fathers, including the four Grutt brothers. Soon a rash of tents covered the sagebrush valley below Grutt Hill. The press espoused Rawhide and a healthy boom attracted the thousands of disappointed individuals who did not get in on the ground floor at either Goldfield or Bullfrog. *(Top: Leo Grutt Collection; bottom: Western History Research Center, University of Wyoming)*

Rawhide quickly grew out of its tent status in the spring of 1908 and handsome wooden buildings were erected along broad streets. In one building in the bottom view are the "bulls and bears" of the Rawhide curb. The people at the right await the distribution of mail. *(Top: Western History Research Center, University of Wyoming; bottom: Mrs. Dorothy Jennings Colllection)*

With block after block of false-fronted buildings (upper right), Rawhide looked like a movie set complete with all the extras: the fashionably attired Easterner, booted prospectors, hustling brokers, promoters, miners, merchants, and "tin-horns." *(Nell Mornsten Collection)*

In the panorama (lower right), taken in August 1908, all structures were less than a year old and the growth seemed endless. The main thoroughfare, Nevada Street, extends across the middle of the picture; Stingaree Gulch is in the background between the hills. There the lower world congregated, and the rattle of pianos and the squeak of dance hall fiddles sounded forth all hours of the night. *(National Archives)*

On September 4, 1908, Rawhide was at the mercy of flames. Nearly $1 million in property went up in smoke and a few thousand people were left homeless. Dynamite was used in an attempt to hold the fire but instead it only scattered the flames over a larger area. Rawhide never rebuilt completely because of lack of financial fuel. *(Two photos: Mrs. Myrtle Myles Collection)*

For days after the fire the town was under martial law to prevent looting. Special relief wagonloads of food and supplies were sent from Reno, Tonopah, Goldfield and other places. (Tonopah *Times-Bonanza*)

The bottom view, taken from an identical spot as the panorama two pages back, shows what little remains of this promoter's paradise. *(Frank Mitrani photo)*

461

Located on the relatively inaccessible west side of Walker Lake, Dutch Creek's unique feature was that it was more easily reached by water than by land. This was one of three places in all of Nevada where steamboats played any serious part in the state's transportation system. The covered arrastra (below) was built to recover gold in Dutch Creek ravine before 1900. (*Top and bottom: Mrs. W. B. Mercer; middle: Mrs. Helen McInnis Collection*)

DUTCH CREEK, on US 95 at a point 11 miles north of Hawthorne.

Conflict between white settlers and Indians was not infrequent in Nevada during the 1860s and 1870s, and the Walker River Indian Reservation was the scene of some of these troubles, particularly with the persistent rumors of gold on this land reserved for the Paiutes.

According to one story, an old Dutchman opened a mine and built an arrastra on the west shore of Walker Lake in the summer of 1867, with the aid of two nephews. Learning of the value of his mine, Indians are said to have come to his cabin to kill him and the two young men. The Dutchman is said to have offered $500 and his own life if the Indians would spare the nephews. The bargain was made, the money changed hands, the Dutchman was duly killed and the nephews departed, presumably safe, but as they started to paddle away the Indians showered them with bullets. The boys' canoe upset and the bodies sank into the murky waters of Walker Lake. The story cannot be verified, but it was widely circulated along with other campfire tales of the allegedly rich ore bodies on the reservation.

Such stories were reported and probably embroidered upon by mining camp journalists and finally on October 29, 1906, the federal government threw open this part of the reservation for appropriation and location. On that day several hundred heavily-armed prospectors and miners, most with the Dutchman's mine as objective, rushed wildly from the starting point four miles north of Hawthorne, over sagebrush and gullies toward the Dutch Creek ravine. A few men imported race horses, believing that they could gain an advantage, but this type of horse was ill-adapted to unimproved terrain. The most daring prospectors had surreptitiously entered the reservation the night before, hoping to escape the vigilance of the Indian police. A touch of Oklahoma!

Amid the excitement of December 1906 the camp of Dutch Creek formed and within a month it boasted over two dozen businesses on the main street which ran up into the foothills. The street was about 70 feet wide and crude signs marked the businesses in tents and false-fronted buildings. Shootings were frequent for awhile, up and down the main street at night; it was said that people moving about in the evening had to go out back doors of structures to avoid stray bullets.

Early in 1907 this boom camp had big plans. Goldfield interests proposed building a $20,000 clubhouse for a yacht club at Walker Lake; a boat service planned importing a large boat from Tiburon, California; Charles Schwab, the Pittsburgh steel magnate, talked of operating his own launches to reach his extensive interests on the lake. Lot-jumpers caused so much trouble that a seven-man vigilance committee was formed to maintain order. Nevertheless, the gold prospects did not live up to anticipation and Dutch Creek died in the spring of 1907. Only a few people were left by 1909. Original buildings have long been removed and a private ranch is located on the site.

GRANITE, 3½ miles west and south of US 95A at a point 4½ miles northwest of Schurz.

Gold mining started in the north end of the Wassuk Range in the spring of 1908 after the Mountain View district had been organized, and the contemporary press described this camp of 250 as rapidly coming to the front. Granite supported a post office, the handwritten *News,* and stores; meanwhile several dozen leasers worked the nearby hills. Late that year the boom subsided and the camp finally folded in mid-1912, though a few mines continued to produce until 1916.

MOUNTAIN VIEW, 4 miles southwest of US 95A at a point 6½ miles northwest of Schurz.

This camp sprang up in 1908 as a companion camp to Granite and had its own post office from April until December of that year. A small stamp mill operated here for awhile before the camp retired early in 1909.

CORYVILLE, or Coreyville, 4 miles west of SR 31 at a point 3 miles south of Hawthorne.

On the basis of promising silver discoveries on the eastern side of Mount Grant, the town of Coryville was laid out and a post office established in April 1883. Several houses were soon erected. A fine road was built to the camp and merchandise and mining supplies were hauled in to begin development work. Intensive operations turned up no permanent veins and the camp folded toward the end of the decade.

ORO CITY, by road and trail 4 miles east of SR 31 at a point 10 miles south of Hawthorne.

This district attracted attention late in 1906 because of a revived interest in nearby mines. Oro City was platted in November 1906 and through the promotional efforts of the Oro City Townsite & Water Co. lot sales and building construction started early in 1907. By March the state legislature granted a franchise to build a railroad from Yerington, and an auto stage service ran from Hawthorne. Over 300 people had come before summer and an application for a post office was submitted; but before the request was fulfilled, Oro City crashed and early in 1908 was deserted. No buildings are left.

WHISKY SPRING, 4½ miles southeast of SR 31 at a point 10 miles south of Hawthorne.

This station at the northern end of Whisky Flat served as a lodging and eating stop for travelers on the Bodie-Candelaria road late in the 1870s. Mining operations below the station on the flat were limited, but important enough after 1882 to warrant construction of a small furnace to smelt silver-copper ore. Only the spring remains.

LUCKY BOY, on the Lucky Boy Pass road 2½ miles west of its junction with SR 31 at a point 4 miles south of Hawthorne.

Two men repairing the Bodie stage road in the summer of 1906 found a chunk of lead-silver ore near the top of Lucky Boy pass, while filling in a small washout caused by a recent rain. The men quit mending the road for the rest of the day and eventually found the ledge from which the piece of ore had rolled, six feet away. Before nightfall they had dug a hole several feet deep and mined a pile of galena.

For nearly two years these men occasionally worked their Lucky Boy mine, and then released it for a store debt in Hawthorne. The new owners leased the mine to the Chicago Exploration Co. in the summer of 1908. During the next few months additional veins were found and early in 1909 a stampede resulted in the formation of a camp. Lucky Boy post office opened in March and during the next month competing newspapers were distributed. Also in April Senator Tasker Oddie of Tonopah secured leases and options on several properties.

Lucky Boy's Labor Day celebration attracted hundreds of visitors who participated in a tug of war, burro races, ladies' nail-driving contest and other sports. A banquet and grand ball in the new miners' union hall that night concluded the camp's finest hour. Several businesses were established and the 1910 census showed a population of 800, but after 1912-13 only leasers whose production was profitable carried on. A new mill was built in the mid-1920s at the foot of Lucky Boy grade, but the district has been quiet since about 1950. No buildings remain.

Lucky Boy sprang up high on the east slope of the Wassuk Range, on the Hawthorne-Bodie road. In 1909 it was one of Nevada's banner camps. But Lucky Boy was not so lucky for Tasker Oddie, who along with others from Tonopah lost much of their fortunes there. Below the camp in the valley (opposite page) are Walker Lake and Hawthorne.

Ore is being removed from a lease at Lucky Boy on the morning or 7 o'clock shift. Leasers worked feverishly on their holdings because they had the right to mine for only a specified amount of time. (Top: Los Angeles County Museum; two others: Mrs. W. B. Mercer Collection)

FLETCHER, 21 miles west of Hawthorne on Lucky Boy Pass road.

When the Carson & Colorado Railroad began running to Hawthorne in 1881 an important flow of connecting traffic developed on the Bodie-Hawthorne road. Fletcher functioned as a stage station on this road after about 1881, and a post office operated at various times between 1883 and 1919. The rock structures that remain are used by the present owners.

AURORA, 4 miles southwest of the Lucky Boy Pass road at a point 23 miles southwest of Hawthorne.

A prospecting party heading southward in August 1860 toward Mono Lake, with Arizona or Mexico as its destination, discovered gold and silver quartz ledges while searching for water and game. Shortly a spectacular rush ensued from Monoville and other California towns, and on Gregory Flats emerged the camp of Esmeralda. A few months later Aurora, named for the goddess of the dawn, was laid out in grid fashion a mile west. Despite the difficulty of obtaining lumber, the new camp grew rapidly into a town with many houses and stores built of fine brick and masonry. After the spring of 1861 the musical sound of eight stamps began reverberating in the upper part of town and Wells, Fargo & Co. hauled out gold. A census in May showed that Aurora had nearly 2000 citizens.

With all these assets, Aurora was aggressively claimed by both Nevada Territory and California. In the spring of 1861 the California legislature created Mono County and fixed the seat here; the following November Nevada declared Aurora to be headquarters of Esmeralda County. This unique double-county-seat status lasted nearly two years, during which two sets of county courts exercised jurisdiction and sat concurrently.

The magic of Aurora even lured Sam Clemens, who mined for gold in the spring of 1862, then worked as a laborer in a stamp mill for ten dollars a week plus board. After only a week on the job he abandoned the pans and batteries, but while in Aurora Clemens sent to the *Territorial Enterprise* in Virginia City, under the pseudonym "Josh," a series of lively sketches which attracted the attention of the editor. Weeks later Clemens was hired as a reporter for the *Enterprise* where he ulti-

mately adopted the famous pen name, Mark Twain.

Strikes on the Wide West claims in 1862-63 kept the Esmeralda district in a state of excitement. By the summer of 1863 Aurora had twenty stores, a dozen hotels, 21 saloons and two newspapers, the semi-weekly *Esmeralda Star* and the daily *Times*. The population approached 10,000, including transients who lived in dugouts or hovels of stone with canvas roofs. About 200 stamps in 16 mills kept up a ceaseless clatter, the largest mill being the Real Del Monte on Bodie Creek.

To resolve the question as to whether Aurora was in California or Nevada, the contending governments jointly sponsored a survey of the border. While this was in progress a lively double county election was held in September 1863; the people voted for a full ticket of Mono County officials in the police station, then walked over to the Armory hall where the polls of Esmeralda were set up. Three weeks later the gang of surveyors reached the district and fixed the boundary four miles west of Aurora. The Mono County officials humbly loaded their records on a wagon and moved to Bodie, then a small camp ten miles southwest and safely within California.

Excesses in promotion and building caught up with the town by summer's end in 1864. Inflated values of mining stocks, extreme speculation in mining properties, the immense sums of money expended in building costly mills that stood idle most of the time, the funds of investors squandered by mismanagement, and a miscalculation of the value of known ore deposits all brought the district into disrepute from which it never recovered. Within a year half the population had moved on and in 1869 surface bonanzas were exhausted after they had yielded over $29 million. In the late 1870s the mines revived with the nearby Bodie boom and produced reasonably well until 1882, but during the next year Aurora again declined and lost the county seat to Hawthorne. The post office was discontinued in 1897.

Resumption of mining early in this century rejuvenated the camp, and by early 1906 another weekly, the Aurora *Borealis*, a post office, and several other businesses served several hundred people. During the World War I years the Aurora Consolidated Mining Co. recovered over $1.8 mil-

Aurora by 1889 (above) had declined drastically from the boom of the early 1860s, when the local mines were thought to be in California, as the stock certificate indicates. Even the newspapers before September 1863 had a Mono County, California byline. The first quartz mills were built at the base of the hill under the Del Monte mine whose shaft buildings can be seen in the mid-background. (*Top: Nevada State Museum; bottom: Mrs. Helen McInnis Collection*)

The Del Monte hoist works (above) fed ore to its mill (below) on Bodie Creek. That handsome $250,000 facility built of brick in 1863 is one of the few Aurora mills whose site can be identified with certainty. Only foundations remain. *(Both photos: Nevada State Museum)*

In 1917 the revival was in full swing at Aurora. A newspaper and post office were re-established, and the streets were alive with activity. Aurorans celebrated holidays by draping the town with patriotic flags and bunting. The center of town was at the Esmeralda Hotel, which in the camp's early years was the courthouse first for Mono and then Esmeralda County.

Around the Aurora Consolidated Mining Co.'s mill, one mile north of town, was a suburb called Mangum. *(Top: Mrs. Helen McInnis Collection; middle: Theron Fox Collection; bottom: Emil Billeb Collection)*

lion in gold, but in the spring of 1919 when Aurora was nearly dead the post office was again removed. After 1946 the town's several abandoned buildings were leveled for their brick in the post World War II used brick market. Still remaining are caved-in cellars, mill foundations, cemetery, and the shell of a mill built early in this century.

BODIE (California), 36 miles west of Hawthorne via Lucky Boy Pass road.

> They say you were wild and woolly, Bodie,
> And fast on the draw as they make 'em;
> That you lived at ease with the bad and the bold,
> Who thought nothing of shooting a man down cold,
> And defying the law to take 'em.
>
> — Lillian Ninnis

A miner named William Bodey found placer gold late in 1859, stayed to face the winter but froze to death in a blizzard that December. In the summer of 1861 an important discovery of lode gold was made on ground which later became the camp's largest producer, and for the next four years Bodie experienced a mild boom and shared in the excitement over nearby Aurora.

Mining met with indifferent success here until 1874 when a rich vein was found in the caving of abandoned workings. Energetic mining men from San Francisco bought that mine in 1876 for $67,500 and continued development as the Standard Mining Co., for which they built a small mill. After phenomenally rich strikes in 1877 a furious rush began, intensifying in 1878, the year that the Comstock played out. Stocks swiftly rose in price and the Bodie activity pumped new life into the San Francisco exchange. Locations were made for miles around and Bodie grew in every direction.

During the severe winter of 1878-79 many people died of exposure and disease. There was little employment, a scarcity of housing and food, and the only pastime was in the saloons. But thousands of eager people came in the spring of 1879 and great quantities of supplies and material were teamed in. The district was caught up in a delirium of excitement, additional mines were opened, new mills built, new structures erected, and the camp was freely spending gold coins.

With government consisting only of a few sheriffs and a justice of the peace, excesses of every kind abounded and the "bad man from Bodie" quickly became a legend throughout the West. Fights and quarrels were alarmingly frequent and shootings by quick-draw artists were so numerous that the common greeting early any day was "Well, have we got a man for breakfast this morning?" Eventually a vigilance committee checked this isolated camp's rowdies and desperadoes, to some degree.

By September 1879 Bodie had five rival daily papers, the *Chronicle*, the *Free Press*, the *News*, the *Standard* and the *Union*, as well as three weeklies, and fraternal organizations furnished social activity in suppers and dances. Other camp diversions included theatrical performances, picnics and sleighing parties. By the end of that year nearly 10,000 people had flocked in, and with the presence of many Chinese and Mexicans the camp was truly cosmopolitan. About fifty companies carried on development work until 1880, when the boom showed signs of cooling off.

A wooden mining camp in a treeless region, Bodie faced inevitable problems. Lumber for construction, timber to shore the mines, and firewood to fuel the furnaces all had to be freighted in at great cost. To connect Bodie with the forests south of Mono Lake, a 32-mile railroad was projected and built in 1881, and began hauling timber to Bodie.

In 1881 a rapid decline had set in. The get-rich-quick craftsmen forsook the town; mines were abandoned except for the proven few; and the lawless left to practice their trades in more active localities. The stock market went to pieces, and by 1883 only 500 people were in the camp which was kept alive by four or five mines. The Standard mine absorbed its former major rival, the Bodie, in 1887 and operated profitably for another score of years. About $30 million in gold and silver was produced from Bodie mines, the Standard accounting for over two-thirds of it; about $7 million was paid in dividends. In 1918 the railroad stopped running and was scrapped.

A fire destroyed most of Bodie in 1932, but small-scale mining continued until the beginning of World War II. In 1962 the California state park system undertook the protection of the Bodie ghost town, and in September 1964 the Bodie State Historical Park was dedicated.

At an altitude of nearly 9000 feet, Bodie was annually blanketed with a soft snow covering. Unlike Aurora with many imposing brick buildings to show the town's wealth, Bodie with its wooden buildings was nevertheless a rich district: over $30 million was produced in this district in over sixty years of mining. *(Emil Billeb Collection)*

In early Nevada, the state legislature gave road franchises to certain individuals who built and maintained roads and collected tolls. At Sunshine Station between Aurora and Bodie, the tollkeeper was especially active in the late 1870s. *(Blevins Hobart Collection)*

In 1877-78 the town of Bodie rose along the western base of Bodie Bluff, a group of wind-swept hills devoid of vegetation except for scrub sagebrush. In less than four years Bodie had run the full cycle of boom to decline. It also had been plagued by many fires before 1884, especially a large one that wiped out the west end of the business district, leading off to the right above. Despite these losses, Main Street by the mid-1890s, when this picture was taken, still contained impressive wooden buildings such as the U. S.

Hotel (at the left), stores and saloons. Off Main Street in the foreground left was Chinatown, the second largest in the West in the days of 1879-1880. Fronting Chinatown and
running off the picture to the left was "Maiden Lane," the domain of Madame Mous-
tache and other ladies of the night. There Kipling's "Fultah Fisher's Boarding House"
was often re-enacted with variations. The twenty-stamp Standard mill at the far left
burned in 1899 but a more modern mill soon took its place. *(Emil Billeb Collection)*

MASONIC (California), 15 miles north of Bodie via graded road (29 miles west-southwest of Hawthorne).

The Masonic district was prospected for many years before the discovery of valuable gold ore in August 1902. Additional lodes found in 1905 encouraged the Pittsburg Liberty Co. to begin large-scale production in 1907, after a ten-stamp steam-powered mill had been erected. A camp then formed with post office, and at the height of operations a few years later Masonic consisted of three camps with a combined population of 500. The company had produced $600,000 in bullion by 1910, when it went bankrupt. Masonic was active again in 1933-38, but is now deserted. Mine ruins, several wooden cabins and the collapsed shell of a mill remain in the tri-sectioned camp.

These views of Masonic show most features of the camp. Uppertown and Middletown are shown at the top and bottom of the opposite page, while the mill and accompanying settlement are shown on this page, in summer and winter scenes. *(William A. Kornmayer Collection)*

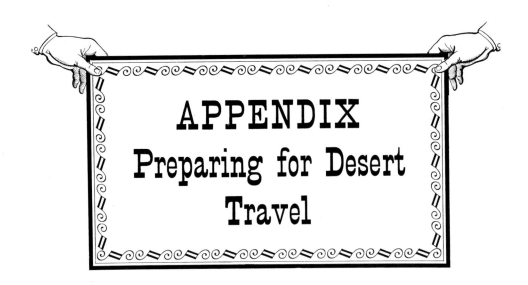

APPENDIX
Preparing for Desert Travel

The basic rule is to keep equipment simple and portable. Personal necessities that should be taken include: hats, gloves, loose-fitting wash and wear clothing, shoes or boots suitable for rough terrain, blankets, canteens, sunglasses, first-aid manual and kit, paper towels and tissue, matches and a food and water supply. Canned foods packed away in the car will be welcome in an emergency.

To help you find your way, carry literature and maps of the area; U.S.G.S. topographical maps are best. Include paper and pencil to record directions. A compass and binoculars may come in handy. A mirror, a flashlight or flares should be taken for signaling in emergencies.

Among the supplies and equipment in the automobile, the following are essential: a spare tire, jack and lug wrench (two tires if on a long trip), a tool box, a pick, a shovel, burlap sacks and tire pump, wood blocks, jumper cables and a gasoline reserve of at least five gallons.

You may want to carry the following camp gear: sleeping bags with air mattresses, a tent, folding chairs and a table, a stove or lantern and fuel, icebox (obtain ice and perishables at the last point of supply), paper bags, aluminum foil, and old newspapers to kindle fires. Food should be stored in cans or plastic containers. Carry butter, cheese and similar foods in coffee cans with lids sealed by adhesive tape. Bottled items should be in plastic containers. Improvise and save time, for instance, by planning meals around one-pan dishes.

Car Preparation and Care

Before leaving home make sure that the car is in top mechanical condition. Flush the engine cooling system. Check the fanbelt, radiator hoses, and wiring. Clean the front of the radiator core. Make sure that the air and oil filters are clean.

At the last point of supply, fill to the brim with gasoline. Check the oil, tires, battery, and radiator pressure cap. Ask about road conditions and directions locally; flash floods can change the terrain overnight.

While on the back roads, keep a written record of mileages, turnoffs, and significant landmarks. On longer journeys travel in two-car parties or tell someone where you are going, your route, and when you will return.

Keep the wheels on the road. Watch for high centers or rocks that the car cannot clear. Watch for gopher holes which are often several inches deep and filled with powdery soil. Avoid driving on dry lakes and around shorelines. Never park in a dry wash; make camp on high ground.

On long downgrades use the engine in low gear as a brake. Check braking power after crossing streams and dust zones.

In general, drive slowly.

Desert Driving Emergencies

When you get stuck in the sand, stop the car at once. Decide whether to go forward or back out. Partially deflate the tires for more traction.

Jack up the end of the car and build a wood, brush or burlap roadway. Never crawl under a car jacked up in the sand! Place weight over the rear wheels by having someone stand on the bumper. Then ease out — heavy on the gas, easy on the clutch. Rock the car backward and forward until the car moves a few feet at a time, then drive off slowly to keep the rear wheels from spinning. If all this fails, further deflate the tires until they bulge at the sides.

Remember always to maintain momentum while driving in sand and keep the front wheels straight. Shift to lower gears or partially deflate the tires before entering a sandy area; never shift gears in sand. Never attempt to *push out* a hopelessly stuck vehicle. It must be *pulled out* by another vehicle on safe ground.

When you see livestock on the road, slow down and creep past. At night flick your headlights rapidly and sound the horn in short staccato bursts.

If you hear a tire blow out, grip the wheel and steer straight. *Do not apply the brakes.* Restore steering control by on, off, on, off applications of the accelerator. After slowing down, apply the brakes.

When in a skid, do not apply the brakes. Turn but do not jerk the steering wheel in the direction of the skid and simultaneously release the accelerator. After gaining control apply the brakes with on-off touches.

If the engine stalls or will not start, check for several things: the gas tank may be empty; the fuel line may have been punctured or the gauge broken; the carburetor may be flooded. Wait a full minute, then hold the accelerator to the floor while trying the starter. Dirt or water may be in the fuel line or carburetor. The butterfly valve may be stuck.

The engine may be overheated. Turn the car into the wind. While the engine is running at fast idle, slowly pour water over the radiator core. After the engine cools, fill the radiator and proceed. You may have electrical trouble. Check the battery connections and terminals to see if the cables are loose or the terminals dirty. Clean or tighten them, or pound them gently with a rock or tool. Look for frayed wires.

If the car comes to a bucking halt while driving at high altitudes or in hot weather, you probably have a vapor lock. Raise the hood and let the engine cool. Apply a wet cloth to the fuel pump. Wait ten to fifteen minutes. Do not run the battery down by repeated efforts to start the engine.

Perils of the Desert

EXPOSURE. Nevada's deserts are subject to extremes of temperature. Only a few hours after the hot sun sets the thermometer drops drastically. Clothing should be adequate to ward off the sun's rays and also to retain body heat during cool nights. Avoid excessive activity in the sun to avoid sunburn, heat exhaustion or sunstroke (heat prostration).

RATTLESNAKES. Many myths concerning snakes have been perpetrated by uninformed individuals. Here are the facts: Snakes do not roam at midday; they prefer early morning or evening shadows and lower temperatures. Rattlesnakes will not provoke a fight; they prefer to remain in hiding unless startled or angered. They will not pursue a victim down a trail and follow him to his camp. A snake seldom bites a human except in self defense. They *will* strike without a signal.

Watch for snakes in hilly areas, especially in washes containing damp soil and shade. When you see small rodents you are in snake country. Old mines and pits are typical snake hangouts. Never handle a snake even if it appears to be dead. Never place your hands and feet in places you cannot see, and do not forget to look at the ground when you get out of your car. While gathering wood or searching through debris, it is wise to wear long gloves, high boots and use a garden tool.

Most snake bites are attributable to carelessness, such as stepping on snakes while hiking. If you should get bitten, avoid unnecessary activity and *get to a hospital immediately.* If professional treatment is not available within a reasonable time, your first aid manual will have helpful instructions. Only as a last resort should the wound be cut and sucked by an untrained person.

INSECTS, SPIDERS AND SCORPIONS. No lethal species live in Nevada, although bites and stings may cause considerable discomfort. None comes to bite you in bed, though during the night they might crawl into your blankets to keep warm, biting you after you roll over.

477

Preventing dehydration before help is available is the main concern; conserve energy and body moisture. Do not bother to look for food; if anything, look for water. Keep the body clothed. Examine the base of cliffs and thickly planted areas for water. Proper squeezing of cactus pulp will furnish some water. Watch and listen for birds that may fly to a spring. Dig around low points or bends in dry stream beds. The cooler the water, the safer to drink without treatment.

If you are stranded with a broken-down car, stay with it unless you are certain of where water sources or a settlement might be found. In sunlight, a flashing mirror is visible for miles; attempt to aim your mirror at the windows of passing aircraft. Even in the most remote areas of Nevada an airplane passes by at least two or three times a week. At night you can light flares, or build three bonfires in a triangle with points at least twelve feet apart. Use any combustible material at hand — sagebrush, greasewood, gasoline, or even the tires from the car.

Drink water in small sips four or five times a day. Remain in a shaded area off the ground. Burrow in the sand or look for a nearby cave. An emergency supply of drinking water is in the radiator, if it has been drained of anti-freeze.

If you go for help, leave a note on the steering wheel and drink water before starting out. Carry as much water as you can. Begin the walk in the early morning or evening and rest in the shade during midday. Follow the course of stream beds downhill. Avoid crossing and recrossing ravines. Always leave notes every few hours; date and time them. Wear clothing for protection against the sun's rays and the cool nights. Do not travel in a storm; seek shelter with your back to the wind.

Glossary of Mining Terms

ADIT. A passage driven into a mine from the side of a hill.

ALLUVIAL. Minerals found associated with deposits made by flowing water.

AMALGAM. An alloy of mercury with one or more other metals.

AMALGAMATION. The process by which mercury is alloyed with gold and silver from pulverized ores.

APEX. The end, edge, or crest of a mineral vein nearest the surface.

ARRASTRA. A circular rock-lined pit in which broken ore is pulverized by stones dragged around the pit attached to horizontal poles fastened in a central pillar.

ASSAY. A means of ascertaining the commercial value of ore.

AURIFEROUS. Containing gold.

BALL MILL. A rotating horizontal cylinder with a diameter almost equal to the length supported by a frame or shaft in which materials are ground using grinding media such as iron or steel balls.

BASE METAL. Any of the nonprecious metals.

BONANZA. In miners' phrase, a body of rich ore.

BORRASCA. In mining, barren rock or non-paying ore. An unproductive mine. Opposite of Bonanza.

CHIMNEY. An ore shoot.

CHLORINATION. The process of dissolving gold ores, after crushing and roasting, by the use of chlorine gas.

CLAIM. A parcel of land legally held for mining purposes, location of which is recorded and marked by monuments.

CLAIM-JUMPING. Taking over mining property after it has been staked by someone else, usually before the claim is recorded.

CONCENTRATE. The product of concentration.

CONCENTRATION. Separation and accumulation of economic minerals from gangue.

CONCENTRATOR. A plant where ore is separated into values and rejects.

COUNTRY ROCK. The rock in which a mineral deposit or an intrusion is enclosed. The common rock of a region.

CRADLE. A wooden box, longer than wide, provided with a movable slide and hopper, and mounted on two rockers. It is used for washing gold-bearing earths.

CROSSCUT. A horizontal opening driven across the course of a vein or in general across the direction of the main workings. A connection from a shaft to a vein.

CYANIDE PROCESS. A process for the extraction of gold from finely crushed ores, concentrates and tailings by means of cyanide of potassium. The gold is dissolved by the solution and subsequently deposited upon metallic zinc or by other means.

DIKE. A tabular body of igneous rock that cuts across the structure of the adjacent country rocks.

DIP. The angle at which a bed, stratum, or vein is inclined from the horizontal.

DISTRICT. In the States and Territories west of the Missouri (prior to 1880), a vaguely bounded and temporary division and organization made by the inhabitants of a mining region.

DREDGE. A large raft or barge on which are mounted either a chain of buckets or suction pumps and other appliances, to elevate and wash alluvial deposits and gravel for gold, tin, platinum, diamonds, etc.

DRIFT. A horizontal passage underground. A drift follows the vein, as distinguished from a crosscut, which intersects it.

DRY WASHING. In placer mining, the separation of heavy valuable materials from lighter waste by a vertical motion technique using air instead of water.

DUMP. A pile or heap of waste rock material or other non-ore refuse near a mine.

FAULT. A break in the continuity of a body of rock. It is accompanied by a movement on one side of the break or the other so that what were once parts of one continuous rock stratum or vein are now separated. The amount of displacement of the parts may range from a few inches to thousands of feet.

FLOAT. The term float or float rock means bunches, blotches, pieces, or boulders of quartz or rock lying detached from, or resting upon the earth's surface without any walls.

FLOTATION. The method of mineral separation in which a froth created in water by a variety of reagents floats some finely crushed minerals, whereas other minerals sink.

FLUX. A substance that promotes the fusing of minerals or metals or prevents the formation of oxides.

FOOTWALL. The wall or rock under a vein.

GALLOWS FRAME. The frame supporting a pulley, over which the hoisting rope passes.

GANGUE. Undesired minerals associated with ore, mostly nonmetallic.

GIANT. The nozzle of a pipe used to convey water for hydraulic mining.

GLORY HOLE. A funnel-shaped excavation the bottom of which is connected to a raise driven from an underground haulage level.

HANGING WALL. The wall or rock on the upper side of an inclined vein.

HARD ROCK. A term used to distinguish between material which can be excavated without blasting and rock having a strong bonded structure.

HARD-ROCK MINE. A mine in hard rock; especially one difficult to drill, blast, and square up.

HEADFRAME. The steel or timber frame at the top of a shaft, which carries the sheave or pulley for the hoisting rope, and serves various other purposes.

HIGH-GRADE. A rich ore.

HIGH-GRADING. Theft of valuable pieces of ore.

HORSE. Waste inclusions within ore deposits.

HYDRAULIC MINING. The process by which a bank of gold-bearing earth and rock is excavated by a jet of water, discharged through the converging nozzle of a pipe under a great pressure.

JEWELRY ROCK. Rich ore.

LAGGING. Heavy planks or timbers used to support the roof of a mine, or for floors of working places and for the accumulation of rock and earth in a stope.

LEACHING. The removal in solution of the more soluble minerals by percolating waters.

LEAD. Commonly used as a synonym for ledge or lode.

LEDGE. A mass of rock that constitutes a valuable mineral deposit.

LENS. A body of ore or of rock thick in the middle and thin at the edges.

LEVEL. Mines are customarily worked from shafts through horizontal passages or drifts called levels. These are commonly spaced at regular intervals in depth and are either numbered from the surface in regular order or designated by their actual elevation, below the top of a shaft.

LODE. The well-defined occurrence of valuable mineral-bearing material.

LONG TOM. A trough for washing gold-bearing earth. It is longer than a rocker.

MERCURY. A heavy, silver-white metallic element that is liquid at ordinary temperatures.

MILL. Reducing plant where ore is concentrated and/or metals recovered.

MINING DISTRICT. A section of country usually designated by name, having described or understood boundaries within which mineral is found and which is worked under rules and regulations prescribed by the miners therein.

MUCKING. The operation of loading broken rock by hand or machine usually in shafts or tunnels.

ORE. A mineral of sufficient value as to quality and quantity which may be mined with profit.

ORE BODY. A solid and fairly continuous mass of ore, which may include low-grade ore and waste as well as pay ore.

ORE SHOOT. A large and usually rich aggregation of mineral in a vein.

OUTCROP. The part of a rock formation that appears at the surface of the ground.

OVERBURDEN. Material of any nature, consolidated or unconsolidated, that overlies a deposit of useful materials or ores.

PAN. A shallow, circular, concave steel dish for washing sand, clay, etc., from gold or tin.

PATENT. A document which conveys titled to the ground, and no further assessment work need be done.

PHILOSOPHER'S STONE. An imaginary stone, or solid substance or preparation, believed by alchemists to have the power of transmuting the base metals into gold or silver.

PICTURE ROCK. Rich ore.

PLACER. A place where gold is obtained by washing.

PLACER MINING. The extraction of heavy mineral from a placer deposit by concentration in running water.

PORPHYRY. Colloquially, the word is used to mean almost any igneous rock, occurring in sheets or dikes, particularly one that is spotted, soft or light color.

PULP. A mixture of ground ore and water capable of flowing through suitably graded channels as a fluid.

QUARTZ. A crystallized silicon dioxide, SiO_2. Any hard, gold or silver ore, as distinguished from gravel or earth. Hence quartz mining as distinguished from hydraulic mining.

QUARTZ MINE. A mine in which the deposits of ore are found in veins or fissures in the rocks forming the earth's crust. Usually applied to lode gold mines.

RAISE. A vertical or inclined opening driven upward from a level to connect with the level above, or to explore the ground for a limited distance above one level. After two levels are connected, the connection may be a winze or a raise, depending upon which level is taken as the point of reference.

RIFFLE. The lining of the bottom of a sluice, made of blocks or slats of wood, or stones, arranged in such a manner that clinks are left between them.

ROCKER. A portable sluicebox used by prospectors.

SHAFT. A vertical or inclined excavation or opening from the surface.

SHOOT. The payable section of a lode; an enriched portion of a continuous ore body.

SKIP. A large hoisting bucket which slides between guides in a shaft, the bail usually connecting at or near the bottom of the bucket so that it may be automatically dumped at the surface. An open iron vehicle or car on four wheels, running on rails and used especially on inclines or in inclined shafts.

SLIME. Ore reduced to a very fine powder and held in suspension in water so as to form a kind of thin ore mud; generally used in the plural.

SLUICEBOX. A wooden trough in which alluvial beds are washed for the recovery of gold.

SQUARE SET. A set of timbers composed of cap, girt, and post. These members meet so as to form a solid 90° angle. They are so framed at the intersection as to form a compression joint, and join with three other similar sets. This system of timbering can be adapted to large or irregular ore bodies.

STAMP MILL. An apparatus in which rock is crushed by descending pestles or stamps operated by water, steam or electric power. Also, the building containing machinery.

STATION. The excavation adjoining the shaft at each of the different levels, where men and material are removed or delivered.

STOPE. An underground excavation from which the ore has been or is being extracted.

STRIKE. The course or bearing of the outcrop of an inclined bed or structure on a level surface; it is perpendicular to the direction of the dip. To find a vein of ore; a valuable discovery.

SULFIDE. A compound of sulfur with more than one element.

SULFURET. In miners' phrase, the undecomposed metallic ores, usually sulfides. Chiefly applied to auriferous pyrites. Concentrate and sulfide are preferable.

TAILINGS. The gangue and other refuse material resulting from the washing, concentration, or treatment of ground ore. Those portions of washed ore that are regarded as too poor to be treated further.

TRAM. To haul or push cars about in a mine.

TUNNEL. A horizontal or nearly horizontal underground passage. Any level or drift in a mine open at one end. Often used as a synonym for adit, drift.

VEIN. A zone or belt of mineralized rock lying within boundaries clearly separating it from neighboring rock.

WHIM. A large capstan or vertical drum turned by horsepower for raising ore from a mine.

WINZE. A subsidiary shaft which starts underground. It is usually a connection between two levels.

SELECTED BIBLIOGRAPHY

The books listed below represent only a portion of the authorities consulted. Research centered on manuscripts and files of newspapers, but to list them all would be exhaustive. The following newspapers deserve mention because they gave coverage to events far beyond their own localities: the *Reese River Reveille* in Austin; the *White Pine News*, the Belmont *Courier*, the *Nevada State Journal* in Reno; and the Elko *Independent*. John Dormer's *True Fissure* in Candelaria and William J. Forbes' *Humboldt Register* in Unionville seemed to write the events of the day with an awareness that history was being preserved. California newspapers such as the Sacramento *Union* and the San Francisco *Alta* had regular correspondents in Nevada's mining areas. Useful, too, were the *Mining & Scientific Press* and the *Engineering & Mining Journal*, along with popular magazines also published in San Francisco.

UNITED STATES GEOLOGICAL SURVEY BULLETINS

Ball, S. H. *A Geological Reconnaissance in Southwestern Nevada and Eastern California*. No. 308, 1907.

Emmons, W. H. *A Reconnaissance of Some Mining Camps in Elko, Lander, and Eureka Counties, Nevada*. No. 408, 1910.

Ferguson, Henry G. *Geology and Ore Deposits of the Manhattan District, Nevada*. No. 723, 1924.

Hewett, D. F. *Geology and Ore Deposits of Goodsprings Quadrangle, Nevada*. Professional Papers No. 162, 1931.

Hill, J. M. *Notes on Some Mining Districts in Eastern Nevada*. No. 648, 1916.

————. *Some Mining Districts in Northeastern California and Northwestern Nevada*. No. 594, 1915.

Ransome, F. L. *Notes on Some Mining Districts in Humboldt County, Nevada*. No. 414, 1909.

————. *Preliminary Account of Goldfield, Bullfrog, and Other Mining Districts in Southern Nevada*, with notes on the Manhattan District by G. H. Garrey and W. H. Emmons. No. 303, 1907.

Schraeder, F. C. *Reconnaissance of the Jarbidge, Contact, and Elk Mountain Districts, Elko County, Nevada*. No. 497, 1912.

Spencer, A. C. *Geology and Ore Deposits of Ely, Nevada*. Professional Papers No. 96, 1917.

Westgate, Lewis G. and Adolph Knopf. *Geology and Ore Deposits of the Pioche District, Nevada*. Professional Papers, No. 171, 1932.

OTHER UNITED STATES GOVERNMENT DOCUMENTS

Browne, J. Ross. *A Report on the Mineral Resources of the States and Territories West of the Rocky Mountains*, for the years 1866 and 1867. G.P.O. 1867, 1868.

Hague, James W. *Mining Industry*, with *Geological Contributions* by Clarence King. U. S. Geological Exploration of the Fortieth Parallel Report, v. 3. Professional Papers of the Engineer Department, U.S. Army, No. 18, 1870.

Raymond, R. W. *Report on the Mineral Resources of the States and Territories West of the Rocky Mountains*, for the years 1868 to 1875, inclusive. G.P.O., 1869-1875.

Vanderburg, W. O. *Reconnaissances of Mining Districts in Pershing, Mineral, Clark, Humboldt, Eureka, Lander and Churchill Counties*. G.P.O., 1936-1940.

Wheeler, Lt. George M. *Preliminary Report Concerning Expeditions and Surveys, Principally in Nevada and Arizona*. G.P.O., 1872.

Wheeler, Lt. G. M. *Report upon United States Geographical Surveys West of the One Hundredth Meridian*, in charge of First Lieutenant George M. Wheeler . . . under the direction of the Chief of Engineers. U.S. Army. G.P.O. 1875-1889.

STATE OF NEVADA DOCUMENTS

Nevada Legislature. *Appendix to the Journals of Senate and Assembly,* 1866 to 1907, for reports of the "State Mineralogist," until 1878; "Surveyor General;" "County Assessors."

Nevada State Historical Society. *Reports.* Published biennially, 1907-1912. S.P.O., 1909-1913.

——. *Papers.* 1913-1926. S.P.O., 1914-1927.

Political History of Nevada, issued by Secretary of State of Nevada. S.P.O., 1965.

Rhulen, Col. George. "Early Nevada Forts," Nevada Historical Society Quarterly, 7:3-4, 1964.

Stuart, E. E. *Nevada's Mineral Resources.* S.P.O., 1909.

UNIVERSITY OF NEVADA PUBLICATIONS

Armstrong, Robert D. *A Preliminary Union Catalog of Nevada Manuscripts,* 1967.

Carpenter, Jay A., Russell R. Elliott, and Byrd F. W. Sawyer. *The History of Fifty Years of Mining at Tonopah, 1900-1950.* Geology and Mining Series, No. 51, 1953.

Couch, B. F. and J. A. Carpenter. *Nevada's Metal and Mineral Production, (1859 to 1940 inclusive).* Geology and Mining Series, No. 38, 1943.

Elliott, Russell R. *Nevada's Twentieth-Century Mining Boom.* 1966.

Kral, V. E. *Mineral Resources of Nye County, Nevada.* Geology and Mining Series, No. 50, 1951.

Overton, T. D. *Mineral Resources of Douglas, Ormsby, and Washoe Counties.* Bulletin, v. 41, No. 9, 1947.

Smith, Grant H. *The History of the Comstock Lode, 1850-1920.* Geology and Mining Series, No. 37, 1943.

Stoddard, Carl and J. A. Carpenter. *Mineral Resources of Storey and Lyon Counties, Nevada.* Geology and Mining Series, No. 49, 1950.

Vanderburg, W. O. *Placer Mining in Nevada.* Geology and Mining Series, No. 27, 1936.

UNPUBLISHED THESES

Berg, Lucile Rae. *A History of the Tonopah Area and Adjacent Region of Central Nevada, 1827-1941.* U. of Nevada 1942.

Hulse, James W. *A History of Lincoln County, Nevada.* U. of Nevada, 1958.

Kersten, Earl W. Jr. *Settlements and Economic Life in the Walker River Country of Nevada and California.* U. of Nebraska, 1961.

King, Buster L. *The History of Lander County.* U. of Nevada, 1954.

Leavitt, Francis H. *The Influence of the Mormon People in the Settlement of Clark County.* U. of Nevada, 1934.

PUBLICATIONS OF HOWELL-NORTH BOOKS, BERKELEY, CALIFORNIA

Angel, Myron, ed. *History of Nevada, 1881,* originally published by Thompson & West; reissued with introduction by David F. Myrick, 1958.

Beebe, Lucius. *The Central Pacific and the Southern Pacific Railroads.* 1963.

Beebe, Lucius, and Charles Clegg. *Steamcars to the Comstock.* 1957.

——. *Virginia & Truckee, a Story of Virginia City and Comstock Times.* 1963.

Billeb, Emil W. *Mining Camp Days.* 1968.

Bloss, Roy S. *Pony Express — The Great Gamble.* 1959.

Lord, Eliot. *Comstock Mining and Miners,* originally printed as U.S. Geological Survey Monographs, v. 4. Reissued with introduction by David F. Myrick and additional illustrations, 1959.

Myrick, David F. *Railroads of Nevada and Eastern California,* 2 vols. 1963.

Stewart, Robert E. Jr. and M. F. Stewart. *Adolph Sutro, a Biography.* 1962.

OTHER BOOKS

Averett, Walter R. *Directory of Southern Nevada Place Names.* Privately printed, 1962.

Bancroft, Hubert H. *History of Arizona and New Mexico.* (1889) Reissued by Horn & Wallace, 1962.

——. *History of Nevada, Colorado, and Wyoming, 1540-1888.* The History Co. (San Francisco), 1890.

Beebe, Lucius M. and Charles Clegg. *U.S. West, the Saga of Wells Fargo.* E. P. Dutton & Co., 1949.

Browne, J. Ross. *Illustrated Mining Adventures: California and Nevada, 1863-1865.* Reissued, Paisano Press (Balboa Island, California), 1961.

——. *A Peep at Washoe and Washoe Revisited.* Paisano Press, 1960.

Buck, Franklin A. *A Yankee Trader in the Gold Rush, the Letters of Franklin A. Buck.* Compiled by Katherine A. White, Houghton Mifflin Co., 1930.

Burton, Richard F. *City of the Saints; and Across the Rocky Mountains to California.* Harper & Brothers, 1862.

Clemens, Samuel L. *Roughing It.* 1871. Many reprints available.

Corbett, Roger. *Unionville, Nevada, Pioneer Mining Camp.* Published by author (Winnemucca, Nevada), 1939.

Crofutt's Trans-continental Tourist's Guide . . . from the Atlantic to the Pacific Ocean. . . . G. A. Crofutt & Co., 1870.

Davis, Sam P., ed. *The History of Nevada.* 2 volumes. Elms Publishing Co. (Los Angeles), 1913.

Egan, Howard. *Pioneering the West, 1846-1878*. Edited by William M. Egan. Howard R. Egan Estate (Richmond, Utah), 1917.

Elliott, Russell R. *The Early History of White Pine County, Nevada, 1861-1887*. Thesis reproduced by White Pine District of Nevada Library Association. Undated.

Fox, Theron. *Nevada Treasure Hunters Ghost Town Guide*. Harlan-Young Press (San Jose), 1961.

Frickstad, W. N., and E. W. Thrall. *A Century of Nevada Post Offices, 1852-1957*. Pacific Rotoprinting Co. (Oakland), 1958.

Glasscock, C. B. *Gold in them Hills*. Bobbs-Merrill Co., 1932.

Greater Nevada, Its Resources and Possibilities. Nevada Chamber of Commerce (Reno), 1905.

Harold's Club. *Pioneer Nevada*, 2 volumes. Harold's Club, 1951, 1956.

Hittell, John S. *Handbook of Pacific Coast Travel*. The Bancroft Co., 1887.

Jackson, W. Turrentine. *Treasure Hill*. University of Arizona Press, 1963.

Kelly, J. Wells, ed. *First Directory of Nevada Territory (1862)*. Talisman Press, 1962.

Labbe, Charles. *Rocky Trails of the Past*. (Las Vegas), 1960.

Lewis, Oscar. *The Town that Died Laughing*. Little, Brown & Co., 1955.

Lillard, Richard G. *Desert Challenge, an Interpretation of Nevada*. Alfred A. Knopf, Inc., 1942.

Lincoln, Francis Church. *Mining Districts and Mineral Resources of Nevada*. Nevada Newsletter Publishing Co., 1923.

Lingenfelter, Richard E. *The Newspapers of Nevada*. John Howell—Books, 1964.

Mack, Effie Mona. *Mark Twain in Nevada*. Charles Scribner's Sons, 1947.

———. *Nevada*. Arthur H. Clark, 1936.

Mills, Lester W. *A Sagebrush Saga*. Art City Publishing Co. (Springfield, Utah), c. 1956.

Morris, Henry Curtis. *Desert Gold and Total Prospecting*. Privately published (Washington, D.C.), 1955.

Muir, John. *Steep Trails*. Edited by William F. Bade. Houghton Mifflin Co., 1918.

Murbarger, Nell. *Ghosts of the Glory Trail*. Desert Magazine Press, 1956.

———. *Sovereigns of the Sage*. Desert Magazine Press, 1958.

Paine, R. D. *The Greater America*. Outing Publishing Co. (New York), 1907.

Paul, Rodman W. *Mining Frontiers of the Far West, 1848-1880*. Holt, Rinehart & Winston, 1963.

Powell, John J. *Nevada: the Land of Silver*. Bacon & Co., Printers (San Francisco), c. 1876.

Rae, William F. *Westward by Rail: the New Route to the East*. Longmans Green & Co., 1870.

Read, Effie O. *White Pine Lang Syne*. Big Mountain Press (Denver), 1965.

Strobridge, Idah Meachim. *In Miners' Mirage-Land*. Baumgardt Publishing Co. (Los Angeles), 1904.

Weight, Harold O. and Lucile Weight. *Rhyolite, the Ghost City of Golden Dreams*. Calico Press (Twentynine Palms, California), 1953.

Williams, Henry T. ed. *The Pacific Tourist*. H. T. Williams (New York), 1879.

The Wonders of Nevada, Where they Are and How to Get to Them. Enterprise Book and Job Printing House (Virginia, Nevada), 1878. Reissued by La Siesta Press (Glendale, California), 1966.

Writers' Program. *Nevada, A Guide to the Silver State*. Binfords & Mort Publishers, 1940. Book of the American Guide Series.

Wright, William (Dan De Quille). *The Big Bonanza*. Introduction by Oscar Lewis. Alfred A. Knopf, Inc., 1947.

———. *A History of the Comstock Mines and the Great Basin Regions, Lake Tahoe and the High Sierra*. F. Boegle (Virginia, Nevada), 1889.

———. *Washoe Rambles*. Westernlore Publishers (Los Angeles), 1963.

INDEX

Morey Mining Co., 353
Morgan mill, 16†, 50°, 51
Mormons and Mormon influence, 35, 45, 55-56, 61, 195, 218, 220, 265, 276, 277, 280, 284, 287-289, 291, 298, 305
Mormon Batallion, 265
Mormon Station, 7, 55, 59°; see Genoa
Morningstar, 85; see Ludwig
Morris, Henry Curtis, 97
Mother Lode mine, 179
Mott, Hiram, 56
Mottsville, 16†, 56
Mound House, 16†, 70°, 71, 433, 435
Mound Station, Elko Co., 216
Mound Station, Lyon Co., 71
Mound Valley, 216
Mountain City, 195, 206, 210, 212, 213°
Mountain City Copper Co., 215
Mountain House, 16†, 61
Mountain View, 463
Mountain Well district, 95; see La Plata
Mt. Airy, 176
Mt. Blitzen, 196°, 198°, 202
Mt. Brougher, Frontispiece, 336°
Mt. Davidson, 17, 18°, 27°
Mt. Diablo mill, 441
Mt. Grant, 463
Mt. Hamilton, 254
Mt. Irish, 301
Mt. Jefferson, 369
Mt. Oddie, 333, 334°, 336°, 340
Mt. Pleasant Point, 17
Mt. Prometheus, 169°
Mt. Tenabo, 165
Muddy (or Moapa) Valley, 287, 288, 289
Muddy River, 287, 288
Muir, John, 177
Mules' Relief, 168, 172
Muncy, 242
Muncy Creek, 242
Murphy mine and mill, 372, 374°
Murry Creek, 229

— N —

Nason, A. W., 124, 125
National, 143, 149, 150°, 151
National Bank mine, 317
National City, 305; see Bristol
National Mining Co., 149
Natomas, 160, 161
Navajo mine, 196, 202
Needles, Calif., 284
Nelson, 280; see Eldorado
Nenzel, Joseph, 126
Nevada Barth Co., 193
Nevada Bunker Hill Mining Co., 215
Nevada & California Railway, 71, 86, 90, 430, 437, 439, 454; see also Carson & Colorado RR.
Nevada Central Railway, 159, 163, 172-174, 380
Nevada City (Colony), 88, 91
Nevada Consolidated Copper Co. (Corp.), 231, 232, 233
Nevada Co., 380
Nevada Copper Belt RR., 63, 80-81, 84-86
Nevada Douglas Copper Co., 84°, 85
Nevada, Emma, 167
Nevadahills Mining Co., 96, 101°

Nevada Keystone Co., 272, 273
Nevada Lucky Tiger Co., 151
Nevada Massachusetts Co., 135, 154, 156, 441
Nevada Mines Co., 176
Nevada National Guard, 199°
Nevada Northern Railway, 222-224, 227, 231, 236, 239
Nevada Packard Mining Co., 129
Nevada Porphyry Gold Mines, 367
Nevada RR., 38
Nevada Reduction Works, 64; see Rock Point mill
Nevada Short Line Railway, 126
Nevada Southern Railway, 266, 272, 285; see also California Eastern Railway
Nevada State Mining Co., 116
Nevada Sulphur Co., 153
Nevada United Mining Co., 93
Nevada Wonder Mining Co., 102, 106°, 107°
Newark, 179, 256
New Boston, 437
New England district, 266
Newland post office, 303
Newlands project, 91
New Mexico Territory, 276
Newmont Mining Co., 121
New Pass, 111, 176
New Pass Range, 177
New Pass Station, 177
New Reveille, 346, 347°
New Ruth, 233; see Ruth
New Seven Troughs, 116; see Tunnel
Newspapers, 29, 300°, 311, 369°, 435
New York Co., 39
New York Giants, 372, 409
New York (state), 192
"Nick of the Woods", 188
Nickel, 109; see Bolivia
Nightingale, 113
Nightingale Range, 113
Nina Tilden, 276
Nivloc, 424, 425°
Nivloc mine, 424
Nixon, George, 96, 345, 386, 396
Nordyke, 16†, 81
North Belle Isle mine, 196°
Northern Belle mine, 444, 452
North Fork, 206
North Fork of the Humboldt River, 206, 220
North, Judge J. W., mill, 44°
North Manhattan, 367
North Twin River district, 376; see Park Canyon
Northumberland, 309, 361
Northumberland Canyon, 361
Northumberland Mining Co., 361
Nye County, 166, 176, 291, 308-381

— O —

Oasis Valley, 309
O'Brien, William S., 15
Oddie, Tasker L., 174, 333, 341, 465
Ogden, Utah, 221, 224
Old Battle Mountain, 159
Old Bottle mine, 284
Old Dominion mill, 353
Old English Gold Corp., 346
Oldham's Station, 195
Old Spanish Trail, 276
"Old Virginny", 17

Olinghouse, 35, 37, 38
Olympic Mines Co., 439
Omco, 439
O'Neil, 220
Oneota district, 430; see Gold Hitt
Oneota post office, 430; see Gold Hitt
Ophir, Washoe Co., 16†, 35, 42†, 43, 45°
Ophir early name for Virginia City 17
Ophir Canyon, 309, 372, 374°
Ophir mill, Virginia City, 27°
Ophir mill, Washoe Co., 42†, 43, 45°
Ophir mine, 17, 19
Ophir Mining Co., 43
Ora post office, 38; see Olinghouse
Oreana, 115, 124°-126, 161
Oreana Station, 124°, 125-126
Ore City Mining Co., 324
Oregon Short Line, see Union Pacific
Oriental, 409
Original Bullfrog mine, 317, 318°
O'Riley, Peter, 17
Orion, 317
Ormsby County, 16†, 31, 42†, 46-53
Ormsby, Major, 79
Oro City, 464
Oro City Townsite & Water Co., 464
Osceola, 229, 261°, 262°, 263
Osceola Placer Mining Co., 261
Osgood Mountains, 157
O'Sullivan, Timothy, 167
Overland mail stations, 75, 89, 91, 111, 174-177, 216, 218, 240, 242, 247
Overland Mail & Telegraph Co., 240
Overland Mail & Telegraph Co., farm, 218
Overland Trail (central route), 79, 89, 90, 93, 166, 216, 218, 240; see also Overland Mail stations
Overland Trail (Humboldt Route), 89
Overton, 288, 289
Owyhee River, 212

— P —

Pachalka Spring, Calif., 276
Pacific Borax Co., 426
Pacific Borax Salt & Soda Co., 454
Pacific Portland Cement Co., 71
Pacific Reclamation Co., 220, 221
Pacific States Mining Co., 346
Pacific Wood, Lumber & Flume Co., 41
Packard, 129°
Packard mine, 129
Pactolus, 381
Pahranagat mining district, 167, 222, 291, 301-303
Pahranagat Valley, 298
Pahrump Valley, 326
Pah-Ute County, Arizona, 276, 288
Pahute Mesa, 332
Paiutes, 77, 79, 90, 130, 148, 153, 265, 291, 433, 435, 463
Palisade, 181, 188, 189°, 190-193°, 256, 291
Palisade Canyon, 192
Palmetto, 383, 406, 411-413°
Palmyra, 16†, 71

Palmyra mining district, 71; see Como
Palo Alto, 367
Pamlico, 440°
Pamlico mine, 440
Panaca, 301
Panama, 129
Pancake Station, 256
Panther mine, 204
Paradise City, 143, 146; see Paradise Valley (town)
Paradise Range, 379
Paradise Valley, 143
Paradise Valley (town), 142°-146
Paradise Well, 146, 147°
Park Canyon, 377
Parran, 93
Patsville, 212
Patterson district, 307
Patterson district, Calif., 87
Paul, Almirin B., 17
Paymaster mine, 259
Peavine, 16†, 35, 38-39
Penelas mine, 379
Penrod, "Manny", 210
Pequop Mountains, 222
Pequop summit, 224
Perry Canyon, 35
Pershing County, 114-141
Petersons, 93; see Salt Wells
Philadelphia Canyon, 160°, 161
Philadelphia district, 355; see Belmont
Phillips, G. H., 385
Phillipsburg, 385
Phonolite, 379
Phonolite Townsite & Water Co., 379
Pickhandle Gulch, 450; see Metallic City
Picotillo, 248†, 252
Piermont, 242
Pigeon Spring, 412°
Pilot Knob, 236
Pine Creek, 361
Pine Forest Gold Mining Co., 149
Pine Grove, 16†, 63, 71, 81-85, 87
Pine Grove Hills, 81
Piñon Range, 190, 215
Pinto Creek Station, 256
Pinto, Eureka Co., 256
Pinto Summit, 256
Pinto, White Pine Co., 256
Pioche, 8, 181, 222, 256, 259, 280, 290†, 290°-296, 298, 301, 303, 305, 307
Pioche & Bullionville RR., 296
Pioche, F. L. A., 291
Pioneer mill, Ione, 379, 380
Pioneer mill, Silver City, 69
Pioneer mine and mill, 330°, 331
Pioneer (mining camp), 311, 326, 330°, 331
Pittman, Key, 341
Pittman Silver Act, 383
Pittsburg, 164
Pittsburg Liberty Co., 474
Pittsburg Mining Co., 164
"Pittsburg of the West", 181
Pittsburgh, Pa., 345
Pittsburgh Silver Peak Gold Mining Co., 422, 423, 424
Placerites (Placeritos), 121
Platina, 274
Platora, 149; see Willow Creek
Pleasant Hill, 17
"Podunk", 39; see Peavine
Poe City, 38; see Peavine

490

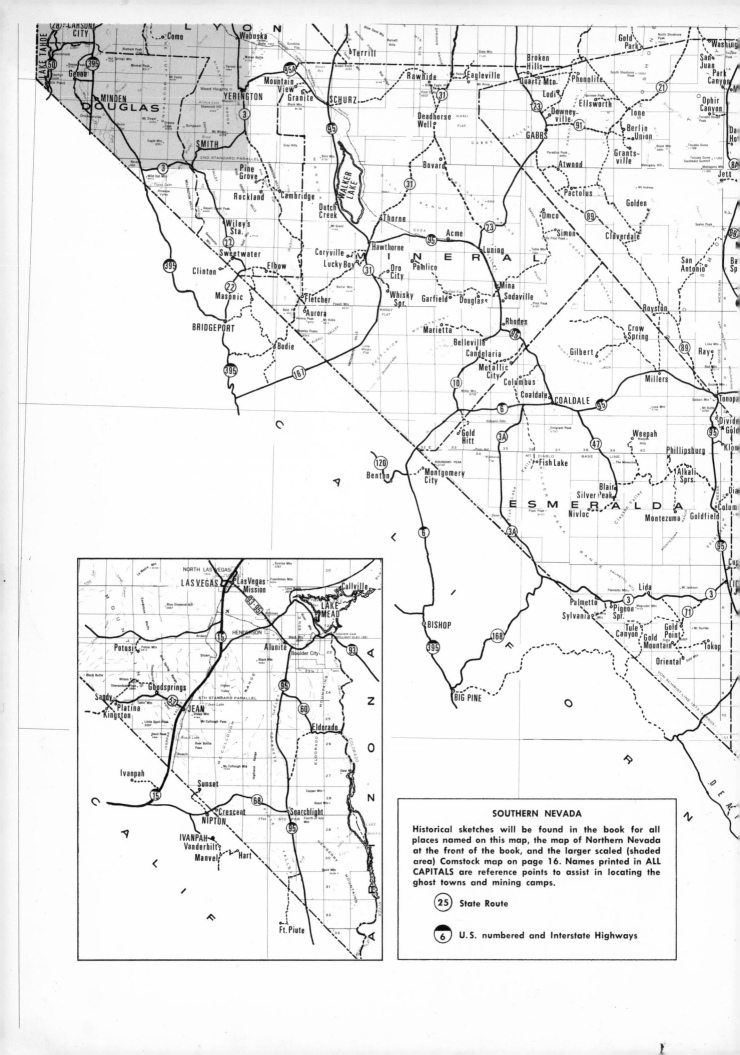

CARSON CITY
(28)
LYON
Como
Wabuska
LAKE TAHOE
50
395
Genoa
Blow Sand Mts.
Terrill
Gold Park
North Shoshone Peak
Washing
95A
Rawhide
Broken Hills
Eagleville
Quartz Mtn.
Phonolite
South Shoshone
San Juan
Peak
Park Canyon
MINDEN
Mountain View
Granite
Lodi
21
Ophir Canyon
YERINGTON
SCHURZ
23
Downeyville
Ellsworth
Ione
DOUGLAS
3
Deadhorse Well
ALKALI FLAT
91
Berlin
Union
Dan
SMITH
95
Bovard
GABBS
Atwood
Grantsville
Jett
2ND STANDARD PARALLEL
Toiyabe Dome

Pine Grove
31
Golden
Pactolus

Rockland
Cambridge
WALKER LAKE
Thorne
Omco
89
Cloverdale
Dutch Creek
Acme
Simon

Wiley's Sta.
23
Luning
MINERAL
San Antonio
22
Sweetwater
Coryville
Hawthorne
Pamlico
Mina
Royston

395
Clinton
Elbow
Lucky Boy
Oro City
Sodaville
Crow Spring
89
Ray

22
Masonic
Fletcher
Whisky Spr.
Garfield
Douglas
Rhodes
95
Gilbert
Millers

BRIDGEPORT
Aurora
Marietta
Belleville
Metallic City
10
Tonopah

Bodie
Candelaria
Columbus
6
COALDALE
95

395
161
Coaldale
Divide Gold

120
Gold Hitt
3A
47
Weepah
Phillipsburg
Klon

Benton
Montgomery City
ESMERALDA
Fish Lake
Blair
Alkali Sprs.

6
3A
Silver Peak
Nivloc
Goldfield
Colum
95

Palmetto
Lida
3
Di

BISHOP
395
168
Pigeon Spr.
Sylvania
Gold Point
Tokop

BIG PINE
Tule Canyon
Gold Mountain
71
3
Oriental

SOUTHERN NEVADA

Historical sketches will be found in the book for all places named on this map, the map of Northern Nevada at the front of the book, and the larger scaled (shaded area) Comstock map on page 16. Names printed in ALL CAPITALS are reference points to assist in locating the ghost towns and mining camps.

(25) State Route

(6) U. S. numbered and Interstate Highways